PRAY CERTAIN

A Daily Devotional for Spiritual Strength, Endurance & Alignment

Dr. Joke Solanke

Copyright © 2026 by Dr. Joke Solanke
All rights reserved.
No part of this book may be reproduced, stored in a retrieval system, or transmitted in any form or by any means—electronic, mechanical, photocopying, recording, or otherwise—without prior written permission of the publisher, except for brief quotations used in reviews or scholarly works.
Scripture quotations are taken from the **New King James Version® (NKJV®)**.
Copyright © 1982 by Thomas Nelson. Used by permission. All rights reserved.

Disclaimer

This devotional is intended for spiritual formation, reflection, and encouragement. It is not a substitute for professional medical, psychological, legal, or financial advice. Readers are encouraged to seek appropriate professional counsel when necessary.

Published by

Purpose and Pathway Publications ISBNs

(Print): 978-1-968717-12-4

(eBook): 978-1-968717-11-7

Printed in the United States of America First Edition

ACKNOWLEDGMENTS

I acknowledge everyone who participated devotedly in the **365 Seeds of Prayer** This devotional emerged from that shared journey and the subsequent quest for deeper understanding, alignment, and endurance in prayer.

PREFACE

Prayer is more than asking for things. It is the primary medium of communication for the human spirit—a sacred platform where alignment with heaven is formed, sustained, and restored. Through prayer, the spirit communes with God, receives instruction, and is recalibrated to divine order.

In Scripture, prayer works most powerfully when it is aligned with God's will: *"If we ask anything according to His will, He hears us"* (1 John 5:14). Alignment gives prayer authority. When prayer aligns with God's design, answers are not forced; they become inevitable.

Pray or Faint is built on this understanding.

This devotional does not approach prayer as a reaction to problems, but as a pathway of formation. It takes the reader back to the genesis of God's will for humanity—how God designed life to function, how alignment was established, how order was disrupted, and how redemption restores clarity, authority, and purpose.

Each day anchors prayer in Scripture, reflection, and wisdom so that prayer is never

detached from truth. As understanding deepens, prayer gains spiritual legitimacy. Requests are no longer random; they are rooted in revelation. Prayer becomes less about persuasion and more about partnership.

This devotional is designed to be used year after year. The truths contained here are generational drawn from timeless biblical foundations, illuminated by the Spirit, and presented through divine perspective. As seasons change, these truths remain relevant, offering clarity for leadership, relationships, purpose, and spiritual growth.

Through this journey, you will find that:

- Prayer becomes clearer as alignment increases
- Answers become consistent when requests align with God's will
- Growth in grace positions you to handle responsibility with wisdom
- Kingdom-based solutions emerge for complex issues of life This is not a devotional to rush through.

It is a **formation journey** to be lived into.

As you pray through these pages, may your prayers find alignment, your faith find footing, and your life reflect the order of the Kingdom you are learning to engage.

TABLE OF CONTENT

Acknowledgments i
Preface ii

Reader Orientation 1
Daily Rhythm (At A Glance) 2
January: Foundation 3
February: Redemption Begins 35
March: Redemption Unfolds (The Patriarchs) 65
April: Covenant Maturity & Identity 98
May: Deliverance & Identity 128
June: Law, Order & Formation 160
July: Proverbs 191
August: Psalms 223
September: Leadership & Kingdom Patterns 255
October: Failure & Path Restoration 286
November: The Kingdom Revealed 318
December: The Kingdom Revealed 349
About The Author 381

READER ORIENTATION

Entering Pray or Faint

This devotional is not designed to rush you—it is designed to **form you**.

Pray or Faint approaches prayer not as a reaction to problems, but as a means of **alignment with God**. Prayer, in its truest form, is the primary medium through which the human spirit communes with heaven, receives instruction, and is recalibrated to divine order.

Many believers struggle in prayer not because they lack sincerity, but because prayer has been reduced to urgency, emotion, or crisis response. Scripture presents a different pattern: prayer gains authority when it is aligned with truth.

> "If we ask anything according to His will, He hears us." — 1 John 5:14

This devotional is built on that foundation.

Across the year, you will journey through Scripture in a deliberate progression—identity, covenant, deliverance, formation, wisdom, healing, leadership, repentance, kingdom life, the cross, and hope. Each season is intentional. Some days will feel clear and affirming. Others may feel confronting or unresolved. This is by design.

Formation does not always resolve tension immediately. Sometimes, growth begins with clarity rather than comfort.

You are not expected to perform, keep pace with others, or extract instant answers from every page. You are invited to **remain**, to listen, to respond honestly, and to allow God to shape your posture over time.

This devotional can be used year after year. The truths are timeless, and different seasons of life will reveal new depth. Return without guilt. Pause without pressure. Continue without pretending.

Prayer is not performance. Prayer is alignment.

DAILY RHYTHM (At a Glance)

How Each Day Is Structured

Each day in *Pray or Faint* follows a simple, intentional formation rhythm grounded in the biblical framework of **2 Timothy 3:16**—teaching, reproof, correction, and instruction in righteousness.

Some days are light. Some are dense. Every day is purposeful.

Begin with Scripture (Teaching)

Start with the anchor Scripture. Read it carefully. Allow God's Word to establish truth before engaging reflection or prayer. Prayer gains clarity and authority when it is anchored in revelation, not reaction.

Read the Devotional Thought (Understanding)

Read slowly. Consider how the truth applies to your current season, responsibilities, relationships, or inner posture. Alignment begins with understanding.

Engage the Key Lessons (Reproof & Correction)

Each day includes guided insights drawn from Scripture to:

- Expose misalignment (reproof)
- Adjust thinking or behavior (correction)

These prompts are not condemnatory—they are formative.

Pray with Intention (Instruction in Righteousness)

Use the prayer points as guidance, not repetition. Let them shape your conversation with God rather than replace it. Prayer is most effective when the heart is receptive to instruction, not merely seeking relief.

Reflect and Journal (Integration)

Where reflection or meditation questions are provided, pause to examine your posture and alignment. Journaling helps solidify transformation and reveals patterns over time. Growth is often the result of consistency, not intensity.

JANUARY FOUNDATION

January 1

Theme: When Life Feels Chaotic

> **Anchor Scripture -** "In the beginning God created the heavens and the earth. The earth was without form, and void; and darkness was on the face of the deep. And the Spirit of God was hovering over the face of the waters." Genesis 1:1–2

Devotional Thought

Our first introduction to God reveals that He faced an unpleasant, disordered, and problematic situation. The world He chose to work with was without form, empty, dark, and deep. If you are facing problems today, you are in good company. God was not discouraged by chaos, nor did He retreat from it. Before He spoke, before He corrected anything, the Spirit of God hovered. *To hover means to brood—to remain present with intention, to protect while preparing, and to stay engaged with purpose until direction is formed.* God's first response to disorder was not action, but presence. In life's adversity—spiritual or physical—God has modeled a template for problem-solving. This passage reveals the first step to take when we find ourselves in unpleasant situations: hover with purpose until clarity emerges. When life feels chaotic, God is not absent—He is present and at work, even before change becomes visible.

Key Lessons & Life Applications

- **Teaching:** Chaos does not mean God is absent; His presence often comes before His instruction.
- **Reproof:** Panic, haste, and impulsive reactions are not spiritual responses to disorder.
- **Correction:** Before trying to fix everything, learn to remain present with God.
- **Instruction:** Some situations require protection and patience before action.
- **Righteous Living:** Waiting with purpose can be an active expression of faith, not weakness.

Prayer Points

1. Father, grant me grace to remain steady when life feels chaotic.
2. Help me resist panic and impulsive decisions in uncertain situations.
3. Teach me how to hover in Your presence until direction is clear.
4. Give me patience to protect what You are forming in this season.
5. Release wisdom, clarity, and strategy as I trust Your timing.

Words of Wisdom: *The first step in solving a chaotic situation is not action but hovering with purpose*

January 2

Theme: What You Say Matters

Anchor Scripture - *"Then God said, 'Let there be light'; and there was light."* Genesis 1:3

Devotional Thought

After hovering over chaos, God spoke. He did not emphasize the chaos, the emptiness, or the darkness before Him. He spoke what He wanted to see. God's speech was not problem-oriented; it was solution-oriented. He did not describe the disorder—He introduced light. What God said came to pass because His words were released from alignment, not reaction. This reveals a vital truth: words carry power when they are spoken with purpose and authority. We speak often, but not all speech produces results. This principle was understood by the centurion who said to Jesus, *"Only speak a word, and my servant will be healed"* (Matthew 8:8). He recognized that authority does not require proximity—only alignment. Words spoken with authority do not negotiate with circumstances; they change them. What you say matters because your words shape outcomes when they are intentional, aligned, and focused on God's desired result.

Key Lessons & Life Applications

- **Teaching:** God speaks outcomes into existence rather than rehearsing problems.
- **Reproof:** Constantly verbalizing problems can reinforce disorder instead of resolving it.
- **Correction:** Shift from problem-focused speech to solution-directed words.
- **Instruction:** Speak in alignment with God's intent, not your emotional reaction.
- **Righteous Living:** Purposeful speech reflects faith in God's authority and wisdom.

Prayer Points

1. Father, align my heart and mind before I speak.
2. Teach me to speak what You desire, not what I fear.
3. Guard my mouth from careless, reactive, or negative words.
4. Help me trust Your authority rather than magnifying problems.
5. Let my words bring light, healing, and clarity.

Words of Wisdom: *Words focused on solutions carry power; words focused on problems sustain confusion.*

January 3

Theme: Light Comes Before Decision

Anchor Scripture - "Then God said, 'Let there be light'; and there was light." Genesis 1:3

Devotional Thought

After hovering over chaos, God did not rush into action. He was not anxious about what to do next. Before any decision was made, **God spoke light into existence**. The light made it possible to see—to recognize what He was dealing with before addressing it. This reveals an important principle for life: decisions require clarity, not panic. God remained present and attentive, and through His word, light revealed the scope of the situation. Only then did creation progress.

This same pattern is echoed in Scripture: *"Your word is a lamp to my feet and a light to my path"* (Psalms 119:105). Light does not illuminate the entire journey at once; it provides enough visibility for the next step. In everyday challenges, meaningful progress begins with proper problem recognition. Light does not immediately resolve the issue, but it reveals it. Before solutions emerge and before direction unfolds, clarity must come first. Wise decisions are made not in haste, but in the presence of light.

Key Lessons & Life Applications

- **Teaching:** God brings clarity before He brings direction.
- **Reproof:** Decisions made without clarity often multiply confusion.
- **Correction:** Not every situation requires immediate action; some require illumination first.
- **Instruction:** Seek light to properly identify what you are facing before responding.
- **Righteous Living:** Wisdom grows when choices are guided by clarity rather than urgency.

Prayer Points

1. Father, speak Your light into every area of confusion in my life.
2. Help me resist haste and emotional reactions when decisions are required.
3. Give me clarity to recognize the true issue before responding.
4. Teach me to wait for illumination before taking action.
5. Let Your Word guide my choices today.

Words of Wisdom: *Clarity guides decisions, without light, choice becomes chance.*

January 4

Theme: Clarity Requires Discernment

Anchor Scripture - "And God saw the light, that it was good; and God divided the light from the darkness." Genesis 1:4

Devotional Thought

Light alone was not the final step. After God spoke light into existence, He examined it—and then He separated it. Scripture says God *saw* the light and declared it good before dividing it from darkness. This reveals a critical principle: illumination must be followed by discernment. Not everything visible is valuable, and not everything present belongs together. Discernment is the ability to distinguish—what is good from what is harmful, what should remain from what must be removed. Many challenges persist not because there is no light, but because there is no separation. God did not destroy the darkness immediately; He defined boundaries. In life, clarity matures when we learn what to keep, what to limit, and what to let go.

Key Lessons & Life Applications

- **Teaching:** Discernment follows illumination; clarity deepens when distinctions are made.
- **Reproof:** Allowing incompatible elements to coexist can undermine stability.
- **Correction:** Not every habit, relationship, or thought that becomes visible should remain.
- **Instruction:** Establish boundaries that protect what is good and life-giving.
- **Righteous Living:** A disciplined life grows where separation is practiced with wisdom.

Prayer Points

1. Lord, help me discern what is good and what must be separated in my life.
2. Give me wisdom to establish healthy boundaries where needed.
3. Reveal what no longer aligns with Your purpose for me.
4. Strengthen me to release what compromises clarity and peace.
5. Teach me to protect what You have declared good.

Words of Wisdom: *Separation and boundaries are not walls; they are guardians of what is important.*

January 5

Theme: The Blueprint of Everything Is in the Name

> **Anchor Scripture** - "God called the light Day, and the darkness He called Night. So the evening and the morning were the first day." Genesis 1:5

Devotional Thought

After separation came naming. God did not leave light and darkness undefined; He named them. By naming, God established order, rhythm, and structure. Naming is not merely labeling—it is the act of defining purpose, limits, and function. When God called the light *Day* and the darkness *Night*, He introduced time and sequence. Evening and morning followed, marking the first day. This reveals a vital truth: clarity is sustained through order, and order is reinforced through naming. What remains unnamed often remains unmanaged. Confusion persists where things are undefined. In life, progress accelerates when we correctly identify seasons, emotions, responsibilities, and priorities. Naming brings structure, and structure allows life to move forward with intention rather than confusion.

Key Lessons & Life Applications

- **Teaching:** God brings order by defining and naming what exists.
- **Reproof:** Avoiding clarity by leaving things undefined sustains confusion.
- **Correction:** Not everything that feels overwhelming is complex—some things simply need to be named.
- **Instruction:** Identify seasons, responsibilities, and challenges accurately to manage them wisely.
- **Righteous Living:** A structured life honors time, boundaries, and God's intended rhythms.

Prayer Points

1. Father, give me clarity to name what You are revealing in my life.
2. Help me recognize the season I am in and respond appropriately.
3. Remove confusion that comes from avoidance or denial.
4. Teach me to respect time, rhythm, and divine order.
5. Let my life reflect intentional structure and peace.

Meditation/Reflection

What name are you answering to—and does it align with your true identity? Take time today to reflect on the names you carry and whether they reflect truth, purpose, and divine order.

Words of Wisdom: *Names are not labels; they are assignments.*

January 6

Theme: Structure Creates Capacity

> **Anchor Scripture -** "Then God said, 'Let there be a firmament in the midst of the waters, and let it divide the waters from the waters.' Thus God made the firmament, and divided the waters which were under the firmament from the waters which were above the firmament; and it was so. And God called the firmament Heaven." **Genesis 1:6–8**

Devotional Thought

Before God introduced life, He established structure. Water already existed, but it was uncontained and undifferentiated. God did not begin by adding content; He created a firmament—a container that defined space, order, and jurisdiction. By separating the waters above from the waters below, God established boundaries that governed function and flow. Scripture later affirms that God *"laid the foundations of the earth upon the waters"* (Psalms 104:5–6), revealing that order precedes manifestation. Structure was not restrictive; it was preparatory. The firmament created an environment where life could emerge without chaos. This reveals a vital principle for life: capacity is determined by structure. When jurisdiction is undefined, pressure overwhelms. When space is ordered, purpose can be sustained. God creates the container before releasing what it must carry.

Key Lessons & Life Applications

- **Teaching:** God establishes structure to create order and jurisdiction before release.
- **Reproof:** Attempting growth without defined space leads to strain and instability.
- **Correction:** Not every delay is denial; some seasons are for building containers.
- **Instruction:** Define boundaries that govern responsibility, access, and function.
- **Righteous Living:** A life with structure honors God by sustaining what He entrusts.

Prayer Points

1. Father, help me build structures that can sustain what You intend to release.
2. Show me where lack of order is limiting my capacity.
3. Teach me to define healthy jurisdiction in my life and responsibilities.
4. Remove confusion that comes from overcrowding and lack of boundaries.
5. Prepare my life as a container fit for Your purpose.

Meditation / Reflection

What structure do I currently have—or need—in my life to support meaning and order?

Could the disorder I am experiencing be the result of building without structure?

Words of Wisdom: *What you are called to carry requires a container designed to hold it.*

January 7

Theme: Stability Requires Grounding

> **Anchor Scripture** - "Then God said, 'Let the waters under the heavens be gathered together into one place, and let the dry land appear'; and it was so. And God called the dry land Earth, and the gathering together of the waters He called Seas. And God saw that it was good." Genesis 1:9–10

Devotional Thought

After establishing structure, God gathered what was scattered. The waters were not removed; they were repositioned. Only then did dry land appear. This reveals an important truth: stability emerges when what is fluid is gathered and given boundaries. Dry land represents footing, permanence, and territory—the ability to stand, build, and grow. God did not create life while everything was still in motion. He created ground first. Many areas of life remain unstable not because effort is lacking, but because grounding is missing. When emotions, priorities, resources, or responsibilities are scattered, progress becomes difficult. God brings order by gathering, and He creates stability by establishing ground. Growth requires a place to stand.

Key Lessons & Life Applications

- **Teaching:** God establishes stability by gathering what is scattered.
- **Reproof:** Constant motion without grounding prevents lasting progress.
- **Correction:** Not everything needs to move at once; some things need to settle.
- **Instruction:** Identify areas of your life that need focus, consolidation, and grounding.
- **Righteous Living:** Stability honors God by creating space for sustainable growth.

Prayer Points

1. Lord, teach me how to gather every scattered area of my life into order.
2. Give me stability where things have felt uncertain or unsettled.
3. Help me establish firm footing in my priorities and decisions.
4. Teach me when to slow down so clarity and grounding can emerge.
5. Let my life be built on what You have established as solid ground.

Meditation / Reflection

Where in my life am I still scattered—emotionally, spiritually, or practically? What would it look like for me to intentionally gather these areas so solid ground can appear?

Consider whether constant movement is preventing stability.

Words of Wisdom: *Every structure requires a foundation; without a solid foundation, collapse is inevitable.*

January 8

Theme: Order Precedes Fruitfulness

Anchor Scripture - "Then God said, 'Let the earth bring forth grass, the herb that yields seed, and the fruit tree that yields fruit according to its kind, whose seed is in itself, on the earth'; and it was so. And the earth brought forth grass, the herb that yields seed according to its kind, and the tree that yields fruit, whose seed is according to its kind. And God saw that it was good." Genesis 1:11–13

Devotional Thought

God did not demand fruit until the environment was prepared. Dry land appeared before the command to produce was given. This reveals a vital principle: fruitfulness is a response to order, not pressure. God never expects output from what He has not first equipped. When the earth was ready, He spoke, and production followed.

Too often, we demand results from people, systems, or seasons that have not been properly prepared. Frustration grows where expectation outpaces structure. Scripture also emphasizes that everything produced fruit according to its kind.

Though all were plants, trees, or fruit-bearing, each produced within its own design. Fruitfulness is governed by identity. You can only produce according to your kind—by innate design or acquired capacity. Order establishes readiness, and identity governs output. Fruitfulness flourishes where preparation and self-understanding are honored.

Key Lessons & Life Applications

- **Teaching:** God establishes order before He commands fruitfulness.
- **Reproof:** Pressuring results without preparation leads to frustration and failure.
- **Correction:** Not every lack of fruit is laziness; some reflect lack of structure or clarity.
- **Instruction:** Equip environments, systems, and people before expecting outcomes.
- **Righteous Living:** Fruitfulness is sustained when identity and preparation are respected.

Prayer Points

1. Father, help me establish order before expecting fruit in my life.
2. Show me where I am demanding results without proper preparation.
3. Give me wisdom to recognize my kind—my design and capacity.
4. Help me plan and prepare rather than pressure and compare.
5. Let my life produce fruit in alignment with Your purpose.

Meditation / Reflection

Where am I expecting results without sufficient preparation?
Do I clearly understand my kind—my design, strengths, and limits—or am I measuring myself against the output of others?

Words of Wisdom: *Fruitfulness follows preparation, not pressure.*

January 9

Theme: Order Requires Measurement, Timing, and Clear Roles

> **Anchor Scripture** - "Then God said, 'Let there be lights in the firmament of the heavens to divide the day from the night; and let them be for signs and seasons, and for days and years...'" Genesis 1:14–19

Devotional Thought

The first light God spoke into existence brought clarity. This next expression of light brought governance. God created different lights, each with a defined purpose—to separate day from night, to mark seasons, and to measure days and years. This was not illumination for visibility alone; it was illumination for order, accountability, and rhythm. Time entered creation as a measuring system, ensuring that growth, activity, and responsibility were regulated rather than chaotic.

Equally important, these lights were not interchangeable. Though all were "lights," each had a distinct assignment and jurisdiction. The sun did not perform the role of the moon, and the moon did not compete with the stars. Order was sustained not only through timing, but through role clarity. God preserved harmony by defining who does what, when, and why. In life, disorder often arises not from lack of effort, but from unclear roles and overlapping responsibilities. Measurement governs progress, and defined roles preserve peace.

Key Lessons & Life Applications

- **Teaching:** God governs creation through time, seasons, and clearly defined roles.
- **Reproof:** Ignoring timing or role boundaries leads to confusion and strain.
- **Correction:** Not every responsibility is yours, and not every season demands the same output.
- **Instruction:** Align your efforts with proper timing and assigned responsibility.
- **Righteous Living:** Accountability and role clarity honor God's design for order.

Prayer Points

1. Lord, teach me to respect timing and seasons in my life.
2. Help me measure progress wisely and pace myself responsibly.
3. Show me where role confusion is creating unnecessary pressure.
4. Give me clarity about my assignments and the grace to honor others'.
5. Align my efforts with Your divine order and rhythm.

Meditation / Reflection

Am I frustrated because of poor timing—or because of unclear roles? Where might I be carrying responsibilities that were never assigned to me? Consider how clarity in timing and function could restore peace and order.

Words of Wisdom: *What is not measured cannot be governed, and what is not assigned cannot be sustained.*

January 10

Theme: Expansion Thrives Within Assigned Boundaries

Anchor Scripture - "Then God said, 'Let the waters abound with an abundance of living creatures, and let birds fly above the earth across the face of the firmament of the heavens.' ... So God created great sea creatures and every living thing that moves, with which the waters abounded, according to their kind, and every winged bird according to its kind. And God saw that it was good. And God blessed them, saying, 'Be fruitful and multiply, and fill the waters in the seas, and let birds multiply on the earth.' Genesis 1:20–23

Devotional Thought

After order, structure, and role definition were established, God released movement and multiplication. Life did not expand randomly; it filled the spaces that had already been assigned. Creatures of the waters multiplied in the waters. Birds multiplied in the air. Each expanded within its domain. This reveals a powerful truth: growth is healthiest when it respects boundaries. God blessed life to be fruitful and multiply, but He also directed *where* that multiplication should occur. Expansion without boundaries leads to chaos; expansion within assignment produces harmony. In life, movement becomes meaningful when it aligns with purpose and place. Progress accelerates when we grow where we are designed to function.

Key Lessons & Life Applications

- **Teaching:** God releases multiplication within clearly defined environments.
- **Reproof:** Growing outside assigned boundaries often creates instability.
- **Correction:** Not all movement is progress; alignment matters.
- **Instruction:** Expand where you are equipped and assigned to function.
- **Righteous Living:** Fruitfulness is sustained when growth honors God-given boundaries.

Prayer Points

1. Father, help me grow within the boundaries You have established for me.
2. Guard me from expanding into areas I am not assigned or prepared for.
3. Align my movement with Your purpose and timing.
4. Bless the work of my hands where You have planted me.
5. Teach me to recognize when restraint is protection, not limitation.

Meditation / Reflection

Am I expanding in the place God has assigned me—or striving in spaces that drain me?

Where might misalignment be disguising itself as ambition or opportunity? Consider whether peace increases when growth stays within its proper domain.

Words of Wisdom: *Healthy growth expands within boundaries, not beyond them.*

January 11

Theme: Responsibility Increases with Complexity

Anchor Scripture - "Then God said, 'Let the earth bring forth the living creature according to its kind: cattle and creeping thing and beast of the earth, each according to its kind'; and it was so. And God made the beast of the earth according to its kind, cattle according to its kind, and everything that creeps on the earth according to its kind. And God saw that it was good." Genesis 1:24–25

Devotional Thought

As creation progresses, complexity increases. God now introduces land animals—creatures that require greater care, interaction, and management. This is not merely more life; it is more responsibility. Each creature is still created according to its kind, reinforcing identity and limits, but the environment now demands greater stewardship. Before humanity is introduced, God establishes a world that requires discernment, balance, and oversight. This reveals an important principle: responsibility grows as complexity increases. God does not assign authority until an environment exists that requires it. In life, growth often brings greater demands—not just more opportunity, but more accountability. Preparation for dominion begins with learning to manage complexity faithfully.

Key Lessons & Life Applications

- **Teaching:** God introduces increasing levels of responsibility as creation matures.
- **Reproof:** Avoid seeking authority without readiness to manage complexity.
- **Correction:** Growth that lacks stewardship can become destructive rather than fruitful.
- **Instruction:** Learn to manage what God places before you before seeking more.
- **Righteous Living:** Faithfulness is proven by responsible care, not just expansion.

Prayer Points

1. Father, prepare me to steward greater responsibility with wisdom.
2. Teach me to manage complexity without fear or avoidance.
3. Help me grow in discernment as my responsibilities increase.
4. Keep me faithful in what You have already entrusted to me.
5. Shape my character before expanding my influence.

Meditation / Reflection

Where in my life has complexity increased recently?
Am I responding with stewardship—or resisting the responsibility it requires?
Consider whether growth is inviting you to mature, not just to advance.

Words of Wisdom: *Growth brings responsibility; stewardship determines sustainability.*

January 12

Theme: Design Precedes Existence: Planning Before Implementation

Anchor Scripture - "Then God said, 'Let Us make man in Our image, according to Our likeness; let them have dominion over the fish of the sea, over the birds of the air, and over the cattle, over all the earth and over every creeping thing that creeps on the earth.' Genesis 1:26

Devotional Thought

Before man was created, his sphere of responsibility was already defined. Genesis 1:26 reveals that God did not introduce humanity into an undefined world.

Dominion was established before existence. Authority was outlined before form. Jurisdiction was assigned before breath. God planned the scope of responsibility before bringing man on board. This shows a foundational truth: God never creates without first defining purpose, boundaries, and assignment.

This framework is echoed throughout Scripture. God later said to Jeremiah, *"Before I formed you in the womb I knew you; before you were born I sanctified you; I ordained you a prophet to the nations"* (Jeremiah 1:5, NKJV). Identity, calling, and assignment preceded manifestation. Many struggles in life arise because we enter spaces, roles, or responsibilities that were never clearly defined. God begins with design, not discovery. Planning is not hesitation; it is wisdom. Stability in life comes when implementation follows intention, not impulse.

Key Lessons & Life Applications

- **Teaching:** God defines purpose, authority, and boundaries before creation.
- **Reproof:** Entering responsibilities without clarity leads to confusion and strain.
- **Correction:** Do not assume roles or territories that were never assigned.
- **Instruction:** Seek understanding of your scope before committing your energy.
- **Righteous Living:** Alignment with God's design brings confidence, restraint, and peace.

Prayer Points

1. Father, help me understand the scope of responsibility You designed for me.
2. Deliver me from entering assignments without clarity or preparation.
3. Teach me to respect boundaries You have set for my life.
4. Align my actions with the purpose You defined before I existed.
5. Give me patience to build according to Your design, not urgency.

Meditation / Reflection

Am I operating within a clearly defined assignment—or assuming responsibilities by pressure or comparison?

Where might confusion be rooted in lack of design clarity?

Consider how peace often follows alignment with God's original intent.

Words of Wisdom: *Conception precedes existence; you cannot deliver what you have not first conceived.*

January 13

Theme: Identity Is Established Before Assignment

Anchor Scripture - "So God created man in His own image; in the image of God He created him; male and female He created them." Genesis 1:27

Devotional Thought

Genesis 1:27 marks the moment design became reality. What God planned in Genesis 1:26, He now executed—but notice the order. Before any instruction, mandate, or responsibility was given, identity was established. Humanity was created in God's image and likeness. Nothing was required of man before this truth was settled. God did not ask man to prove his worth, earn his place, or demonstrate capacity. Identity came first.

This principle is woven throughout creation. Flight was built into the birds, and swimming was built into the fish. They were not trained to function; they were designed to function. Creation did not struggle to become what it was made to be—it thrived by remaining within its assigned environment. In the same way, you do not need to learn how to be who you are; you need to stay where who you are was meant to operate. Confusion often comes not from lack of ability, but from misalignment. When identity is settled and environment is right, function becomes natural and sustainable. God anchored humanity's confidence, value, and dignity in identity—not activity—so that assignment would flow without strain.

Key Lessons & Life Applications

- **Teaching:** God establishes identity before responsibility or action.
- **Reproof:** Defining yourself by performance leads to insecurity and comparison.
- **Correction:** Stop seeking validation from assignments identity should provide.
- **Instruction:** Align your environment with who you are designed to be.
- **Righteous Living:** Stability grows when identity, not pressure, leads your choices.

Prayer Points

1. Father, anchor my confidence in who You created me to be.
2. Deliver me from striving to earn worth through performance.
3. Help me recognize environments that align with my design.
4. Give me courage to step away from spaces that distort my identity.
5. Let my actions flow naturally from who I am in You.

Meditation / Reflection

Am I struggling because of lack of ability—or because of misalignment?
Where might I be functioning outside the environment that supports my design?
Pause today to reaffirm that your identity was settled before your assignment.

Words of Wisdom: *Who you are precedes what you do. When identity is settled, assignment becomes a pleasure.*

January 14

Theme: Purpose Is Progressive

> **Anchor Scripture -** "Then God blessed them, and God said to them, 'Be fruitful and multiply; fill the earth and subdue it; have dominion over the fish of the sea, over the birds of the air, and over every living thing that moves on the earth.'" **Genesis 1:28**

Devotional Thought

Genesis 1:28 reveals God's agenda for humanity clearly and deliberately. The verse begins with a blessing before any instruction is given. The Hebrew word translated *blessed* is **bārak**, which does not mean encouragement or approval. It means to **endow, empower, and authorize**. When God blessed them, He was saying, *I authorize you to be what I am about to require.* The command that followed did not demand effort without capacity; it flowed from empowerment already released.

Purpose in this verse unfolds progressively. God did not compress responsibility into a single expectation. He said, *be fruitful*, then *multiply; fill the earth*, then *subdue it; have dominion* within defined boundaries. Each instruction builds on the previous one. This shows that purpose is not instant—it develops as capacity grows. God's original intent was never pressure, but progression. When blessing is understood as authorization, purpose becomes a journey of growth rather than a burden of performance.

Key Lessons & Life Applications

- **Teaching:** God releases authorization before assigning responsibility.
- **Reproof:** Striving without empowerment leads to exhaustion.
- **Correction:** Purpose is meant to unfold in stages, not be rushed.
- **Instruction:** Walk faithfully in each level of responsibility as it develops.
- **Righteous Living:** Progress flows naturally when purpose is aligned with God's design.

Prayer Points

1. Father, help me receive Your blessing as authorization, not pressure.
2. Teach me to honor the progressive nature of purpose in my life.
3. Deliver me from striving to prove what You have already empowered.
4. Give me grace to grow through each stage of responsibility.
5. Align my expectations with Your timing and intent.

Meditation / Reflection

Am I trying to force outcomes instead of allowing purpose to unfold? Where might God be inviting me to grow gradually rather than rush ahead? Consider whether peace increases when you embrace progression instead of pressure.

Words of Wisdom: *God's blessing authorizes growth—purpose unfolds as capacity develops.*

January 15

Theme: Rest Is Part of the Process

> **Anchor Scripture -** "Thus the heavens and the earth, and all the host of them, were finished. And on the seventh day God ended His work which He had done, and He rested on the seventh day from all His work which He had done. Then God blessed the seventh day and sanctified it, because in it He rested from all His work which God had created and made." Genesis 2:1–3

Devotional Thought

Genesis 2 does not introduce rest as an ending, but as a **pause within progression**.

God rested after a milestone—not because creation was over forever, but because a phase was complete. Purpose was still unfolding, stewardship was still ahead, and humanity had not yet begun its assignment. Rest was inserted into the process, not postponed until everything was finished.

This reveals a vital truth: rest is meant to be scheduled, not accidental. When rest is ignored, the body eventually demands it—sometimes at a devastating cost. Jesus demonstrated this when He rested in the boat while the mission was still active. The storm did not mean the assignment was over; it meant rest was already built into the journey. Rest does not signal abandonment of purpose; it preserves capacity for what comes next. When rest is delayed indefinitely, burnout replaces longevity, and collapse replaces completion.

Key Lessons & Life Applications

- **Teaching:** God designed rest as a rhythm within purpose, not a reward after life is over.
- **Reproof:** Neglecting rest often reflects misunderstanding, not dedication.
- **Correction:** Rest should be intentional and scheduled, not forced by exhaustion.
- **Instruction:** Pause after milestones to restore strength and clarity.
- **Righteous Living:** Honoring rest protects the life God intends to use.

Prayer Points

1. Father, help me recognize rest as part of Your design, not a sign of
2. weakness.
3. Teach me to pause intentionally after seasons of labor.
4. Deliver me from postponing rest until damage occurs.
5. Give me wisdom to steward my body, mind, and spirit well.
6. Help me build rhythms that preserve longevity in purpose.

Meditation / Reflection

Have I delayed rest until exhaustion forced it?
What milestones have I passed without pausing to restore capacity?
Consider how intentional rest could strengthen—not slow—your journey.

Words of Wisdom: *Rest is not the end of purpose; it is what sustains it.*

January 16

Theme: Life Begins With Breath

Anchor Scripture - "This is the history of the heavens and the earth when they were created… for the LORD God had not caused it to rain on the earth, and there was no man to till the ground; but a mist went up from the earth and watered the whole face of the ground. And the LORD God formed man of the dust of the ground, and **breathed into his nostrils the breath of life; and man became a living being.**" Genesis 2:4–7

Devotional Thought

In Genesis 2, Scripture makes a careful distinction between provision and life. The mist that rose from the ground was not about animation—it was about preparation. The earth was sustained before man appeared, by divine design. Life did not emerge from soil, water, or environment. Life began only when God breathed into man.

Among all of creation, man alone received God's breath. This is intentional. Plants grew, the ground was watered, and systems were in place—but none were called *living souls* until God breathed.

This reveals a profound truth: function can exist without life, but life requires divine breath. Man was fully formed before he was alive. Dust became a body, but breath made him a being. Job later affirmed this when he said, *"The breath of the Almighty gives me life"* (Job 33:4). Jesus echoed this same reality after His resurrection when He breathed on His disciples. Life—true life—flows from God's breath, not from environment, effort, or preparation. Without breath, existence remains operational but lifeless.

Key Lessons & Life Applications

- **Teaching:** Life originates from God's breath, not from form or function.
- **Reproof:** Productivity without divine breath leads to emptiness.
- **Correction:** Do not confuse preparation with life or activity with vitality.
- **Instruction:** Seek God's breath daily to sustain true life.
- **Righteous Living:** Spiritual vitality is preserved through ongoing connection with God.

Prayer Points

1. Father, breathe Your life into every area of my being.
2. Deliver me from living by effort without divine vitality.
3. Renew my spirit with the breath of the Almighty.
4. Help me recognize when I am functioning without life.
5. Restore intimacy that sustains true living.

Meditation / Reflection

Am I merely functioning, or am I truly alive?
Where might I be relying on structure, preparation, or effort without God's breath?
Pause today to invite the breath of God into every part of your life.

Words of Wisdom: *Form can exist without life, but breath is what makes us alive.*

January 17

Theme: Life Is Placed with Purpose

> **Anchor Scripture** - "The LORD God planted a garden eastward in Eden, and there He put the man whom He had formed... Then the LORD God took the man and put him in the garden of Eden to tend and keep it." Genesis 2:8–14

Devotional Thought

After forming man and breathing life into him, God did not leave him unplaced. Scripture says, *"There He put the man..."* Life was not released into randomness; it was positioned intentionally. God planted the garden before placing the man, and then assigned him to it. This reveals a vital principle: life flourishes best where it is properly placed. Purpose is not abstract—it is geographic, relational, and functional.

The garden was not merely a place of beauty; it was a place of responsibility. Man was placed there *to tend and to keep it*. These words imply cultivation and protection. Work was introduced before the fall, not as punishment, but as purpose. God did not give man life and leave him idle; He gave him life and entrusted him with care. Placement precedes productivity. Responsibility follows life, not as burden, but as meaning. When people feel unfulfilled, it is often not because life lacks value, but because it lacks proper placement.

Key Lessons & Life Applications

- **Teaching:** God places life intentionally, not randomly.
- **Reproof:** Discontent can stem from misplacement, not lack of ability.
- **Correction:** Purpose is discovered where God positions you, not where pressure pushes you.
- **Instruction:** Tend what God has entrusted to you before seeking elsewhere.
- **Righteous Living:** Stewardship brings fulfillment when aligned with God's placement.

Prayer Points

1. Father, help me recognize where You have placed me for this season.
2. Deliver me from despising the environment You have assigned.
3. Teach me to tend and protect what You have entrusted to me.
4. Align my sense of purpose with where You are working in my life.
5. Give me grace to be faithful in the place You have planted me.

Meditation / Reflection

Am I honoring the place God has positioned me, or constantly looking elsewhere? What responsibility has God already entrusted to my care?
Consider whether fulfillment might come from tending where you are planted.

Words of Wisdom: *Purpose is not only what you do—it is where you are placed.*

January 18

Theme: Responsibility Requires Guardianship

> **Anchor Scripture -** "Then the LORD God took the man and put him in the garden of Eden to tend and keep it." Genesis 2:15

Devotional Thought

Placement came with responsibility. Genesis 2:15 reveals that Adam was not placed in the garden as a guest, but as a steward. He was assigned to **tend** and to **keep** it. These two words define the nature of responsibility entrusted to humanity from the beginning.

To *tend* means to cultivate, develop, and cause something to flourish. To *keep* means to guard, protect, and preserve. Adam's assignment was productive and protective. He was responsible not only for what grew in the garden, but for what was allowed to enter it. This establishes an important truth: **responsibility is proactive, not reactive**.

Guardianship existed before temptation. Authority was exercised before testing. Disorder does not enter because responsibility was unclear; it enters when guardianship is neglected. Genesis 2:15 shows that stewardship is not optional—it is the price of placement.

Key Lessons & Life Applications

- **Teaching:** Responsibility accompanies placement.
- **Reproof:** Neglected guardianship invites disorder.
- **Correction:** Stewardship includes protection, not just productivity.
- **Instruction:** Guard what God has entrusted to you.
- **Righteous Living:** Faithfulness is demonstrated through vigilance.

Prayer Points

1. Father, help me understand the responsibilities attached to my placement.
2. Teach me to cultivate what You have entrusted to me.
3. Give me discernment to guard my life, relationships, and influence.
4. Deliver me from passivity in areas requiring vigilance.
5. Strengthen my commitment to faithful stewardship.

Meditation / Reflection

What has God entrusted to me that requires guarding, not just managing? Where might neglect be opening the door to disorder?

Words of Wisdom: *What you fail to guard, you will eventually lose.*

January 19

Theme: Freedom Comes with Responsibility

> **Anchor Scripture** – "And the LORD God commanded the man, saying, 'Of every tree of the garden you may freely eat; but of the tree of the knowledge of good and evil you shall not eat, for in the day that you eat of it you shall surely die." Genesis 2:16–17

Devotional Thought

Before temptation ever appeared, instruction was already given. Genesis 2:16–17 shows that freedom was never unconditional. God began with permission—*"Of every tree you may freely eat"*—but He followed it with instruction and consequence. Freedom was real, but it was framed by responsibility. God did not remove choice; He clarified what choice carried.

This passage teaches a vital truth: **freedom of choice is not freedom from consequences**. Every freedom God gives comes with instruction, and every instruction carries responsibility. God was not restricting life; He was protecting it. The boundary was not about control, but trust. Moral maturity begins when freedom is exercised with awareness of consequence. Where instruction is ignored, responsibility is forfeited. God's intent was never to limit joy, but to preserve life through obedience.

Key Lessons & Life Applications

- **Teaching:** God grants freedom with clear instruction and defined consequence.
- **Reproof:** Ignoring boundaries often reflects carelessness, not ignorance.
- **Correction:** Freedom without responsibility exposes life to loss.
- **Instruction:** Wise choices are guided by understanding, not impulse.
- **Righteous Living:** Obedience safeguards freedom and preserves life.

Prayer Points

1. Father, help me exercise freedom with wisdom and responsibility.
2. Teach me to honor Your instructions, even when choice feels easier.
3. Guard my heart from careless decisions that carry hidden consequences.
4. Strengthen my trust in Your boundaries as protection, not restriction.
5. Align my choices with Your design for life and peace.

Meditation / Reflection

Do I view instruction as guidance or limitation?
Where might I be exercising freedom without considering consequence?
Consider how responsibility transforms freedom from risk into wisdom.

Words of Wisdom: *Freedom of choice does not cancel responsibility for consequence.*

January 20

Theme: Every conversation you entertain has the potential to shape your destiny.

Anchor Scripture - "Now the serpent was more cunning than any beast of the field which the LORD God had made. And he said to the woman, 'Has God indeed said, "You shall not eat of every tree of the garden"?" Genesis 3:1–5

Devotional Thought

Genesis 3 does not begin with sin—it begins with **access**. Before any action was taken, a conversation was allowed. The serpent did not force disobedience; he was given audience. He did not begin with instruction, but with a question. The first failure was not eating the fruit—it was permitting unauthorized influence within a governed space.

This passage reveals a critical life principle: **what you allow access to will eventually influence action**. Adam had been assigned to *keep* the garden—to guard it. Yet an unfamiliar voice entered unchecked and was entertained. The serpent questioned God's instruction, reframed His words, and subtly introduced doubt—not through force, but through dialogue.

Destiny is often compromised not by dramatic rebellion, but by unmanaged conversations. Discernment is not only about choosing right over wrong; it is about controlling who has permission to speak into your decisions. Every voice is not neutral. Every question is not innocent. Influence begins where access is granted.

Key Lessons & Life Applications

- **Teaching:** Influence begins with access, not action.
- **Reproof:** Entertaining unauthorized voices weakens clarity.
- **Correction:** Not every question deserves engagement.
- **Instruction:** Guard conversations that shape belief and direction.
- **Righteous Living:** Wisdom protects destiny by managing influence.

Prayer Points

1. Father, sharpen my discernment over who has access to my thoughts and decisions.
2. Help me recognize voices that question Your truth without authority.
3. Teach me when to disengage rather than explain.
4. Guard my heart from conversations that weaken conviction.
5. Surround me with voices that reinforce wisdom and truth.

Meditation / Reflection

Who currently has access to influence my thinking and decisions?
Have I allowed conversations that challenge clarity rather than strengthen truth?
Consider whether silence or disengagement is the wisest response.

Words of Wisdom: *Not every voice deserves access, and not every question requires an answer.*

January 21

Theme: When Identity Is Forgotten, Choice Becomes Costly

Anchor Scripture - "So when the woman saw that the tree was good for food, that it was pleasant to the eyes, and a tree desirable to make one wise, she took of its fruit and ate. She also gave to her husband with her, and he ate. Then the eyes of both of them were opened, and they knew that they were naked; and they sewed fig leaves together and made themselves coverings." Genesis 3:6–7

Devotional Thought

Genesis 3:6–7 marks the moment where influence becomes action. Nothing new was introduced—no new information, no new authority, no new command. What changed was **identity awareness**. Adam and Eve did not eat because they lacked instruction; they ate because identity was no longer being actively remembered and defended.

Before the fall, Adam had authority, clarity, responsibility, and placement. But in this moment, desire replaced discernment, and perception replaced truth. The tree was evaluated based on appearance and personal benefit rather than God's instruction. When identity is forgotten, choice becomes vulnerable.

The immediate result was not empowerment, but exposure. *"Their eyes were opened"*—yet what they saw was not wisdom, but shame. They became aware of what they had never noticed before because identity had shifted. The attempt to cover themselves reveals another change: self-correction replaced trust in God. Shame entered where authority once stood. When identity collapses, people don't stop acting—they start compensating.

Key Lessons & Life Applications

- **Teaching:** Actions follow identity awareness, not information alone.
- **Reproof:** Decisions made outside identity often lead to exposure.
- **Correction:** Perception should never replace instruction.
- **Instruction:** Remember who you are before responding to desire.
- **Righteous Living:** Identity anchored in God protects against costly choices.

Prayer Points

1. Father, anchor my identity in what You have spoken, not what I perceive.
2. Help me remember who I am before making decisions.
3. Guard me from choices driven by desire rather than truth.
4. Deliver me from compensating behaviors rooted in shame.
5. Restore clarity where identity has been weakened.

Meditation / Reflection

Am I evaluating situations by truth or by appearance? Have recent choices been shaped by identity or by desire? Pause to reaffirm who God says you are before acting.

Words of Wisdom: *When identity is forgotten, perception replaces truth—and choice becomes costly.*

January 22

Theme: Where Are You?

> **Anchor Scripture** - "And they heard the sound of the LORD God walking in the garden in the cool of the day, and Adam and his wife hid themselves from the presence of the LORD God among the trees of the garden. Then the LORD God called to Adam and said to him, 'Where are you?' So he said, 'I heard Your voice in the garden, and I was afraid because I was naked; and I hid myself.'" Genesis 3:8–10

Devotional Thought

God's question, *"Where are you?"*, was not about physical location. It was an identity question. Adam had not moved far geographically, but he had shifted profoundly in standing. Before the fall, God's presence was familiar and welcomed. After identity was displaced, that same presence felt threatening. What changed was not God's location—but Adam's position.

In life, access is often determined by identity. Certain spaces require authorization; without the right identity, access is restricted. Adam once stood freely in God's presence, but displaced identity resulted in lost access. Fear—an emotion that had never existed before—entered the human experience and replaced fellowship.

Hiding followed. One misstep created a chain reaction: identity displacement led to loss of standing, which produced fear, which resulted in withdrawal.

This passage reveals a sobering truth: **identity determines location**. When identity shifts, access changes. God's question was an invitation—not condemnation—to recognize what had moved. Restoration does not begin with hiding or explanation, but with answering honestly where we now stand.

Key Lessons & Life Applications

- **Teaching:** God's presence was designed for fellowship, not fear.
- **Reproof:** Fear often signals displaced identity, not divine rejection.
- **Correction:** Hiding addresses symptoms; realignment addresses the cause.
- **Instruction:** Identity must be restored before access can be regained.
- **Righteous Living:** Right standing restores confidence and communion.

Prayer Points

1. Father, help me answer honestly when You ask, "Where are you?"
2. Reveal any areas where my identity has been displaced.
3. Heal fears that emerged from misalignment rather than truth.
4. Restore my confidence to stand where You placed me.
5. Realign me quickly when missteps occur.

Meditation / Reflection

Where do I feel withdrawn, restricted, or disconnected—and why? Is fear pointing to an identity issue rather than an external threat?

Consider how one unaddressed misstep can create spiraling consequences.

Words of Wisdom: *Identity determines location, access, and standing.*

January 23

Theme: The Blame Game Does Not Excuse Consequences

Anchor Scripture - "And He said, 'Who told you that you were naked? Have you eaten from the tree of which I commanded you that you should not eat?' Then the man said, 'The woman whom You gave to be with me, she gave me of the tree, and I ate.' And the LORD God said to the woman, 'What is this you have done?' The woman said, 'The serpent deceived me, and I ate.' Genesis 3:11–13

Devotional Thought

After fear came hiding, and after hiding came blame. God's questions were direct and purposeful—not to accuse, but to invite ownership. Yet instead of taking responsibility, Adam shifted blame to Eve and indirectly to God. Eve, in turn, shifted blame to the serpent. Each response moved accountability further away from the individual who acted. This pattern repeats throughout Scripture and human history. The difference between failure that destroys and failure that restores is not the mistake—it is the response when confronted. This is clearly seen in the lives of **Saul** and **David**. Saul was confronted by **Samuel** and responded by blaming the people and justifying his disobedience, losing the opportunity for correction and ultimately forfeiting his kingdom. David, however, was confronted by **Nathan**. He took ownership, acknowledged his sin, accepted correction, and submitted to consequence—and fellowship was restored.

The lesson is unmistakable: **blame may explain behavior, but it does not excuse consequences**. Responsibility delayed is restoration delayed. God's questions are invitations to alignment, but alignment requires ownership. Healing and growth begin not when fault is redistributed, but when responsibility is reclaimed.

Key Lessons & Life Applications

- **Teaching:** God seeks ownership, not explanations.
- **Reproof:** Blame protects pride but blocks correction.
- **Correction:** Ownership creates space for mercy and restoration.
- **Instruction:** Respond to correction with humility, not justification.
- **Righteous Living:** Integrity is revealed by how we respond when confronted.

Prayer Points

1. Father, give me grace to respond with honesty when corrected.
2. Deliver me from the habit of shifting blame.
3. Help me take ownership without fear or defensiveness.
4. Restore areas where pride has delayed correction.
5. Teach me to value alignment over self-protection.

Meditation / Reflection

When confronted, do I explain—or do I own my actions?
Am I responding more like Saul or like David when correction comes?
Consider how ownership could restore alignment and fellowship.

Words of Wisdom: *Blame is often a shield for shame; genuine remorse opens the door to correction and restoration*

January 24

Theme: Judgment Did Not Cancel Hope

Anchor Scripture - "So the LORD God said to the serpent: 'Because you have done this, You are cursed more than all cattle, And more than every beast of the field; On your belly you shall go, And you shall eat dust All the days of your life. And I will put enmity Between you and the woman, And between your seed and her Seed; He shall bruise your head, And you shall bruise His heel.'" Genesis 3:14–15

Devotional Thought

Genesis 3:14–15 reveals something profound about God's character: **judgment and hope are not opposites**. Consequences were pronounced, but God did not abandon His purpose. Before Adam or Eve spoke another word, God addressed the source of deception. Responsibility was established, order was restored, and direction was given.

Verse 15 quietly introduces the first promise embedded within judgment. Conflict was declared—but so was victory. God acknowledged the reality of struggle while announcing its eventual resolution. The bruise to the heel speaks of pain; the crushing of the head speaks of defeat. God made it clear that deception would not have the final word.

This passage teaches us that failure does not end the story. Even in moments of correction, God is already working toward restoration. Consequences may shape the journey, but they do not cancel destiny. God does not wait for perfection to introduce hope—He speaks it into brokenness.

Key Lessons & Life Applications

- **Teaching:** God addresses the root of deception before restoring order.
- **Reproof:** Consequences are real, but they are not the end.
- **Correction:** God confronts what caused the fall, not just those affected by it.
- **Instruction:** Hope can exist even in the presence of judgment.
- **Righteous Living:** Trust God's promise even when the path includes pain.

Prayer Points

1. Father, thank You that judgment does not cancel Your purpose.
2. Help me trust Your plan even when consequences remain.
3. Strengthen me to walk through pain without losing hope.
4. Remind me that deception does not define my future.
5. Anchor my faith in Your promise of victory.

Meditation / Reflection

Where have I assumed that failure ended God's plan for me? Can I recognize hope even while consequences are unfolding? Consider how God may already be working toward restoration.

Words of Wisdom: *God's correction may shape the journey, but His promise—rooted in love—secures the destination.*

January 25

Theme: You Are Ultimately Responsible for Your Actions

> **Anchor Scripture** – "To the woman He said, "I will greatly multiply your sorrow and your conception; in pain you shall bring forth children; your desire shall be for your husband, and he shall rule over you." Then to Adam He said, "Because you have heeded the voice of your wife, and have eaten from the tree of which I commanded you, saying, 'You shall not eat of it': cursed is the ground for your sake; in toil you shall eat of it all the days of your life. Both thorns and thistles it shall bring forth for you" Genesis 3:16–19

Devotional Thought

Genesis 3:16–19 delivers a sobering truth: **influence does not remove responsibility**. Adam pointed to Eve—*"She gave me…"*—but God did not debate the influence; He addressed the decision. The presence of influence did not cancel accountability. Adam was still responsible for what he chose to do.

God's response reveals a leadership and life principle that remains true today: **you are ultimately responsible for your actions**. Counsel, pressure, emotions, or relationships may explain why a choice was made, but they do not erase its consequences. God acknowledged the influence, yet He held Adam accountable for yielding authority over his decision-making.

This passage teaches the necessity of discernment and boundaries. Not every voice should carry equal weight, and not every influence should be allowed to govern action. Maturity is revealed by knowing who to listen to—and who to obey. Responsibility cannot be delegated, even when influence is real.

Key Lessons & Life Applications

- **Teaching:** Accountability remains personal, regardless of influence.
- **Reproof:** Shifting blame delays growth and healing.
- **Correction:** Responsibility begins where excuses end.
- **Instruction:** Guard the voices that shape your decisions.
- **Righteous Living:** Ownership strengthens integrity and wisdom.

Prayer Points

1. Father, help me take responsibility for my choices without excuse.
2. Teach me discernment in the influences I allow into my life.
3. Strengthen me to obey Your voice above all others.
4. Deliver me from blaming circumstances or people.
5. Align my decisions with truth and accountability.

Meditation / Reflection

Where have I blamed influence instead of owning responsibility? Are there voices in my life that carry authority they should not have? Consider how boundaries protect both freedom and integrity.

Words of Wisdom: *Consequences follow the one who chooses, not the influence that persuades.*

January 26

Theme: God's Correction Is Governed by Love

> **Anchor Scripture** - "And Adam called his wife's name Eve, because she was the mother of all living. Also for Adam and his wife the LORD God made tunics of skin, and clothed them" **Genesis 3:20–21**

Devotional Thought

After consequence was pronounced and accountability established, Scripture records something deeply revealing about God's disposition: **He covered them.** Genesis 3:20–21 shows that correction did not end God's care. Judgment did not exhaust His compassion. Before exile, before restriction, and before guarded access, God addressed their exposure. Adam's act of naming his wife *Eve*—"the mother of all living"—was a declaration of hope in the midst of loss. Though death had entered the human story, Adam still spoke life forward. God then responded not with distance, but with provision. He replaced their inadequate, self-made coverings with garments He Himself provided. This covering required sacrifice, signaling that restoration is costly and intentional, not sentimental or permissive.

This passage reveals a vital truth: **God's correction is governed by love.** He does not correct to humiliate, abandon, or expose. He corrects to restore order while preserving dignity. Consequences remained real, but shame was not allowed to define them. God addressed the failure without stripping humanity of worth.

In life, correction often feels like rejection—but Scripture shows otherwise. Divine correction is structured, purposeful, and compassionate. God does not ignore failure, yet He refuses to leave people uncovered in it. Love does not cancel correction; it governs how correction is carried out.

Key Lessons & Life Applications

- **Teaching:** God's love remains active even when correction is necessary.
- **Reproof:** Shame thrives when people rely on self-made coverings.
- **Correction:** God addresses failure without exposing dignity.
- **Instruction:** Receive God's provision instead of hiding behind self-protection.
- **Righteous Living:** Restoration begins where correction is received with humility.

Prayer Points

1. Father, thank You for correcting me without abandoning me.
2. Help me receive Your correction without interpreting it as rejection.
3. Remove every form of shame that hides me from Your care.
4. Teach me to trust Your love even when discipline is required.
5. Restore dignity and hope where failure once spoke loudly.

Meditation / Reflection

Where have I mistaken correction for rejection?

Have I relied on self-made coverings instead of God's provision? Consider how God's love governs even the moments that feel painful.

Words of Wisdom: *Even when God judges, His compassion remains active.*

January 27

Theme: Boundaries Are a Form of Mercy

Anchor Scripture – "Then the LORD God said, "Behold, the man has become like one of Us, to know good and evil. And now, lest he put out his hand and take also of the tree of life, and eat, and live forever"—therefore the LORD God sent him out of the garden of Eden to till the ground from which he was taken. So He drove out the man; and He placed cherubim at the east of the garden of Eden, and a flaming sword which turned every way, to guard the way to the tree of life." **Genesis 3:22–24**

Devotional Thought

Genesis 3:22–24 reveals a side of God that is often misunderstood: **restriction as protection**. After the fall, God did not merely remove humanity from Eden; He restricted access to the Tree of Life. This was not an act of cruelty, but mercy. To live forever in a fallen state would have meant eternal brokenness. God intervened to prevent permanent damage.

The placement of the cherubim and the flaming sword was not vengeance—it was governance. God guarded what humanity was no longer prepared to steward. This passage teaches a profound truth: **loss of access is sometimes an act of love**.

When capacity changes, access must be adjusted. What was once safe can become dangerous when identity, alignment, or obedience is compromised.

God did not destroy Eden. He protected it. And He did not abandon humanity; He redirected them. Being sent out was painful, but it preserved the possibility of restoration. Boundaries did not end God's relationship with humanity—they preserved it. God knew that unrestricted access without readiness would lead to greater harm.

In life, closed doors are often interpreted as rejection. Scripture reframes them as mercy. God restricts access not to punish, but to protect what is sacred and to protect us from what we are no longer equipped to handle.

Key Lessons & Life Applications

- **Teaching:** God sets boundaries to protect life, not to withhold love.
- **Reproof:** Loss of access is not always loss of favor.
- **Correction:** Some doors close because capacity has changed.
- **Instruction:** Respect boundaries God establishes, even when they are painful.
- **Righteous Living:** Wisdom discerns when restriction is preservation.

Prayer Points

1. Father, help me trust You when access is restricted.
2. Give me wisdom to see boundaries as protection, not rejection.
3. Heal any resentment I carry toward closed doors.
4. Teach me to grow in capacity before seeking restored access.
5. Align my desires with Your wisdom and timing.

Meditation / Reflection

What access in my life may God be protecting me from right now? Have I mistaken restriction for punishment instead of mercy? Consider whether growth is required before access can be restored.

Words of Wisdom: *What God guards, He values—and what He restricts, He protects.*

January 28

Theme: God Responds to Problems with Questions, Not Panic

Anchor Scripture - "Then the LORD God called to Adam and said to him, 'Where are you?'" Genesis 3:9

Devotional Thought

God's first response to human failure was not punishment, accusation, or reaction— it was a question. *"Where are you?"* This was not a request for information, but an invitation to awareness. God modeled a critical principle for leadership and life: **clarity precedes correction**. Before addressing behavior, God addressed position—relational, spiritual, and moral.

Effective problem-solving begins with diagnosis, not reaction. God did not rush to fix the damage until responsibility was surfaced. Questions create space for truth, ownership, and alignment. Panic escalates problems; questions expose them. Leaders who respond emotionally often miss the real issue. God responded strategically.

Key Lessons & Life Applications (2 Timothy 3:16)

- **Teaching:** Awareness is the first step toward restoration.
- **Reproof:** Avoiding self-examination delays healing.
- **Correction:** Ask the right questions before taking action.
- **Instruction:** Seek clarity before assigning blame.
- **Righteous Living:** Truth grows where honesty is welcomed.

Prayer Points

1. Lord, help me respond to problems with wisdom, not panic.
2. Give me clarity to identify where I truly am.
3. Teach me to ask the right questions in difficult moments.
4. Remove fear that hides me from truth.
5. Restore alignment where I have drifted.

Words of Wisdom: *Wise leadership begins with the courage to ask honest questions.*

January 29

Theme: Discipline Preserves Order

Anchor Scripture - "So the LORD God said to the serpent… To the woman He said… Then to Adam He said…" Genesis 3:14–19

Devotional Thought

Genesis 3 reveals that God addressed failure with **measured and specific discipline**. Each party received a response appropriate to their role and responsibility. The serpent, the woman, and the man were not treated the same—but none were ignored. This demonstrates a critical leadership principle: **discipline must be timely, intentional, and proportional**.

God did not postpone correction, minimize the issue, or avoid discomfort. He addressed the matter decisively to prevent further breakdown. Discipline was not an emotional reaction; it was a strategic intervention designed to stabilize the system. Where discipline is delayed or avoided, disorder multiplies. What is not corrected early becomes harder to change later.

This principle applies across every level of life—parenting, leadership, organizations, and personal growth. When issues are ignored, patterns harden. When correction is avoided, dysfunction normalizes. God's example teaches that discipline, though uncomfortable, preserves order and makes restoration possible. Change often begins at the moment correction is accepted.

Key Lessons & Life Applications

- **Teaching:** Discipline is a necessary tool for maintaining order.
- **Reproof:** Avoiding correction allows dysfunction to grow.
- **Correction:** Address issues decisively before they become entrenched.
- **Instruction:** Apply discipline proportionally and with purpose.
- **Righteous Living:** Growth follows correction that is received with humility.

Prayer Points

1. Father, give me wisdom to address issues without delay.
2. Help me apply discipline with clarity and fairness.
3. Remove fear that causes me to avoid necessary correction.
4. Teach me to accept discipline as a pathway to growth.
5. Restore order in areas where correction was postponed.

Meditation / Reflection

Where have I delayed correction—personally or in leadership?
What issue requires decisive action before it becomes harder to change? Consider how timely discipline can preserve peace and order.

Words of Wisdom: *Discipline applied early prevents disorder from becoming permanent.*

January 30

Theme: Delegation Requires Governance

Anchor Scripture - "Because you have done this..." Genesis 3:14–19

Devotional Thought

God delegated authority to humanity, but Genesis 3 reveals that delegation did not remove governance. When delegated authority was misused, God did not abandon the system—He governed it. Consequences were introduced not as punishment alone, but as structural correction. God adjusted responsibility, environment, and access to preserve what remained and prevent further collapse.

This passage teaches a vital leadership principle: **delegation without governance leads to disorder**. Freedom without accountability produces instability. Authority without boundaries invites misuse. God did not revoke humanity's existence or purpose, but He recalibrated the system. Governance stepped in where self-regulation failed.

In leadership, parenting, ministry, and life, problems often arise not because authority was given, but because governance was absent or weak. God modeled how to respond: intervene, correct, redefine boundaries, and restore order—without destroying the people involved. Governance is not control; it is protection. It ensures that delegated authority functions within safe and sustainable limits.

Key Lessons & Life Applications

- **Teaching:** Delegation does not eliminate the need for governance.
- **Reproof:** Unchecked autonomy invites disorder.
- **Correction:** Boundaries stabilize authority after failure.
- **Instruction:** Govern systems when self-regulation breaks down.
- **Righteous Living:** Accountability preserves purpose and peace.

Prayer Points

1. Father, teach me to steward authority with wisdom and restraint.
2. Help me recognize where governance is needed in my life.
3. Give me courage to enforce boundaries that preserve order.
4. Protect me from misusing freedom You have entrusted to me.
5. Align my leadership with Your principles of accountability.

Meditation / Reflection

Where has authority been exercised without adequate governance?
Have I confused freedom with absence of accountability?
Consider how boundaries can restore stability and trust.

Words of Wisdom: *Delegation without governance creates disorder; governance preserves purpose.*

January 31

Theme: Love Does Not Cancel Accountability

Anchor Scripture - "So He drove out the man; and He placed cherubim at the east of the garden of Eden, and a flaming sword which turned every way, to guard the way to the tree of life." Genesis 3:24

Devotional Thought

Genesis 3 closes with a difficult but necessary leadership decision. God did not act in anger or haste. Scripture records divine deliberation—*"The man has become like one of Us..."*—before action was taken. This reveals intentional governance, not emotional reaction. Humanity was not expelled from Eden because God stopped loving them, but because **love demanded accountability and protection of a greater purpose**.

Eating from the Tree of Life in a compromised state would have locked humanity into permanent brokenness. Eden had to be guarded—not destroyed—and access had to be restricted until a lasting solution could be provided. God chose restraint over indulgence, protection over permission. This was not rejection; it was leadership.

Leadership often requires decisions that are painful to explain and misunderstood by those affected. Accountability sometimes demands action even when affection remains. Love does not remove responsibility, and compassion does not override consequence. God modeled a leadership truth many struggle to accept: **you can care deeply and still enforce boundaries**. Accountability preserves the integrity of the system, even when individual desires are disappointed.

This passage reminds us that leadership must consider the bigger picture—long-term impact, future restoration, and collective responsibility. Love that avoids accountability ultimately endangers what it claims to protect.

Key Lessons & Life Applications

- **Teaching:** Love and accountability are not opposites; they work together.
- **Reproof:** Avoiding hard decisions for emotional comfort weakens leadership.
- **Correction:** Restrict access when capacity is compromised.
- **Instruction:** Govern with foresight, not sentiment.
- **Righteous Living:** Integrity requires protecting the greater good.

Prayer Points

1. Father, give me wisdom to lead with both love and accountability.
2. Help me make difficult decisions without bitterness or fear.
3. Teach me to see the bigger picture when emotions are involved.
4. Strengthen me to protect what must be preserved for the future.
5. Align my leadership decisions with Your wisdom and timing.

Meditation / Reflection

Have I avoided necessary accountability to preserve comfort or approval? Do I recognize that restriction can be an act of love?

Consider where leadership requires courage to protect long-term purpose.

Words of Wisdom: *Love that avoids accountability eventually undermines what it seeks to protect.*

FEBRUARY
REDEMPTION BEGINS

February 1

Theme: Amazing Grace

> **Anchor Scripture** - "And I will put enmity between you and the woman, and between your seed and her Seed; He shall bruise your head, and you shall bruise His heel." Genesis 3:15

Devotional Thought

God did not wait for sin to be resolved before revealing His plan of redemption. Grace entered the story while sin was still active and consequences were still unfolding. Genesis 3:15 was spoken in the midst of judgment, not after restoration. While discipline was being enforced, God introduced hope. This reveals the nature of grace—it speaks to the future even when the present remains broken.

God did not deny the seriousness of failure, nor did He suspend its consequences. Humanity was still expelled, the ground was still cursed, and life was still altered. Yet in that same moment, God declared that evil would not have the final word.

The promise of the Seed revealed that redemption was already woven into God's response to failure. Grace was not God reacting to repentance; it was God committing to restoration long before humanity understood the depth of its loss.

Amazing grace is not the absence of consequence—it is the presence of promise. It assures us that failure does not cancel destiny and that brokenness does not exhaust God's purpose. Grace speaks forward. It anchors hope while change is still in process and secures the end even when the journey remains difficult.

Key Lessons & Life Applications

- **Teaching:** Grace operates even while brokenness remains.
- **Reproof:** Expecting grace only after improvement misunderstands God's heart.
- **Correction:** Consequences do not negate God's redemptive plan.
- **Instruction:** Trust God's promise while transformation is still unfolding.
- **Righteous Living:** Hope grows when we anchor our future in God's word, not our past.

Prayer Points

1. Father, thank You for grace that meets me in the midst of my process.
2. Help me trust Your redemptive plan even while consequences remain.
3. Remove shame that causes me to doubt Your promises.
4. Strengthen my faith in what You have already spoken.
5. Let hope rise where failure once tried to define me.

Meditation / Reflection

Do I believe God's grace is active even when my life is still being corrected? Am I allowing unresolved issues to silence future hope?

Reflect on how God speaks redemption before restoration becomes visible.

Words of Wisdom: *Grace secures the future even while the present is still unfolding.*

February 2

Theme: Grace Is God Initiating, Not Man Fixing

Anchor Scripture - "And also for Adam and his wife the LORD God made tunics of skin, and clothed them." Genesis 3:21

Devotional Thought

Grace is never humanity's idea—it is always God's initiative. After Adam and Eve failed, they attempted to cover themselves with fig leaves. Their effort was sincere but insufficient. God did not wait for them to perfect their solution before intervening. He stepped in and provided what they could not produce for themselves.

This moment reveals a defining characteristic of grace: **God acts first**. Grace is not a response to human improvement; it is God moving toward humanity while brokenness remains. Adam and Eve did not ask for covering—God provided it. Their failure did not trigger abandonment; it triggered divine involvement.

In life, many people try to fix what only God can redeem. Grace interrupts self-reliance and replaces it with divine provision. God's covering was not cosmetic—it was costly. Grace required sacrifice, revealing that restoration is intentional and deliberate, not accidental. Grace begins where human solutions end.

Key Lessons & Life Applications

- **Teaching:** Grace originates with God, not human effort.
- **Reproof:** Self-made solutions cannot resolve spiritual brokenness.
- **Correction:** Stop striving to fix what requires God's intervention.
- **Instruction:** Receive what God provides instead of hiding behind effort.
- **Righteous Living:** Freedom grows when grace replaces self-reliance.

Prayer Points

1. Father, thank You for initiating grace when I could not help myself.
2. Help me release self-made solutions and trust Your provision.
3. Cover areas of shame I have tried to manage on my own.
4. Teach me to receive Your grace without resistance.
5. Let Your provision speak louder than my past mistakes.

Meditation / Reflection

Where have I relied on effort instead of grace? Am I allowing God to provide what I cannot fix? Reflect on areas where grace is inviting you to rest.

Words of Wisdom: *Grace begins where human effort ends.*

February 3

Theme: Grace Covers Before It Confronts

Anchor Scripture - "And also for Adam and his wife the LORD God made tunics of skin, and clothed them." Genesis 3:21

Devotional Thought

Before God sent Adam and Eve out of Eden, He covered them. Before boundaries were enforced, dignity was restored. This sequence reveals an essential truth about grace: **God covers before He confronts the future.** Correction followed, but exposure was not permitted.

Grace does not ignore failure, but it refuses to humiliate. God addressed the consequences of sin, yet He ensured that Adam and Eve were not sent forward uncovered. Their shame was not allowed to define them. Grace provided protection even as responsibility was enforced.

In life, correction without covering leads to discouragement and fear. God's model shows that restoration begins with dignity. Grace creates safety so truth can be faced without collapse. When God corrects, He does so from a place of care, not condemnation.

Key Lessons & Life Applications

- **Teaching:** Grace restores dignity before enforcing consequence.
- **Reproof:** Shame hinders growth and healing.
- **Correction:** Address failure without stripping worth.
- **Instruction:** Allow God to cover areas of vulnerability.
- **Righteous Living:** Healing flows where grace precedes correction.

Prayer Points

1. Father, thank You for covering me even when I fail.
2. Heal areas where shame has taken root.
3. Teach me to receive correction without fear.
4. Restore dignity where failure has wounded me.
5. Let Your grace prepare me for growth.

Meditation / Reflection

As a parent, leader, or someone in authority, do I preserve dignity while enforcing correction?

Do my actions restore order without diminishing worth?

Reflect on how grace can guide both truth and compassion.

Words of Wisdom: *Grace restores dignity before it delivers punishment.*

February 4

Theme: Grace Warns Before It Judges

> **Anchor Scripture -** "So the LORD said to Cain, 'Why are you angry? And why has your countenance fallen? If you do well, will you not be accepted? And if you do not do well, sin lies at the door. And its desire is for you, but you should rule over it.'" Genesis 4:6–7

Devotional Thought

Before Cain acted, God spoke. Before judgment occurred, grace warned. God did not ignore Cain's emotional state or dismiss his inner conflict. He confronted it directly, offering clarity and an opportunity for self-correction. This reveals an important truth about grace: **grace speaks, but it does not compel**.

Cain's response was not ignorance—it was indifference. Grace was extended, but it was not received. God exposed the danger ahead and clearly defined Cain's responsibility, yet Cain chose self-will over submission. This moment reveals that grace can be **frustrated**. It can be resisted, ignored, and rendered ineffective—not because grace is weak, but because it honors human choice.

The apostle Paul later affirms this reality, teaching that grace is not a license for sin and does not abound where sin is willfully embraced. Grace does not cooperate with rebellion. It warns, instructs, and provides a way out—but it does not override the will. When grace is ignored, judgment feels sudden, but it is never unjust.

Grace always speaks first. What follows depends on the response.

Key Lessons & Life Applications

- **Teaching:** Grace warns to protect, not to threaten.
- **Reproof:** Indifference can frustrate grace.
- **Correction:** Self-will resists transformation.
- **Instruction:** Respond to grace with humility and obedience.
- **Righteous Living:** Grace empowers righteousness, not rebellion.

Prayer Points

1. Father, help me recognize when You are warning me in love.
2. Deliver me from indifference toward Your instruction.
3. Teach me to submit my will when grace speaks.
4. Guard my heart from resisting Your correction.
5. Help me respond to grace before consequences escalate.

Meditation / Reflection

Am I attentive when grace confronts my attitudes and emotions? Have I mistaken grace for permission instead of instruction?

Reflect on areas where self-will may be resisting transformation.

Words of Wisdom: *Grace instructs and warns, but it will not override a resistant will.*

February 5

Theme: Grace Speaks Even When Ignored

Anchor Scripture - "And the LORD said to Cain, 'Why are you angry? And why has your countenance fallen?'" Genesis 4:6

Devotional Thought

Grace does not speak once and withdraw—it often speaks repeatedly before judgment unfolds. God engaged Cain before the act, not after. He addressed Cain's emotions, not just his behavior. This reveals a compassionate truth about grace: **God speaks even when He knows He may be ignored.**

Cain's anger was evident, and God did not pretend it wasn't there. He invited Cain to self-awareness and reflection. Grace is patient, but it is not passive. It confronts internal disorder before it becomes external damage. God's question was an invitation to pause, examine, and choose differently.

In life, grace often speaks through inner conviction, wise counsel, or gentle correction. When these prompts are ignored, the consequences feel harsh—but grace had already made its appeal. God's willingness to speak, even when rejection is likely, reflects His desire for restoration, not punishment.

Key Lessons & Life Applications

- **Teaching:** Grace engages the heart before addressing behavior.
- **Reproof:** Ignoring conviction hardens the heart.
- **Correction:** Emotional awareness is critical to wise choices.
- **Instruction:** Pause and reflect when grace speaks.
- **Righteous Living:** Growth begins with honest self-examination.

Prayer Points

1. Father, help me recognize when You are speaking to my heart.
2. Give me humility to listen before reacting.
3. Teach me to address inner unrest early.
4. Guard me from ignoring conviction.
5. Lead me in wisdom and self-awareness.

Meditation / Reflection

Am I attentive when God speaks to my emotions and attitudes? Do I pause to reflect, or do I rush past conviction?

Consider how listening early can prevent deeper pain.

Words of Wisdom: *Grace often speaks quietly before consequences speak loudly*

February 6

Theme: Grace Does Not Force Compliance

Anchor Scripture - "If you do well, will you not be accepted? And if you do not do well, sin lies at the door. And its desire is for you, but you should rule over it." **Genesis 4:7**

Devotional Thought

Grace provides instruction, but it does not remove choice. God clearly outlined the path before Cain—acceptance through obedience, danger through neglect. Yet God did not force Cain's response. This reveals an essential aspect of grace: **it respects human will.**

Grace does not manipulate or coerce. It empowers choice while clarifying consequence. God described sin as something waiting at the door—near, persistent, and opportunistic. Cain was warned, equipped, and informed, yet still free to choose. Grace never violates responsibility.

In life, grace often provides clarity without compulsion. God gives insight, warnings, and direction, but He allows individuals to decide. Obedience is meaningful only when it is chosen. Grace honors dignity by honoring choice, even when that choice leads to loss.

Key Lessons & Life Applications

- **Teaching:** Grace clarifies responsibility without removing choice.
- **Reproof:** Freedom without discipline invites harm.
- **Correction:** Recognize danger before it gains control.
- **Instruction:** Take responsibility for mastering harmful impulses.
- **Righteous Living:** True obedience flows from willing submission.

Prayer Points

1. Father, help me choose obedience when grace gives me insight.
2. Strengthen my will to resist what seeks to control me.
3. Teach me to act wisely with the freedom You give.
4. Help me recognize danger before it overtakes me.
5. Align my choices with Your truth.

Meditation / Reflection

Do I expect grace to remove responsibility instead of empowering it? Where do I need to exercise self-control today?

Reflect on how choice shapes outcomes.

Words of Wisdom: *Grace informs the will, but it never replaces it.*

February 7

Theme: Grace Can Be Rejected

> **Anchor Scripture** - "And Cain talked with Abel his brother; and it came to pass, when they were in the field, that Cain rose against Abel his brother and killed him." **Genesis 4:8**

Devotional Thought

The tragedy of Cain's story is not that grace was absent—it is that grace was rejected. God warned Cain, instructed him, and gave him opportunity to choose differently. Yet Cain ignored grace and acted from anger and self-will. This passage reveals a sobering truth: **grace can be refused.**

Grace does not guarantee transformation; response does. When grace is ignored, the consequences are often irreversible. Cain's act did not occur in isolation—it followed ignored warnings, unaddressed emotions, and resisted instruction. Grace had spoken, but Cain chose otherwise.

This reminds us that grace is powerful, but it is not automatic. It invites, instructs, and empowers—but it must be received. Rejection of grace leads not only to personal loss, but often to harm beyond oneself.

Key Lessons & Life Applications

- **Teaching:** Grace must be received to be effective.
- **Reproof:** Ignored warnings lead to deeper consequences.
- **Correction:** Address issues early before damage occurs.
- **Instruction:** Respond promptly when grace speaks.
- **Righteous Living:** Humility keeps the heart open to grace.

Prayer Points

1. Father, help me receive Your grace when it is offered.
2. Guard my heart from stubbornness and pride.
3. Teach me to respond quickly to Your instruction.
4. Heal areas where I have resisted correction.
5. Lead me in humility and obedience.

Meditation / Reflection

Have I ignored grace in any area of my life? What warnings have I postponed addressing?
Consider how responding early could change outcomes.

Words of Wisdom: *Grace rejected becomes an opportunity lost.*

February 8

Theme: Grace Invites Ownership Before Judgment

Anchor Scripture - "And the LORD said, 'Where is Abel your brother?' He said, 'I do not know. Am I my brother's keeper?' And He said, 'What have you done? The voice of your brother's blood cries out to Me from the ground.'" Genesis 4:9–10

Devotional Thought

Grace does not withdraw when sin occurs—it speaks. When God asked Cain, *"Where is Abel your brother?"* He was not seeking information; He was extending an opportunity for ownership. Grace created space for confession before judgment followed.

Cain's response revealed deflection rather than repentance. Instead of owning his actions, he attempted to evade responsibility. At that moment, God revealed a sobering truth: *"The voice of your brother's blood cries out to Me from the ground."* This shows that when ownership is refused, truth still testifies. Silence does not erase reality.

Ownership does not cancel consequences, but it delays damage and opens the door to mercy and restoration. Scripture later affirms this pattern: those who cover their sins do not prosper, but those who confess and forsake them find mercy. Grace always invites ownership before consequences escalate. When that invitation is ignored, restoration becomes harder, and damage deepens.

Key Lessons & Life Applications

- **Teaching:** Grace invites confession before judgment.
- **Reproof:** Deflection prolongs damage.
- **Correction:** Ownership creates space for mercy.
- **Instruction:** Respond honestly when grace confronts you.
- **Righteous Living:** Integrity restores alignment.

Prayer Points

1. Father, help me respond with honesty when You confront me.
2. Deliver me from covering my errors with excuses.
3. Give me courage to take responsibility for my actions.
4. Let confession lead me toward restoration, not fear.
5. Teach me to embrace grace through humility.

Meditation / Reflection

Am I owning my errors, or attempting to hide them?
Where might confession open the door to mercy and restoration?
Reflect on how ownership can prevent deeper damage.

Words of Wisdom: *Owning our errors does not cancel consequences, but it opens the door to mercy and restoration.*

February 9

Theme: Grace Limits Damage Even When It Judges

Anchor Scripture - "So the LORD said to him, 'Therefore, whoever kills Cain, vengeance shall be taken on him sevenfold.' And the LORD set a mark on Cain, lest anyone finding him should kill him." Genesis 4:15

Devotional Thought

Even in judgment, grace is active. Cain's punishment was real—he lost his place, his peace, and his proximity. Yet God did not allow destruction to continue unchecked. He placed a mark on Cain, not as approval, but as protection. This reveals a profound truth: **grace limits damage even when judgment is necessary.**

God addressed the wrongdoing without permitting endless retaliation. The mark was not honor; it was restraint. Grace ensured that consequence would not escalate into chaos. Judgment corrected the course, but grace preserved life.

In our lives, God's correction often includes boundaries that prevent further harm. Grace does not always restore immediately, but it stabilizes. It keeps consequences from multiplying beyond their purpose.

Key Lessons & Life Applications

- **Teaching:** God's judgments are measured, not reckless.
- **Reproof:** Consequences are meant to correct, not destroy.
- **Correction:** Grace sets limits even in discipline.
- **Instruction:** Accept boundaries as protection.
- **Righteous Living:** God's restraint reveals His mercy.

Prayer Points

1. Father, thank You for limiting harm in my life.
2. Help me recognize Your grace even in correction.
3. Teach me to respect the boundaries You establish.
4. Protect me from unnecessary loss.
5. Let Your discipline produce wisdom.

Meditation / Reflection

Can I see God's grace within His correction?

Have boundaries protected me from greater harm? Reflect on how restraint can be an expression of love.

Words of Wisdom: *Even in judgment, grace works to contain destruction.*

February 10

Theme: Grace Preserves the Future

> **Anchor Scripture -** "Then Cain went out from the presence of the LORD and dwelt in the land of Nod on the east of Eden." Genesis 4:16

Devotional Thought

Cain's departure from God's presence marked a turning point. Fellowship was broken, and distance followed. Yet Cain's story did not end there. Life continued. This reveals a sobering but hopeful truth: **grace preserves the future even when intimacy is lost**.

God allowed Cain to live, build, and move forward—though no longer from the same place. Grace did not restore fellowship immediately, but it preserved opportunity. Cain's choices altered his access, but not God's overarching commitment to humanity.

In life, disobedience can affect closeness with God, but grace ensures that failure does not end the story. Distance is not the same as abandonment. Grace keeps the future possible, even when restoration requires time.

Key Lessons & Life Applications

- **Teaching:** Choices affect proximity, not God's faithfulness.
- **Reproof:** Loss of intimacy has consequences.
- **Correction:** Restoration may require distance and time.
- **Instruction:** Seek renewal even after missteps.
- **Righteous Living:** Grace sustains hope beyond failure.

Prayer Points

1. Father, draw me back when distance grows.
2. Help me value Your presence above all else.
3. Restore intimacy where it has been damaged.
4. Keep my future secure in Your grace.
5. Teach me to walk humbly toward restoration.

Meditation / Reflection

Has distance replaced intimacy in any area of my life? What steps can I take toward renewed fellowship?

Reflect on how grace keeps hope alive.

Words of Wisdom: *Grace keeps the future open, even when intimacy is broken.*

February 11

Theme: Grace Operates Within Boundaries

> **Anchor Scripture** - "And Adam knew his wife again, and she bore a son and named him Seth, 'For God has appointed another seed for me instead of Abel, whom Cain killed.'" Genesis 4:25

Devotional Thought

Grace does not erase boundaries; it works within them. Adam and Eve were removed from Eden because the requirements for occupancy were no longer met. Eden demanded innocence, obedience, and unhindered fellowship—conditions that could not be sustained after the fall. Yet removal from Eden did not mean removal from God's agenda.

Though disqualified from Eden, Adam and Eve remained relevant. Grace preserved their role in humanity's future, even if at a different level. Their access changed, but their purpose did not end. Likewise, Cain's failure, though severe, did not terminate the human story. Grace ensured continuity through Seth.

This reveals an important principle: **there are measures of grace**. Grace restores direction, but not always position. God honors structure and order, even while sustaining purpose. Boundaries are not rejection; they are protection. Grace does not force access where conditions are unmet, but it never abandons the future.

In life, some doors close not because God is done with us, but because the environment requires maturity we have not yet regained. Grace redirects without discarding.

Key Lessons & Life Applications

- **Teaching:** Grace operates within divine boundaries.
- **Reproof:** Disqualification from one place does not equal rejection.
- **Correction:** Accept redirection without resentment.
- **Instruction:** Honor the requirements of every environment.
- **Righteous Living:** Growth restores access over time.

Prayer Points

1. Father, help me accept Your boundaries without bitterness.
2. Teach me to grow into environments You prepare for me.
3. Restore purpose even when access is restricted.
4. Help me recognize grace in redirection.
5. Align my expectations with Your wisdom and timing.

Meditation / Reflection

Am I resisting boundaries God has placed for my growth? Have I confused redirection with rejection?

Reflect on how grace may be repositioning you, not removing you.

Words of Wisdom: *Grace has boundaries—to preserve purpose, maintain order, and protect God's standards.*

February 12

Theme: Grace Rebuilds What Failure Disrupted

Anchor Scripture - "And as for Seth, to him also a son was born; and he named him Enosh. Then men began to call on the name of the LORD." Genesis 4:26

Devotional Thought

With Seth's lineage came a spiritual reset. Scripture records that people began again to call on the name of the Lord. Grace did more than replace loss—it **restored worship**. Where violence and self-will once dominated, reverence re-emerged.

Grace rebuilds what failure disrupts. It restores spiritual rhythm, not by ignoring the past, but by re-centering the heart. The return to worship signals renewed alignment. Grace does not just preserve life; it restores relationship.

In personal and communal life, grace re-establishes spiritual priority. After seasons of confusion or compromise, grace invites people back to God—not with shame, but with renewal.

Key Lessons & Life Applications

- **Teaching:** Grace restores spiritual alignment.
- **Reproof:** Loss of worship weakens identity.
- **Correction:** Re-establish spiritual focus after disruption.
- **Instruction:** Let grace draw you back to God.
- **Righteous Living:** Worship sustains alignment.

Prayer Points

1. Father, restore my devotion to You.
2. Re-center my heart where distractions crept in.
3. Renew my hunger for Your presence.
4. Heal spiritual drift caused by past failures.
5. Let grace restore my worship.

Meditation / Reflection

Has my devotion weakened due to disappointment?
What would restored worship look like in my life?

Words of Wisdom: *Grace restores worship before it restores momentum.*

February 13

Theme: Grace Re-Establishes Spiritual Lineage

Anchor Scripture - "This is the book of the genealogy of Adam. In the day that God created man, He made him in the likeness of God." Genesis 5:1

Devotional Thought

After the fall, after violence, after loss, Scripture deliberately pauses to restate identity. Genesis does not begin this chapter by rehearsing sin; it reaffirms origin. Humanity is reintroduced not by failure, but by design—*made in the likeness of God*. This is a foundational truth: **sin did not change who humanity was created to be.**

Sin can hinder purpose, delay destiny, and disrupt direction, but it does not erase identity. A wrinkled or dirty bill may look damaged, but its value remains unchanged. In the same way, failure may distort function, but it does not cancel worth. A son does not stop being a son because he behaves foolishly. An illegitimate label does not negate lineage.

This understanding is what empowered the prodigal son to return home. He remembered who he was before he remembered what he had done. Many people stay distant from God not because grace is unavailable, but because they believe their past disqualifies them from being recognized. Yet God's grace re-establishes lineage—even when boundaries are required. God can identify with you without condoning your choices. Grace restores identity while correcting behavior.

Key Lessons & Life Applications

- **Teaching:** Identity is rooted in creation, not performance.
- **Reproof:** Shame falsely convinces people they are disqualified.
- **Correction:** Separate who you are from what you have done.
- **Instruction:** Return to God on the basis of identity, not perfection.
- **Righteous Living:** Transformation begins with identity clarity.

Prayer Points

1. Father, thank You that my identity is rooted in Your design.
2. Heal distortions caused by shame and past failure.
3. Help me separate my mistakes from who I am in You.
4. Restore confidence in my spiritual lineage.
5. Teach me to receive correction without rejecting my identity.

Meditation / Reflection

Have I allowed my past to redefine who I am?
Do I approach God as a disqualified servant or as a returning child? Reflect on how identity clarity changes access and confidence.

Words of Wisdom: *Failure may wrinkle destiny and stall purpose, but it does not erase identity.*

February 14

Theme: Grace Preserves God's Image

> **Anchor Scripture** - "This is the book of the genealogy of Adam. In the day that God created man, He made him in the likeness of God. He created them male and female, and blessed them and called them Mankind in the day they were created." **Genesis 5:1–2**

Devotional Thought

After sin altered behavior, God reaffirmed identity. Genesis pauses to remind humanity that creation was intentional and identity was bestowed before failure occurred. Grace preserves what sin attempts to distort. God restated that humanity was still created in His likeness—failure had not revoked design.

Grace does not rewrite identity; it restores awareness of it. Before humanity could move forward, God re-established the truth of who they were. Identity anchored the future, not performance. Grace ensured that humanity was not defined by its fall, but by its Creator.

In life, grace often reminds us of truths we forgot under pressure. When shame attempts to redefine identity, grace restores clarity. The image of God remains the foundation for restoration.

Key Lessons & Life Applications

- **Teaching:** God's image is preserved through grace.
- **Reproof:** Failure does not erase identity.
- **Correction:** Reject definitions rooted in shame.
- **Instruction:** Live from divine identity, not past mistakes.
- **Righteous Living:** Identity clarity stabilizes purpose.

Prayer Points

1. Father, thank You for preserving Your image in me.
2. Heal distortions caused by shame or failure.
3. Restore my confidence in who You created me to be.
4. Help me live from identity, not insecurity.
5. Anchor my future in Your truth.

Meditation / Reflection

Am I allowing failure to redefine my identity?
How does knowing I bear God's image change my perspective?

Words of Wisdom: *Grace preserves identity when failure tries to rewrite it.*

February 15

Theme: Grace Measures Life by Faithfulness, Not Speed

Anchor Scripture - "So all the days that Adam lived were nine hundred and thirty years; and he died." Genesis 5:5

Devotional Thought

Genesis records long lives with simple summaries. No achievements are listed, no accolades highlighted—only faithfulness through time. Grace reframes success. It values endurance over acceleration and consistency over spectacle.

Grace measures life by alignment, not pace. Adam lived, walked, and endured through change, loss, and consequence. His life reminds us that progress is not always dramatic. Sometimes grace is seen in sustained obedience over time.

In a world obsessed with speed and visibility, grace honors faithfulness. God records what matters, not what impresses. Longevity with God is itself a testimony.

Key Lessons & Life Applications

- **Teaching:** Faithfulness matters more than speed.
- **Reproof:** Rushing can compromise alignment.
- **Correction:** Measure progress by obedience, not comparison.
- **Instruction:** Embrace steady growth.
- **Righteous Living:** Endurance honors God.

Prayer Points

1. Father, teach me to value faithfulness over urgency.
2. Help me remain steady in obedience.
3. Guard me from comparison and impatience.
4. Strengthen my endurance.
5. Let my life honor You consistently.

Meditation / Reflection

Do I value speed more than alignment?
What would faithfulness look like in my current season?

Words of Wisdom: *Grace honors endurance more than acceleration.*

February 16

Theme: Grace Walks With Those Who Choose Alignment

Anchor Scripture - "Enoch walked with God; and he was not, for God took him." Genesis 5:24

Devotional Thought

Enoch's life is summarized in one phrase: *he walked with God*. Grace is relational before it is positional. Enoch's story reveals that closeness with God is possible even in imperfect generations. Grace empowers intimacy amid broken contexts.

Walking with God implies agreement, pace, and direction. Enoch aligned his life with God's movement. Grace does not remove responsibility; it invites relationship. Alignment creates intimacy.

In life, grace calls us not merely to survive, but to walk with God. It is possible to live differently—even when surrounded by compromise—when alignment is chosen.

Key Lessons & Life Applications

- **Teaching:** Grace invites relational alignment.
- **Reproof:** Distance grows where alignment is neglected.
- **Correction:** Restore intimacy through intentional walk.
- **Instruction:** Match your pace with God's direction.
- **Righteous Living:** Intimacy flows from agreement.

Prayer Points

1. Father, teach me to walk closely with You.
2. Align my steps with Your will.
3. Remove distractions that disrupt intimacy.
4. Help me choose alignment daily.
5. Draw me into deeper fellowship.

Meditation / Reflection

What does walking with God look like in my daily life?
Where do I need to adjust my pace or direction?

Words of Wisdom: *Grace draws near to those who choose alignment.*

February 17

Theme: Grace Distinguishes Before It Delivers

Anchor Scripture - "But Noah found grace in the eyes of the LORD." Genesis 6:8

Devotional Thought

This verse marks a turning point in Scripture. For the first time, the word *grace* is formally introduced—not in a moment of peace, but in a world overwhelmed by corruption and violence. Grace appears not as an escape from reality, but as God's deliberate distinction within it. **Grace did not remove Noah from the world; it distinguished him within it.**

To *find grace* means to be recognized, regarded, and positioned by God for purpose. Grace set Noah apart before deliverance ever came. The flood had not yet begun, the ark had not yet been built, and obedience had not yet been demonstrated—yet grace had already identified its carrier. This reveals a profound truth: **grace precedes action, but it demands response**.

Grace did not make Noah passive; it made him responsible. Grace did not cancel judgment; it created a path of preservation. In a generation marked by disorder, grace located a man willing to walk differently. Grace always finds expression through someone who will steward it faithfully.

In life, grace often shows up as divine distinction before visible change occurs. It identifies, positions, and entrusts—long before outcomes are seen.

Key Lessons & Life Applications

- **Teaching:** Grace identifies before it delivers.
- **Reproof:** Grace is not accidental; it is intentional recognition.
- **Correction:** Do not confuse grace with exemption from responsibility.
- **Instruction:** Steward the distinction grace brings.
- **Righteous Living:** Grace invites obedience, not passivity.

Prayer Points

1. Father, thank You for the grace that distinguishes and positions.
2. Help me recognize the responsibility grace carries.
3. Teach me to steward grace faithfully.
4. Separate me from patterns that oppose Your purpose.
5. Let my life reflect the grace I have received.

Meditation / Reflection

Have I recognized how grace has distinguished me?

Am I responding to grace with obedience or complacency? Reflect on what responsibility grace is inviting you to carry.

Words of Wisdom: *Grace distinguishes before it delivers—and entrusts before it preserves.*

February 18

Theme: Grace Operates Within Order

Anchor Scripture - "These are the generations of Noah. Noah was a just man, perfect in his generations. Noah walked with God." Genesis 6:9

Devotional Thought

Grace did not operate randomly in Noah's life—it aligned with character and order. Scripture emphasizes Noah's walk, not just God's favor. Grace flowed through structure, discipline, and alignment.

Grace does not oppose order; it requires it. Noah's righteousness was not perfection without flaw, but consistency without compromise. His walk with God created stability in a corrupt world.

In life, grace flourishes where order is honored. Disorder frustrates grace, while alignment sustains it. God's grace rests comfortably on lives that are structured, disciplined, and intentional.

Key Lessons & Life Applications

- **Teaching:** Grace functions best within order.
- **Reproof:** Disorder weakens spiritual effectiveness.
- **Correction:** Restore alignment where compromise exists.
- **Instruction:** Build disciplined habits that support grace.
- **Righteous Living:** Consistency protects calling.

Prayer Points

1. Father, align my life with Your order.
2. Help me walk consistently with You.
3. Remove patterns that disrupt alignment.
4. Strengthen my discipline and obedience.
5. Let grace rest fully on my life.

Meditation / Reflection

Does my lifestyle support or frustrate grace? Where does God invite me to restore order?

Words of Wisdom: *Grace thrives where order is honored.*

February 19

Theme: Grace Preserves Through Obedience

Anchor Scripture - "And Noah did according to all that the LORD commanded him." Genesis 6:22

Devotional Thought

Grace provided instruction, but obedience preserved life. Noah's faith was proven not by belief alone, but by action sustained over time. Grace revealed what to do; obedience carried it through.

This verse captures the simplicity and weight of obedience. Noah did not negotiate, delay, or reinterpret God's instructions. Grace gave clarity; obedience ensured survival.

In life, grace provides direction, but obedience secures outcome. Preservation is often the fruit of sustained obedience rather than dramatic faith moments. Grace initiates, but obedience completes the process.

Key Lessons & Life Applications

- **Teaching:** Obedience activates preservation.
- **Reproof:** Partial obedience undermines outcomes.
- **Correction:** Follow instruction without alteration.
- **Instruction:** Remain faithful through the process.
- **Righteous Living:** Obedience honors grace.

Prayer Points

1. Father, help me obey fully and faithfully.
2. Strengthen my resolve to follow Your instruction.
3. Remove hesitation and compromise from my response.
4. Teach me to trust the process You establish.
5. Let obedience secure what grace has begun.

Meditation / Reflection

Am I obedient in both instruction and endurance?
Where might delayed obedience be weakening outcomes?

Words of Wisdom: *Grace reveals the path; obedience preserves the future.*

February 20

Theme: Grace Prepares Before Crisis Arrives

Anchor Scripture - "And God said to Noah, 'The end of all flesh has come before Me, for the earth is filled with violence through them; and behold, I will destroy them with the earth.'" Genesis 6:13

Devotional Thought

Grace does not wait for crisis to arrive before preparing a solution. God informed Noah of what was coming long before the flood began. This was not panic—it was preparation. Grace gave advance insight so obedience could begin early.

God did not reveal the problem without also revealing the plan. Grace equips ahead of time, allowing responsibility to replace fear. Preparation is a gift of grace, not a sign of anxiety.

In life, grace often gives foresight—through conviction, instruction, or wisdom—so we can act before situations escalate. Ignoring preparation is not faith; it is vulnerability.

Key Lessons & Life Applications

(2 Timothy 3:16)

- **Teaching:** Grace provides foresight for preparation.
- **Reproof:** Waiting until crisis arrives invites unnecessary loss.
- **Correction:** Respond early to divine instruction.
- **Instruction:** Prepare faithfully even when others do not.
- **Righteous Living:** Obedience begins before urgency.

Prayer Points

1. Father, help me recognize Your preparation moments.
2. Teach me to act on insight before pressure comes.
3. Deliver me from procrastination disguised as faith.
4. Strengthen my discipline in seasons of calm.
5. Let preparation protect my future.

Meditation / Reflection

Have I ignored preparation because the crisis has not yet arrived?
What instruction has God already given me?

Words of Wisdom: *Grace prepares long before urgency demands action.*

February 21

Theme: Grace Gives Specific Instructions

Anchor Scripture - "Make yourself an ark of gopherwood; make rooms in the ark, and cover it inside and outside with pitch." Genesis 6:14

Devotional Thought

Grace is not vague. When God instructed Noah, He gave specific details—materials, structure, and method. Grace did not leave room for guesswork. Precision protected preservation.

Specific instruction reveals that grace values clarity. God did not say, "Build something." He said, "Build this." Obedience thrives where instruction is clear. Ambiguity weakens outcomes.

In life, grace often provides detailed direction through Scripture, counsel, or inner conviction. Ignoring specifics while claiming obedience leads to compromised results. Grace speaks clearly to those willing to listen carefully.

Key Lessons & Life Applications

- **Teaching:** Grace communicates with clarity.
- **Reproof:** Vague obedience weakens effectiveness.
- **Correction:** Follow instruction as given, not as preferred.
- **Instruction:** Pay attention to details God provides.
- **Righteous Living:** Precision honors divine wisdom

Prayer Points

1. Father, help me value Your specific instructions.
2. Remove resistance to details that challenge my comfort.
3. Teach me to obey fully, not selectively.
4. Sharpen my discernment to hear clearly.
5. Let accuracy protect my assignment.

Meditation / Reflection

Do I follow God's instructions precisely or partially? Where might details matter more than I realized?

Words of Wisdom: *Grace speaks clearly; obedience listens carefully.*

February 22

Theme: Grace Assigns Responsibility for Others

Anchor Scripture - "And you shall bring into the ark two of every sort of living thing, to keep them alive with you; they shall be male and female." Genesis 6:19

Devotional Thought

Grace extended beyond Noah—it included others. God entrusted Noah with responsibility not only for himself, but for life beyond him. Grace assigns stewardship that impacts generations.

Preservation required cooperation. Noah's obedience affected creation itself. Grace often places responsibility on individuals so others may benefit. Leadership is stewardship shaped by grace.

In life, grace frequently entrusts us with responsibility for people, systems, or outcomes beyond personal interest. Faithfulness affects more than one life. Grace expands responsibility because it trusts character.

Key Lessons & Life Applications

- **Teaching:** Grace entrusts responsibility beyond self.
- **Reproof:** Self-centered obedience limits impact.
- **Correction:** Embrace stewardship that serves others.
- **Instruction:** Lead with awareness of broader influence.
- **Righteous Living:** Responsibility reflects maturity.

Prayer Points

1. Father, help me steward what affects others wisely.
2. Teach me to lead with responsibility and care.
3. Remove selfishness from my obedience.
4. Strengthen me to carry influence faithfully.
5. Let grace shape my leadership.

Meditation / Reflection

Who benefits from my obedience?

Am I stewarding responsibility beyond myself?

Words of Wisdom: *Grace entrusted to one often preserves many.*

February 23

Theme: Grace Has a Window

Anchor Scripture - "My Spirit shall not strive with man forever…" Genesis 6:3

Devotional Thought

Grace is generous, but it is not indefinite. Before the flood came, grace warned, instructed, and waited. God gave humanity time to respond, space to repent, and a visible provision for refuge. The ark did not appear suddenly; it stood as a testimony of grace in plain sight.

Grace strives before it judges. It speaks before it acts. But grace also honors human choice. When grace is consistently resisted, it does not disappear—it withdraws its striving. Judgment is not the absence of grace; it is the consequence of ignored grace.

In life, grace often arrives with opportunity and timing. Delayed obedience can become missed opportunity. Grace opens a door, but it does not force entry. Wisdom recognizes when grace is inviting a response.

Key Lessons & Life Applications

- **Teaching:** Grace operates within time and response.
- **Reproof:** Presuming grace will always wait is dangerous.
- **Correction:** Respond promptly to God's instruction.
- **Instruction:** Recognize seasons of divine invitation.
- **Righteous Living:** Obedience honors grace.

Prayer Points

1. Father, help me recognize when grace is inviting action.
2. Deliver me from delaying obedience.
3. Teach me to respond while opportunity remains.
4. Keep my heart sensitive to Your warnings.
5. Help me value grace with urgency.

Meditation / Reflection

Have I delayed responding to God's instruction?
What door of grace may be open right now?

Words of Wisdom: *Grace opens a door—but it does not hold it open forever.*

February 24

Theme: Grace Provides Refuge, Not Perfection

Anchor Scripture - "And Noah went in, and his sons and his wife and his sons' wives with him, into the ark, because of the waters of the flood." Genesis 7:7

Devotional Thought

Those who entered the ark were not preserved because they were perfect, but because they were positioned. Grace did not require flawlessness; it required alignment. Refuge was found inside what God provided, not in personal righteousness.

Grace often works through association. Noah found grace, and those connected to his obedience were covered. Protection flowed through alignment, not merit. This pattern echoes throughout Scripture: salvation comes through entering what God provides.

In life, grace invites us into safety through obedience. Perfection is not the requirement—positioning is. Refuge is found not in who we are, but in where we stand.

Key Lessons & Life Applications

- **Teaching:** Grace preserves through alignment, not perfection.
- **Reproof:** Self-righteousness misunderstands grace.
- **Correction:** Enter what God provides rather than trusting self.
- **Instruction:** Align with obedience that brings protection.
- **Righteous Living:** Safety flows from submission.

Prayer Points

1. Father, help me align with what You have provided.
2. Remove pride that resists instruction.
3. Teach me to trust Your provision.
4. Cover those connected to my obedience.
5. Let grace position me for preservation.

Meditation / Reflection

Am I trusting my effort or God's provision?
Where is God inviting me to step into safety?

Words of Wisdom: *Grace protects those who position themselves within its provision.*

February 25

Theme: Grace Does Not Cancel Accountability

Anchor Scripture - "And the LORD shut him in." Genesis 7:16

Devotional Thought

The same God who opened the door also shut it. This moment reveals a sobering truth: grace and accountability are not opposites. Grace provided access; accountability enforced consequence. Once the door closed, opportunity ended.

Grace does not eliminate boundaries—it establishes them. The closing of the door was not cruelty; it was finality. Protection for those inside required separation from those outside. Love does not cancel accountability; it upholds it.

In leadership, parenting, and personal responsibility, this principle remains. Failing to enforce boundaries in the name of compassion creates disorder. God models decisive leadership—gracious, yet firm.

Key Lessons & Life Applications

- **Teaching:** Grace and accountability coexist.
- **Reproof:** Avoiding boundaries weakens protection.
- **Correction:** Enforce limits when necessary.
- **Instruction:** Lead with clarity and courage.
- **Righteous Living:** Obedience respects boundaries.

Prayer Points

1. Father, help me honor boundaries You establish.
2. Teach me to enforce accountability with wisdom.
3. Remove fear of decisive leadership.
4. Help me balance compassion with responsibility.
5. Strengthen my discernment in difficult decisions.

Meditation / Reflection

Where do I avoid enforcing necessary boundaries? How does accountability protect what matters most?

Words of Wisdom: *Love does not cancel accountability—it gives it purpose.*

February 26

Theme: Grace Restores After Judgment

Anchor Scripture - "Then God spoke to Noah and to his sons with him, saying, 'And as for Me, behold, I establish My covenant with you and with your descendants after you.'" Genesis 9:8–9

Devotional Thought

Judgment was not God's final word—restoration was. After the flood subsided, God initiated covenant. Grace did not end with survival; it moved toward relationship. God spoke again, not in anger, but in promise.

This reveals a powerful truth: **grace restores after judgment**. Correction may shape the journey, but grace secures the future. God did not leave humanity in fear or uncertainty; He anchored them with covenant.

In life, seasons of correction are not conclusions. Grace follows discipline with reassurance. God's desire is not to punish endlessly, but to restore stability and trust. Covenant speaks of continuity beyond failure.

Key Lessons & Life Applications

- **Teaching:** God's heart moves toward restoration.
- **Reproof:** Judgment is not abandonment.
- **Correction:** Do not mistake discipline for rejection.
- **Instruction:** Receive God's promises after correction.
- **Righteous Living:** Hope grows where covenant is embraced.

Prayer Points

1. Father, thank You for restoring after correction.
2. Help me trust Your promises beyond past discipline.
3. Heal areas wounded by fear or loss.
4. Anchor my future in Your covenant.
5. Teach me to move forward with confidence.

Meditation / Reflection

Have I viewed correction as final rather than formative? How does covenant change my outlook?

Words of Wisdom

February 27

Theme: Grace Establishes Stability

Anchor Scripture - "I set My rainbow in the cloud, and it shall be for the sign of the covenant between Me and the earth." Genesis 9:13

Devotional Thought

After chaos, God established stability. The rainbow was not merely a sign of beauty—it was a declaration of assurance. Grace does not leave humanity guessing; it provides visible reminders of faithfulness.

God anchored the future with a sign that transcended emotion and circumstance. Grace stabilizes by reminding us of God's commitment. Even when storms return, the promise remains.

In life, grace often establishes anchors—truths, assurances, and reminders—that restore confidence after disruption. Stability is not the absence of storms; it is the presence of promise.

Key Lessons & Life Applications

- **Teaching:** Grace establishes assurance after disruption.
- **Reproof:** Fear thrives where assurance is forgotten.
- **Correction:** Re-anchor life in God's promises.
- **Instruction:** Remember what God has declared.
- **Righteous Living:** Confidence flows from covenant.

Prayer Points

1. Father, thank You for signs of Your faithfulness.
2. Help me remember Your promises during uncertainty.
3. Restore my confidence after past storms.
4. Anchor my heart in truth, not fear.
5. Let grace stabilize my life.

Meditation / Reflection

What promises has God already given me?
How can I remember them during storms?

Words of Wisdom: *Grace establishes stability by anchoring us in promise.*

February 28

Theme: Grace Preserves Purpose Across Generations

> **Anchor Scripture -** "And God blessed Noah and his sons, and said to them: 'Be fruitful and multiply, and fill the earth.'" Genesis 9:1

Devotional Thought

Grace does not stop with survival—it restores purpose. After the flood, God reaffirmed humanity's original mandate. Failure had interrupted progress, but grace preserved destiny. God's blessing reintroduced fruitfulness, expansion, and responsibility. Grace reactivates assignment after crisis. The past did not cancel the future; it refined it.

In life, grace restores calling after seasons of loss or correction. Purpose is not revoked by failure—it is reestablished through grace. God's agenda continues.

Key Lessons & Life Applications

- **Teaching:** Grace restores purpose after disruption.
- **Reproof:** Do not abandon calling due to past failure.
- **Correction:** Re-engage destiny with humility.
- **Instruction:** Walk forward with renewed responsibility.
- **Righteous Living:** Purpose thrives under grace.

Prayer Points

1. Father, thank You for restoring purpose in my life.
2. Heal discouragement caused by past failures.
3. Reignite vision and calling.
4. Help me steward purpose faithfully.
5. Let grace guide my future.

Meditation / Reflection

Have I disengaged from purpose due to past disruption? How does grace invite me to re-engage?

Words of Wisdom: *Grace does not erase purpose—it restores it.*

February 29 — Bonus Day

Theme: Grace Secures What Judgment Could Not Destroy

Anchor Scripture - "For the gifts and the calling of God are irrevocable." Romans 11:29

Devotional Thought

The flood reshaped the world, but it did not cancel God's intent. Grace carried humanity forward despite judgment. God's calling endured beyond failure, correction, and loss.

This bonus day reminds us that grace is not reactive—it is redemptive. What judgment corrects, grace preserves. God's plan is not fragile. Even when humanity falters, grace secures destiny.

As this month closes, we stand on a powerful truth: **grace sustains God's purpose through every season**.

Key Lessons & Life Applications

- **Teaching:** God's calling is preserved by grace.
- **Reproof:** Failure does not disqualify destiny.
- **Correction:** Release fear of permanent loss.
- **Instruction:** Trust God's long-term plan.
- **Righteous Living:** Hope anchors endurance.

Prayer Points

1. Father, thank You for securing my calling by grace.
2. Heal fear of disqualification.
3. Strengthen my trust in Your redemptive plan.
4. Help me walk confidently into the future.
5. Let grace sustain me through every season.

Meditation / Reflection

What fear of loss has grace already answered?
How does knowing God's calling is secure change my outlook?

Words of Wisdom: *Grace preserves what judgment corrects.*

March
Redemption Unfolds
(The Patriarchs)

March 1

Theme: Redemption Begins With Covenant

Anchor Scripture - "Then God spoke to Noah and to his sons with him, saying: 'And as for Me, behold, I establish My covenant with you and with your descendants after you, and with every living creature that is with you... Never again shall all flesh be cut off by the waters of the flood.'" Genesis 9:8–11

Devotional Thought

Redemption does not begin with correction; it begins with covenant. After judgment had run its course, God did not retreat from humanity—He bound Himself to them. Covenant was God's way of saying that failure would not have the final word. Redemption would unfold within relationship, not distance.

God's covenant was not based on human perfection but on divine commitment. Humanity had proven fragile, yet God chose faithfulness. This marks a shift in the story: grace preserved life, and covenant now directs it. Redemption begins when God commits Himself to restoring what was broken.

In life, redemption often starts when God reaffirms His commitment to us—even while growth and maturity are still in process. Covenant provides stability while transformation unfolds.

Key Lessons & Life Applications

- **Teaching:** Redemption is rooted in God's commitment, not human consistency.
- **Reproof:** Failure does not nullify God's covenant.
- **Correction:** Stop interpreting discipline as abandonment.
- **Instruction:** Build life on God's promises, not past mistakes.
- **Righteous Living:** Covenant provides confidence for growth.

Prayer Points

1. Father, thank You for committing Yourself to my restoration.
2. Help me trust Your promises even while I am still growing.
3. Heal places where I feared abandonment.
4. Anchor my life in Your covenant faithfulness.
5. Let redemption unfold through obedience and trust.

Meditation / Reflection

Do I live as someone secured by covenant or haunted by failure? How does knowing God is committed to me change my outlook?

Words of Wisdom: *Redemption begins when God commits Himself to restoring what was broken.*

March 1

Theme: Unity Without God Leads to Confusion

Anchor Scripture - "Now the whole earth had one language and one speech… And they said, 'Come, let us build ourselves a city, and a tower whose top is in the heavens; let us make a name for ourselves.'" Genesis 11:1–4

Devotional Thought

Unity is powerful—but only when rightly aligned. At Babel, humanity achieved unity without submission to God. They spoke one language, shared one goal, and worked with remarkable cooperation. Yet their unity was self-centered, not God-directed.

This passage reveals an important truth about redemption: **not all togetherness is healthy**. When unity is driven by pride and self-preservation, it leads to confusion rather than progress. God intervened not to punish unity, but to redirect humanity toward purpose.

In life, collaboration without alignment produces instability. Redemption requires unity that honors God's design. God disrupts misplaced unity to preserve long-term purpose.

Key Lessons & Life Applications

- **Teaching:** Unity must be aligned with God's purpose.
- **Reproof:** Self-centered ambition distorts collaboration.
- **Correction:** Reevaluate motives behind collective efforts.
- **Instruction:** Build unity around obedience, not ego.
- **Righteous Living:** Alignment sustains true progress.

Prayer Points

1. Father, align my pursuits with Your will.
2. Guard me from unity rooted in pride.
3. Teach me to collaborate with humility.
4. Disrupt plans that oppose Your purpose.
5. Let my efforts honor Your design.

Meditation / Reflection

Am I pursuing unity for purpose or for recognition?
What motivations drive my collaboration with others?

Words of Wisdom: *Unity without alignment produces confusion, not progress.*

March 3

Theme: Redemption Requires Separation

Anchor Scripture - "Now the LORD had said to Abram: 'Get out of your country, from your family and from your father's house, to a land that I will show you.'" **Genesis 12:1**

Devotional Thought

Redemption often begins with a call to separate. God did not start Abram's journey with explanation—He began with instruction. Separation was not rejection; it was preparation. To move Abram into promise, God had to move him out of familiarity.

This moment introduces a defining principle of redemption: **what God redeems, He redirects**. New futures require new alignments. Abram could not carry old frameworks into new assignments.

In life, redemption frequently requires leaving what is comfortable to embrace what is purposeful. Separation creates space for transformation. God's call is not meant to diminish life, but to reposition it.

Key Lessons & Life Applications

- **Teaching:** Redemption often begins with obedience, not clarity.
- **Reproof:** Familiarity can hinder transformation.
- **Correction:** Let go of environments that resist growth.
- **Instruction:** Trust God's direction even without full details.
- **Righteous Living:** Separation positions destiny.

Prayer Points

1. Father, give me courage to obey Your call.
2. Help me release what no longer serves Your purpose.
3. Teach me to trust You beyond familiarity.
4. Reposition my life for growth and alignment.
5. Lead me into the future You have prepared.

Meditation / Reflection

What might God be asking me to leave in order to grow?
How does obedience create space for redemption?

Words of Wisdom: *Redemption often begins where familiarity ends.*

March 4

Theme: Partial Obedience Delays Progress

Anchor Scripture - "So Abram departed as the LORD had spoken to him, and Lot went with him. And Abram was seventy-five years old when he departed from Haran." Genesis 12:4

Devotional Thought

Abram obeyed God's call—but he did not obey it completely. Scripture records a subtle yet significant detail: *"and Lot went with him."* God's instruction was clear—leave your country, your family, and your father's house. Yet Abram carried part of his past into his future.

Abram's decision was understandable. He had no biological son at the time, and Lot, his nephew, may have represented continuity, responsibility, and emotional attachment. Compassion and sentiment influenced his obedience. However, redemption often requires clarity, not sentiment. What God intended to separate was carried along, and it later became a source of conflict, delay, and distraction.

Lot represented Abram's past—family ties, inherited obligations, and unfinished transitions. As long as Lot remained, God's communication with Abram stalled. Only after separation did God resume speaking clearly and expansively about the promise. Partial obedience still moves you forward, but it often introduces unnecessary complications.

In life, God's call is rarely vague. What He asks us to leave behind is not always sinful—but it may be misaligned. Carrying what belongs to the past into the future can delay clarity, strain relationships, and complicate destiny.

Key Lessons & Life Applications

- **Teaching:** Obedience requires alignment, not sentiment.
- **Reproof:** Carrying unresolved attachments can delay progress.
- **Correction:** Reevaluate what God asked you to leave behind.
- **Instruction:** Complete separation creates space for clarity.
- **Righteous Living:** Full obedience preserves peace and direction.

Prayer Points

1. Father, reveal areas where my obedience has been partial.
2. Help me release attachments that delay Your purpose.
3. Teach me to honor Your instruction above sentiment.
4. Restore clarity where compromise has clouded direction.
5. Give me courage to complete the separation You require.

Meditation / Reflection

Is there something from my past I carried into a new season?
Could unresolved attachments be delaying clarity or peace?
Ask God to show you what belongs to the past and what belongs to the future.

Words of Wisdom: *What God asks you to leave behind is often what delays what lies ahead.*

March 5

Theme: Redemption Grows Through Worship

> **Anchor Scripture** - "Then Abram moved his tent and went and dwelt by the terebinth trees of Mamre... and built an altar there to the LORD." Genesis 13:18

Devotional Thought

As Abram journeyed, he paused to worship. He did not treat movement as more important than devotion. Altars marked his progress. Redemption was not only unfolding geographically—it was being nurtured spiritually.

Worship grounds redemption. Altars remind us that progress without presence leads to pride. Abram built altars not because life was perfect, but because God was faithful.

In life, worship keeps redemption aligned. When seasons change and paths shift, worship stabilizes the heart. Altars help us remember who leads the journey.

Key Lessons & Life Applications

- **Teaching:** Worship sustains alignment during transition.
- **Reproof:** Progress without devotion weakens perspective.
- **Correction:** Pause to honor God along the journey.
- **Instruction:** Build spiritual rhythms that support growth.
- **Righteous Living:** Worship anchors obedience.

Prayer Points

1. Father, teach me to worship as I progress.
2. Keep my heart aligned through devotion.
3. Help me pause and acknowledge Your faithfulness.
4. Restore my altar of worship.
5. Let worship guide my journey.

Meditation / Reflection

Do I prioritize worship during seasons of change? Where do I need to rebuild my altar?

Words of Wisdom: *Redemption flourishes where worship remains central.*

March 6

Theme: Redemption Requires Letting Go

> **Anchor Scripture -** "And Abram said to Lot, 'Please let there be no strife between you and me… If you take the left, then I will go to the right; or, if you go to the right, then I will go to the left.'" Genesis 13:8–9

Devotional Thought

The conflict between Abram and Lot revealed a deeper issue than land—it exposed misalignment. Abram recognized that redemption could not continue in an environment where strife threatened fellowship. Rather than negotiate endlessly, he established clear boundaries: *left or right*. No ambiguity. No shared space for continued tension.

Letting go was not Abram's loss; it was his preservation. He allowed Lot to choose first, even if that meant Lot walked away with what appeared to be the better portion. Abram chose clarity over control and peace over possession. Redemption often requires decisive separation, not prolonged compromise.

Boundaries are not rejection; they are protection. Abram understood that some relationships cannot coexist without conflict, and alignment sometimes demands distance. Once the separation was complete, God resumed speaking to Abram, reaffirming the promise. Blessing had been present before, but clarity and restored fellowship followed obedience.

In life, redemption advances when we are willing to release what disrupts alignment—even when release feels costly. Letting go creates space for God to speak again.

Key Lessons & Life Applications

- **Teaching:** Redemption requires clear boundaries.
- **Reproof:** Shared space without alignment breeds conflict.
- **Correction:** Prolonged compromise delays clarity.
- **Instruction:** Establish boundaries that protect fellowship.
- **Righteous Living:** Letting go creates room for restoration.

Prayer Points

1. Father, give me wisdom to recognize when letting go is necessary.
2. Help me establish boundaries that protect peace and alignment.
3. Remove fear that keeps me holding onto what You ask me to release.
4. Restore clarity where compromise has created confusion.
5. Teach me to value fellowship with You above all else.

Meditation / Reflection

Is there an environment or relationship I need to exit to restore peace? Have I avoided boundaries out of fear of loss?

What might God be waiting to say after separation is complete?

Words of Wisdom: *What you refuse to release may be what delays clarity and restoration.*

March 7

Theme: Redemption Is Preserved Through Peace

> **Anchor Scripture** - "So Abram said to Lot, 'Please let there be no strife between you and me… for we are brethren.'" Genesis 13:8

Devotional Thought

Being related does not automatically mean being aligned. Abram and Lot were brethren, yet their values, priorities, and capacity for peace had begun to differ. Abram recognized that redemption cannot thrive in an atmosphere of strife—even when the relationship is legitimate.

Peace is not always maintained through closeness. Sometimes, it is preserved through distance without malice. Abram did not deny their brotherhood; he acknowledged it. But he also understood that fellowship with God could not flourish where contention was tolerated. The demand of redemption was clear: *"Let there be no strife."*

Abram chose peace over proximity. He did not accuse, dominate, or manipulate. He communicated clearly, established boundaries, and protected alignment. Scripture later affirms this principle: *"As much as depends on you, live peaceably with all men."* Peace does not always mean agreement—it often means wisdom.

In life, choosing peace may require stepping back, not because love has failed, but because purpose must be protected. Redemption is preserved when peace is prioritized over personal preference.

Key Lessons & Life Applications

- **Teaching:** Redemption requires an environment of peace.
- **Reproof:** Brotherhood does not guarantee shared values.
- **Correction:** Distance without malice can preserve alignment.
- **Instruction:** Communicate boundaries clearly and early.
- **Righteous Living:** Fellowship with God thrives where strife is removed.

Prayer Points

1. Father, help me recognize when peace requires boundaries.
2. Teach me to pursue peace without guilt or hostility.
3. Remove fear that keeps me in environments of strife.
4. Give me wisdom to communicate clearly and honorably.
5. Preserve my fellowship with You through peace.

Meditation / Reflection

Am I tolerating strife to preserve proximity?
Is God calling me to choose peace—even if it means distance?
Does my current environment support fellowship with God?

Words of Wisdom: *Peace is not avoidance—it is alignment preserved with wisdom.*

March 8

Theme: Alignment Unlocks the Next Phase of the Promise

Anchor Scripture - "And the LORD said to Abram, *after Lot had separated from him*: 'Lift your eyes now and look from the place where you are—northward, southward, eastward, and westward; for all the land which you see I give to you and your descendants forever.'" Genesis 13:14–15

Devotional Thought

Scripture is deliberate with timing: *"after Lot had separated from him."* This was not coincidence—it was condition. Once alignment was completed, heaven responded. God did not merely resume fellowship; **He unveiled the next phase of the promise**.

Abram had walked in obedience before. He had blessings before. But vision expansion waited for alignment. When Lot departed, God instructed Abram to lift his eyes and look—not narrowly, but in every direction. What had been promised before was now revealed with greater clarity, scope, and permanence.

This moment marks a transition. Separation was not the end of relationship—it was the beginning of expansion. God did not introduce a new promise; He unfolded what had been waiting. Alignment unlocked access to what was next.

In life, God often withholds *revelation*, not because He is unwilling, but because preparation is incomplete. The next phase of the journey is frequently revealed only after the current one is properly concluded. When alignment is restored, vision expands. When vision expands, destiny advances.

Key Lessons & Life Applications

- **Teaching:** Alignment precedes revelation.
- **Reproof:** Carrying unresolved attachments can delay future clarity.
- **Correction:** Complete separation unlocks expanded vision.
- **Instruction:** Lift your eyes—obedience reveals what's next.
- **Righteous Living:** God unfolds promise progressively.

Prayer Points

1. Father, complete every alignment You require in my life.
2. Reveal the next phase of Your promise as I walk in obedience.
3. Restore vision where compromise once limited clarity.
4. Help me finish seasons properly so the next may unfold.
5. Expand my capacity to see what You are preparing.

Meditation / Reflection

What season may God be waiting for me to close before revealing what's next? Is there an alignment that would unlock greater clarity or vision?

Words of Wisdom: *Alignment does not just restore what was lost—it unlocks what was waiting.*

March 9

Theme: Faith Is Credited in a Restored Relationship

Anchor Scripture - "And he believed in the LORD, and He accounted it to him for righteousness." Genesis 15:6

Devotional Thought

Genesis 15:6 did not occur in isolation. It followed restored alignment, renewed fellowship, and expanded vision. After Abram separated from Lot, God spoke again. After God revealed the next phase of the promise, Abram believed. **Faith was credited in the context of restored relationship, not confusion.**

Abram did not believe blindly. He believed *after* God clarified direction and reaffirmed the promise. Scripture affirms this principle clearly: *"Faith comes by hearing, and hearing by the word of God"* (Romans 10:17). Faith requires an object, and Abram's faith was anchored in what God had spoken. **Faith is not the denial of reality; it is trust grounded in revelation.**

God accounted Abram's belief as righteousness—not because Abram was flawless, but because his heart was aligned and responsive to the Word he had heard. Where God speaks, faith becomes possible. Where revelation is clear, trust becomes reasonable. Righteousness flowed not from perfection, but from believing God.

Key Lessons & Life Applications

- **Teaching:** Faith responds to what God has spoken.
- **Reproof:** Belief without revelation becomes fragile.
- **Correction:** Restore alignment before forcing faith.
- **Instruction:** Let God's Word define the object of your faith.
- **Righteous Living:** Righteousness flows from trusting God's Word.

Prayer Points

1. Father, help me hear and respond to Your Word.
2. Strengthen my faith through revelation, not assumption.
3. Restore alignment where trust has weakened.
4. Teach me to believe what You have spoken.
5. Let my faith be credited as righteousness before You.

Meditation / Reflection

What Word from God is inviting my trust right now?
Am I responding to revelation—or trying to manufacture faith?

Words of Wisdom: *Faith is not imagination; it is a response to what God has revealed.*

March 10

Theme: Redemption Is Sustained by Reassurance and Intimacy

Anchor Scripture - "After these things the word of the LORD came to Abram in a vision, saying, 'Do not be afraid, Abram. I am your shield, your exceedingly great reward.'" Genesis 15:1

Devotional Thought

After alignment was restored and faith was credited, God did not immediately fulfill the promise—He reassured the relationship. Scripture says, *"the word of the LORD came to Abram in a vision."* This signals access, intimacy, and continued fellowship.

Redemption is not sustained by activity alone; it is sustained by communication.

God addressed Abram's inner state before addressing outcomes: *"Do not be afraid."* Fear often creeps in after obedience, when expectations rise but results are not yet visible. God responded not with explanation, but with presence. He reminded Abram that protection (*"your shield"*) and fulfillment (*"your reward"*) were found in Him, not merely in what He would give.

This reveals a redemptive pattern: God reassures before He advances. Intimacy precedes execution. When fear threatens confidence, God reaffirms access.

Redemption remains secure when relationship is nurtured, even when fulfillment is still unfolding.

Key Lessons & Life Applications

- **Teaching:** God sustains redemption through ongoing communication.
- **Reproof:** Fear often follows obedience when assurance is lacking.
- **Correction:** Seek God's presence, not just His promises.
- **Instruction:** Allow intimacy with God to stabilize your journey.
- **Righteous Living:** Confidence grows where fellowship is maintained.

Prayer Points

1. Father, thank You for continual access to Your presence.
2. Reassure my heart when fear tries to rise.
3. Help me value intimacy with You above outcomes.
4. Restore confidence through Your Word and presence.
5. Let fellowship with You sustain my faith.

Meditation / Reflection

Am I drawing confidence from God's presence or from expected outcomes? How does ongoing communication with God stabilize my faith?

Words of Wisdom: *Redemption is sustained not by speed, but by intimacy with God.*

March 11

Theme: Impatience Often Misreads God's Timing

Anchor Scripture - "So Sarai said to Abram, 'See now, the LORD has restrained me from bearing children. Please, go in to my maid; perhaps I shall obtain children by her.' And Abram heeded the voice of Sarai." Genesis 16:2

Devotional Thought

God had reassured Abram of His presence, protection, and promise—but reassurance did not eliminate pressure. Time passed, and Sarai interpreted delay as restraint: *"The LORD has restrained me…"* What God had not said, Sarai concluded. What God had not denied, she assumed.

This moment reveals a subtle danger: **impatience often misreads God's timing as God's intention**. Sarai did not reject the promise; she attempted to manage it. Abram did not rebel; he agreed. Yet agreement outside God's instruction can still introduce unnecessary complexity.

Human solutions often appear reasonable when waiting becomes uncomfortable. But God's promise includes God's process. When timing is forced, consequences multiply—not because God withdraws, but because alignment is disrupted.

In life, impatience rarely announces itself loudly. It often comes dressed as practicality, compassion, or logic. Redemption continues, but the path becomes heavier when trust gives way to control.

Key Lessons & Life Applications

- **Teaching:** God's promises include His timing and method.
- **Reproof:** Delay does not mean denial or restraint.
- **Correction:** Do not interpret silence as permission.
- **Instruction:** Wait for God's process, not human substitutes.
- **Righteous Living:** Trust honors God's wisdom over convenience.

Prayer Points

1. Father, guard my heart from impatience.
2. Help me trust Your timing without forcing outcomes.
3. Deliver me from conclusions You never spoke.
4. Teach me discernment during delayed seasons.
5. Strengthen my trust in Your process.

Meditation / Reflection

Have I interpreted delay as denial?
Am I tempted to manage what God promised to fulfill?

Words of Wisdom: *Impatience does not cancel God's promise—but it complicates the journey.*

March 12

Theme: God Protects Covenant While Extending Blessing

Anchor Scripture - "And the Angel of the LORD said to her, 'I will multiply your descendants exceedingly, so that they shall not be counted for multitude.'" **Genesis 16:10**

Devotional Thought

Hagar did not initiate the decision that altered the course of Abram's household. She responded to authority, not ambition. Scripture does not assign her guilt—and neither does God. Instead of correction, God met her with protection, clarity, and measured blessing.

This encounter reveals an important redemptive distinction: **God is generous with blessing, but deliberate with covenant.** Hagar was not the covenant bearer, yet she was not excluded from God's care. God acknowledged Ishmael's future without redefining the covenant promise given to Abram. Compassion was extended, but the covenant line remained protected.

This distinction helps explain a reality we often observe in life: **people can be blessed outside of covenant.** Provision, increase, influence, and success are not exclusive evidence of alignment. God causes rain to fall on the just and the unjust. Blessing flows from God's generosity; covenant flows from God's intention.

Covenant blessing is restricted. It carries responsibility, demands obedience, and requires boundaries. It is not merely received—it is stewarded. While many may experience blessing, only those aligned with God's purpose are entrusted with covenant responsibility. Behavior matters in covenant because covenant carries weight.

Understanding this truth guards the heart from confusion, comparison, and offense when those without godly values appear to prosper. God is not unjust—He is orderly. Redemption advances not by expanding qualification, but by preserving alignment.

Key Lessons & Life Applications

- **Teaching:** God distinguishes between blessing and covenant assignment.
- **Reproof:** Prosperity does not automatically indicate alignment.
- **Correction:** Covenant requires compliance, not convenience.
- **Instruction:** Honor the boundaries covenant demands.
- **Righteous Living:** Alignment governs responsibility, not visibility.

Prayer Points

1. Father, help me discern blessing from covenant assignment.
2. Teach me to honor Your distinctions without comparison.
3. Thank You for Your generosity beyond covenant lines.
4. Guard my heart from entitlement or confusion.
5. Align my choices with the responsibility covenant requires.

Meditation / Reflection

Have I assumed that blessing automatically means calling?
Do I respect God's right to distinguish roles, responsibilities, and access?

Words of Wisdom: *Blessing may be generous, but covenant is governed.*

March 13

Theme: Covenant Requires Clarified Identity

Anchor Scripture - "And God said to Abram: 'As for Me, behold, My covenant is with you, and you shall be a father of many nations.'" Genesis 17:4

Devotional Thought

After human interference complicated the journey, God did not abandon His covenant—He clarified it. God re-entered the conversation with precision, not emotion. He reaffirmed His covenant and restated Abram's identity within it.

Covenant always begins with identity. Before expansion, God clarifies who carries responsibility. Abram was not merely promised descendants; he was defined as a father of nations. This was not aspirational language—it was covenant assignment.

Redemption does not progress on vague identity. God establishes *who* before He expands *what*. When identity is unclear, responsibility becomes distorted. But when identity is clarified, covenant can advance without confusion.

In life, God often reasserts identity after misalignment—not to shame, but to realign purpose. Covenant requires knowing who you are and what you are responsible to carry.

Key Lessons & Life Applications

- **Teaching:** Covenant begins with clarified identity.
- **Reproof:** Confusion about identity leads to missteps.
- **Correction:** God restates identity to restore alignment.
- **Instruction:** Know who you are before expanding responsibility.
- **Righteous Living:** Identity anchors covenant responsibility.

Prayer Points

1. Father, clarify my identity in Your purpose.
2. Restore alignment where confusion has crept in.
3. Help me carry responsibility consistent with who You say I am.
4. Guard me from defining myself by outcomes alone.
5. Anchor my identity in Your covenant.

Meditation / Reflection

Do I clearly understand who I am called to be in God's plan? Has confusion about identity affected my decisions?

Words of Wisdom: *Covenant advances where identity is settled.*

March 14

Theme: Transformation Precedes Expansion

Anchor Scripture - "No longer shall your name be called Abram, but your name shall be Abraham; for I have made you a father of many nations." Genesis 17:5

Devotional Thought

God did not expand Abram's influence without first transforming his identity. The name change was not cosmetic—it was covenantal. Abram meant *exalted father*; Abraham meant *father of many nations*. God changed the name before the manifestation.

This reveals a redemptive order: **transformation precedes expansion**. God reshapes identity before enlarging assignment. The name Abraham carried the blueprint of destiny long before fulfillment appeared.

Names in Scripture define boundaries, authority, and assignment. God did not wait for Abraham to *become* a father of nations to rename him; He renamed him so he could grow into it. Identity was adjusted to sustain what was coming.

In life, expansion without transformation creates strain. God often changes who we are internally before He increases what we carry externally.

Key Lessons & Life Applications

- **Teaching:** Identity transformation comes before expansion.
- **Reproof:** Growth without transformation is unsustainable.
- **Correction:** Embrace identity change before seeking increase.
- **Instruction:** Let God redefine you before He enlarges you.
- **Righteous Living:** Identity sustains destiny.

Prayer Points

1. Father, transform my identity to match my assignment.
2. Help me embrace change before expansion.
3. Remove resistance to growth that reshapes me.
4. Align who I am becoming with what You are releasing.
5. Prepare me inwardly for outward increase.

Meditation / Reflection

Is God redefining something about who I am?
Am I resisting transformation while asking for expansion?

Words of Wisdom: *What you carry tomorrow requires who you become today.*

March 15

Theme: Covenant Blessing Requires Compliance

Anchor Scripture - "And God said to Abraham: 'As for you, you shall keep My covenant, you and your descendants after you throughout their generations.'" **Genesis 17:9**

Devotional Thought

After identity was clarified and transformation initiated, God introduced responsibility. Covenant blessing is never detached from compliance. God's promise was sure, but participation required obedience.

This moment underscores a critical truth: **covenant is not entitlement; it is stewardship**. God does not negotiate covenant terms after alignment. Compliance protects covenant integrity.

Blessing may be generous, but covenant is governed. Covenant demands boundaries, discipline, and accountability. This is why not everyone who is blessed carries covenant authority. Covenant blessing requires obedience—not perfection, but submission.

In life, resisting covenant responsibility weakens access. Redemption advances when obedience is honored, not avoided.

Key Lessons & Life Applications

- **Teaching:** Covenant includes responsibility and obedience.
- **Reproof:** Entitlement weakens covenant alignment.
- **Correction:** Compliance preserves covenant blessing.
- **Instruction:** Honor God's terms without negotiation.
- **Righteous Living:** Obedience sustains divine trust.

Prayer Points

1. Father, help me honor covenant responsibility.
2. Strengthen my obedience without resistance.
3. Guard me from entitlement disguised as faith.
4. Teach me to steward what You entrust to me.
5. Align my life with covenant boundaries.

Meditation / Reflection

Am I embracing covenant responsibility or only covenant benefit?
Where might obedience be required for alignment to continue?

Words of Wisdom: *Covenant blessing flows where obedience is honored.*

March 16

Theme: Covenant Requires Shared Alignment

Anchor Scripture - "Then God said to Abraham, 'As for Sarai your wife, you shall not call her name Sarai, but Sarah shall be her name. And I will bless her and also give you a son by her...'" Genesis 17:15–16

Devotional Thought

God did not advance the covenant with Abraham alone—He aligned Sarah as well. Covenant fulfillment required **shared alignment**, not individual faith in isolation. This explains why Hagar could not substitute for Sarah. Hagar was not part of the divine agenda; Sarah was. The promise was not transferable.

Sarah's name change was not a coincidence—it was alignment. God redefined her identity because she was a covenant carrier, not merely a companion. Covenant fulfillment required her qualification, participation, and agreement. What God intended to bring forth could only come through those He had aligned.

This reveals a sobering redemptive truth: **association can either expedite or hinder covenant fulfillment**. Wrong partnerships—whether in marriage, business, ministry, or leadership—have stalled many destinies. Not because those involved were evil, but because they were misaligned with covenant terms.

Even good and godly relationships are not automatically covenant-compatible. Covenant carries responsibility, boundaries, and specific qualifications. If someone cannot grow with you, they cannot go with you. God does not bypass essential carriers, nor does He allow substitutes for alignment.

Scripture reinforces this principle elsewhere. Paul and Barnabas were both called and anointed, yet they could no longer function together after disagreement. Their separation did not cancel either calling—but it clarified covenant function. Scripture continued to trace the covenant assignment through Paul. Separation preserved purpose.

If you are a covenant carrier, **association matters**. God may require separation not because love has failed, but because alignment must be protected. Covenant does not accommodate every relationship; it preserves destiny.

Key Lessons & Life Applications

- **Teaching:** Covenant fulfillment requires shared alignment.
- **Reproof:** Substitutes cannot fulfill divine intention.
- **Correction:** God aligns people, not just outcomes.
- **Instruction:** Discern associations through covenant responsibility.
- **Righteous Living:** Alignment protects destiny.

Prayer Points

1. Father, align every relationship connected to my assignment.
2. Help me discern who is qualified to walk this journey with me.
3. Give me courage to release substitutes for alignment.
4. Prepare me—and others—for covenant responsibility.
5. Preserve my destiny through wisdom and discernment.

Meditation / Reflection

Are there relationships I've allowed to substitute for alignment? Who is God redefining or repositioning in my journey?

Am I willing to let go if growth is no longer mutual?

Words of Wisdom: *If they cannot grow with you, they cannot go with you.*

March 17

Theme: Faith Is Tested Where Logic Ends

Anchor Scripture - "Then Abraham fell on his face and laughed, and said in his heart, 'Shall a child be born to a man who is one hundred years old?'" **Genesis 17:17**

Devotional Thought

Abraham believed God—yet he laughed. This was not mockery; it was the collision of promise and limitation. Faith does not eliminate human reasoning; it often confronts it.

God did not rebuke Abraham for laughing. Instead, He clarified the promise. This reveals an important truth: **faith can coexist with questions, but it cannot be governed by them**. Covenant faith is not the absence of logic—it is the submission of logic to divine authority.

At this stage, the promise had outgrown Abraham's natural framework. Age, biology, and timing argued against fulfillment. Yet God remained firm. Covenant does not retreat when reason hesitates.

In life, faith is often tested at the edge of possibility. God does not demand denial of reality; He invites trust beyond it.

Key Lessons & Life Applications

- **Teaching:** Faith is often tested where logic fails.
- **Reproof:** Overreliance on reason can limit trust.
- **Correction:** Allow God's Word to override natural conclusions.
- **Instruction:** Bring questions to God, not excuses.
- **Righteous Living:** Faith grows by trusting beyond evidence.

Prayer Points

1. Father, help me trust You beyond natural limitations.
2. Strengthen my faith when logic resists promise.
3. Teach me to submit understanding to Your Word.
4. Guard my heart from doubt disguised as reasoning.
5. Let faith govern my response to Your promises.

Meditation / Reflection

Where has logic challenged my faith?
Am I allowing questions to clarify trust—or to weaken it?

Words of Wisdom: *Faith begins where human reasoning reaches its limit.*

March 18

Theme: God Reaffirms What He Intends to Fulfill

> **Anchor Scripture** - "And the LORD said, 'Is anything too hard for the LORD? At the appointed time I will return to you, according to the time of life, and Sarah shall have a son.'" Genesis 18:14

Devotional Thought

God did not withdraw the promise in response to hesitation—He reaffirmed it. He addressed the core issue directly: *"Is anything too hard for the LORD?"* Redemption does not advance by pressure, but by divine certainty.

God also introduced a critical element: **appointed time**. Covenant fulfillment is not random; it is scheduled. God's promises are governed by timing as much as by power. What God intends, He fulfills—when preparation is complete.

Reaffirmation is often God's response to wavering faith. He restates what He has already said, not because the promise changed, but because the hearer needs strengthening.

In life, when faith wavers, God often responds with reassurance—not urgency. His agenda does not shift; it waits for alignment.

Key Lessons & Life Applications

- **Teaching:** God reaffirms promises when faith is tested.
- **Reproof:** Doubt does not cancel divine intention.
- **Correction:** Trust God's timing, not pressure.
- **Instruction:** Expect fulfillment at the appointed time.
- **Righteous Living:** Confidence grows through reassurance.

Prayer Points

1. Father, reaffirm what You have spoken over my life.
2. Strengthen my trust when fulfillment feels delayed.
3. Help me rest in Your appointed timing.
4. Remove anxiety that pressures promise.
5. Let reassurance anchor my faith.

Meditation / Reflection

What promise has God reaffirmed to me over time? Am I trusting His timing as much as His power?

Words of Wisdom: *What God intends, He reaffirms—and fulfills in due time.*

March 19

Theme: Covenant Carriers Are Invited Into God's Counsel

Anchor Scripture - "And the LORD said, 'Shall I hide from Abraham what I am doing...?'" Genesis 18:17

Devotional Thought

After covenant identity was clarified and alignment restored, God did something profound—He invited Abraham into His counsel. This was not information sharing; it was relational access. Covenant carriers are not merely recipients of promises; they are entrusted with insight.

God revealed His intentions because Abraham was positioned to steward responsibility. Covenant creates proximity, and proximity invites participation. God was not seeking Abraham's permission—He was honoring Abraham's role.

This moment reveals a leadership truth: **God shares His plans with those aligned to carry them responsibly**. Access is granted where trust exists. Revelation follows relationship.

In life, intimacy with God often expands beyond personal benefit into shared concern. Covenant carriers begin to feel the weight of what God feels—not to control outcomes, but to intercede faithfully.

Key Lessons & Life Applications

- **Teaching:** Covenant invites access to God's counsel.
- **Reproof:** Distance limits insight.
- **Correction:** Alignment precedes revelation.
- **Instruction:** Steward access with humility.
- **Righteous Living:** Proximity carries responsibility.

Prayer Points

1. Father, draw me closer into Your counsel.
2. Teach me to steward access with humility.
3. Align my heart with what concerns You.
4. Help me carry responsibility faithfully.
5. Guard me from entitlement to revelation.

Meditation / Reflection

Am I positioned to steward the insight God gives?
How do I respond when God entrusts me with responsibility?

Words of Wisdom: *Access increases with alignment, not ambition.*

March 20

Theme: Intercession Is a Covenant Responsibility

Anchor Scripture - "Far be it from You to do such a thing as this… Shall not the Judge of all the earth do right?" Genesis 18:25

Devotional Thought

Abraham did not remain silent once God revealed His intentions. He interceded.

Covenant relationship did not make him passive—it made him responsible. Abraham stood in the gap, not to challenge God's justice, but to appeal to God's mercy.

This moment shows that **intercession is not emotional pleading; it is informed engagement.** Abraham understood God's character and spoke accordingly. His questions were rooted in trust, not accusation.

Covenant carriers are called to stand between judgment and mercy, not to excuse wrongdoing, but to appeal for grace where possible. Intercession reflects maturity—it recognizes both justice and compassion.

In life, leadership often requires speaking up for others, even when outcomes are uncertain. Intercession is not about control; it is about alignment with God's heart.

Key Lessons & Life Applications

- **Teaching:** Covenant invites intercession, not silence.
- **Reproof:** Indifference weakens responsibility.
- **Correction:** Engage God with reverence and confidence.
- **Instruction:** Appeal to God's character in prayer.
- **Righteous Living:** Mature faith intercedes wisely.

Prayer Points

1. Father, teach me to intercede with understanding.
2. Align my prayers with Your character.
3. Help me stand in the gap responsibly.
4. Remove fear that silences advocacy.
5. Shape my heart to reflect Yours.

Meditation / Reflection

Do I intercede from knowledge or emotion?

How does understanding God's character shape my prayers?

Words of Wisdom: *Intercession flows from alignment with God's heart.*

March 21

Theme: Justice and Mercy Are Not Opposites

Anchor Scripture - "And the LORD said, 'Because the outcry against Sodom and Gomorrah is great… I will go down now and see…'" Genesis 18:20–21

Devotional Thought

God's response to Abraham's intercession reveals balance, not contradiction. God did not ignore justice to extend mercy, nor did He rush judgment without examination. He said, *"I will go down now and see."* This reflects careful governance.

Justice and mercy are not opposites; they are companions in God's character. God investigates before acting. He listens before deciding. Covenant leadership reflects this same posture—measured, discerning, and fair.

This passage teaches that **righteous judgment requires understanding, not assumption**. God models restraint and responsibility. Covenant carriers must learn to lead with both truth and compassion.

In life, authority must be exercised with care. Decisions that affect others require clarity, patience, and integrity. God's example shows us how to lead without haste and judge without cruelty.

Key Lessons & Life Applications

- **Teaching:** God balances justice with mercy.
- **Reproof:** Rushed judgment lacks wisdom.
- **Correction:** Seek understanding before deciding.
- **Instruction:** Lead with discernment and integrity.
- **Righteous Living:** Authority requires accountability.

Prayer Points

1. Father, teach me to lead with justice and mercy.
2. Guard me from haste in judgment.
3. Help me seek understanding before decisions.
4. Shape my leadership after Your example.
5. Give me discernment in matters of authority.

Meditation / Reflection

Do I rush conclusions without full understanding?
How can I better reflect God's balance of justice and mercy?

Words of Wisdom: *True justice is informed by discernment and governed by mercy.*

March 22

Theme: Influence Does Not Cancel Accountability

Anchor Scripture - "Then the men said to Lot, 'Have you anyone else here? Son-in-law, your sons, your daughters, and whomever you have in the city—take them out of this place!'" Genesis 19:12

Devotional Thought

Lot lived in Sodom, yet he was not of Sodom. He had influence, a household, and a position at the city gate. But influence does not cancel accountability. Proximity to righteousness does not replace obedience to instruction.

The angels urged urgency, but Lot hesitated. His influence could not shield him from the consequences of delayed action. Leadership without decisive obedience exposes those under its care.

This passage teaches a sobering truth: **being connected to the right people does not exempt us from personal responsibility**. Influence may open doors, but accountability determines outcomes. Redemption requires response, not reputation.

In life, leadership carries weight. When warning is clear, delay becomes dangerous. God's mercy provides opportunity—but opportunity demands action.

Key Lessons & Life Applications

- **Teaching:** Influence does not replace obedience.
- **Reproof:** Delay weakens leadership responsibility.
- **Correction:** Respond promptly to divine instruction.
- **Instruction:** Lead decisively when responsibility is entrusted.
- **Righteous Living:** Accountability follows authority.

Prayer Points

1. Father, help me respond promptly to Your instruction.
2. Deliver me from hesitation when obedience is required.
3. Teach me to lead responsibly under pressure.
4. Guard those entrusted to my care.
5. Strengthen my resolve to act when You speak.

Meditation / Reflection

Where might hesitation be undermining responsibility?
Am I relying on position instead of obedience?

Words of Wisdom: *Influence opens doors; obedience determines outcomes.*

March 23

Theme: Intercession Can Trigger Deliverance

Anchor Scripture - "And while he lingered, the men took hold of his hand… the LORD being merciful to him, and they brought him out." Genesis 19:16

Devotional Thought

Lot lingered, but deliverance did not wait for his readiness. Scripture shows the angels *grabbing* Lot and leading him out. This sudden intervention did not happen in isolation—it followed Abraham's intercession. What prayer could not change in Sodom, it secured for Lot.

Intercession often operates behind the scenes, triggering mercy others did not ask for themselves. Abraham's appeal for righteousness created a window for rescue. Lot benefited from a prayer he did not pray and a relationship he did not steward as carefully as Abraham did.

This reveals a sobering and hopeful truth: **intercession can activate mercy, but it cannot replace obedience.** The angels removed Lot from danger, but Lot still had to leave. Mercy intervened, yet responsibility remained.

In life, prayers from others may open doors of escape, delay judgment, or create opportunity—but redemption still requires response. Intercession can pull you out, but it cannot walk forward for you.

Key Lessons & Life Applications

- **Teaching:** Intercession can activate divine mercy.
- **Reproof:** Lingering delays what prayer secures.
- **Correction:** Deliverance must be followed by obedience.
- **Instruction:** Honor the prayers that created your escape.
- **Righteous Living:** Mercy invites response, not complacency.

Prayer Points

1. Father, thank You for prayers that covered me unknowingly.
2. Help me respond fully to mercy extended through others.
3. Teach me not to linger where You have opened a way out.
4. Strengthen my obedience after deliverance.
5. Make me sensitive to intercessory grace.

Meditation / Reflection

Who may have prayed for my deliverance when I hesitated? Am I honoring mercy by responding decisively?

Words of Wisdom: *Intercession may pull you out, but obedience must carry you forward.*

March 24

Theme: Redemption Requires Full Departure

Anchor Scripture - "But his wife looked back behind him, and she became a pillar of salt." Genesis 19:26

Devotional Thought

Lot's wife left Sodom physically but not fully. Her glance backward revealed unresolved attachment. Jesus later referenced this moment with a sober warning: *"Remember Lot's wife."* Redemption demands more than movement—it requires separation.

There is no neutral ground in redemption. Looking back is not harmless reflection; it is divided allegiance. Scripture consistently warns against living between worlds. Playing the middle ground produces loss, not safety.

Redemption calls for leaving and cleaving. Partial obedience creates permanent consequences. Jesus reinforced this principle when He warned that lukewarm commitment is unacceptable. **Being half-in and half-out is not stability—it is danger.**

In life, God's call requires full departure. Attachment to what God is judging undermines what He is saving. The warning remains loud: choose direction, not compromise.

Key Lessons & Life Applications

- **Teaching:** Redemption requires full separation.
- **Reproof:** Divided allegiance weakens deliverance.
- **Correction:** Middle ground is not a safe place.
- **Instruction:** Leave fully to live freely.
- **Righteous Living:** Commitment sustains redemption.

Prayer Points

1. Father, help me leave what You've delivered me from.
2. Heal lingering attachments that compete with obedience.
3. Strengthen my resolve to move forward without compromise.
4. Guard my heart from divided loyalty.
5. Anchor me firmly in Your direction.

Meditation / Reflection

Am I fully out—or emotionally lingering behind?
What does obedience require me to release completely?

Words of Wisdom: *Redemption demands total allegiance—there is no middle ground.*

March 25

Theme: Delayed Obedience Still Has Consequences

Anchor Scripture - "And Lot said to them, 'Please, no, my lords! … See now, this city is near enough to flee to, and it is a little one; please let me flee there…' … Then Lot went up out of Zoar and dwelt in the mountains." Genesis 19:18–22, 30

Devotional Thought

Lot was instructed to flee to the mountains, but he resisted the instruction and proposed an alternative destination—Zoar. God did not override his will. Instead, God respected Lot's agency. This was not mercy redefining the plan; it was permissive will allowing choice.

Mercy rescued Lot from Sodom. Alignment was required for what came next.

Later, Scripture records that Lot eventually left Zoar and ended up in the mountains anyway. The destination did not change—only the outcome did. What could have been obedience became survival. What could have preserved clarity resulted in isolation.

This passage reveals a sobering truth: **delayed obedience still has consequences**. God does not violate human will, but He also does not import misalignment into covenant advancement. Permission does not equal approval. God may allow a choice, but alignment determines trajectory.

In life, permissive will explains why many survive without advancing. Rescue may come through mercy, but progression requires cooperation. Destiny unfolds where obedience meets instruction.

Key Lessons & Life Applications

- **Teaching:** God respects human agency.
- **Reproof:** Permission does not equal alignment.
- **Correction:** Obedience determines progression.
- **Instruction:** Choose God's direction, not personal comfort.
- **Righteous Living:** Alignment protects purpose.

Prayer Points

1. Father, help me distinguish permission from alignment.
2. Deliver me from choices that delay purpose.
3. Teach me to cooperate fully with Your instruction.
4. Align my will with Your direction.
5. Preserve my future through obedience.

Meditation / Reflection

Where might I be living in permissive will instead of alignment?
What next level requires my active cooperation?

Words of Wisdom: *Permission may allow survival; alignment enables advancement*

March 26

Theme: Deliverance Without Renewal Creates Distortion

Anchor Scripture - "Now the firstborn said to the younger, 'Our father is old... come, let us make our father drink wine...'" Genesis 19:31–35

Devotional Thought

Lot and his daughters left Sodom, but Sodom did not leave them. Though physically removed from the city, the values, reasoning patterns, and survival instincts they had absorbed were never confronted or unlearned. What unfolded in the cave was not merely moral failure—it was the manifestation of unresolved exposure.

Redemption rescued them from destruction, but **renewal had not yet taken place**. Deliverance removed them from danger, but it did not remove distortion from within. This reveals a sobering truth: leaving an environment does not automatically erase what that environment has taught you.

Scripture later warns that new wine poured into old wineskins creates chaos. Freedom without renewal produces confusion, not clarity. When people are rescued without being re-formed, old patterns resurface under pressure. What is not intentionally unlearned eventually expresses itself—often in destructive ways.

This passage invites honest self-examination. Redemption is not only about escape; it is about transformation. God's design includes both rescue and renewal.

Key Lessons & Life Applications

- **Teaching:** Deliverance must be followed by renewal.
- **Reproof:** Unaddressed exposure resurfaces under pressure.
- **Correction:** Freedom requires intentional unlearning.
- **Instruction:** Renew the mind after leaving harmful systems.
- **Righteous Living:** Transformation protects deliverance.

Prayer Points

1. Father, cleanse me from patterns formed in unhealthy environments.
2. Help me unlearn what no longer aligns with Your truth.
3. Heal distortions created by past exposure.
4. Renew my mind as You restore my life.
5. Let freedom be sustained through transformation.

Meditation / Reflection

What have I left physically but not mentally or emotionally?
What patterns need intentional renewal?

Words of Wisdom: *Deliverance removes chains; renewal removes patterns.*

March 27

Theme: Unresolved Patterns Can Shape Generations—But Alignment Can Redeem Them

Anchor Scripture - "Thus both the daughters of Lot were with child by their father... and they bore sons." Genesis 19:36–38

Devotional Thought

The consequences of unresolved exposure did not end with Lot—they extended into generations. The sons born from this moment became the founders of the Moabites and Ammonites. These nations later reflected many of the same moral distortions, boundary breakdowns, and spiritual confusion seen in Sodom—not because they lived there, but because the patterns were never unlearned.

This passage reveals a sobering generational truth: **what is not healed in one generation often becomes normalized in the next**. Learned behavior, unresolved trauma, and distorted reasoning can quietly become culture.

Yet Scripture does not end in despair. Redemption does not excuse distortion, but it responds to alignment. From Moab came Ruth—a woman who chose a different path. She rejected inherited patterns, aligned herself with the God of Israel, and became part of the lineage of redemption. Her story proves that origin does not imprison destiny. **Choice and alignment can interrupt generational cycles.**

God's grace does not erase responsibility, but it always leaves room for repentance, renewal, and redirection. Legacy is not only inherited—it is also chosen.

Key Lessons & Life Applications

- **Teaching:** Unresolved patterns can shape generations.
- **Reproof:** Ignoring distortion allows it to multiply.
- **Correction:** Alignment can interrupt generational cycles.
- **Instruction:** Examine what has been inherited and choose wisely.
- **Righteous Living:** Renewal redeems legacy.

Prayer Points

1. Father, reveal patterns passed down that need healing.
2. Help me reject what does not align with Your truth.
3. Give me courage to choose a different path.
4. Heal my lineage through repentance and renewal.
5. Let my legacy reflect alignment, not residue.

Meditation / Reflection

What patterns have I inherited that require examination?
Where is God inviting me to choose alignment over familiarity?

Words of Wisdom: *What is not healed becomes heritage—but alignment can rewrite legacy.*

March 28

Theme: Authority Without Structure Creates Chaos

Anchor Scripture - "Now the two angels came to Sodom in the evening, and Lot was sitting in the gate of Sodom…" Genesis 19:1

Devotional Thought

Lot sat at the city gate—a place of authority, influence, and civic leadership. Yet when crisis came, his position could not restrain evil, protect his household, or enforce order. He had access, but no structure. Presence, but no power.

This reveals a leadership truth many learn too late: **authority without structure collapses under pressure.** Titles, positions, and proximity to power do not equal governing capacity. When structure is absent, chaos fills the vacuum.

Lot negotiated instead of enforcing. He pleaded where command was required. The result was exposure, not safety. Leadership without structure does not fail quietly—it fails publicly.

In life, authority must be reinforced with systems, boundaries, and clarity. Otherwise, responsibility becomes a burden rather than a tool for protection.

Key Lessons & Life Applications

- **Teaching:** Authority must be supported by structure.
- **Reproof:** Position alone does not secure outcomes.
- **Correction:** Build systems before crisis arrives.
- **Instruction:** Lead with clarity, not negotiation.
- **Righteous Living:** Structure protects those under authority.

Prayer Points

1. Father, help me build structure where You've given authority.
2. Expose areas where position has replaced preparation.
3. Teach me to govern wisely, not react emotionally.
4. Strengthen my leadership capacity.
5. Let my authority bring order, not confusion.

Meditation / Reflection

Where do I have influence without structure?
What needs reinforcement before pressure exposes weakness?

Words of Wisdom: *Access without structure creates exposure, not safety.*

March 29

Theme: Delayed Correction Hardens Dysfunction

Anchor Scripture - "So Lot went out and spoke to his sons-in-law… but to his sons-in-law he seemed to be joking." Genesis 19:14

Devotional Thought

When Lot finally spoke with urgency, he was not taken seriously. Correction came too late. Authority had not been established early, so warning sounded like humor.

This reveals a painful leadership lesson: **delayed correction weakens credibility**. What is tolerated long enough becomes normalized. When boundaries are absent early, discipline later feels foreign—even offensive.

Correction is not most effective in crisis; it is most effective in consistency. Leadership that avoids discomfort today often inherits dysfunction tomorrow. Respect must be built before it is needed. In families, workplaces, and personal growth, unresolved issues do not disappear—they harden. Silence is not neutrality; it is permission.

Key Lessons & Life Applications

- **Teaching:** Authority must be established early.
- **Reproof:** Avoiding correction breeds contempt.
- **Correction:** Address issues before they escalate.
- **Instruction:** Lead consistently, not reactively.
- **Righteous Living:** Discipline preserves dignity.

Prayer Points

1. Father, give me courage to address issues promptly.
2. Deliver me from avoiding necessary correction.
3. Restore credibility where authority has weakened.
4. Teach me to lead with wisdom and consistency.
5. Help me protect relationships through timely discipline.

Meditation / Reflection

What issue have I delayed correcting?
How might early intervention change outcomes?

Words of Wisdom: *What you refuse to correct early will resist correction later.*

March 30

Theme: Walking by Sight Undermines Covering

Anchor Scripture - "And Lot lifted his eyes and saw all the plain of Jordan, that it was well watered everywhere... Then Lot chose for himself all the plain of Jordan." **Genesis 13:10–11**

Devotional Thought

Lot had an opportunity many never receive—he lived under Abram's covering. He walked with a covenant carrier, witnessed divine favor, and benefited from spiritual protection he did not cultivate himself. Yet when the moment of decision came, Lot chose by sight, not by discernment.

Scripture is clear: *Lot lifted his eyes and saw.* What he saw appeared prosperous, convenient, and promising. What he did not see was the moral decay beneath the surface. Greed narrowed his vision. Self-interest overruled wisdom.

This moment explains everything that followed. **When covering is rejected for convenience, exposure is inevitable.** Lot's decision was not neutral; it was formative. He exchanged alignment for advantage, proximity to covenant for immediate gain.

In life, walking by sight often feels practical, even smart—but it quietly removes us from protection. Selfish choices may look harmless at first, but they carry delayed consequences. Taking advantage of opportunity without regard for alignment is terminal; it always catches up.

Key Lessons & Life Applications

- **Teaching:** Covering provides protection beyond visibility.
- **Reproof:** Greed distorts judgment.
- **Correction:** Choose alignment over appearance.
- **Instruction:** Discern beyond what looks good.
- **Righteous Living:** Wisdom sees consequences ahead.

Prayer Points

1. Father, deliver me from choices driven by appearance alone.
2. Help me value covering and alignment.
3. Expose hidden costs behind attractive options.
4. Guard my heart from selfish ambition.
5. Teach me to walk by wisdom, not sight.

Meditation / Reflection

Have I chosen convenience over covering?
What decision am I making based only on what looks good?

Words of Wisdom: *What seems harmless on the outside may carry darkness within.*

March 31

Theme: Private Disorder Eventually Becomes Public

Anchor Scripture - "So Lot went out and spoke to his sons-in-law... but to his sons-in-law he seemed to be joking." Genesis 19:14

Devotional Thought

When crisis came, Lot's voice carried no weight. His sons-in-law treated his warning as a joke. This was not a sudden failure—it was the result of long-standing compromise.

Lot had lived in Sodom long enough for its culture to shape his household. He lacked moral authority, spiritual credibility, and relational influence. Even his wife's divided loyalty revealed a deeper truth: **Lot could not lead what he had slowly absorbed**.

This family gives us a window into Sodom's disorder—blurred boundaries, weakened authority, fractured values. What was normal in the city became normal in the home. And when leadership is compromised privately, it collapses publicly.

This pattern is not ancient; it is current. Societal dysfunction often begins as tolerated compromise. Families lose influence when values are negotiated away. **You cannot confront what you have normalized**.

Redemption may rescue a person, but leadership credibility must be rebuilt. Influence requires integrity, consistency, and courage.

Key Lessons & Life Applications

- **Teaching:** Influence is built over time.
- **Reproof:** Compromise erodes authority.
- **Correction:** Address dysfunction before crisis exposes it.
- **Instruction:** Lead with conviction, not convenience.
- **Righteous Living:** Integrity sustains influence.

Prayer Points

1. Father, restore my moral authority where compromise weakened it.
2. Help me confront what I have tolerated.
3. Heal dysfunction within my household and sphere.
4. Rebuild credibility through integrity.
5. Let my life speak with clarity and weight.

Meditation / Reflection

Where might compromise have weakened my influence?
What values need to be re-established in my life or home?

Words of Wisdom: *What you tolerate privately will eventually undermine you publicly.*

APRIL
COVENANT MATURITY & IDENTITY

April 1

Theme: Covenant Does Not Cancel Accountability

Anchor Scripture - "But God came to Abimelech in a dream by night, and said to him, 'Indeed you are a dead man because of the woman whom you have taken, for she is a man's wife.'" Genesis 20:3

Devotional Thought

Genesis 20 exposes a space that is neither absolute truth nor absolute falsehood—**a gray area** Abraham believed he could manage. Sarah *was* his wife, but she was *also* his sister. Abraham did not lie outright; he **withheld truth**, trusting that partial disclosure would protect him.

This reveals a sobering reality: **spiritual maturity is not automatic**, even for great people of faith. Growth in calling does not guarantee growth in trust. Abraham had walked with God, seen miracles, and carried covenant promises—yet fear still shaped his decisions.

The most troubling question emerges here: *What if Abimelech had violated Sarah?* Was Sarah's safety a calculated risk Abraham was willing to take? Or was Abraham quietly hoping that God would intervene while he acted from fear?

Fear-based decisions place others at risk. They shift responsibility from obedience to assumption. Abraham's fear turned Sarah into collateral damage and exposed how fear **ensnares judgment**, just as Scripture warns.

"The fear of man brings a snare…" (Proverbs 29:25, NKJV) Fear is not neutral—it is a form of bondage that compromises trust in God's protection and replaces faith with self-preservation.

Key Lessons & Life Applications

- **Teaching:** Covenant does not eliminate fear; it reveals whether trust has matured.
- **Reproof:** Partial truth driven by fear can endanger others.
- **Correction:** God exposes gray areas where faith is compromised by self-protection.
- **Instruction:** Trust in God's protection must replace calculated risk-taking.
- **Righteous Living:** Righteousness requires courage to act fully in truth, not convenience.

Prayer Points

1. Father, expose fear-based decisions I have justified as wisdom.
2. Deliver me from the bondage of the fear of man.
3. Heal areas where trust in Your protection is incomplete.
4. Teach me to protect others through obedience, not assumption.
5. Let my faith mature beyond partial truth into full alignment.

Meditation / Reflection

Where have I relied on "gray areas" instead of full trust in God's covering?

Words of Wisdom: *Fear-based decisions are a form of bondage—the fear of man brings a snare.*

April 2

Theme: Fear Revisited at a Higher Level

Anchor Scripture - "And Abraham said, 'Because I thought, surely the fear of God is not in this place; and they will kill me on account of my wife.'" Genesis 20:11

Devotional Thought

Genesis 20 invites us to consider not only Abraham's fear, but the **environment that amplified it**. Abraham had moved into Gerar, a territory where the fear of God was unfamiliar to him. The question lingers: *Was this a place he should have settled in?*

Spiritual maturity does not make us immune to environmental pressure. Certain territories **test convictions**, awaken dormant fears, and expose areas where trust in God has not fully matured. Abraham's fear was not new—but the environment gave it permission to resurface.

Abraham assumed danger based on perception rather than instruction. His fear-based judgment led him to compromise truth, risking Sarah and entangling an entire nation. Environment matters—what we tolerate geographically, relationally, or culturally can subtly erode spiritual confidence.

God allowed Abraham to feel the tension so that hidden fear could be confronted. Growth often reveals itself not in ideal settings, but in **unfamiliar and uncomfortable territories**.

Key Lessons & Life Applications

- **Teaching:** Environment can either reinforce faith or amplify fear.
- **Reproof:** Assumptions about people and places can lead to compromise.
- **Correction:** God exposes fear when surroundings challenge trust.
- **Instruction:** Discernment is required before relocating or settling.
- **Righteous Living:** Trust in God must govern decisions, regardless of territory.

Prayer Points

1. Lord, sharpen my discernment concerning environments I enter.
2. Reveal how surroundings may be influencing my decisions.
3. Heal fear that resurfaces under pressure.
4. Teach me to rely on Your voice, not assumptions.
5. Establish me in places that strengthen obedience and trust.

Meditation / Reflection

Are there environments in my life that subtly weaken my trust in God?

Words of Wisdom: *Environment does not create fear—it reveals what faith has not yet resolved.*

April 3

Theme: God Defends What He Initiated

Anchor Scripture - "Yes, I know that you did this in the integrity of your heart. For I also withheld you from sinning against Me; therefore I did not let you touch her." **Genesis 20:6**

Devotional Thought

At a surface level, Abimelech appears to be an unintended victim—warned, interrupted, and restrained by God. Yet a deeper examination reveals that his action was likely part of a **normalized cultural practice**: powerful men taking women without scrutiny or consent. Ignorance did not make the act righteous; it only delayed judgment.

Sarah stands as the **primary violated party**. Even without physical contact, being taken into another man's house under royal authority constituted violation. The intention was possession, and God judged the motive before the act.

Abraham failed through fear. Abimelech failed through entitlement. Sarah was placed in harm's way by both.

All were wrong—but not equally.

What reshapes the entire narrative is **covenant**. God's response was swift and decisive, not because the people involved were righteous, but because covenant was in place. The redemptive line carried through Sarah could not be negotiated, delayed, or contaminated.

The level of divine defense is different when covenant is in place.

God restrained Abimelech not to affirm innocence, but to preserve His agenda. Where covenant exists, heaven intervenes early, forcefully, and without negotiation.

Key Lessons & Life Applications

- **Teaching:** Covenant activates a higher level of divine intervention.
- **Reproof:** Cultural normalization does not excuse moral violation.
- **Correction:** God restrains actions when His purposes are threatened.
- **Instruction:** Power must submit to covenant, not exploit it.
- **Righteous Living:** God defends covenant carriers to preserve redemption, not convenience.

Prayer Points

1. Thank You, Lord, for the covenant that invokes Your defense.
2. Father, take me into the realm of covenant relationship.
3. Keep me aligned so I do not abuse divine protection.
4. Expose cultural practices that violate dignity and truth.
5. Let my life remain positioned for Your redemptive purposes.

Meditation / Reflection

How does understanding covenant reshape my view of divine protection and accountability?

Words of Wisdom: *The level of divine defense is different when covenant is in place.*

April 4

Theme: Intercession Restores Order

Anchor Scripture - "So Abraham prayed to God; and God healed Abimelech, his wife, and his female servants. Then they bore children." Genesis 20:17

Devotional Thought

After God intervened to stop destruction, He required **intercession to restore order**. Abraham—the one whose fear initiated the crisis—was also the one God appointed to pray for healing and restoration.

This reveals a profound principle of covenant maturity: **those involved in disruption are often assigned responsibility for restoration**. God did not bypass Abraham; He repositioned him. Intercession was not optional—it was necessary to realign what fear had disturbed.

Intercession is more than prayer; it is **participation in God's repair work**. Abraham's prayer reopened wombs, healed households, and restored order to a nation affected by one man's private decision.

God does not only correct through confrontation—He restores through intercession.

Key Lessons & Life Applications

- **Teaching:** God uses intercession to restore what was disrupted.
- **Reproof:** Fear-based decisions often require intentional repair.
- **Correction:** God assigns responsibility, not avoidance, after failure.
- **Instruction:** Intercession is a leadership function, not a weakness.
- **Righteous Living:** Maturity accepts responsibility for restoration.

Prayer Points

1. Lord, give me grace to repair what my decisions have affected.
2. Teach me to intercede with humility and responsibility.
3. Restore order where fear has caused disruption.
4. Heal relationships impacted by misalignment.
5. Use me as an agent of restoration, not withdrawal.

Meditation / Reflection

Where is God asking me to intercede instead of retreat?

Words of Wisdom: *God restores order through intercession, not denial.*

April 5

Theme: Leadership Requires Integrity Under Exposure

Anchor Scripture - *"Then Abimelech called Abraham and said to him, 'What have you done to us? How have I offended you, that you have brought on me and on my kingdom a great sin?'"* Genesis 20:9

Devotional Thought

One of the most humbling moments in Genesis 20 is when a pagan king confronts God's covenant carrier. Abraham is exposed—not privately, but publicly—and must account for his actions.

Leadership maturity is tested not by perfection, but by **integrity under exposure**. When mistakes are revealed, character determines whether influence is lost or refined. Abraham did not argue covenant privilege; he faced responsibility.

Exposure is not the enemy of leadership—**defensiveness is**. God allowed Abraham to be confronted because integrity must be visible, not assumed. Covenant authority without integrity erodes trust and weakens witness.

God refines leaders by allowing truth to surface.

Key Lessons & Life Applications

- **Teaching:** Leadership accountability applies across spiritual boundaries.
- **Reproof:** Covenant status does not excuse unethical conduct.
- **Correction:** God permits exposure to refine character.
- **Instruction:** Leaders must respond to confrontation with humility.
- **Righteous Living:** Integrity sustains authority under scrutiny.

Prayer Points

1. Father, help me walk in integrity regardless of visibility.
2. Remove defensiveness when correction comes.
3. Strengthen my character where exposure is uncomfortable.
4. Teach me to lead with humility and accountability.
5. Let my life reflect Your righteousness publicly and privately.

Meditation / Reflection

How do I respond when my actions are questioned or exposed?

Words of Wisdom: *Integrity is revealed not in secrecy, but under exposure.*

April 6

Theme: Promise Without Striving

Anchor Scripture - "And the LORD visited Sarah as He had said, and the LORD did for Sarah as He had spoken." Genesis 21:1

Devotional Thought

Genesis 21 marks a transition from Abraham's striving years to **Isaac's season of fulfillment**. Isaac represents a promise fulfilled without manipulation, fear, or effort. What God promised, He performed—**in His time**.

The delay was not punishment; it was preparation. God allowed time to mature Abraham's trust so that fulfillment would not be contaminated by control or fear. Isaac arrived not when Abraham forced the outcome, but when alignment was complete.

Scripture affirms, *"He has made everything beautiful in its time"* (Ecclesiastes 3:11, NKJV). Beauty in fulfillment is inseparable from obedience in waiting. What is birthed prematurely carries strain; what is birthed in God's timing carries peace.

Covenant maturity learns to trust God not only for **what** He promised, but for **when** He will perform it.

Key Lessons & Life Applications

- **Teaching:** God fulfills His promises according to divine timing.
- **Reproof:** Striving often signals distrust in God's schedule.
- **Correction:** Waiting realigns the heart with God's process.
- **Instruction:** Trust God's timing as much as His promise.
- **Righteous Living:** Peace accompanies obedience to divine timing.

Prayer Points

1. Lord, deliver me from striving to fulfill what You have promised.
2. Teach me to trust Your timing as much as I trust Your word.
3. Heal impatience that leads to manipulation or fear.
4. Align my expectations with Your divine schedule.
5. Let what You have promised manifest in peace and order.

Meditation / Reflection

Where am I tempted to rush what God intends to unfold in His time?

Words of Wisdom: *What God promises, He fulfills—beautifully, and in His time.*

April 7

Theme: Some Things Cannot Coexist

Anchor Scripture - "Then God said to Abraham, 'Do not let it be displeasing in your sight because of the lad or because of your bondwoman. Whatever Sarah has said to you, listen to her voice; for in Isaac your seed shall be called.'" Genesis 21:12

Devotional Thought

April 7 unveils one of the most critical truths in the redemptive narrative: **some things cannot coexist without threatening God's eternal plan**. Separation was not about favoritism or rejection—it was about preservation.

Before Isaac, every attempt to preserve God's redemptive line had failed.

Abel was the first righteous option, lost not by personal error but by the envy and violence of his brother Cain.

Noah carried hope after the flood, yet ended compromised when he became drunk, lay uncovered in his tent, and exposed his household to shame and moral disorder (Genesis 9:20–24).

Abraham himself, though chosen, repeatedly faltered under fear and compromise.

By the time Isaac was born, **there was no margin left for contamination**. Isaac was not merely a promised son—he was the vessel through whom the continuation of redemption depended at that stage of history.

Ishmael represents compromise, substitution, and human intervention. Though loved, provided for, and blessed by God, he could not grow alongside Isaac without conflict. **Compromise always competes with covenant**. This mirrors an earlier truth revealed with Lot—Lot could not grow with Abraham, not because Lot lacked blessing, but because covenant advancement cannot coexist with mixture.

Separation did not cancel God's provision for Ishmael. God sustained him. God multiplied him. But **inheritance and redemption required exclusivity**.

Some things can be blessed—but cannot be allowed to remain connected to destiny.

Key Lessons & Life Applications

- **Teaching:** Covenant advancement requires separation, not coexistence.
- **Reproof:** Compromise will always compete with covenant purpose.
- **Correction:** God separates to protect what cannot be replaced.
- **Instruction:** Provision does not equal inheritance or redemptive assignment.
- **Righteous Living:** Obedience sometimes requires releasing what God still blesses.

Prayer Points

1. Father, help me discern what cannot coexist with my destiny.
2. Give me courage to obey separation without guilt or fear.
3. Deliver me from compromise disguised as compassion.
4. Protect what You are preserving for redemption through my life.
5. Align me fully with what You have ordained to continue.

Meditation / Reflection

What has God blessed in my life that cannot continue with my destiny?

Words of Wisdom: *What God is preserving for redemption cannot coexist with compromise.*

April 8

Theme: Inheritance Requires Discernment

Anchor Scripture - "But My covenant I will establish with Isaac, whom Sarah shall bear to you at this set time next year." Genesis 17:21

Devotional Thought

One of the most misunderstood truths in Scripture is the difference between **blessing and inheritance**. Ishmael was blessed. He was preserved. He multiplied. Yet inheritance followed covenant, not compassion, effort, or order of birth.

Inheritance is not determined by who came first, who worked hardest, or who feels entitled—it is determined by **divine assignment**. Abraham had to learn that discernment, not affection, governs legacy. Without discernment, what is merely blessed will compete with what is divinely ordained.

God made it clear: the covenant would pass through Isaac at an appointed time. This was not favoritism; it was precision. Redemption requires clarity. Confusion about inheritance always produces conflict, delay, or distortion of purpose.

Covenant maturity understands this: **everything God blesses is not authorized to carry legacy**.

Key Lessons & Life Applications

- **Teaching:** Inheritance follows covenant, not emotion or effort.
- **Reproof:** Confusing blessing with entitlement distorts legacy.
- **Correction:** God clarifies inheritance to prevent rivalry and confusion.
- **Instruction:** Discernment is required to steward covenant accurately.
- **Righteous Living:** Faith honors God's order, even when it is costly.

Prayer Points

1. Father, sharpen my discernment concerning inheritance and assignment.
2. Help me distinguish blessing from covenant responsibility.
3. Remove emotional bias that clouds spiritual clarity.
4. Teach me to steward legacy according to Your design.
5. Align my decisions with covenant precision.

Meditation / Reflection

Where might I be confusing blessing with inheritance in my life?

Words of Wisdom: *Not everything blessed is assigned to carry inheritance.*

April 9

Theme: Growth Attracts Conflict

Anchor Scripture - "And the Philistines envied him." Genesis 26:14

Devotional Thought

Isaac's growth did not produce applause—it provoked opposition. Scripture is intentional in its wording: envy followed increase. This reveals a sobering truth of covenant life—**growth often exposes unresolved insecurity in others**.

Conflict is not always a sign of error. Sometimes it is evidence of advancement. When God prospers someone, contrast becomes visible. What others have learned to tolerate in themselves becomes uncomfortable when confronted by another person's obedience, discipline, or favor.

Isaac's maturity is revealed in his response. He did not retaliate. He did not explain himself. He did not shrink to maintain peace. He chose restraint, trusting that the God who caused the increase would also secure the outcome.

Covenant growth attracts conflict—but wisdom determines whether conflict becomes warfare or a doorway into greater expansion.

Key Lessons & Life Applications

- **Teaching:** Increase often provokes envy rather than affirmation.
- **Reproof:** Not all resistance is a call to self-correction.
- **Correction:** God trains restraint and discernment during seasons of growth.
- **Instruction:** Respond to opposition with wisdom, not self-reduction.
- **Righteous Living:** Peace preserves progress when growth invites scrutiny.

Prayer Points

1. Father, help me recognize conflict without fear or offense.
2. Give me discernment to understand the root of resistance.
3. Guard my heart from shrinking to preserve comfort.
4. Teach me to remain at peace while continuing to grow.
5. Establish me firmly as You increase me.

Meditation / Reflection

Do I take time to discern the root cause of conflict?

Is this resistance inviting correction—or is it simply a reaction to growth?

Am I shrinking, apologizing, or slowing down to make others comfortable, when the real issue is that my growth is confronting their insecurity?

How do I usually respond when increase attracts resistance—do I retreat, retaliate, or remain at peace and continue forward?

Words of Wisdom: *Do not apologize for becoming who God is forming you to be.*

April 10

Theme: Peace as a Covenant Strategy

> **Anchor Scripture** - "So Isaac departed from there and pitched his tent in the Valley of Gerar, and dwelt there." Genesis 26:17

Devotional Thought

After Isaac's prosperity provoked envy and hostility, his response was unexpected—**he moved**. He did not argue, retaliate, or defend his success. Isaac understood something covenant carriers must learn: **peace is not weakness; it is strategy**.

Isaac's peace was not avoidance—it was wisdom. He recognized that some conflicts are not meant to be won but outgrown. By choosing peace, Isaac preserved momentum and protected what God was building through him.

Covenant maturity knows when to stand and when to relocate. Fighting every battle drains focus and delays progress. Peace becomes strategic when it preserves purpose and positions you for continued increase.

Sometimes, the most powerful response to resistance is not confrontation, but confident movement forward.

Key Lessons & Life Applications

- **Teaching:** Peace can be an intentional covenant strategy.
- **Reproof:** Not every conflict requires engagement.
- **Correction:** God often leads forward, not into unnecessary battles.
- **Instruction:** Choose environments that support continued growth.
- **Righteous Living:** Wisdom preserves peace without compromising purpose.

Prayer Points

1. Father, teach me when peace is the wiser response.
2. Deliver me from the need to prove or defend myself.
3. Help me discern battles You have not assigned to me.
4. Preserve my focus as You increase me.
5. Position me where peace and purpose align.

Meditation / Reflection

Am I fighting conflicts God is asking me to move beyond?

Words of Wisdom: *Peace is not retreat when it preserves purpose.*

April 11

Theme: The Price of Peace

Anchor Scripture - "And Isaac's servants dug in the valley, and found a well of running water there. But the herdsmen of Gerar quarreled with Isaac's herdsmen, saying, 'The water is ours!' So he called the name of the well Esek, because they quarreled with him." Genesis 26:19–20

Devotional Thought

Genesis 26 reveals a difficult but powerful truth: **peace often has a cost**. Isaac was not yielding because he was weak. He was yielding because he was wise.

The wells Isaac dug were **rightfully his**—they were inherited, lawful, and essential to his economic survival. Yet each time envy surfaced, his resources were contested and sabotaged. These were not misunderstandings; they were deliberate provocations meant to force Isaac into conflict.

The Philistines wanted a fight. Isaac refused to give them what they wanted.

This is emotional maturity at its highest level: **the ability to absorb loss without reacting in rage**, especially when you are right. Isaac chose not to fight impossible troublemakers. He chose his battles and allowed God to take over the fight.

Peace came at a price—temporary economic loss, public misunderstanding, and restraint under pressure. But Isaac understood that **winning the argument could cost him the future**, while yielding preserved momentum.

Some battles are designed to distract you. Maturity knows when to walk away and let God defend what He has already established.

Key Lessons & Life Applications

- **Teaching:** Peace sometimes requires absorbing unjust loss.
- **Reproof:** Not every provocation deserves a response.
- **Correction:** God trains emotional maturity through restraint.
- **Instruction:** Choose battles that preserve destiny, not ego.
- **Righteous Living:** Trust God to vindicate you when envy targets your progress.

Prayer Points

1. Father, give me wisdom to choose my battles carefully.
2. Strengthen me to walk in peace when provoked unjustly.
3. Heal emotional reactions that crave vindication.
4. Teach me to trust You with battles I refuse to fight.
5. Let my restraint create room for Your intervention.

Meditation / Reflection

Am I fighting battles God is asking me to release to Him?
How do I respond when my rightful progress is sabotaged by envy?

Words of Wisdom: *Peace often costs what is rightfully yours—but preserves what truly matters.*

April 12

Theme: Abraham Releases What He Loves

Anchor Scripture - "Take now your son, your only son Isaac, whom you love... and offer him there as a burnt offering." Genesis 22:2

Devotional Thought

Genesis 22 is not primarily about sacrifice—it is about **capacity**. What God was preparing to entrust to Abraham was **deeper, weightier, and more consequential than Isaac**. Before Abraham could steward what was next, his love had to be proven **without competition**.

Isaac was not just a son; he was the fulfillment of promise, the carrier of legacy, and the embodiment of hope. Yet God required Abraham to demonstrate that **even fulfilled promise would not rival devotion to the Promise-Giver**.

This was not a test of trust alone—it was a test of **supremacy of love**. God was measuring whether Abraham's affection for Isaac had quietly become a competing allegiance. Love for God had to stand alone—unshared, uncontested, and unrivaled.

What Abraham released was not what God wanted to take; it was what God needed Abraham not to cling to. Capacity for what comes next is determined by what we are willing to place back on the altar.

You cannot carry the next dimension of God's purpose if your heart is already full.

Key Lessons & Life Applications

- **Teaching:** God entrusts greater purpose to those whose love is undivided.
- **Reproof:** Fulfilled promises can quietly compete with devotion to God.
- **Correction:** God confronts attachments that threaten capacity.
- **Instruction:** Release what you love to make room for what is next.
- **Righteous Living:** Love for God must remain supreme and uncontested.

Prayer Points

1. Father, purify my love so nothing competes with You.
2. Expose attachments that limit my capacity for what is next.
3. Teach me to release even what You have given me.
4. Prepare my heart to carry greater responsibility and purpose.
5. Let my devotion to You remain without rivalry.

Meditation / Reflection

What do I love deeply that could unintentionally compete with my devotion to God?

Words of Wisdom: *God tests love not to take from us, but to expand our capacity for what is next.*

April 13

Theme: Obedience Redefines Trust

Anchor Scripture - "So Abraham rose early in the morning… and went to the place of which God had told him." Genesis 22:3

Devotional Thought

This act of obedience did more than prove Abraham's faith—it **sealed his identity**. Genesis 22 is the moment Abraham truly became *the father of faith*. Not by confession, but by **action under weight**.

Abraham rose early. He delayed nothing. He negotiated nothing. Obedience became the language of his trust.

This was not blind obedience; it was informed obedience. Abraham had history with God. He knew God's character well enough to obey without explanation. Trust had matured beyond understanding.

There is also a sobering detail in this narrative: **Abraham carried this instruction alone**. Scripture records his words to the servants, *"Stay here with the donkey; the lad and I will go yonder and worship, and we will come back to you"* (Genesis 22:5, NKJV). At that point, Abraham separated himself from everyone—including those closest to him.

Did Abraham tell Sarah? Scripture is silent. What it does reveal is this truth: **some obediences are solitary by design**. There are instructions God gives that cannot be processed by committee, shared prematurely, or negotiated relationally. Not because others lack faith—but because the test is **personal and capacity-specific**. Some exams are group assignments.

Others are taken alone.

Obedience redefines trust when it is no longer conditional on clarity, consensus, or emotional reinforcement. Abraham trusted that even if he did not understand *how*, God would remain faithful to *what* He promised.

Delayed obedience often reveals unresolved negotiation. Immediate obedience reveals settled trust.

Key Lessons & Life Applications

- **Teaching:** Obedience is trust expressed through decisive action.
- **Reproof:** Delay often signals internal negotiation, not wisdom.
- **Correction:** God matures trust through solitary obedience.
- **Instruction:** Act on God's word even when understanding is incomplete.
- **Righteous Living:** Faith is proven through obedience, not explanation.

Prayer Points

1. Lord, strengthen my obedience when understanding is limited.
2. Give me grace to obey You even when the journey is solitary.
3. Remove hesitation rooted in fear or emotional dependence.
4. Mature my trust beyond the need for explanation or approval.
5. Let my obedience reflect confidence in Your character.

Meditation / Reflection

Are there instructions God has given me that require obedience without consensus or applause?

Words of Wisdom: *Trust is not proven by what we say, but by what we obey.*

April 14

Theme: You Cannot Outgive God

Anchor Scripture - "And Abraham lifted his eyes and looked, and there behind him was a ram caught in a thicket by its horns. So Abraham went and took the ram, and offered it up for a burnt offering instead of his son." Genesis 22:13

Devotional Thought

Genesis 22 reveals a covenant truth that reshapes our understanding of giving, surrender, and obedience: **you cannot outgive God.**

Abraham did not give Isaac to impoverish himself; he released what was already received. Scripture makes this principle clear: *"For who makes you differ from another? And what do you have that you did not receive?"* (1 Corinthians 4:7, NKJV). God never asks for what He did not first give.

The ram was already prepared. Provision did not follow sacrifice—it preceded it. Abraham's obedience simply unveiled what God had already supplied. As Scripture affirms, *"Now may He who supplies seed to the sower…"* (2 Corinthians 9:10, NKJV).

God gives before He requires. He entrusts before He asks.

This moment teaches us that surrender is not loss—it is recognition of source. What Abraham placed on the altar was not ownership relinquished, but stewardship acknowledged. Every act of obedience returns to this truth: **God always gives more than He receives.**

You cannot outgive the One from whom all things come.

Key Lessons & Life Applications

- **Teaching:** Everything we have is received from God.
- **Reproof:** Fear of loss reveals misunderstanding of God as source.
- **Correction:** God reshapes ownership into stewardship through obedience.
- **Instruction:** Release confidently what God has entrusted to you.
- **Righteous Living:** Faith gives freely, knowing God's supply is endless.

Prayer Points

- Father, thank You for being the source of all I have.
- Deliver me from fear that resists obedience.
- Help me give and release with confidence, not anxiety.
- Teach me to live as a faithful steward, not an owner.
- Let my life testify that I cannot outgive You.

Meditation / Reflection

Is there anything I am holding tightly out of fear of loss rather than trust in God's provision?

Words of Wisdom: *You cannot outgive God—everything you release returns to Him as trust.*

April 15

Theme: Stewarding What Was Secured

Anchor Scripture - "Then Isaac sowed in that land, and reaped in the same year a hundredfold; and the LORD blessed him." Genesis 26:12

Devotional Thought

Isaac must not be misunderstood. He was not called to replicate Abraham's journey, nor to outperform it. **Isaac's assignment was stewardship, not pioneering**. What Abraham secured through obedience, Isaac was entrusted to preserve, stabilize, and transmit.

One man is too small to carry the full weight of God's agenda. God works through **continuity**, not exhaustion of a single vessel. Covenant advances like a relay race—each generation runs its leg faithfully, then passes the baton forward. The goal is not individual completion, but **unbroken transmission**.

Isaac's greatness lay in his restraint. He did not innovate the covenant; he **maintained it**. He did not expand recklessly; he stabilized faithfully. He re-opened wells, preserved names, and remained rooted where God planted him. His obedience ensured that what Abraham received did not deteriorate, distort, or disappear.

This relay continued through Jacob, Israel, David, and the prophets—until **Christ**, the fulfillment of covenant, restored access to what was lost in Eden. Through Christ, humanity was delivered from the bondage of sin, and access to the **tree of life** was restored. That was the whole race. That was the goal.

Isaac teaches us this truth: **faithfulness is not measured by visibility, but by continuity**.

Key Lessons & Life Applications

- **Teaching:** God advances His agenda through generational stewardship.
- **Reproof:** Measuring impact only by innovation undervalues faithfulness.
- **Correction:** God assigns different roles—securing, stewarding, or fulfilling.
- **Instruction:** Preserve what others paid to establish.
- **Righteous Living:** Faithfulness sustains what obedience has secured.

Prayer Points

1. Father, help me steward faithfully what others labored to establish.
2. Deliver me from the pressure to compete with previous generations.
3. Teach me to value continuity as much as breakthrough.
4. Align my obedience with Your long-term agenda.
5. Let my life faithfully pass the baton forward.

Meditation / Reflection

Am I trying to replace what God has called me to preserve, or steward what He has already secured?

Words of Wisdom: *God's purposes are too vast for one life—faithfulness keeps the race alive.*

April 16

Theme: Digging Wells, Not Fighting Battles

Anchor Scripture - "And Isaac dug again the wells of water which they had dug in the days of Abraham his father… and he gave them the same names which his father had given them." Genesis 26:18

Devotional Thought

Inheritance is often misunderstood. Many assume that receiving from a father means resting from labor. Scripture teaches the opposite: **inheritance is not relief from responsibility—it is the beginning of stewardship.**

Isaac inherited what Abraham secured, but inheritance did not grant him an idle life. It placed upon him the burden to **preserve, repair, rebuild, and advance** what had already been established. Wells that Abraham dug had been stopped up. Isaac had to reopen them, restore their names, and ensure their function for the future.

This is inheritance values. What is inherited must be maintained, not merely enjoyed. Legacy deteriorates when stewards confuse inheritance with entitlement. Isaac did not sit back and live off Abraham's obedience—he labored to keep it alive.

Instead of fighting battles to prove ownership, Isaac invested energy in sustaining sources of life. He understood that **legacy is preserved through faithful labor, not passive possession.**

True inheritance is work handed forward, not comfort handed down.

Key Lessons & Life Applications

- **Teaching:** Inheritance carries responsibility, not exemption from labor.
- **Reproof:** Expecting ease from inheritance reflects entitlement, not honor.
- **Correction:** God calls heirs to steward, not idle.
- **Instruction:** Preserve, repair, and advance what was entrusted to you.
- **Righteous Living:** Faithfulness sustains legacy across generations.

Prayer Points

1. Father, teach me to honor inheritance through stewardship.
2. Deliver me from entitlement disguised as blessing.
3. Give me grace to preserve what others labored to establish.
4. Strengthen me to rebuild what time or conflict has damaged.
5. Let my life advance the legacy You entrusted to me.

Meditation / Reflection

Am I treating what I inherited as entitlement—or as responsibility to steward and advance?

Words of Wisdom: *Inheritance is not permission to rest; it is a call to steward legacy.*

April 17

Theme: Desire vs Discipline

> **Anchor Scripture** - "So Esau said, 'Look, I am about to die; so what is this birthright to me?' Then Jacob said, 'Swear to me as of this day.' So he swore to him, and sold his birthright to Jacob." Genesis 25:32–33

Devotional Thought

This encounter between Jacob and Esau was not a casual family dispute—it was a **destiny test**. What Isaac was positioned to pass on, having been established by Abraham, went far beyond the traditional blessing of the firstborn. It represented **covenant stewardship**—a responsibility tied to God's unfolding redemptive agenda.

Esau's failure was not hunger; it was **disdain**. His words reveal contempt: *"What is this birthright to me?"* In that moment, Esau disqualified himself—not because he was imperfect, but because he lacked the capacity to **subdue the flesh and think beyond himself**.

This was not about moral flaw versus moral excellence. It was about **value alignment**. The covenant required a steward who could carry weight, restrain appetite, and preserve purpose across time. Esau's untamed desire could not coexist with what lay ahead.

Jacob, though flawed in method, understood the value of what was at stake. His discipline of focus—though needing refinement in character—revealed capacity for long-range vision.

Scripture later echoes this principle plainly: *"Those who despise Me I will despise"* (1 Samuel 2:30, NKJV). What you despise, you cannot preserve. What you do not value, you will eventually trade away.

Covenant maturity is not about perfection; it is about **capacity**—the ability to honor, protect, and steward what God entrusts beyond personal comfort.

Key Lessons & Life Applications

- **Teaching:** Covenant inheritance requires disciplined stewardship, not entitlement.
- **Reproof:** Appetite unchecked reveals contempt for long-term purpose.
- **Correction:** God exposes value systems through daily choices.
- **Instruction:** Discipline preserves what desire alone cannot sustain.
- **Righteous Living:** What you honor, you protect; what you despise, you lose.

Prayer Points

1. Father, align my values with what You are entrusting to me.
2. Deliver me from appetites that undermine destiny.
3. Teach me discipline that honors covenant responsibility.
4. Help me think beyond self and immediate comfort.
5. Guard my inheritance from careless or shortsighted decisions.

Meditation / Reflection

Am I allowing immediate desire to override long-term calling or responsibility?

Words of Wisdom: *What you do not value, you cannot preserve.*

April 18

Theme: Value Determines Destiny

Anchor Scripture - "Lest there be any fornicator or profane person like Esau, who for one morsel of food sold his birthright." Hebrews 12:16

Devotional Thought

Destiny is not decided in dramatic moments alone—it is revealed in what we consistently **value**. Esau did not lose his inheritance because of one bad day; that day merely exposed a heart posture that already existed.

Scripture later describes Esau as *profane*—not immoral in the obvious sense, but **common** in his estimation of sacred things. He treated what was holy as ordinary and what was eternal as expendable. His destiny unraveled not through rebellion, but through **disregard**.

Jacob's story teaches the opposite lesson. Though flawed in character and method, Jacob valued what Esau despised. Value shaped pursuit, and pursuit shaped destiny. God entrusted the future not to the flawless, but to the one who understood the weight of what was being carried.

This is the governing principle: **destiny aligns itself with value**. What you honor expands in your life. What you treat lightly diminishes. God does not force destiny on those who despise its cost.

You cannot preserve what you do not value—and you will never steward what you treat as optional.

Key Lessons & Life Applications

- **Teaching:** Destiny responds to value, not entitlement.
- **Reproof:** Treating sacred things casually invites loss.
- **Correction:** God exposes destiny alignment through everyday choices.
- **Instruction:** Guard what God entrusts by honoring its weight.
- **Righteous Living:** Honor sustains what calling introduces.

Prayer Points

1. Father, align my values with Your purposes.
2. Deliver me from treating sacred assignments casually.
3. Teach me to honor what You are preparing me to steward.
4. Guard my destiny from indifference and neglect.
5. Let my values qualify me for what lies ahead.

Meditation / Reflection

What do my daily choices reveal about what I truly value?

Words of Wisdom: *Destiny follows value—what you honor, you are trusted to carry.*

April 19

Theme: Deception Produces Delay

Anchor Scripture - "Now therefore, my son, obey my voice according to what I command you." Genesis 27:8

Devotional Thought

Genesis 27 cannot be read honestly by placing the burden of deception on Jacob alone. This was not merely an individual failure—it was a **family system dysfunction**. Scripture makes it clear: deception was learned, affirmed, and mentored.

Rebekah did not see anything wrong with her actions. She believed she was helping God fulfill prophecy. Yet her interpretation of *"the older shall serve the younger"* was flawed. She assumed it referred to the **traditional blessing of the firstborn**, when in reality, God was doing something **entirely new—without precedent or prototype**.

Rebekah herself was raised in deception. Her brother Laban would later reveal the same pattern. What she modeled, she transferred. What she normalized, she initiated Jacob into. In trying to secure destiny, she trained him in manipulation—and the very blessing she sought to protect was delayed by the method she chose.

This teaches a sobering truth: **many delays in destiny are rooted in homes, not hearts alone**. Dysfunctional mentoring can distort interpretation. Good intentions do not excuse flawed methods. Love without wisdom can initiate children into cycles they must later unlearn.

Jacob did not suffer because he valued covenant—he suffered because he pursued it through inherited deception. His destiny was not canceled, but it was stalled until **with God** replaced inherited deception. God honored the promise—but He required transformation before peace.

Key Lessons & Life Applications

- **Teaching:** Destiny delays often originate in family systems, not individuals alone.
- **Reproof:** Good intentions do not sanctify deceptive methods.
- **Correction:** God exposes inherited patterns that distort purpose.
- **Instruction:** New things from God require new ways, not recycled strategies.
- **Righteous Living:** Alignment, not manipulation, accelerates destiny.

Prayer Points

1. Father, expose patterns I inherited that hinder alignment.
2. Heal distortions caused by flawed mentoring or interpretation.
3. Deliver me from repeating familiar but unapproved methods.
4. Teach me to pursue destiny through obedience, not strategy.
5. Align my heart and methods with what You are doing now.

Meditation / Reflection

Are there inherited patterns or learned behaviors influencing how I pursue God's promises?

Words of Wisdom: *Destiny is delayed when inherited deception replaces divine alignment.*

April 20

Theme: God Does Not Wait for Perfection to Work with Humanity

Anchor Scripture - "And behold, the LORD stood above it and said: 'I am the LORD God of Abraham your father and the God of Isaac; the land on which you lie I will give to you and your descendants.'" Genesis 28:13

Devotional Thought

Genesis 28 marks a profound moment of divine engagement. Jacob is fleeing the consequences of deception. His character is still unrefined, his methods still flawed, and his alignment incomplete. Yet **God meets him**.

This encounter reveals a critical covenant truth: **God does not wait for perfection to begin working with humanity.** Jacob had not yet been transformed into Israel, but God initiated relationship anyway. Promise followed him even while correction lay ahead.

This does not mean God endorsed Jacob's methods. It means God distinguishes between **purpose and process**. God works *through* imperfect vessels while simultaneously working *on* them. Usage is not approval; engagement is not endorsement.

The apostle Paul would later explain this principle clearly: *"We have this treasure in earthen vessels, that the excellence of the power may be of God and not of us"* (2 Corinthians 4:7, NKJV). The vessel remains human; the power remains divine.

God's grace allows movement before maturity—but **rest comes only after alignment**. Jacob would carry the promise forward, but peace would wait until transformation replaced manipulation.

Understanding this truth guards us from two extremes: pride when God uses us, and despair when we see our flaws. God's work advances because He is faithful—not because we are finished.

Key Lessons & Life Applications

- **Teaching:** God engages people before they are perfected.
- **Reproof:** Being used by God does not equal divine approval of all methods.
- **Correction:** God refines character even while advancing purpose.
- **Instruction:** Cooperate with God's transforming work, not just His calling.
- **Righteous Living:** Humility keeps the vessel open to correction and growth.

Prayer Points

1. Father, thank You for working through imperfect vessels.
2. Guard my heart from pride when You use me.
3. Help me embrace Your correction as part of Your grace.
4. Align my character with the purpose You are advancing.
5. Let Your power be evident beyond my limitations.

Meditation / Reflection

Am I mistaking God's engagement with my life for full alignment with His ways?

Words of Wisdom: *God works through imperfection—but alignment is what brings rest.*

April 21

Theme: Leaving Home to Find Identity

Anchor Scripture - "So Jacob went out from Beersheba and went toward Haran." Genesis 28:10

Devotional Thought

Jacob did not leave home because he was ready—he left because staying would have kept him misaligned. Sometimes God allows displacement not as punishment, but as **repositioning**. What familiar environments protect can also prevent transformation.

Home had shaped Jacob's methods—strategy, manipulation, inherited patterns, and flawed mentoring. To become who God intended, Jacob had to step outside the systems that reinforced who he had been. Identity could not be formed where old patterns were constantly affirmed.

Leaving home did not immediately fix Jacob, but it **created space for encounter**. On the journey—alone, exposed, and without advantage—God met him. Not after perfection. Not after repentance. But at the point of vulnerability. God's agenda had not changed; Jacob's alignment had to.

This teaches a sobering truth: **God may keep speaking, blessing, and protecting, while still waiting for us to align**. Distance from familiar voices often makes room for God's voice to become clear. Identity is not discovered in comfort; it is formed in transition.

Jacob would not fully become Israel until later, but this step marked the beginning—leaving what shaped him so he could be reshaped by God.

Key Lessons & Life Applications

- **Teaching:** Identity formation often requires separation from familiar systems.
- **Reproof:** Comfort can preserve misalignment.
- **Correction:** God repositions people to reshape character.
- **Instruction:** Allow distance from old patterns to create space for encounter.
- **Righteous Living:** Alignment begins when God's voice outweighs familiar influence.

Prayer Points

1. Father, give me courage to leave environments that hinder alignment.
2. Help me recognize when familiarity is preserving old patterns.
3. Create space in my life for fresh encounter with You.
4. Align my identity with Your purpose, not my past.
5. Lead me through transition with humility and trust.

Meditation / Reflection

Is there a place, pattern, or influence I may need to leave in order to truly align with God?

Words of Wisdom: *Sometimes you must leave what formed you to become who God intended.*

April 22

Theme: Encounter Changes Trajectory

> **Anchor Scripture** - "Then Jacob awoke from his sleep and said, 'Surely the LORD is in this place, and I did not know it.'" Genesis 28:16

Devotional Thought

Jacob's life did not change because he traveled farther—it changed because he **encountered God**. The ladder, the angels, and the divine declaration revealed a truth Jacob had never fully grasped: **God was present even when Jacob was misaligned**.

This encounter did not immediately correct Jacob's character, but it **reoriented his trajectory**. God reaffirmed covenant promises not to reward Jacob's methods, but to anchor Jacob's future. Encounter precedes transformation. God meets people where they are, but He never leaves them where He finds them.

Jacob discovered something vital: God's agenda was active even when Jacob was unaware. Human ignorance does not negate divine presence. The revelation—*"the LORD is in this place"*—marked the moment Jacob's journey shifted from survival to significance.

Encounters do not eliminate process; they **give direction to it**. After this moment, Jacob would still walk through years of refinement, but he would never again be without reference. Encounter gave him orientation.

God often changes the course of a life not by removing struggle, but by **revealing Himself within it**.

Key Lessons & Life Applications

- **Teaching:** Divine encounters realign direction before they transform character.
- **Reproof:** Living unaware of God's presence limits discernment.
- **Correction:** God reveals Himself to redirect trajectory, not just behavior.
- **Instruction:** Seek encounter, not just answers.
- **Righteous Living:** Awareness of God's presence shapes faithful living.

Prayer Points

1. Father, awaken my awareness to Your presence.
2. Let divine encounter redirect my life's trajectory.
3. Help me recognize You even in unfamiliar places.
4. Anchor my journey in revelation, not circumstance.
5. Align my path with Your ongoing work in my life.

Meditation / Reflection

Where might God be present in my life that I have not yet recognized?

Words of Wisdom: *Encounter does not remove the journey—it gives it direction.*

April 23

Theme: Formation Through Process

Anchor Scripture - "So Jacob served seven years for Rachel, and they seemed only a few days to him because of the love he had for her." Genesis 29:20

Devotional Thought

Encounter changes direction, but **process forms character**. After Jacob's encounter at Bethel, his life did not immediately become easier—it became instructional. God led him into a season where time, labor, and repetition would reshape what encounter had exposed.

Jacob entered Laban's house carrying the promise but lacking refinement. Ironically, he now lived under the authority of a man who mirrored his own methods. What Jacob had practiced at home, he now experienced from the other side. This was not coincidence—it was formation.

Process teaches what revelation alone cannot. Years of service disciplined Jacob's impatience, confronted his manipulation, and trained him in endurance. God was not punishing Jacob; He was **preparing him to carry weight without distortion**.

Formation is rarely quick. It unfolds slowly, often invisibly, shaping the inner life while outward activity continues. God uses time to remove shortcuts, repetition to build consistency, and pressure to refine integrity.

The promise remained intact, but Jacob had to be reshaped to sustain it. Destiny matures not only through encounter, but through **faithful endurance in process**.

Key Lessons & Life Applications

- **Teaching:** God forms character through time and responsibility.
- **Reproof:** Impatience resists the work process is meant to accomplish.
- **Correction:** God uses repetition to refine internal posture.
- **Instruction:** Submit to process as part of divine preparation.
- **Righteous Living:** Endurance produces stability and maturity.

Prayer Points

1. Father, help me embrace process without resentment.
2. Teach me patience while You are forming my character.
3. Remove shortcuts that undermine long-term growth.
4. Strengthen me to endure seasons of repetition faithfully.
5. Shape me to carry destiny with integrity.

Meditation / Reflection

How am I responding to the process God is using to shape me?

Words of Wisdom: *Encounter reveals direction; process builds capacity.*

April 24

Theme: What You Sow Returns

Anchor Scripture - *"Yet your father has deceived me and changed my wages ten times, but God did not allow him to hurt me."* Genesis 31:7

Devotional Thought

Jacob's years under Laban reveal a sobering but redemptive truth: **what you sow eventually returns—not to destroy you, but to instruct you.** The deceiver became the deceived. The manipulator lived under manipulation. The methods Jacob once used were now used on him.

The turning point came quietly but powerfully: *"So it came to pass in the morning, that behold, it was Leah"* (Genesis 29:25, NKJV). In that moment, Jacob encountered himself. The shock was not merely relational—it was revelatory. The harvest had arrived.

This was not divine revenge; it was divine correction. God was allowing Jacob to experience the weight of his own methods so they could be uprooted. Yet even within this return, mercy was present. Though Laban deceived him repeatedly, **God did not allow Jacob to be destroyed.** Correction was firm, but protection remained.

What Paul would later articulate—*"whatever a man sows, that he will also reap"* (Galatians 6:7, NKJV)—was already operating in Jacob's life long before it was written. The law was not introduced by Paul; it was **revealed through Jacob.**

This principle is not about punishment—it is about alignment. God allows the return so transformation can occur. The harvest exposes what must change. Jacob was not abandoned; he was being reshaped.

What returns to us is often God's invitation to maturity.

Key Lessons & Life Applications

- **Teaching:** God governs life through the law of sowing and reaping.
- **Reproof:** Deceptive methods eventually return as experience.
- **Correction:** God uses consequence to refine character, not cancel destiny.
- **Instruction:** Change the seed to change the future harvest.
- **Righteous Living:** Integrity produces peace; manipulation produces delay.

Prayer Points

1. Father, help me recognize the seeds I have sown.
2. Give me grace to learn from what has returned to me.
3. Heal patterns that no longer align with Your ways.
4. Align my actions and methods with righteousness.
5. Let my future harvest reflect obedience and transformation.

Meditation / Reflection

What recurring experiences in my life might be revealing seeds I once planted?

Words of Wisdom: *What returns to you is not always judgment—it is often instruction.*

April 25

Theme: Wrestling Produces Identity

Anchor Scripture - "And He said, 'Your name shall no longer be called Jacob, but Israel; for you have struggled with God and with men, and have prevailed.'" **Genesis 32:28**

Devotional Thought

There are transformations that will never occur until **everything else is released**. Genesis 32 reveals Jacob's most defining moment—not a blessing received, but an **identity surrendered**. This was Jacob's Moriah.

For years, Jacob carried promise without peace, blessing without rest, movement without alignment. On this night, he was stripped of advantage—no family, no possessions, no strategy. Alone, vulnerable, and desperate, Jacob finally stopped running and **engaged God directly**.

The wrestling exposed a critical truth: the identity Jacob had been living from could not carry the blessing God intended to release. When God asked, *"What is your name?"* it was not for information—it was for confession. *Jacob* meant supplanter, strategist, manipulator. That identity had served survival, but it could not steward destiny.

God did not recognize *Jacob* as the identity aligned with His agenda. The man existed, but the name—the constructed personality shaped by fear, family patterns, and self-preservation—could not continue. Blessing could only align with **Israel**, the identity formed through surrender and dependence on God.

This is the turning point: Jacob never again appears as the governing identity in God's redemptive plan. Israel does. Not because God rejected the man, but because **God transformed him**. Wrestling did not destroy Jacob; it revealed who he was never meant to remain.

Identity precedes destiny. Until the old name is released, the new future cannot be sustained.

Key Lessons & Life Applications

- **Teaching:** God blesses identity aligned with His purpose.
- **Reproof:** Survival identities cannot steward covenant destiny.
- **Correction:** God confronts false coverings to reveal true identity.
- **Instruction:** Surrender precedes transformation.
- **Righteous Living:** True identity is formed through dependence on God, not self-strategy.

Prayer Points

1. Father, bring me to the place where I release false identities.
2. Expose patterns and names I've lived under that You did not give me.
3. Strip away strategies that replace dependence on You.
4. Align my identity with Your eternal purpose.
5. Let transformation, not survival, define my life.

Meditation / Reflection

What identity might God be asking me to release so I can step fully into who He created me to be?

Words of Wisdom: *Blessing aligns with identity—and identity is revealed in surrender.*

April 26

Theme: Renaming Signals Alignment

> **Anchor Scripture** - "Then God said to him, 'Your name is Jacob; your name shall not be called Jacob anymore, but Israel shall be your name.' So He called his name Israel." Genesis 35:10

Devotional Thought

Renaming in Scripture is never cosmetic—it is **covenantal**. When God renames a person, He is not improving behavior; He is **affirming alignment**. Genesis 35 confirms what began at Peniel: Jacob's transformation was not temporary, emotional, or situational—it was sealed by God.

Jacob had already wrestled and surrendered, but renaming finalized identity. God publicly affirmed what had been formed privately. The old name—Jacob, the supplanter—no longer represented who the man had become. The new name—Israel—signified one who prevails by dependence on God, not by strategy.

Renaming signals that alignment has been achieved. God does not release covenant authority until identity is settled. This is why the name Jacob no longer governs God's agenda. The man remained, but the identity that once covered him was retired.

This teaches a sobering truth: **God cannot advance destiny through misaligned identity**. Names matter because they define posture, authority, and function. Once alignment is complete, God confirms it with clarity.

What God names, He authorizes.

Key Lessons & Life Applications

- **Teaching:** God confirms alignment through identity, not activity.
- **Reproof:** Carrying an old name can hinder new authority.
- **Correction:** God seals transformation with clarity and affirmation.
- **Instruction:** Live from the identity God assigns, not the one you inherited.
- **Righteous Living:** Alignment precedes authorization.

Prayer Points

1. Father, align my identity fully with Your purpose.
2. Remove names and labels You did not assign to me.
3. Seal the transformation You have begun in my life.
4. Help me live consistently from who You say I am.
5. Authorize my steps as I walk in alignment with You.

Meditation / Reflection

Am I living from the identity God has affirmed—or from a name shaped by past patterns?

Words of Wisdom: *What God names, He authorizes.*

April 27

Theme: Israel Emerges from Conflict

> **Anchor Scripture** - "So Jacob lifted his eyes and looked, and there, Esau was coming... But Esau ran to meet him, and embraced him... and they wept." **Genesis 33:1, 4**

Devotional Thought

Israel did not emerge in isolation—he emerged **in confrontation**. Genesis 33 reveals that transformation is tested not in private encounters alone, but in **real-world conflict**. The true measure of identity is how it responds when faced with old threats.

Jacob had feared this moment for years. Esau represented unresolved guilt, past manipulation, and the consequences of old identity. But Jacob no longer approached as the same man. Israel stood where Jacob once strategized.

Notice the shift: no deception, no bargaining, no schemes. Israel approached in humility, clarity, and peace. The conflict that once threatened his survival became the stage on which transformation was revealed.

This moment teaches a powerful truth: **identity transformation does not erase history, but it redeems how history is faced**. Israel did not avoid Esau; he confronted the past from a new posture. What once had power to destroy now lost its grip.

God often allows us to revisit old conflicts—not to punish us, but to prove that we are no longer who we used to be. Israel emerged not because the conflict disappeared, but because **the man had changed**.

Transformation is complete when what once controlled you can no longer define you.

Key Lessons & Life Applications

- **Teaching:** True identity is revealed in how conflict is handled.
- **Reproof:** Avoiding unresolved conflict can delay confirmation of growth.
- **Correction:** God redeems past wounds by changing present posture.
- **Instruction:** Face old challenges from your new identity.
- **Righteous Living:** Peace flows from transformation, not avoidance.

Prayer Points

1. Father, help me face past conflicts from a renewed identity.
2. Heal fears rooted in old versions of myself.
3. Strengthen me to walk in humility and truth.
4. Redeem unresolved relationships through transformation.
5. Let my life testify that You have changed me.

Meditation / Reflection

How do I respond when confronted with situations that once defined or intimidated me?

Words of Wisdom: *Transformation is proven when old conflicts lose their power.*

April 28

Theme: Family Dysfunction Without Covenant Loss

Anchor Scripture - "Now Israel loved Joseph more than all his children… and they hated him and could not speak peaceably to him." Genesis 37:3–4

Devotional Thought

Scripture does not present transformed people living in flawless families. Even after Jacob became Israel, dysfunction persisted within his household. Favoritism re-emerged. Rivalry intensified. Peace fractured among brothers.

Yet covenant was not withdrawn.

This reveals a sobering but hopeful truth: **family dysfunction does not automatically cancel covenant purpose.** God's promises are sustained by His faithfulness, not by perfect parenting or ideal family systems. Israel's alignment restored covenant continuity, even while God continued addressing unresolved household disorder.

This does not excuse dysfunction—it explains divine patience. Covenant does not deny reality; it works through it. God preserves purpose while correcting patterns. He remains committed to redemption even when families are still in process.

What changed was not the absence of problems, but the **presence of divine direction**. God continued to move His agenda forward—not because the family was healed, but because the covenant carrier was aligned.

This guards us from despair: ongoing family challenges do not mean covenant failure. They often signal **unfinished formation**, not forfeited promise.

Key Lessons & Life Applications

- **Teaching:** Covenant continuity depends on God's faithfulness, not family perfection.
- **Reproof:** Favoritism and unresolved conflict create generational wounds.
- **Correction:** God confronts dysfunction without abandoning purpose.
- **Instruction:** Lead families toward alignment even while healing is ongoing.
- **Righteous Living:** Faith trusts God to redeem broken systems over time.

Prayer Points

1. Father, help me trust You amid unresolved family challenges.
2. Heal patterns of favoritism and rivalry.
3. Give wisdom to steward covenant responsibly within my household.
4. Bring order and healing where dysfunction persists.
5. Let Your faithfulness sustain what human weakness complicates.

Meditation / Reflection

Am I interpreting family challenges as covenant failure—or as part of ongoing formation?

Words of Wisdom: *Covenant survives imperfection because God is faithful while He heals.*

April 29

Theme: Covenant Survives Imperfect Generations

Anchor Scripture - "And Jacob said to Simeon and Levi, 'You have troubled me by making me obnoxious among the inhabitants of the land…'" Genesis 34:30

Devotional Thought

Genesis 34 is intentionally disturbing. It exposes the unresolved dysfunction within Israel's household: Dinah's vulnerability, deception cloaked in religion, and Simeon and Levi's uncontrolled violence. This was not covenant zeal—it was reckless retaliation that endangered the entire family.

Yet covenant was not revoked.

This reveals a sobering truth: **covenant survives imperfect generations—not because dysfunction is tolerated, but because God is faithful.** God did not approve of what happened in Shechem. Jacob himself condemned it. Still, God restrained retaliation, preserved the family, and continued His redemptive agenda.

This teaches us something critical about covenant. Covenant is the highest level of relationship God establishes with humanity. It is not casual or permissive—it is weighty and governed by divine terms. Covenant does not excuse disorder; it **pulls God into the process of correction, restraint, and preservation**.

God's faithfulness often delays destruction to allow repentance and alignment. This restraint must never be mistaken for approval. Covenant mercy does not cancel accountability—it postpones final judgment so transformation can occur.

Israel's family was still in formation, yet God remained involved. Covenant did not fail because the family was messy; covenant endured because **God does not abandon what He has sworn**.

Genesis closes **April** with honesty: covenant does not require perfect generations—it requires a faithful God and aligned leadership willing to submit to correction.

Key Lessons & Life Applications

- **Teaching:** Covenant continuity is sustained by God's faithfulness, not human perfection.
- **Reproof:** Unrestrained anger and deception violate covenant values.
- **Correction:** God restrains harm while confronting disorder.
- **Instruction:** Covenant invites responsibility, not entitlement.
- **Righteous Living:** Reverence for covenant produces humility and discipline.

Prayer Points

1. Father, thank You for Your faithfulness amid human weakness.
2. Correct disorder in my life without withdrawing Your presence.
3. Teach me to honor covenant with reverence and restraint.
4. Heal generational wounds without interrupting Your purpose.
5. Align my life with the responsibilities covenant demands.

Meditation / Reflection

Do I interpret God's patience as permission—or as an invitation to alignment?

Words of Wisdom: *Covenant mercy delays judgment for repentance; it does not remove accountability.*

MAY
DELIVERANCE &
IDENTITY

May 1

Theme: Dreams Without Clarity

Anchor Scripture - "Now Joseph had a dream, and he told it to his brothers; and they hated him even more." Genesis 37:5

Devotional Thought

Joseph's story begins not with maturity, authority, or understanding—but with **revelation without clarity**. God showed Joseph his future before Joseph had the wisdom, timing, or restraint to steward it well.

The dream was real. The interpretation was accurate. But Joseph lacked discernment. He spoke what God revealed without understanding **who**, **when**, or **how** it should be shared. Revelation preceded formation.

This introduces an important principle: **God often reveals destiny before He develops capacity**. Dreams announce direction, not readiness. Seeing the future does not mean one is prepared to handle it.

Joseph's mistake was not dreaming—it was assuming revelation equals permission. His brothers' hatred intensified, not because the dream was false, but because wisdom had not yet caught up with insight.

God allowed this gap intentionally. The distance between revelation and fulfillment becomes the training ground for humility, restraint, and character. Dreams initiate calling; process builds credibility.

Clarity does not always accompany calling. Often, clarity is earned through obedience, endurance, and silence.

Key Lessons & Life Applications

- **Teaching:** God reveals purpose before providing full understanding.
- **Reproof:** Sharing revelation prematurely can create unnecessary resistance.
- **Correction:** Wisdom must govern how revelation is handled.
- **Instruction:** Allow time and process to mature insight.
- **Righteous Living:** Humility preserves what pride can endanger.

Prayer Points

1. Father, help me steward revelation with wisdom.
2. Teach me when to speak and when to remain silent.
3. Mature my character to match the future You have shown me.
4. Guard me from pride when You reveal purpose.
5. Prepare me for fulfillment through obedience and restraint.

Meditation / Reflection

Am I seeking clarity before formation—or allowing God to develop me in His time?

Words of Wisdom: *Revelation announces destiny; process prepares the soul.*

May 2

Theme: Betrayal Is Not Disqualification

Anchor Scripture - "Then Midianite traders passed by; so the brothers pulled Joseph up and lifted him out of the pit, and sold him to the Ishmaelites for twenty shekels of silver. And they took Joseph to Egypt." Genesis 37:28

Devotional Thought

Joseph's journey into destiny passed first through betrayal. Those closest to him—his own brothers—became the instruments of his descent. Yet Scripture makes something unmistakably clear: **betrayal did not cancel God's plan.**

Being betrayed does not mean God has rejected you. Often, betrayal is the door God uses to relocate you into purpose you could not reach on your own. Joseph did not choose Egypt, but Egypt was chosen for Joseph.

This moment teaches a hard but necessary truth: **God's agenda is not dependent on human loyalty.** People may violate trust, distort narratives, and act out of envy, but God remains faithful to His word. Betrayal may wound the heart, but it cannot void divine calling.

Joseph's story also guards us from bitterness. Had Joseph allowed betrayal to define him, he would have carried resentment into destiny—and resentment always corrupts authority. God allowed the betrayal, not to break Joseph, but to refine him.

Destiny is not proven by how well you are treated, but by how well you remain aligned when treated unjustly.

Key Lessons & Life Applications

- **Teaching:** God's purpose survives human betrayal.
- **Reproof:** Allowing bitterness to take root can derail destiny.
- **Correction:** God repositions through pain without abandoning purpose.
- **Instruction:** Guard your heart when trust is violated.
- **Righteous Living:** Faithfulness to God must outlast disappointment with people.

Prayer Points

1. Father, heal wounds caused by betrayal.
2. Help me trust Your purpose beyond human actions.
3. Remove bitterness that could corrupt my future.
4. Strengthen my heart to remain aligned with You.
5. Use every painful experience for Your glory.

Meditation / Reflection

Am I allowing betrayal to redefine me—or trusting God to redeem it?

Words of Wisdom: *Betrayal may redirect your path, but it cannot disqualify your destiny.*

May 3

Theme: Integrity in Hidden Places

> **Anchor Scripture** - "The LORD was with Joseph, and he was a successful man; and he was in the house of his master the Egyptian." Genesis 39:2

Devotional Thought

Joseph's public story begins in private places. Before authority, visibility, or influence, Scripture emphasizes one critical truth: **the Lord was with Joseph**. Not because Joseph was promoted—but because Joseph remained faithful where no one was watching.

Integrity is revealed most clearly in hidden places. Joseph had every reason to abandon character—betrayed, displaced, and stripped of status. Yet he chose consistency over resentment. His integrity was not situational; it was rooted in his relationship with God.

Hidden places test motives. There are no crowds to impress, no titles to validate effort, and no recognition to reward discipline. Yet it is in these unseen spaces that God forms leaders capable of carrying authority without corruption.

Joseph's success was not the result of favorable conditions; it was the product of faithful conduct. God trusted Joseph in obscurity before entrusting him with influence.

Integrity does not require visibility to be valuable. Heaven takes careful note of what earth overlooks.

Key Lessons & Life Applications

- **Teaching:** God's presence sustains faithfulness in unseen places.
- **Reproof:** Compromising integrity in private weakens public credibility.
- **Correction:** God tests character before releasing authority.
- **Instruction:** Serve faithfully even when recognition is absent.
- **Righteous Living:** Integrity aligns daily conduct with divine purpose.

Prayer Points

1. Father, help me remain faithful where no one sees.
2. Strengthen my integrity beyond external validation.
3. Guard my heart from resentment in hidden seasons.
4. Teach me to honor You consistently.
5. Prepare me for responsibility through unseen obedience.

Meditation / Reflection

Am I as faithful in hidden places as I am in visible ones?

Words of Wisdom: *Integrity is proven where recognition is absent.*

May 4

Theme: Authority Is Forged Before It Is Seen

Anchor Scripture - "And the LORD was with Joseph and showed him mercy, and He gave him favor in the sight of the keeper of the prison." Genesis 39:21

Devotional Thought

Authority is not conferred at the moment of promotion—it is **forged long before visibility arrives**. Joseph's transition from Potiphar's house to prison may appear like regression, but Scripture reveals continuity: *the LORD was with Joseph.*

Prison did not diminish Joseph's calling; it **deepened his formation**. In confinement, stripped of reputation and reward, Joseph learned governance without position and leadership without title. Authority was being shaped internally while circumstances suggested limitation.

God often uses restricted environments to refine internal authority. When influence is removed, character is tested. Joseph's faithfulness under unjust conditions demonstrated that his leadership was not dependent on comfort, affirmation, or fairness.

Notice the pattern: wherever Joseph went, responsibility followed—not because he pursued it, but because **authority recognizes integrity**. God entrusted Joseph with stewardship in hidden, confined spaces before releasing him into public authority.

What is forged in obscurity can withstand exposure. Authority that is rushed into visibility often collapses under pressure. Authority that is forged patiently endures.

Key Lessons & Life Applications

- **Teaching:** God forges authority through process before promotion.
- **Reproof:** Resisting hidden seasons weakens future leadership.
- **Correction:** God refines authority through restraint and testing.
- **Instruction:** Lead faithfully even without recognition or reward.
- **Righteous Living:** True authority flows from character shaped by God.

Prayer Points

1. Father, form authority in me before You reveal it through me.
2. Help me remain faithful in restrictive seasons.
3. Refine my character where pressure is greatest.
4. Prepare me to lead with humility and integrity.
5. Align my heart with Your timing and purpose.

Meditation / Reflection

Am I allowing God to forge authority in hidden places, or am I rushing visibility?

Words of Wisdom: *Authority revealed too early is fragile; authority forged patiently endures.*

May 5

Theme: Promotion Without Compromise

Anchor Scripture - "How then can I do this great wickedness, and sin against God?" Genesis 39:9

Devotional Thought

Joseph's refusal in Potiphar's house was not simply a moral decision—it was a **qualification test for power**. What stood before him was not just temptation, but the possibility of **unaccountable access**. If Joseph failed here, he would not merely lose credibility; he would be **disqualified** from the future God was preparing him for.

The position Joseph would later occupy in Egypt would place him above systems of accountability. Pharaoh would depend on Joseph to govern the economy, preserve the nation, and manage people's survival. When a leader becomes indispensable, external controls weaken. Only **internal restraint** can prevent exploitation.

This is why the test was private and severe. God was not testing sexuality alone—He was testing whether Joseph could govern himself before governing others. Had Joseph exploited secrecy in Potiphar's house, he would later exploit authority in Pharaoh's court. Power reveals what restraint has—or has not—been formed in secret.

This pattern runs through covenant history. Abraham was tested on releasing what he loved most. Isaac was tested in enduring unjust loss without retaliation. Jacob was tested in identity and restitution before encounter came. Joseph was tested in private access to power. Each test matched the assignment.

Joseph understood something vital: no promotion is worth forfeiting alignment. Advancement that requires compromise is not progress—it is **delay disguised as opportunity**. God does not promote skill alone; He promotes those who have proven they will not misuse power when no one is watching.

Key Lessons & Life Applications

- **Teaching:** God tests covenant carriers at the point of potential power abuse.
- **Reproof:** Compromise in secret disqualifies public authority.
- **Correction:** God forms internal restraint before releasing external power.
- **Instruction:** Govern yourself faithfully before seeking influence over others.
- **Righteous Living:** Integrity is the foundation of sustainable authority.

Prayer Points

1. Father, form restraint in me before You release authority through me.
2. Guard my heart where access and secrecy intersect.
3. Disqualify every desire that could corrupt future responsibility.
4. Align my ambition with Your standards of righteousness.
5. Prepare me to steward power without exploiting people.

Meditation / Reflection

If no one could hold me accountable, would my choices still honor God?

Words of Wisdom: *God does not promote potential—He promotes proven restraint.*

May 6

Theme: God Preserves Many Through One

Anchor Scripture - "But the LORD was with Joseph and showed him mercy, and He gave him favor in the sight of the keeper of the prison." Genesis 39:21

Devotional Thought

God's method of preservation is often **personal before it is corporate**. Long before Joseph stood before Pharaoh, God was shaping one life to become the instrument through which many would be preserved. Preservation did not begin with policy—it began with character.

Joseph's confinement did not pause God's plan; it positioned it. Even in prison, the Lord's presence remained active, opening doors of responsibility and favor. This teaches a vital truth: **God preserves many through one who has learned restraint, faithfulness, and alignment.**

Preservation requires trustworthiness. God does not place the fate of nations in careless hands. Joseph's earlier tests—betrayal, integrity in hidden places, refusal to compromise—were not detours; they were prerequisites. God was ensuring that when Joseph gained access to power, he would use it to preserve life, not exploit it.

This principle reveals the weight of individual obedience. One aligned life can become a refuge for many. Conversely, one compromised leader can endanger multitudes. God's focus on Joseph was never narrow—it was strategic.

God prepares preservers in obscurity so they can serve faithfully in visibility. What Joseph carried was not ambition; it was **assignment**. And assignment always carries others in view.

Key Lessons & Life Applications

- **Teaching:** God uses aligned individuals to preserve many.
- **Reproof:** Personal compromise limits corporate preservation.
- **Correction:** God develops preservers through hidden faithfulness.
- **Instruction:** Remain faithful even when impact is not yet visible.
- **Righteous Living:** Obedience positions one life to bless many.

Prayer Points

1. Father, align my life to serve Your purpose beyond myself.
2. Prepare me to carry responsibility that affects others.
3. Form faithfulness in me during hidden seasons.
4. Guard me from self-centered ambition.
5. Use my obedience to bring preservation to many.

Meditation / Reflection

Am I living with the awareness that my obedience may preserve others?

Words of Wisdom: *God shapes one life carefully because many lives depend on it.*

May 7

Theme: Reconciliation Without Revenge

> **Anchor Scripture** - "And he turned himself away from them and wept. Then he returned to them again, and talked with them. And he took Simeon from them and bound him before their eyes." Genesis 42:24

Devotional Thought

Reconciliation without revenge is one of the highest demonstrations of emotional and spiritual maturity. When Joseph finally stood face-to-face with his brothers, he held absolute power over those who once betrayed him. Yet Scripture reveals restraint, not retaliation.

Joseph felt deeply. He wept privately. He struggled internally. Emotional maturity does not mean absence of feeling—it means **mastery over impulse**. Joseph's response shows that healing is not instant, but it is governed.

Simeon, identified by many scholars as the ring leader in Joseph's earlier betrayal, became the focal point of Joseph's testing. Detaining Simeon was not revenge; it was measured accountability. Joseph was discerning hearts, not settling scores.

At the same time, Joseph's affection for Benjamin exposed another layer of maturity. He was sentimental, protective, and deeply moved—yet he did not allow emotion to override discernment. Favoritism had once fractured the family. Joseph refused to repeat that mistake.

This season mattered. Had Joseph remained with his brothers in immaturity, he would never have been prepared for the weight of global leadership. Separation was not cruelty—it was **preparation**. Growing apart allowed Joseph to be shaped for a level of authority that required emotional regulation, justice without bitterness, and compassion without compromise.

Reconciliation does not demand amnesia. It requires wisdom, timing, and healed authority. Joseph chose restoration over revenge, but he did not bypass process.

Key Lessons & Life Applications

- **Teaching:** True reconciliation requires emotional restraint and wisdom.
- **Reproof:** Power exercised through revenge corrupts leadership.
- **Correction:** Healing does not eliminate discernment or accountability.
- **Instruction:** Separate emotion from decision-making in moments of authority.
- **Righteous Living:** Maturity restores without exploiting power.

Prayer Points

1. Father, mature my emotions so I do not misuse authority.
2. Heal wounds without allowing bitterness to guide decisions.
3. Teach me to reconcile wisely, not impulsively.
4. Help me distinguish justice from revenge.
5. Prepare my heart to lead with restraint and compassion.

Meditation / Reflection

When I have power, do I seek restoration—or vindication?

Words of Wisdom: *Revenge proves power; restraint proves maturity.*

May 8

Theme: A Family Becomes a Nation

Anchor Scripture - "So He said, 'I am God, the God of your father; do not fear to go down to Egypt, for I will make of you a great nation there.'" Genesis 46:3

Devotional Thought

The movement from family to nation is never accidental—it is **intentional and orchestrated by God**. Genesis 46 marks a decisive shift. What began with one man (Abraham), then a household (Isaac and Jacob), now expands into a people with national destiny.

God's words to Jacob are striking: *"I will make of you a great nation there."* Egypt was not merely a place of survival; it was a **womb for nationhood**. God used displacement to multiply identity. What could not grow safely within Canaan would mature in Egypt.

This teaches a vital truth: **nationhood requires structure, scale, and separation**. Families can survive informally; nations cannot. Egypt provided the environment—though imperfect and eventually oppressive—where Israel would grow numerically, culturally, and organizationally.

Joseph's presence ensured protection and provision, but God's purpose extended beyond comfort. The goal was not prosperity alone; it was **peoplehood**. God was transitioning covenant carriers from relational units into a collective identity.

Fear often accompanies transitions of scale. Jacob was leaving familiarity for uncertainty. God reassured him that growth would occur in the unfamiliar. Nationhood often begins in places that do not look like promise.

God does not just preserve families—He **forms nations**.

Key Lessons & Life Applications

- **Teaching:** God intentionally transitions families into nations.
- **Reproof:** Comfort zones can limit growth into collective purpose.
- **Correction:** God uses unfamiliar environments to mature identity.
- **Instruction:** Trust God through transitions of change and scale.
- **Righteous Living:** Faith embraces growth even when it requires relocation.

Prayer Points

1. Father, help me trust You through seasons of transition.
2. Prepare me for growth beyond personal or familial boundaries.
3. Remove fear associated with unfamiliar environments.
4. Align my life with Your purposes for collective impact.
5. Let my obedience contribute to something larger than myself.

Meditation / Reflection

Am I resisting a transition God is using to grow me beyond my current capacity?

Words of Wisdom: *God often grows nations in places that first feel like exile.*

May 9

Theme: Favor Turns Into Affliction

Anchor Scripture - "But the more they afflicted them, the more they multiplied and grew." Exodus 1:12

Devotional Thought

Israel's transition from favor to affliction was not accidental—it was **formational**. They entered Egypt under honor and protection, but growth eventually produced fear. What began as hospitality ended as oppression.

Yet Scripture reveals a paradox: **affliction became the womb of multiplication**. This echoes a timeless truth later captured by the psalmist: *"It is good for me that I have been afflicted, that I may learn Your statutes"* (Psalms 119:71, NKJV). God often births strength, clarity, and identity from the furnace of affliction.

Affliction did not mean covenant failure. It meant **nationhood was being forged**. Comfort would have preserved survival; pressure would produce structure, unity, and dependence on God. Egypt became a furnace where identity hardened and numbers increased.

God allows favor to give way to affliction when comfort would weaken destiny. What feels like loss of privilege may actually be preparation for deliverance. The furnace does not destroy covenant people—it **reveals and refines them**.

Israel multiplied not in ease, but in endurance. Their suffering did not silence them; it strengthened them. God was not absent in affliction—He was **at work within it**.

Key Lessons & Life Applications

- **Teaching:** God uses affliction as a tool of formation.
- **Reproof:** Comfort can hinder growth when identity is still forming.
- **Correction:** Affliction refines purpose rather than negating promise.
- **Instruction:** Trust God's work even when favor shifts to pressure.
- **Righteous Living:** Endurance produces maturity and spiritual strength.

Prayer Points

1. Father, help me discern Your purpose in seasons of affliction.
2. Strengthen me to grow rather than shrink under pressure.
3. Teach me what comfort could not teach me.
4. Refine my character in the furnace of adversity.
5. Prepare me for deliverance through endurance and faith.

Meditation / Reflection

Can I trust that God is forming something in me even when circumstances are difficult?

Words of Wisdom: *God often births destiny from the furnace of affliction.*

May 10

Theme: Growth Without Freedom

Anchor Scripture - "But the children of Israel were fruitful and increased abundantly, multiplied and grew exceedingly mighty; and the land was filled with them." Exodus 1:7

Devotional Thought

Growth does not always mean freedom. Israel multiplied rapidly in Egypt, yet remained bound. Numbers increased, strength expanded, and capacity grew—but liberty did not follow. This reveals a critical distinction: **growth can occur without freedom, but freedom requires formation.**

Egypt allowed Israel to grow numerically while denying them autonomy. Productivity thrived, but purpose was constrained. God permitted this paradox because unchecked freedom without identity would have produced fragmentation. Growth was necessary; freedom would come later.

This season teaches a sobering truth: **capacity can expand while chains remain.** Many grow in skill, influence, and strength while still confined by systems they did not choose. God allows this stage to build endurance, unity, and dependence before deliverance.

Growth without freedom creates pressure. Pressure produces a cry. And the cry invites divine intervention. Until identity matures, freedom can become dangerous. God was not delaying liberation out of neglect—He was preparing a people to sustain it.

Freedom is not granted simply because growth has occurred. It is released when a people are ready to live responsibly beyond constraint.

Key Lessons & Life Applications

- **Teaching:** Growth and freedom are not the same.
- **Reproof:** Expansion without formation can lead to collapse.
- **Correction:** God allows restraint to mature identity.
- **Instruction:** Develop discipline and unity while growth occurs.
- **Righteous Living:** Faith trusts God's timing for freedom.

Prayer Points

1. Father, help me grow responsibly even when freedom is limited.
2. Teach me patience in seasons of restraint.
3. Mature my identity to sustain future liberty.
4. Guard me from frustration that leads to rebellion.
5. Prepare me for freedom through obedience and endurance.

Meditation / Reflection

Am I mistaking growth for freedom—or allowing God to prepare me for both?

Words of Wisdom: *Growth builds capacity; freedom tests maturity.*

May 11

Theme: Identity Lost in Bondage

Anchor Scripture - "So the Egyptians made the children of Israel serve with rigor. And they made their lives bitter with hard bondage…" Exodus 1:13–14

Devotional Thought

Bondage does more than restrict movement—it **reconditions the mind**. Over time, Israel's labor shifted from meaningful contribution to oppressive servitude. What began as growth under constraint became existence defined by survival.

This is the danger of prolonged oppression: **psychological and mental deconditioning**. When pressure is constant, the mind adapts in order to cope. Expectations shrink. Resistance weakens. Captivity becomes normal.

Israel was still multiplying, but their identity was eroding. They were no longer thinking like covenant heirs, but functioning like enslaved laborers. Purpose faded. Memory dulled. Identity narrowed to quotas and survival.

This reveals a sobering truth: **external bondage produces internal captivity when the mind is reshaped by fear and repetition**. When people are trained to expect limitation, they stop imagining freedom—even when it becomes possible.

God allowed this season not to erase Israel, but to expose how deeply bondage had penetrated their thinking. Deliverance would require more than escape; it would require **retraining the mind to remember who they were**. This is why freedom would later be slow, contested, and resisted from within.

Before God could lead Israel out of Egypt, He had to **reintroduce Israel to themselves**—by covenant, by promise, and by identity.

Key Lessons & Life Applications

- **Teaching:** Prolonged bondage reshapes identity through mental conditioning.
- **Reproof:** Normalizing oppression weakens resistance.
- **Correction:** God exposes internal captivity before external deliverance.
- **Instruction:** Guard the mind against narratives that redefine identity.
- **Righteous Living:** Freedom must be sustained by renewed thinking.

Prayer Points

1. Father, break mental patterns formed by prolonged pressure.
2. Restore my identity where fear and survival have reshaped my thinking.
3. Heal psychological wounds created by oppression and limitation.
4. Renew my mind with Your truth and promises.
5. Prepare me for freedom by restoring how I think.

Meditation / Reflection

Have I adapted mentally to pressure in ways that limit how I see myself?

Words of Wisdom: *Bondage is most effective when it trains the mind to accept captivity as normal.*

May 12

Theme: God Hears the Cry of the Oppressed

Anchor Scripture - "And the children of Israel groaned because of the bondage, and they cried out; and their cry came up to God because of the bondage." **Exodus 2:23**

Devotional Thought

Deliverance begins not with escape, but with **awareness**. For years, Israel endured oppression in silence—conditioned to survive rather than resist. But Exodus marks a turning point: *they cried out.*

This cry was not polished prayer. It was raw, unfiltered anguish rising from awareness that bondage was not normal and suffering was not acceptable. The moment Israel cried, something shifted—not in God, but in them. **Silence broke. Normalization ended. Awareness awakened faith.**

Scripture emphasizes that their cry reached God *because of the bondage*. God was not uninformed; He was waiting for alignment. Crying out was the first act of resistance against mental and spiritual captivity.

This teaches a vital truth: **God responds when people recognize their condition and turn toward Him**. Oppression loses power when it is named. Prayer becomes powerful when it is honest.

God hears more than words—He hears posture. The cry signaled readiness for intervention, not merely relief. It marked the transition from endurance to expectation. Before chains can fall, the soul must acknowledge that it was never meant to live bound.

Key Lessons & Life Applications

- **Teaching:** Awareness precedes deliverance.
- **Reproof:** Silence can prolong oppression.
- **Correction:** God responds when bondage is acknowledged before Him.
- **Instruction:** Turn pain into prayer rather than resignation.
- **Righteous Living:** Faith begins when suffering is brought to God.

Prayer Points

1. Father, awaken my awareness where I have normalized bondage.
2. Give me the courage to cry out rather than remain silent.
3. Hear my cry and respond according to Your mercy.
4. Break patterns of endurance that suppress faith.
5. Align my heart with expectation of deliverance.

Meditation / Reflection

Where might silence be delaying the intervention God is ready to bring?

Words of Wisdom: *A cry to God is the first sound of freedom.*

May 13

Theme: Deliverance Begins with Awareness

Anchor Scripture - "So God heard their groaning, and God remembered His covenant with Abraham, with Isaac, and with Jacob." Exodus 2:24

Devotional Thought

Deliverance does not begin with power—it begins with **awareness**. Scripture says God *heard* and God *remembered*. This does not mean God had forgotten; it means **the time for covenant action had arrived**.

God responds when awareness aligns with covenant. Israel's groaning was not new, but their posture had shifted. They were no longer enduring silently—they were acknowledging bondage and calling on God. Awareness activated remembrance.

This teaches a critical truth: **covenant promises remain active, but deliverance requires engagement**. God does not override human awareness; He responds to it. When people recognize that their condition violates covenant intent, divine intervention follows.

Awareness dismantles psychological captivity. It reframes suffering from normalcy to injustice. Once awareness is restored, identity begins to surface, and expectation replaces resignation.

God remembered His covenant—not because Israel deserved rescue, but because covenant was still binding. Deliverance flows from God's faithfulness, not human perfection.

Before Pharaoh was confronted, awareness had to be restored. Before miracles were released, identity had to awaken.

Key Lessons & Life Applications

- **Teaching:** Deliverance begins when awareness aligns with covenant.
- **Reproof:** Ignorance and normalization delay intervention.
- **Correction:** God responds to awakened identity, not silent endurance.
- **Instruction:** Name bondage honestly before God.
- **Righteous Living:** Awareness restores expectation and faith.

Prayer Points

1. Father, awaken awareness where I have adapted to limitation.
2. Restore remembrance of covenant promises over my life.
3. Align my understanding with Your intention for freedom.
4. Break internal resignation that delays deliverance.
5. Let awareness lead me into transformation.

Meditation / Reflection

What conditions in my life have I accepted that God never intended?

Words of Wisdom: *God's power responds when awareness aligns with covenant.*

May 14

Theme: God Reveals Himself to Deliver

Anchor Scripture - "And the LORD said, 'I have surely seen the oppression of My people who are in Egypt, and have heard their cry... for I know their sorrows. So I have come down to deliver them...'" Exodus 3:7–8

(Notice: God speaks of Himself, His awareness, and His action — not yet His servant.)

Devotional Thought

Before God sends a deliverer, He **reveals Himself as Deliverer**. Exodus makes this clear: deliverance does not begin with a human solution; it begins with divine self-disclosure.

God declares three things about Himself:
- I have seen
- I have heard
- I have come down

This revelation corrects a dangerous misconception formed during prolonged bondage — the belief that God is distant, indifferent, or uninvolved. Before chains can break externally, this image of God must be healed internally.

Deliverance requires a people who know **who God is**, not just what they want Him to do. God reveals His compassion, awareness, and intention *before* He reveals His strategy.

This is crucial: **God does not outsource deliverance without first owning it.** He establishes Himself as the source, the authority, and the initiator. Human instruments will come later, but the power and purpose remain divine.

When God reveals Himself rightly, faith becomes possible again. Hope is restored. Expectation rises. Deliverance becomes imaginable.

God does not move until people know *who* is moving on their behalf.

Key Lessons & Life Applications

- **Teaching:** God reveals His nature before releasing deliverance.
- **Reproof:** Misunderstanding God delays trust and faith.
- **Correction:** God restores the knowledge of Himself before breaking chains.
- **Instruction:** Learn who God is, not just what He can do.
- **Righteous Living:** Faith rests in God's character, not circumstances.

Prayer Points

1. Father, reveal Yourself to me beyond my circumstances.
2. Heal distorted images of who You are.
3. Restore my confidence in Your involvement.
4. Help me trust Your character as Deliverer.
5. Prepare my heart to recognize Your hand at work.

Meditation / Reflection

Do I truly know God as Deliverer—or only as distant authority?

Words of Wisdom: *Deliverance begins when God is rightly known.*

May 15

Theme: Authority Confronts Power

> **Anchor Scripture** - "Now Moses and Aaron went in and told Pharaoh, 'Thus says the LORD God of Israel: "Let My people go, that they may hold a feast to Me in the wilderness."'" Exodus 5:1

Devotional Thought

When authority confronts power, the confrontation is never accidental—it is **strategically prepared**. Moses did not appear before Pharaoh as an uninformed outsider. He stood there as a man who had been **raised inside the very system that sought to destroy him**.

God's strategy was deliberate. Moses was born under a death sentence, preserved by divine intervention, and then raised in Pharaoh's household. The same empire that ordered his execution unknowingly financed his education, trained his intellect, and gave him unrestricted access to Egyptian culture, governance, and intelligence.

This reveals a profound truth: **God sometimes prepares deliverers inside the systems they are later sent to confront**. Moses understood Egypt's power structures, language, protocols, and psychology. When authority finally confronted power, it did so with insight, not ignorance.

Moses did not challenge Pharaoh with equal force, but with divine authority. Pharaoh had power—political, military, and economic—but Moses carried legitimacy from a higher throne. Authority does not negotiate identity; it declares jurisdiction. *"Let My people go."*

Deliverance is not merely escape—it is **transfer of ownership and authority**. God did not bypass Egypt's power; He confronted it openly through a man who understood it from the inside.

When authority confronts power, resistance intensifies—but collapse becomes inevitable.

Key Lessons & Life Applications

- **Teaching:** God prepares authority strategically before public confrontation.
- **Reproof:** Power without divine legitimacy is temporary.
- **Correction:** God positions His servants to understand systems before challenging them.
- **Instruction:** Confront oppression from alignment, not impulse.
- **Righteous Living:** Authority exercised under God honors both wisdom and obedience.

Prayer Points

1. Father, help me recognize how You are preparing me strategically.
2. Give me understanding of systems I am called to confront.
3. Align my voice with Your authority, not my emotions.
4. Teach me to move with wisdom, courage, and obedience.
5. Let Your authority prevail over every opposing power.

Meditation / Reflection

Could God be preparing me within environments I will one day be sent to challenge?

Words of Wisdom: *God often trains deliverers inside the systems they are called to confront.*

May 16

Theme: Resistance Does Not Cancel Purpose

Anchor Scripture - "And Pharaoh said, 'Who is the LORD, that I should obey His voice to let Israel go? I do not know the LORD, nor will I let Israel go.'" Exodus 5:2

Devotional Thought

Resistance is not evidence of failure—it is often confirmation that purpose has been properly engaged. Pharaoh's response reveals arrogance, not authority. He rejected God's command because he did not recognize God's jurisdiction.

Yet this resistance did not surprise God, nor did it cancel deliverance. It exposed the nature of power when confronted by authority: **power resists before it collapses**.

This moment also highlights an important contrast in Moses' life. Years earlier, Moses attempted to confront injustice in Egypt **without divine authorization**. He killed an Egyptian in anger and became a fugitive (Exodus 2:11–15). That action, though emotionally justified, lacked mandate—and it failed.

Now the difference is unmistakable. Moses did not return as a self-appointed liberator. He returned as a **sent one**. Authority had replaced impulse. Alignment had replaced ambition. What once produced exile now initiated confrontation.

This teaches a crucial truth: **purpose does not fail because of resistance; it fails when it is pursued without authority**. Resistance refines obedience, clarifies jurisdiction, and exposes whether one is acting in God's timing or their own.

Pharaoh's resistance was not a setback—it was a setup. God was about to demonstrate that no resistance can withstand divine purpose when it is carried by authorized obedience.

Key Lessons & Life Applications

- **Teaching:** Resistance does not negate divine purpose.
- **Reproof:** Acting without authority produces unnecessary loss.
- **Correction:** God trains His servants to wait for alignment before action.
- **Instruction:** Engage resistance with obedience, not reaction.
- **Righteous Living:** Purpose advances through authorized submission to God.

Prayer Points

1. Father, help me discern the difference between impulse and authority.
2. Teach me patience when resistance arises.
3. Align my actions with Your timing and mandate.
4. Strengthen my faith when opposition intensifies.
5. Let Your purpose prevail despite resistance.

Meditation / Reflection

Am I interpreting resistance as failure—or as confirmation that purpose is being engaged?

Words of Wisdom: *Resistance cannot cancel purpose—but action without authority can delay it.*

May 17

Theme: The Cost of Hardened Hearts

Anchor Scripture - "But when Pharaoh saw that there was relief, he hardened his heart and did not heed them, as the LORD had said." Exodus 8:15

Devotional Thought

A hardened heart is not formed in a moment—it is **trained through repeated resistance**. Pharaoh's story reveals a dangerous pattern: relief without repentance leads to resistance without restraint.

Each time pressure eased, Pharaoh hardened his heart again. He acknowledged God's power briefly, but never surrendered to God's authority. This exposes a sobering truth: **temporary relief can deceive people into thinking change is unnecessary**.

Hardening is not merely stubbornness; it is **moral and spiritual calcification**. The heart becomes less responsive, less reflective, and less capable of discernment. Pharaoh was not ignorant—he was resistant. Knowledge without submission only strengthens pride.

This cost was not limited to Pharaoh. Hardened leadership multiplied suffering for others. Entire systems remained trapped because one man refused to yield. Hardened hearts never suffer alone; they **export pain**.

God did not harden Pharaoh arbitrarily. Pharaoh hardened himself repeatedly before God confirmed that posture. Divine judgment often ratifies choices already made.

This passage warns us that resisting God does not neutralize His power—it **intensifies consequence**. Soft hearts repent. Hardened hearts double down.

Key Lessons & Life Applications

- **Teaching:** Hardened hearts develop through repeated resistance.
- **Reproof:** Relief without repentance reinforces pride.
- **Correction:** God confirms choices already embraced.
- **Instruction:** Respond to conviction before resistance becomes habit.
- **Righteous Living:** Humility keeps the heart responsive to God.

Prayer Points

1. Father, keep my heart soft and responsive to You.
2. Expose areas where resistance is hardening my heart.
3. Teach me to repent fully, not temporarily.
4. Guard me from pride disguised as control.
5. Let humility preserve my discernment.

Meditation / Reflection

Have I mistaken relief for repentance in any area of my life?

Words of Wisdom: *A heart that resists truth eventually loses the capacity to hear it.*

May 18

Theme: Life Is in the Blood — Exemption Before Freedom

Anchor Scripture - "Now the blood shall be a sign for you on the houses where you are. And when I see the blood, I will pass over you; and the plague shall not be on you to destroy you…" Exodus 12:13

Devotional Thought

The Passover was not only about deliverance from Egypt—it was about **exemption from judgment**. The blood on the doorposts guaranteed that what came upon Egypt would **not come upon Israel**.

This establishes a timeless covenant principle: **judgment recognizes blood**. Where blood was applied, destruction had no jurisdiction. God did not ask Israel to escape judgment through effort, defense, or negotiation. He provided a means of exemption.

The blood did not remove Israel from Egypt immediately—it protected them *within* Egypt while judgment passed through the land. This teaches a profound truth: **God's people can live in the same environment as judgment and yet be exempt by covenant.**

This moment points forward. Exemption precedes freedom. Protection comes before movement. God secures His people before He relocates them.

The blood was a sign—not for Israel, but for God. *"When I see the blood…"* Judgment does not consult emotions or intentions; it responds to covenant markers.

Passover reveals that redemption is not merely rescue—it is **divine distinction**.

God knows how to separate His people without removing them prematurely.

Key Lessons & Life Applications

- **Teaching:** Blood establishes exemption from judgment.
- **Reproof:** Good intentions cannot replace covenant obedience.
- **Correction:** God protects His people before moving them forward.
- **Instruction:** Trust God's provision for protection in times of judgment.
- **Righteous Living:** Covenant alignment secures divine covering.

Prayer Points

1. Father, thank You for the provision of exemption through covenant.
2. Cover me and my household in seasons of judgment.
3. Teach me to trust Your protection before my circumstances change.
4. Help me walk in obedience that honors covenant.
5. Prepare me for what You are bringing me out of—and into.

Meditation / Reflection

Do I trust God's provision for protection even before I see deliverance?

Words of Wisdom: *Exemption is secured before freedom is experienced.*

May 19

Theme: Obedience Activates Protection

Anchor Scripture - "Then Moses called for all the elders of Israel and said to them, 'Pick out and take lambs for yourselves according to your families, and kill the Passover lamb.'" Exodus 12:21

Devotional Thought

Protection was provided by God—but it was **activated by obedience**. The blood had power, but only when it was applied. God did not force protection upon Israel; He instructed them, and they had to respond.

This reveals a critical covenant principle: **provision does not replace participation**. God supplied the lamb, defined the process, and promised exemption—but each household had to act. Obedience became the bridge between promise and protection.

Israel was not protected because they were special, strong, or sinless. They were protected because they obeyed. Faith was demonstrated not by emotion, but by **alignment with instruction**.

This moment also exposes the danger of partial obedience. Knowing about the blood was not enough. Believing in the blood was not enough. The blood had to be applied exactly as God instructed. Protection responds to obedience, not familiarity.

God's instructions were not burdensome; they were lifesaving. Obedience positioned Israel under divine covering while judgment passed through the land.

In every generation, God's protection remains available—but it is consistently activated through obedient trust.

Key Lessons & Life Applications

- **Teaching:** Obedience activates what God has already provided.
- **Reproof:** Familiarity with truth does not guarantee protection.
- **Correction:** God honors precise obedience, not assumption.
- **Instruction:** Act fully on God's instructions, especially in crisis.
- **Righteous Living:** Faith is demonstrated through obedient action.

Prayer Points

1. Father, help me obey You fully and promptly.
2. Guard me from partial obedience or assumption.
3. Teach me to trust Your instructions even when I do not fully understand.
4. Align my actions with Your covenant provision.
5. Let my obedience position me under Your protection.

Meditation / Reflection

Am I relying on familiarity with God's promises rather than obedience to His instructions?

Words of Wisdom: *Protection responds to obedience, not assumption.*

May 20

Theme: Leaving Egypt Is Not Freedom

Anchor Scripture - "And it came to pass, when Pharaoh had let the people go, that God did not lead them by way of the land of the Philistines... for God said, 'Lest perhaps the people change their minds when they see war, and return to Egypt.'" **Exodus 13:17**

Devotional Thought

Leaving Egypt marked the end of bondage—but it did not complete freedom. God intentionally led Israel away from the shortest route, not because He lacked power, but because **freedom requires readiness, not speed.**

Egypt was behind them, yet Egypt still lived within them. God understood that unprocessed fear could undo deliverance. Had Israel faced war too soon, they would have retreated—not because they were incapable, but because their identity was still forming.

This reveals a vital truth: **physical exit does not equal internal liberation.** God prioritizes transformation over convenience. The wilderness was not punishment; it was protection.

God often delays direct confrontation not to frustrate us, but to mature us. He leads us away from battles we are not yet prepared to fight—not because He doubts His power, but because He honors process.

Freedom is not merely about what you leave; it is about what leaves you. Until fear, dependency, and mental conditioning are addressed, true freedom remains incomplete.

God does not just remove His people from Egypt—He removes Egypt from His people.

Key Lessons & Life Applications

- **Teaching:** Deliverance precedes formation.
- **Reproof:** Speed without readiness can reverse progress.
- **Correction:** God values transformation over shortcuts.
- **Instruction:** Trust God's path even when it seems indirect.
- **Righteous Living:** Freedom matures through obedience and process.

Prayer Points

1. Father, free me from internal bondage even after external change.
2. Teach me patience in seasons of formation.
3. Remove fear that could draw me backward.
4. Help me trust Your process for lasting freedom.
5. Prepare me for battles at the right time.

Meditation / Reflection

What internal patterns might still need healing after external change?

Words of Wisdom: *Freedom is not complete until fear no longer controls direction.*

May 21

Theme: Fear After Deliverance

Anchor Scripture - "And when Pharaoh drew near, the children of Israel lifted their eyes, and behold, the Egyptians **March**ed after them. So they were very afraid, and the children of Israel cried out to the LORD." Exodus 14:10

Devotional Thought

Fear does not disappear simply because deliverance has occurred. Israel had left Egypt, yet when they saw the Egyptians pursuing them, fear resurfaced immediately. This moment exposes a hard truth: **fear often outlives bondage**.

Deliverance changed Israel's location, but it had not yet fully transformed their mindset. The sight of familiar oppressors triggered old survival instincts. What they feared most was not death—it was uncertainty.

Fear after deliverance is common because freedom introduces responsibility. Bondage tells you what to do; freedom demands trust. When pressure returned, Israel defaulted to fear instead of faith.

This teaches us that fear is not always a sign of unbelief—it is often a sign of **unhealed memory**. God did not rebuke Israel for feeling fear; He addressed what fear could do if left unchecked.

God allows moments like this to surface what still needs healing. Fear reveals what deliverance has not yet touched. The Red Sea was not just a geographic obstacle—it was a test of whether Israel would trust God beyond rescue.

Deliverance removes chains. Formation removes fear.

Key Lessons & Life Applications

- **Teaching:** Fear can resurface even after deliverance.
- **Reproof:** Old memories can overpower new realities.
- **Correction:** God exposes fear to heal it, not shame it.
- **Instruction:** Bring fear to God instead of retreating backward.
- **Righteous Living:** Faith grows as fear is confronted honestly.

Prayer Points

1. Father, heal fear that remains after deliverance.
2. Help me trust You when old threats reappear.
3. Remove fear rooted in past trauma.
4. Strengthen my faith beyond my memories.
5. Teach me to move forward even when afraid.

Meditation / Reflection

What fears resurface when I face uncertainty after breakthrough?

Words of Wisdom: *Deliverance removes chains; faith removes fear.*

May 22

Theme: God Makes a Way Through Impossibility

> **Anchor Scripture** - "Then Moses said to the people, 'Do not be afraid. Stand still, and see the salvation of the LORD, which He will accomplish for you today... The LORD will fight for you, and you shall hold your peace.'" Exodus 14:13-14

Devotional Thought

The Red Sea presented Israel with undeniable impossibility. Behind them was Egypt. Before them was the sea. There was no strategy left—only God.

In this moment, Moses' instruction echoes a timeless truth later captured in Scripture: *"Be still, and know that I am God"* (Psalms 46:10, NKJV). Stillness was not inactivity; it was **recognition of divine supremacy.**

God often waits until all human options are exhausted before revealing His way—not to humiliate His people, but to establish clarity. At the Red Sea, movement would have meant panic. Stillness created space for revelation.

Standing still was an act of faith. Silence became alignment. Israel did not part the sea; God did. The command to be still was an invitation to **know God beyond theory—through encounter.**

The sea opened only after fear yielded to trust. What appeared to be an ending became a pathway. God did not remove the obstacle; He transformed it.

This moment teaches us that impossibility is often the stage God uses to reveal who He is. When striving ceases, knowing begins. When control is surrendered, deliverance appears.

Key Lessons & Life Applications

- **Teaching:** God reveals Himself most clearly in impossible moments.
- **Reproof:** Striving can block perception of God's intervention.
- **Correction:** Stillness positions the heart for revelation.
- **Instruction:** Learn when to stop moving and start trusting.
- **Righteous Living:** Faith rests in who God is, not in what we can do.

Prayer Points

1. Father, teach me to be still in moments of fear.
2. Help me recognize Your sovereignty in impossible situations.
3. Quiet my striving so I can see Your salvation.
4. Build my trust beyond logic and strategy.
5. Reveal Yourself to me in new ways.

Meditation / Reflection

Where is God inviting me to be still so I can truly know Him?

Words of Wisdom: *Stillness is often the doorway to revelation.*

May 23

Theme: Praise Before Understanding

Anchor Scripture - "Then Moses and the children of Israel sang this song to the LORD, and spoke, saying: 'I will sing to the LORD, for He has triumphed gloriously!'" Exodus 15:1

Devotional Thought

Israel's first response after crossing the Red Sea was not explanation—it was **praise**. They did not yet understand the wilderness ahead, the tests to come, or the journey required. But they understood one thing: **God had acted**.

Praise preceded clarity. Worship came before comprehension. This reveals a powerful truth: **praise is not the result of understanding—it is the recognition of God's faithfulness**.

In this moment, Israel praised not because everything was resolved, but because God had proven Himself trustworthy. The song of Moses was not a conclusion; it was a declaration of confidence in God's character.

Praise anchored their identity in what God had done, not in what they still feared. It marked the transition from survival to acknowledgment. Even before the path was clear, worship affirmed who God is.

This teaches us that praise stabilizes faith between deliverance and destination. When praise waits for full understanding, fear often fills the gap. But when praise comes first, trust grows.

God does not require complete comprehension to deserve worship. He invites praise as a response to His revealed faithfulness.

Key Lessons & Life Applications

- **Teaching:** Praise flows from recognition of God's faithfulness.
- **Reproof:** Waiting for full understanding can delay worship.
- **Correction:** God deserves praise even when the journey is unclear.
- **Instruction:** Respond to deliverance with gratitude and worship.
- **Righteous Living:** Worship anchors the heart in trust.

Prayer Points

1. Father, teach me to praise You before everything makes sense.
2. Help me worship You for what You have already done.
3. Guard my heart from fear during seasons of transition.
4. Let praise strengthen my faith for what lies ahead.
5. Make worship my first response, not my last resort.

Meditation / Reflection

Do I wait to understand before I praise—or do I praise because God has proven faithful?

Words of Wisdom: *Praise declares trust before understanding arrives.*

May 24

Theme: God always completes what He begins.

Anchor Scripture - "Thus the LORD saved Israel that day out of the hand of the Egyptians, and Israel saw the Egyptians dead on the seashore." Exodus 14:30

Devotional Thought

Deliverance is not complete until **pursuit is terminated**. Israel crossed the Red Sea, but Egypt pursued them into the same waters. What Israel feared followed them—yet it could not survive where God made a way.

This moment reveals a powerful truth: **what God delivers you from cannot follow you into your future**. The same waters that became a pathway for Israel became a grave for Egypt. God did not merely create distance between Israel and bondage—He ended its ability to pursue.

Fear often convinces us that what once dominated us will always have access. But Exodus declares otherwise. God knows how to shut doors permanently. When He delivers, He does so decisively.

Israel did not fight Egypt. They did not negotiate closure. God handled pursuit completely. This teaches us that **closure is a divine work, not a human struggle**.

What once had authority over you may attempt one final chase—but it cannot survive the boundary God establishes. Deliverance reaches its fullness when fear is replaced by finality.

God does not only rescue—He **concludes**.

Key Lessons & Life Applications

- **Teaching:** God ends pursuit when deliverance is complete.
- **Reproof:** Fear exaggerates the power of former bondage.
- **Correction:** God handles closure that humans cannot achieve.
- **Instruction:** Trust God to finish what He began.
- **Righteous Living:** Freedom includes final separation from the past.

Prayer Points

1. Father, thank You for completing my deliverance fully.
2. Remove fear of what once pursued me.
3. Establish permanent boundaries between me and bondage.
4. Help me trust You for closure, not self-defense.
5. Let my future be free from the shadows of my past.

Meditation / Reflection

Am I still fearing what God has already defeated?

Words of Wisdom: *What God delivers you from cannot follow you into freedom.*

May 25

Theme: Freedom Restores Awareness of Identity

Anchor Scripture - "So the LORD saved Israel that day out of the hand of the Egyptians… Thus Israel saw the great work which the LORD had done in Egypt; so the people feared the LORD, and believed the LORD and His servant Moses." **Exodus 14:30–31**

Devotional Thought

Identity is not created at rescue—it is **remembered**. Israel's identity did not change when they crossed the Red Sea; what changed was their **awareness** of who they were.

Bondage had deconditioned them. Years of oppression reshaped how they saw themselves, not who they truly were. Slavery trained their minds to think like captives, even though they were covenant people. Deliverance broke external chains, but restoration required **renewal of awareness**.

After the Red Sea, Israel encountered God not just as Deliverer, but as **Owner, Protector, and Covenant Keeper**. Fear shifted—from fear of Egypt to reverence for God. Belief resurfaced, but identity still needed to be consciously reclaimed.

This teaches us a critical truth: **freedom restores awareness; formation restores confidence**. God rescues quickly to secure life, then patiently reconditions the mind to sustain freedom.

Identity after rescue is not about becoming someone new—it is about remembering who you were before life trained you otherwise.

God does not redefine His people after deliverance. He **reintroduces them to themselves**.

Key Lessons & Life Applications

- **Teaching:** Identity exists before deliverance; awareness follows rescue.
- **Reproof:** Life experiences can distort self-perception without changing identity.
- **Correction:** God restores awareness before He entrusts responsibility.
- **Instruction:** Allow God to recondition how you see yourself.
- **Righteous Living:** Freedom is sustained by renewed awareness of identity.

Prayer Points

1. Father, restore my awareness of who You say I am.
2. Heal distortions formed by hardship and survival.
3. Recondition my thinking with covenant truth.
4. Help me live from identity, not experience.
5. Anchor my freedom in truth, not memory.

Meditation / Reflection

In what ways has life conditioned me to forget who I truly am in God?

Words of Wisdom: *Deliverance removes chains; restored awareness revives identity.*

May 26

Theme: Provision in Transition

Anchor Scripture - "Then the LORD said to Moses, 'Behold, I will rain bread from heaven for you. And the people shall go out and gather a certain quota every day...'" Exodus 16:4

Devotional Thought

Transition exposes a new kind of vulnerability. Israel was no longer enslaved, but they were not yet settled. Freedom introduced uncertainty, and uncertainty demanded trust. In this in-between space, God revealed Himself not only as Deliverer, but as **Sustainer**.

Manna was not merely food—it was **training**. God provided daily to teach Israel dependence without regression. They could not store it, hoard it, or control it. Provision came consistently, but only for the day.

This reveals a critical truth: **God often provides differently in transition than in bondage or settlement**. In Egypt, provision came through labor. In the wilderness, provision came through trust. God was reconditioning their expectations—shifting them from self-reliance under oppression to daily dependence under covenant.

Provision in transition is intentionally measured. God gives enough to sustain faith, not enough to eliminate it. This daily rhythm retrained Israel to look upward rather than backward.

Transition is uncomfortable because it strips away familiar systems. But it is also sacred—because it is where God teaches His people how to live free without becoming fearful. God does not abandon His people in transition. He **feeds them while He forms them**.

Key Lessons & Life Applications

- **Teaching:** God provides consistently during seasons of transition.
- **Reproof:** Anxiety often emerges when old systems no longer apply.
- **Correction:** God retrains dependence through daily provision.
- **Instruction:** Trust God for today's needs without hoarding tomorrow.
- **Righteous Living:** Daily dependence strengthens covenant relationship.

Prayer Points

1. Father, help me trust You in seasons of transition.
2. Teach me daily dependence without fear.
3. Remove anxiety rooted in uncertainty.
4. Recondition my expectations around provision.
5. Feed me as You form me.

Meditation / Reflection

How do I respond when God provides daily instead of all at once?

Words of Wisdom: *Transition teaches trust through daily provision.*

May 27

Theme: Dependence vs. Complaining

Anchor Scripture - "And the whole congregation of the children of Israel complained against Moses and Aaron in the wilderness." Exodus 16:2

Devotional Thought

Complaining did not begin in the wilderness—it was **learned in slavery**. In Egypt, complaining was how pain was expressed, how frustration was released, and how survival emotions were managed. It was a conditioned response formed under oppression.

The tragedy is that Israel **carried the same strategy into a totally different experience**. They were no longer enslaved. They were no longer working for provision. Manna came freely—yet the language of bondage remained.

This reveals a sobering truth: **people often bring old coping mechanisms into new freedoms**. Complaining became reflexive, not reflective. It was no longer a cry for help; it was resistance to trust.

God was not angered by hunger. He was provoked by posture. Complaining questioned God's intent, not His ability. It suggested that freedom was less trustworthy than bondage, and that daily dependence was inferior to forced predictability.

Some people, no matter how much they are blessed, will still complain—because the issue is not provision, but conditioning. Complaining becomes dangerous when it replaces gratitude and undermines trust.

In Scripture, complaining repeatedly triggers divine displeasure because it **reverses the work of deliverance internally**. It keeps the heart anchored in slavery while the body is free.

God's goal was not to silence Israel, but to **retrain their language from complaint to dependence**.

Key Lessons & Life Applications

- **Teaching:** Complaining is often a learned behavior from past oppression.
- **Reproof:** Old survival strategies can sabotage new freedoms.
- **Correction:** God retrains expression from complaint to trust.
- **Instruction:** Replace conditioned complaining with conscious dependence.
- **Righteous Living:** Gratitude reflects freedom of the heart.

Prayer Points

1. Father, break patterns of complaining learned through hardship.
2. Retrain my responses in seasons of provision.
3. Help me recognize when old habits no longer serve new realities.
4. Replace complaint with gratitude and trust.
5. Align my language with freedom, not fear.

Meditation / Reflection

Am I using coping strategies from past bondage in a season of freedom?

Words of Wisdom: *Complaining is often the language of slavery spoken in freedom.*

May 28

Theme: God Tests the Redeemed

Anchor Scripture - "Then the LORD said to Moses, 'Behold, I will rain bread from heaven for you. And the people shall go out and gather a certain quota every day, **that I may test them, whether they will walk in My law or not.**'" Exodus 16:4

Devotional Thought

Redemption removes bondage, but **testing reveals readiness**. God did not test Israel to expose weakness; He tested them to **train obedience**. The wilderness became a classroom where daily choices mattered more than dramatic miracles.

The test was simple: gather daily, trust God, do not hoard, and rest when instructed. There was no threat, no enemy, no emergency—only obedience. This reveals a profound truth: **God often tests the redeemed through ordinary faithfulness, not extraordinary crises.**

Testing exposed whether Israel would live by trust or control. Hoarding revealed fear. Disobedience revealed lingering bondage. Rest tested whether they believed provision would continue.

God tests not to disqualify, but to form. Passing the test required alignment, not perfection. The goal was to establish a rhythm of trust that could sustain freedom long-term.

Testing after redemption is a mercy. It prevents future collapse by addressing hidden fractures early. God cares enough to examine obedience before entrusting greater responsibility.

Key Lessons & Life Applications

- **Teaching:** God tests obedience after redemption.
- **Reproof:** Control and fear undermine trust.
- **Correction:** God retrains daily dependence through simple instructions.
- **Instruction:** Obey consistently, not selectively.
- **Righteous Living:** Faithfulness in small things sustains freedom.

Prayer Points

1. Father, help me pass the tests that follow deliverance.
2. Expose fear that leads me to control outcomes.
3. Teach me obedience in daily routines.
4. Align my heart with Your instructions.
5. Form my character through faithful obedience.

Meditation / Reflection

How do I respond to God's instructions when there is no immediate pressure?

Words of Wisdom: *Redemption removes chains; testing builds trust.*

May 29

Theme: Trust Is Learned Daily

Anchor Scripture - "And Moses said, 'Let no one leave any of it till morning.' Notwithstanding they did not heed Moses…" Exodus 16:19–20

Devotional Thought

The wilderness was designed as a **curriculum for refinement**, not a permanent residence. God intended to retrain Israel's trust through daily dependence. What should have been a short, intensive formation season became prolonged because the lesson was resisted.

Manna was God's training tool. Each day invited Israel to practice trust, obedience, and restraint. The instruction was simple, but the implications were deep: *trust Me today, and I will be faithful tomorrow.*

Yet fear overrode faith. Many chose hoarding over obedience. What they stored spoiled, revealing that **trust cannot be stockpiled**. God was not testing survival skills; He was refining identity and posture.

This moment reveals a sobering truth: **opportunities for refinement, when resisted, become seasons of delay**. What could have been a brief transition extended into decades—not because God failed, but because the lesson was never fully learned.

The wilderness was meant to form a people ready for promise. Instead, resistance to daily trust turned formation into frustration. A curriculum designed for forty days expanded into forty years—and still, many never entered.

God's intention was refinement, not punishment. Delay was not the goal; readiness was. But trust must be learned—or time stretches.

Key Lessons & Life Applications

- **Teaching:** God designs seasons of refinement with clear intent.
- **Reproof:** Resistance to trust prolongs transition.
- **Correction:** God extends time when lessons remain unlearned.
- **Instruction:** Embrace refinement before delay sets in.
- **Righteous Living:** Daily obedience shortens unnecessary seasons.

Prayer Points

1. Father, help me recognize seasons of refinement.
2. Give me grace to learn quickly what You are teaching.
3. Remove fear that resists daily trust.
4. Prevent unnecessary delay in my journey.
5. Refine my heart for readiness, not resistance.

Meditation / Reflection

What lesson might God be teaching me that I am resisting—and prolonging?

Words of Wisdom: *Unlearned lessons extend seasons meant to be brief.*

May 30

Theme: Deliverance Is the Beginning

Anchor Scripture - "So the LORD saved Israel that day out of the hand of the Egyptians..." Exodus 14:30

Devotional Thought

Deliverance marks a decisive moment—but it is never the destination. Exodus 14 records Israel's rescue, yet the chapters that follow reveal a sobering truth: **coming out is easier than going in.**

God delivered Israel powerfully, but deliverance only created opportunity. What followed required formation, obedience, trust, and endurance. Freedom removed chains, but it exposed responsibility. Without internal transformation, external rescue could still end in loss.

The wilderness made this clear. A people who experienced miracles struggled to steward freedom. Complaining, fear, resistance to instruction, and refusal to trust prolonged what was meant to be brief. Deliverance opened the door; formation determined whether they would walk through it fully.

God's intention was never just escape from Egypt—it was entry into promise. Yet many settled into survival instead of growth. The tragedy was not lack of power or provision, but **failure to mature**.

Deliverance is God's initiative. Completion requires human response. Rescue gives a beginning; obedience determines the outcome.

God saves decisively—but He forms patiently. The question after deliverance is not *"What did God do?"* but *"What will I do with what He has done?"*

Key Lessons & Life Applications

- **Teaching:** Deliverance initiates a journey of formation.
- **Reproof:** Freedom without growth leads to stagnation.
- **Correction:** God expects transformation after rescue.
- **Instruction:** Steward deliverance with obedience and humility.
- **Righteous Living:** Freedom matures through responsibility.

Prayer Points

1. Father, help me see deliverance as a beginning, not an end.
2. Give me grace to grow beyond rescue into maturity.
3. Guard me from complacency after breakthrough.
4. Teach me to steward freedom wisely.
5. Complete the work You began in my life.

Meditation / Reflection

How am I responding to the freedom God has already given me?

Words of Wisdom: *Deliverance opens the door; formation determines the future.*

May 31

Theme: A Free People Must Be Formed

Anchor Scripture - "And said, 'If you diligently heed the voice of the LORD your God and do what is right in His sight, give ear to His commandments and keep all His statutes, I will put none of the diseases on you which I have brought on the Egyptians. For I am the LORD who heals you.'" Exodus 15:26

Devotional Thought

Freedom without formation is fragile. After the Red Sea, Israel was free—but not yet formed. God immediately began the work of shaping a people who could sustain liberty without collapsing into rebellion, fear, or disorder.

This verse reveals God's intent clearly: deliverance was complete, but **formation had just begun**. God introduced structure, instruction, and expectation. Freedom did not eliminate responsibility; it increased it.

God was not trying to control Israel—He was teaching them how to live healthy, ordered lives outside oppression. Formation was necessary to prevent Egypt from re-emerging internally. A free people without discipline will recreate bondage in new forms.

This moment marks a shift: God moved from dramatic acts of power to consistent instruction. Miracles secured freedom; obedience would preserve it. Healing here was not merely physical—it was **systemic restoration** of how a people lived, thought, and related to God.

The wilderness was not a mistake. It was a **training ground**. God knew that freedom must be protected by formation, or it would be squandered.

Deliverance rescues individuals. Formation builds a people.

Key Lessons & Life Applications

- **Teaching:** Freedom must be sustained through formation.
- **Reproof:** Liberty without structure leads to instability.
- **Correction:** God introduces instruction to preserve freedom.
- **Instruction:** Learn to live free through obedience and discipline.
- **Righteous Living:** Formation safeguards long-term wholeness.

Prayer Points

1. Father, form me to steward the freedom You have given.
2. Teach me obedience that preserves liberty.
3. Heal patterns formed under bondage.
4. Establish discipline that honors covenant freedom.
5. Shape me into someone who can carry responsibility well.

Meditation / Reflection

In what ways is God forming me so my freedom will last?

Words of Wisdom: *Freedom survives only where formation is embraced.*

JUNE
LAW, ORDER & FORMATION

June 1

Theme: Freedom Requires Structure

> **Anchor Scripture -** "And the whole congregation of the children of Israel complained against Moses and Aaron in the wilderness." Exodus 16:2

Devotional Thought

Freedom exposes what structure once concealed. Israel had been delivered from Egypt, yet quickly became unsettled. Without imposed schedules, quotas, and commands, uncertainty surfaced—and with it, confusion and complaint.

This moment reveals a foundational truth: **freedom without structure breeds anxiety**. Bondage may be oppressive, but it is predictable. Freedom demands internal order where external control once existed.

God allowed this tension to surface intentionally. Complaining revealed not hunger alone, but the absence of structure. Israel had not yet learned how to govern themselves under freedom. Their longing for Egypt was not love for slavery, but familiarity with order—even if unjust.

God's goal was not to return them to bondage, but to **replace forced order with chosen discipline**. Formation begins when freedom is paired with structure.

Freedom is sustained not by escape, but by alignment.

Key Lessons & Life Applications

- **Teaching:** Freedom requires intentional structure.
- **Reproof:** Absence of order invites confusion and fear.
- **Correction:** God exposes disorder to introduce formation.
- **Instruction:** Learn to govern yourself under freedom.
- **Righteous Living:** Discipline preserves liberty.

Prayer Points

1. Father, help me embrace structure as a gift, not a restriction.
2. Reveal areas where freedom has produced disorder.
3. Teach me self-governance under Your authority.
4. Replace confusion with godly discipline.
5. Form habits that sustain freedom.

Meditation / Reflection

How do I respond when freedom removes familiar structure?

Words of Wisdom: *Freedom flourishes only where discipline is learned.*

June 2

Theme: God Feeds Before He Governs

Anchor Scripture - "Then the LORD spoke to Moses, saying, 'I have heard the complaints of the children of Israel… You shall eat meat in the evening, and you shall be filled with bread in the morning.'"Exodus 16:11–12

Devotional Thought

Before God introduced law, He introduced provision. He fed Israel **before** He governed them. This reveals the heart of God's leadership: **care precedes command**. God did not respond to complaints with rebuke first, but with sustenance. He addressed their need so their hearts could receive instruction. Formation cannot begin where trust has not been established.

This teaches us that God is not eager to control, but to **stabilize**. Hunger clouds judgment. Fear distorts perception. God met physical need to prepare Israel for spiritual responsibility.

Provision was not endorsement of complaining—it was preparation for instruction. God feeds first so obedience is not driven by desperation, but by trust. True governance flows from relationship, not coercion.

Key Lessons & Life Applications

- **Teaching:** God establishes trust before issuing commands.
- **Reproof:** Complaining reveals unmet trust, not just unmet need.
- **Correction:** God stabilizes before He disciplines.
- **Instruction:** Receive God's care as preparation for obedience.
- **Righteous Living:** Gratitude opens the heart to instruction.

Prayer Points

1. Father, thank You for meeting my needs before correcting me.
2. Help me recognize Your care even when I am unsettled.
3. Remove fear that blocks obedience.
4. Teach me to trust Your heart as You guide my life.
5. Prepare me for responsibility through gratitude.

Meditation / Reflection

Do I recognize God's provision as preparation for instruction?

Words of Wisdom: *God feeds hearts before He forms habits.*

June 3

Theme: Daily Obedience Builds Discipline

Anchor Scripture - "Then they gathered it every morning, every man according to his need. And when the sun became hot, it melted." Exodus 16:21

Devotional Thought

Formation rarely comes through dramatic moments—it comes through **daily obedience**. Manna required Israel to gather every morning, consistently and humbly. There were no shortcuts, no stockpiles, no exceptions.

This rhythm trained discipline. Each day reinforced trust. Each morning demanded obedience. God was building capacity through repetition.

Discipline is formed when obedience becomes habitual, not heroic. God was not just feeding Israel—He was teaching them how to live responsibly under freedom.

The melting manna reinforced urgency. Delay led to loss. Obedience had a window. Discipline respects timing.

Daily obedience builds internal order. It replaces chaos with rhythm and fear with trust.

Key Lessons & Life Applications

- **Teaching:** Discipline is formed through daily obedience.
- **Reproof:** Irregular obedience weakens formation.
- **Correction:** God trains responsibility through repetition.
- **Instruction:** Obey consistently, even in small things.
- **Righteous Living:** Faithfulness is proven daily.

Prayer Points

1. Father, help me obey You consistently.
2. Build discipline through daily faithfulness.
3. Remove the desire for shortcuts.
4. Teach me to honor timing and rhythm.
5. Establish habits that reflect trust.

Meditation / Reflection

Am I practicing obedience daily—or only when it feels urgent?

Words of Wisdom: *Discipline is obedience practiced repeatedly.*

June 4

Theme: Rest Is Part of God's Order

Anchor Scripture - "Six days you shall gather it, but on the seventh day, the Sabbath, there will be none." Exodus 16:26

Devotional Thought

Rest was not introduced as a reward—it was introduced as **order**. God built rest into the rhythm of freedom to retrain a people who had only known relentless labor.

In Egypt, rest was forbidden. Productivity defined worth. In freedom, God redefined value: obedience mattered more than output. The Sabbath tested whether Israel trusted God enough to stop striving.

Some disobeyed. They went out to gather on the seventh day and found nothing. This reveals a sobering truth: **restlessness often masks distrust**. The inability to rest signals fear of lack.

God was not limiting Israel; He was liberating them from compulsive survival. Rest became a declaration: *God is my source, not my effort.*

True freedom includes the discipline to stop.

Key Lessons & Life Applications

- **Teaching:** Rest is a divine command, not a suggestion.
- **Reproof:** Inability to rest often reveals fear.
- **Correction:** God restores trust through ordered rhythms.
- **Instruction:** Learn to stop when God says stop.
- **Righteous Living:** Rest honors God as Provider.

Prayer Points

1. Father, teach me to rest without fear.
2. Break striving learned through past pressure.
3. Help me trust You enough to stop.
4. Establish healthy rhythms in my life.
5. Let rest renew my trust in You.

Meditation / Reflection

What fears surface when I am told to rest?

Words of Wisdom: *Rest is faith expressed through restraint.*

June 5

Theme: Obedience Reveals Readiness

Anchor Scripture - "But some of them left part of it until morning, and it bred worms and stank." Exodus 16:20

Devotional Thought

God's instructions around manna were simple, but they revealed deep truths about readiness. Obedience was not complex—yet disobedience persisted.

The spoiled manna exposed a lack of trust. Hoarding was fear disguised as wisdom. God allowed consequences to teach that **disobedience always corrodes what God provides**. Readiness is not measured by intention, but by response. Israel's inability to obey simple instructions signaled they were not yet ready for greater responsibility.

God does not entrust much to those who resist small obedience. Formation requires alignment in the ordinary before authority is granted in the extraordinary.

Obedience reveals capacity.

Key Lessons & Life Applications

- **Teaching:** Obedience reveals readiness for responsibility.
- **Reproof:** Fear often drives disobedience.
- **Correction:** God allows consequences to teach trust.
- **Instruction:** Honor God's instructions precisely.
- **Righteous Living:** Faithfulness prepares the heart for increase.

Prayer Points

1. Father, expose fear that undermines obedience.
2. Teach me to trust You in small instructions.
3. Help me obey without reservation.
4. Prepare me for greater responsibility.
5. Align my heart with Your commands.

Meditation / Reflection

What small instructions might God be using to assess my readiness?

Words of Wisdom: *Capacity is revealed by obedience in small things.*

June 6

Theme: God Trains Trust Under Pressure

> **Anchor Scripture** - "Therefore the people quarreled with Moses and said, 'Give us water, that we may drink.'" Exodus 17:2

Devotional Thought

Pressure reveals what training has not yet completed. When Israel faced thirst, old patterns resurfaced. Complaining returned. Accusation replaced trust.

God allowed pressure to test whether formation was taking root. Provision in the past did not guarantee trust in the present. Trust must be exercised repeatedly under new stress.

This moment teaches us that **pressure does not create fear—it exposes it**. God was not absent; He was observing posture.

God still provided water, but the lesson was clear: formation is incomplete until trust replaces reaction. Pressure is not punishment—it is assessment.

God trains His people to trust Him not only when provision flows, but when it is temporarily unseen.

Key Lessons & Life Applications

- **Teaching:** Pressure tests formation.
- **Reproof:** Old reactions resurface under stress.
- **Correction:** God exposes trust gaps through difficulty.
- **Instruction:** Respond to pressure with prayer, not accusation.
- **Righteous Living:** Trust matures through repeated testing.

Prayer Points

1. Father, help me respond rightly under pressure.
2. Heal reactions rooted in fear.
3. Teach me to trust You when provision is delayed.
4. Replace accusation with prayer.
5. Complete the work of formation in me.

Meditation / Reflection

How do I usually respond when pressure interrupts provision?

Words of Wisdom: *Pressure reveals what training has not yet finished.*

June 7

Theme: Battles Reveal Dependence

Anchor Scripture - "So it was, when Moses held up his hand, that Israel prevailed; and when he let down his hand, Amalek prevailed." Exodus 17:11

Devotional Thought

Israel's first battle after deliverance revealed something crucial: **victory depends on posture, not strength alone**. Joshua fought in the valley, but the outcome was decided on the hill. When Moses' hands were raised, Israel prevailed; when they dropped, the enemy gained ground.

This battle teaches that freedom does not eliminate conflict—it **redefines how conflict is won**. God trained Israel to see that success flows from dependence on Him, not merely from effort or numbers.

Dependence requires partnership. Moses needed support to keep his hands raised. God was forming a people who understood intercession, cooperation, and sustained trust. Victory was collective, not individual.

Battles expose whether a people rely on God consistently or only initially. Dependence must be maintained, not assumed.

God was teaching Israel that **how you fight matters as much as what you fight**.

Key Lessons & Life Applications

- **Teaching:** Victory flows from dependence on God.
- **Reproof:** Self-reliance weakens spiritual authority.
- **Correction:** God trains people to maintain posture under pressure.
- **Instruction:** Support one another in spiritual responsibility.
- **Righteous Living:** Sustained dependence preserves victory.

Prayer Points

1. Father, teach me to depend on You in every battle.
2. Help me maintain spiritual posture consistently.
3. Surround me with godly support.
4. Guard me from self-reliance.
5. Let victory flow from alignment with You.

Meditation / Reflection

What posture do I maintain when the battle is prolonged?

Words of Wisdom: *Victory is sustained by dependence, not momentum.*

June 8

Theme: Leadership Needs Support Systems

Anchor Scripture - "When Moses' father-in-law saw all that he did for the people, he said, 'What is this thing that you are doing for the people?'" Exodus 18:14

Devotional Thought

Calling does not eliminate limitation. Moses was faithful, anointed, and obedient—yet overwhelmed. Leadership without support becomes unsustainable, no matter how sincere the intention.

Jethro's observation was not criticism; it was wisdom. God often uses outside perspective to reveal blind spots leaders cannot see from within responsibility. Moses' problem was not devotion—it was **isolation**.

This moment reveals a key formation truth: **God does not design leadership to be carried alone.** Burnout is not a badge of faithfulness; it is often a sign of missing structure.

God values longevity over heroics. Support systems are not signs of weakness—they are expressions of wisdom. Leadership that refuses help eventually collapses under its own weight.

Formation includes learning how to receive counsel.

Key Lessons & Life Applications

- **Teaching:** God values sustainable leadership.
- **Reproof:** Isolation weakens effectiveness.
- **Correction:** Wise counsel preserves strength.
- **Instruction:** Invite trusted voices into leadership decisions.
- **Righteous Living:** Humility protects long-term impact.

Prayer Points

1. Father, help me receive wisdom without defensiveness.
2. Show me where support is needed.
3. Remove pride that resists counsel.
4. Strengthen my leadership through structure.
5. Preserve my effectiveness over time.

Meditation / Reflection

Where might God be offering help that I have resisted?

Words of Wisdom: *Calling flourishes where support is welcomed.*

June 9

Theme: Delegation Is God's Design

Anchor Scripture - "Moreover you shall select from all the people able men... and place such over them to be rulers of thousands, hundreds, fifties, and tens." **Exodus 18:21**

Devotional Thought

Delegation was not Moses' idea—it was **God's design** revealed through counsel. God never intended one man to carry the weight of a nation. Authority was meant to be shared, not hoarded.

Delegation does not diminish leadership; it multiplies it. By distributing responsibility, Moses preserved both his strength and the people's access to justice. Order replaced exhaustion.

This passage teaches that **structure is spiritual**. Delegation reflects trust, develops others, and protects leaders from collapse. Refusing to delegate often masks fear—fear of loss of control, relevance, or trust.

God forms nations by training leaders to empower others. True leadership builds capacity beyond itself.

Formation matures when responsibility is shared wisely.

Key Lessons & Life Applications

- **Teaching:** Delegation reflects God's design for leadership.
- **Reproof:** Control undermines growth.
- **Correction:** God values order over overload.
- **Instruction:** Share responsibility intentionally.
- **Righteous Living:** Empowerment strengthens community.

Prayer Points

1. Father, teach me to delegate with wisdom.
2. Help me trust others with responsibility.
3. Remove fear that resists shared leadership.
4. Develop capacity in those around me.
5. Establish order that honors You.

Meditation / Reflection

What responsibility might God be asking me to release to others?

Words of Wisdom: *Delegation is leadership expressed through trust.*

June 10

Theme: Order Preserves Leadership Longevity

Anchor Scripture - "So Moses heeded the voice of his father-in-law and did all that he had said." Exodus 18:24

Devotional Thought

Longevity in leadership is preserved by **order**, not passion alone. Moses' willingness to implement structure protected both him and the people. What zeal could not sustain, order secured.

God's work was never threatened by delegation; it was strengthened by it. Moses did not lose authority—he gained capacity. Order ensured continuity, clarity, and sustainability.

This moment teaches a vital truth: **disorder exhausts even the most anointed leaders.** Without structure, vision collapses under its own weight. God honors obedience that embraces wisdom, even when it requires change.

Leadership that endures is leadership that adapts.

Key Lessons & Life Applications

- **Teaching:** God values leadership sustainability.
- **Reproof:** Passion without order leads to burnout.
- **Correction:** Wise structure protects vision.
- **Instruction:** Implement systems that support longevity.
- **Righteous Living:** Obedience includes adapting when God provides wisdom.

Prayer Points

1. Father, help me embrace order that preserves longevity.
2. Remove resistance to wise change.
3. Teach me to steward leadership responsibly.
4. Protect me from burnout through structure.
5. Align my leadership with Your design.

Meditation / Reflection

What structure might God be asking me to implement for longevity?

Words of Wisdom: *Order is the guardian of longevity.*

June 11

Theme: God Calls a People Into Covenant Order

Anchor Scripture - "Now therefore, if you will indeed obey My voice and keep My covenant, then you shall be a special treasure to Me above all people… a kingdom of priests and a holy nation." Exodus 19:5–6

Devotional Thought

God did not deliver Israel merely to free them—He delivered them to **form them into a nation**. Exodus 19 marks a pivotal transition: from rescued people to covenant community.

Covenant order established identity before law. God named who they were *before* instructing how they should live. Obedience was not about earning favor; it was about aligning with identity.

This teaches us that **law flows from relationship, not restriction**. God's commands were meant to preserve a people who carried His presence.

Freedom without covenant order dissolves into chaos. Covenant order anchors identity, purpose, and responsibility.

God forms nations by shaping identity first.

Key Lessons & Life Applications

- **Teaching:** Covenant identity precedes instruction.
- **Reproof:** Freedom without identity lacks direction.
- **Correction:** God establishes order to protect relationship.
- **Instruction:** Live in alignment with covenant identity.
- **Righteous Living:** Obedience reflects belonging, not fear.

Prayer Points

1. Father, anchor my identity in covenant truth.
2. Help me live from who You say I am.
3. Align my obedience with relationship, not obligation.
4. Shape me as part of Your holy people.
5. Preserve my identity through covenant order.

Meditation / Reflection

Do I see obedience as alignment with identity or as restriction?

Words of Wisdom: *Identity anchors obedience.*

June 12

Theme: God Establishes Boundaries for Encounter

> **Anchor Scripture** - "You shall set bounds for the people all around, saying, 'Take heed to yourselves that you do not go up to the mountain or touch its base.'" **Exodus 19:12**

Devotional Thought

Encounter without boundaries is dangerous. As God prepared to reveal Himself, He established limits—not to exclude the people, but to protect them.

This moment teaches a profound truth: **access to God requires order**. God is near, but He is also holy. Boundaries preserve life and reverence.

God was training Israel to understand that intimacy without respect leads to irreverence. Boundaries do not signal distance; they define safe proximity.

Formation includes learning how to approach God rightly. Without boundaries, encounter becomes reckless. With boundaries, encounter becomes transformative.

God does not lower His holiness to accommodate disorder—He raises His people to meet Him safely.

Key Lessons & Life Applications

- **Teaching:** Boundaries preserve sacred encounter.
- **Reproof:** Familiarity can breed irreverence.
- **Correction:** God sets limits to protect relationship.
- **Instruction:** Approach God with reverence and obedience.
- **Righteous Living:** Healthy boundaries honor God's holiness.

Prayer Points

1. Father, teach me reverence in Your presence.
2. Help me honor boundaries You establish.
3. Guard me from casual familiarity with holy things.
4. Shape my approach to You with humility.
5. Preserve my life through obedience.

Meditation / Reflection

How do I approach God—with reverence or familiarity?

Words of Wisdom: *Boundaries make encounter safe.*

June 13

Theme: God Reveals Himself in Holiness

Anchor Scripture - "Then it came to pass on the third day, in the morning, that there were thunderings and lightnings… and Mount Sinai was completely in smoke, because the LORD descended upon it in fire." Exodus 19:16–18

Devotional Thought

God's holiness was not hidden—it was revealed. At Sinai, God did not soften His presence to accommodate fear; He revealed Himself fully to **recalibrate reverence**.

Holiness is not distance—it is distinction. God's manifestation taught Israel that encounter with Him requires awe, not casual familiarity. The trembling mountain was not intimidation; it was instruction.

This moment corrected a dangerous misconception: freedom does not mean informality with God. Deliverance invites relationship, but holiness defines how that relationship is approached.

God revealed His holiness before giving the law to establish a foundation: **obedience flows from reverence**. Without awe, instruction becomes negotiable. With awe, obedience becomes worship.

Formation deepens when God is seen rightly.

Key Lessons & Life Applications

- **Teaching:** God reveals Himself as holy to shape reverence.
- **Reproof:** Casual familiarity weakens obedience.
- **Correction:** Awe restores proper posture before God.
- **Instruction:** Approach God with humility and honor.
- **Righteous Living:** Reverence fuels faithful obedience.

Prayer Points

1. Father, restore awe in my approach to You.
2. Remove casual attitudes toward holy things.
3. Teach me to honor Your presence rightly.
4. Deepen my reverence without fear.
5. Let holiness shape my obedience.

Meditation / Reflection

How do I respond when God reveals His holiness?

Words of Wisdom: *Holiness recalibrates reverence.*

June 14

Theme: Law as Protection, Not Punishment

> **Anchor Scripture** - "And God spoke all these words, saying: 'I am the LORD your God, who brought you out of the land of Egypt, out of the house of bondage.'" **Exodus 20:1–2**

Devotional Thought

The law did not begin with commands—it began with **identity and deliverance**. Before God told Israel what to do, He reminded them who He was and what He had already done.

This framing matters. The law was not given to control freed slaves, but to **protect a redeemed people**. It established boundaries to preserve freedom, not restrict it.

God introduced law as a safeguard against chaos, exploitation, and regression into bondage. Law was not punishment—it was protection.

Obedience was never meant to earn deliverance; it was meant to **preserve it**. When law is separated from relationship, it becomes legalism. When rooted in covenant, it becomes life-giving order.

Formation requires guardrails.

Key Lessons & Life Applications

- **Teaching:** God's law flows from relationship.
- **Reproof:** Viewing law as punishment distorts God's heart.
- **Correction:** Law protects freedom and order.
- **Instruction:** Obey God as a response to deliverance.
- **Righteous Living:** Boundaries preserve liberty.

Prayer Points

1. Father, help me see Your instructions as protection.
2. Remove fear-based views of obedience.
3. Anchor my obedience in gratitude.
4. Teach me to honor Your boundaries.
5. Preserve my freedom through discipline.

Meditation / Reflection

Do I see God's instructions as restriction—or as protection?

Words of Wisdom: *Law protects what love delivers.*

June 15

Theme: The Ten Commandments: Order for Freedom

Anchor Scripture - "You shall have no other gods before Me." Exodus 20:3

Devotional Thought

The Ten Commandments were not designed to constrain life—they were given to **order freedom**. They defined how a redeemed people could live without self-destruction.

The first commandment sets the tone: freedom collapses when allegiance is divided. God knew that misplaced devotion would eventually reintroduce bondage in new forms.

Each commandment protects relationship—with God and with others. They establish a moral framework where freedom can flourish without chaos.

God was not imposing control; He was **preserving alignment**. Order is not the enemy of freedom—disorder is.

True freedom thrives within boundaries that honor God and protect people.

Key Lessons & Life Applications

- **Teaching:** God's commands preserve freedom.
- **Reproof:** Divided allegiance undermines liberty.
- **Correction:** Order prevents spiritual regression.
- **Instruction:** Live free within God's design.
- **Righteous Living:** Obedience safeguards relationships.

Prayer Points

1. Father, align my heart with You alone.
2. Protect me from divided devotion.
3. Help me honor boundaries that sustain freedom.
4. Teach me to live responsibly under liberty.
5. Let obedience preserve my relationships.

Meditation / Reflection

Where might divided allegiance be threatening my freedom?

Words of Wisdom: *Freedom survives where allegiance is undivided.*

June 16

Theme: Fear vs Reverence

Anchor Scripture - "So the people stood afar off, but Moses drew near the thick darkness where God was." **Exodus 20:21**

Devotional Thought

The giving of the law exposed a divide—not in God's intention, but in human response. While God invited Israel into reverent alignment, fear drove them backward. They stood afar off, not because God rejected them, but because **fear distorted perception**.

Fear and reverence are not the same. Fear pushes God away; reverence draws near. Reverence acknowledges holiness while trusting God's goodness. Fear sees danger where God intends transformation.

God's law was meant to become a way of life, not a source of terror. But when fear dominates, obedience feels forced instead of natural. Israel's retreat revealed immaturity, not divine distance.

Moses' approach modeled God's desire: **closeness governed by reverence, not avoidance driven by fear**. The law was never meant to intimidate; it was meant to instruct a people still learning how to stand in God's presence.

Key Lessons & Life Applications

- **Teaching:** Reverence draws near; fear retreats.
- **Reproof:** Fear distorts God's intent.
- **Correction:** God invites approach, not avoidance.
- **Instruction:** Learn to stand before God with reverence.
- **Righteous Living:** Obedience flows from trust, not terror.

Prayer Points

1. Father, replace fear with reverence in my heart.
2. Heal distorted views of Your holiness.
3. Teach me to draw near without fear.
4. Help me trust Your intentions.
5. Align my obedience with love and awe.

Meditation / Reflection

Do I respond to God's holiness with fear—or with reverent trust?

Words of Wisdom: *Fear retreats; reverence remains.*

June 17

Theme: God Invites Mediated Access

Anchor Scripture - "Speak with us, and we will hear; but let not God speak with us, lest we die." Exodus 20:19

Devotional Thought

Israel's request for mediation revealed both wisdom and limitation. Recognizing their fear, they asked Moses to stand between them and God. This was not rebellion—it was an admission of unreadiness.

God accommodated their request, not because mediation was His original desire, but because **mercy meets people where maturity has not yet arrived**. God adjusted access without abandoning relationship.

This moment teaches that mediation is often a concession, not an ideal. God desired direct relationship, but the people lacked the internal readiness to sustain it. Mediation preserved connection while formation continued.

God's agenda did not change—only the method. He remained committed to forming a people capable of alignment. Until then, mediated access became a bridge, not a barrier.

Key Lessons & Life Applications

- **Teaching:** God accommodates immaturity without abandoning purpose.
- **Reproof:** Fear limits access to God's presence.
- **Correction:** Mediation preserves relationship during formation.
- **Instruction:** Grow toward direct alignment with God.
- **Righteous Living:** Maturity expands access.

Prayer Points

1. Father, mature my heart for deeper access.
2. Heal fear that limits intimacy with You.
3. Thank You for meeting me where I am.
4. Lead me toward greater alignment.
5. Prepare me for direct relationship with You.

Meditation / Reflection

Where might fear be limiting my access to God?

Words of Wisdom: *Mediation is mercy for the maturing.*

June 18

Theme: Justice Reflects God's Character

Anchor Scripture - "If you buy a Hebrew servant, he shall serve six years; and in the seventh he shall go out free and pay nothing." Exodus 21:2

Devotional Thought

God's laws immediately turned toward justice—not ritual. This reveals a critical truth: **God's character governs His legal system.** Justice was not abstract; it was practical, humane, and protective.

God regulated power so it would not become abuse. He established accountability so freedom would not degenerate into exploitation. Justice ensured dignity, restraint, and restoration.

These laws demonstrate that covenant order extends into daily life. God's concern was not merely worship, but **how people treated one another.** True righteousness is lived socially, not just spiritually.

Justice was a reflection of who God is. Law expressed His heart for fairness, mercy, and responsibility. Formation was now moving from reverence to relationships.

Key Lessons & Life Applications

- **Teaching:** God's justice reflects His character.
- **Reproof:** Power without restraint leads to injustice.
- **Correction:** Law protects dignity and equity.
- **Instruction:** Live justly in everyday relationships.
- **Righteous Living:** Faith expresses itself through fairness.

Prayer Points

1. Father, align my actions with Your justice.
2. Guard me from abusing authority or advantage.
3. Teach me to reflect Your character in relationships.
4. Form my heart for fairness and mercy.
5. Let my life express covenant righteousness.

Meditation / Reflection

Do my daily interactions reflect God's justice and character?

Words of Wisdom: *Justice is holiness expressed in human relationships.*

June 19

Theme: Responsibility in Community Living

Anchor Scripture - "If men contend with each other, and one strikes the other... he shall surely pay for the loss of his time, and shall provide for him to be thoroughly healed." Exodus 21:18–19

Devotional Thought

Freedom does not remove responsibility—it **relocates it into community**. God's laws addressed real-life conflicts to teach Israel how to live together without reproducing oppression.

This instruction reveals that accountability is relational. Actions have consequences because people matter. God regulated conflict to prevent cycles of retaliation and escalation. Justice was not about punishment alone; it was about **restoration and responsibility**.

Community living requires maturity—the willingness to own outcomes and repair harm. God was forming a people who understood that freedom thrives where responsibility is embraced.

Formation is proven in how we treat one another when tensions arise.

Key Lessons & Life Applications

- **Teaching:** Community requires shared responsibility.
- **Reproof:** Irresponsible actions damage freedom.
- **Correction:** God requires restoration where harm occurs.
- **Instruction:** Take responsibility for the impact of your actions.
- **Righteous Living:** Accountability preserves community health.

Prayer Points

1. Father, teach me responsibility in my relationships.
2. Help me repair harm where I have caused it.
3. Guard me from careless actions.
4. Form my heart for restoration, not retaliation.
5. Make me a responsible member of my community.

Meditation / Reflection

How do I respond when my actions affect others?

Words of Wisdom: *Freedom survives where responsibility is practiced.*

June 20

Theme: Ownership Comes With Consequences

Anchor Scripture - "But if the ox tended to thrust with its horn in times past... and it kills a man or a woman, the ox shall be stoned and its owner also shall be put to death." Exodus 21:29

Devotional Thought

Ownership in God's kingdom is never neutral. Authority, possession, and influence carry moral weight. God held owners accountable not only for actions, but for **neglect and foreknowledge.**

This law reveals a sobering principle: what you oversee, you are responsible for. Ignorance is not always innocence when warning signs are present. God expected vigilance, stewardship, and preventive care.

Freedom expands responsibility. Authority demands foresight. God was training Israel to think beyond personal rights toward communal safety.

Formation matures when ownership is stewarded, not ignored.

Key Lessons & Life Applications

- **Teaching:** Ownership carries moral responsibility.
- **Reproof:** Neglect can be as harmful as action.
- **Correction:** God calls owners to accountability.
- **Instruction:** Steward what you control with diligence.
- **Righteous Living:** Responsibility protects life and order.

Prayer Points

1. Father, teach me to steward what You've entrusted to me.
2. Expose areas of neglect.
3. Give me foresight and wisdom.
4. Help me guard others through responsibility.
5. Align my authority with Your justice.

Meditation / Reflection

What am I responsible for that I may be neglecting?

Words of Wisdom: *Authority without responsibility becomes danger.*

June 21

Theme: Compassion Regulates Power

Anchor Scripture - "If you ever take your neighbor's garment as a pledge, you shall return it to him before the sun goes down." Exodus 22:26

Devotional Thought

Power unchecked becomes cruelty. God built compassion into His laws to prevent justice from becoming oppression. Even when debt was owed, dignity was protected.

This instruction reveals God's heart: **justice must be tempered with mercy**. The law acknowledged vulnerability and insisted that power not strip others of basic humanity.

Compassion was not optional—it was required. God regulated power so that freedom would not devolve into dominance. Formation required learning restraint, empathy, and care.

True strength is revealed in how power is exercised—not in how much is held.

Key Lessons & Life Applications

- **Teaching:** God requires compassion in the use of power.
- **Reproof:** Power without mercy becomes oppressive.
- **Correction:** Law restrains dominance to preserve dignity.
- **Instruction:** Exercise authority with empathy.
- **Righteous Living:** Mercy reflects God's character.

Prayer Points

1. Father, temper my strength with compassion.
2. Guard me from abusing power or advantage.
3. Teach me empathy in decision-making.
4. Help me protect the dignity of others.
5. Let my authority reflect Your mercy.

Meditation / Reflection

How do I use power when I have the advantage?

Words of Wisdom: *Power is proven by restraint.*

June 22

Theme: God Protects the Vulnerable

Anchor Scripture - "You shall neither mistreat a stranger nor oppress him, for you were strangers in the land of Egypt." Exodus 22:21

Devotional Thought

God's laws consistently tilt toward protecting the vulnerable. He reminded Israel of their own history so compassion would become a way of life, not a legal obligation.

This instruction reveals that memory is a moral safeguard. Forgetting where you came from hardens the heart; remembering keeps power in check. God did not want Israel to reproduce Egypt's cruelty under a new name.

Justice in God's kingdom includes empathy. Power must be exercised with awareness of human fragility. Formation requires learning to govern strength with compassion.

God protects the vulnerable not because they are weak, but because **power must answer to righteousness**.

Key Lessons & Life Applications

- **Teaching:** God values the protection of the vulnerable.
- **Reproof:** Forgetting past bondage breeds oppression.
- **Correction:** Compassion restrains misuse of power.
- **Instruction:** Govern authority with empathy and memory.
- **Righteous Living:** Justice honors dignity.

Prayer Points

1. Father, keep my heart sensitive to the vulnerable.
2. Guard me from reproducing past oppression.
3. Teach me to wield strength with compassion.
4. Help me remember where You brought me from.
5. Align my actions with Your justice.

Meditation / Reflection

How does remembering my past shape how I treat others?

Words of Wisdom: *Memory is the guardian of mercy.*

June 23

Theme: Angelic Guidance on the Journey

Anchor Scripture - "Behold, I send an Angel before you to keep you in the way and to bring you into the place which I have prepared." Exodus 23:20

Devotional Thought

God did not leave Israel to navigate promise alone. He assigned guidance, protection, and direction through divine agency. This reveals a profound truth: **God provides oversight where maturity is still forming**.

The angel's role was not to replace obedience, but to support alignment. Guidance did not cancel responsibility; it required attentiveness and submission.

God knows that transitions are dangerous seasons. Protection is increased when capacity is still developing. Divine guidance ensures that promise is reached without unnecessary loss.

Formation includes learning to follow guidance—not just power.

Key Lessons & Life Applications

- **Teaching:** God provides guidance during formation.
- **Reproof:** Independence can derail destiny.
- **Correction:** Submission keeps alignment intact.
- **Instruction:** Pay attention to God's direction.
- **Righteous Living:** Guidance preserves promise.

Prayer Points

1. Father, help me discern Your guidance clearly.
2. Teach me submission during transition.
3. Protect me from premature independence.
4. Keep me aligned with Your direction.
5. Lead me safely into what You have prepared.

Meditation / Reflection

How attentive am I to God's guidance during transition?

Words of Wisdom: *Guidance preserves what power initiates.*

June 24

Theme: Gradual Possession Requires Maturity

Anchor Scripture - "Little by little I will drive them out from before you, until you have increased, and you inherit the land." Exodus 23:30

Devotional Thought

God's pace is intentional. He did not promise instant possession because capacity had not yet caught up with promise. Expansion without maturity leads to collapse.

This verse reveals a vital kingdom principle: **God grows territory at the speed of stewardship**. Increase must match readiness. Rapid expansion without formation exposes weakness.

God protects His people from success they cannot sustain. Delay is not denial—it is preparation. Maturity determines timing.

Formation ensures that what is gained can be governed.

Key Lessons & Life Applications

- **Teaching:** God expands territory gradually.
- **Reproof:** Impatience threatens sustainability.
- **Correction:** Growth must align with capacity.
- **Instruction:** Embrace God's timing for expansion.
- **Righteous Living:** Maturity safeguards increase.

Prayer Points

1. Father, grow my capacity before increasing my territory.
2. Remove impatience that resists Your timing.
3. Prepare me for what You have promised.
4. Teach me to value formation over speed.
5. Align my growth with Your wisdom.

Meditation / Reflection

Am I prepared to govern what I am asking God to give me?

Words of Wisdom: *God grows territory at the pace of maturity.*

June 25

Theme: Covenant Confirmed by Blood

Anchor Scripture - "And Moses took the blood, sprinkled it on the people, and said, 'This is the blood of the covenant which the LORD has made with you according to all these words.'" Exodus 24:8

Devotional Thought

Covenant is never casual. It is sealed with seriousness—and in Scripture, that seriousness is marked by blood. This moment established Israel not merely as a governed people, but as a **covenanted nation**.

Blood signified life, accountability, and permanence. God was binding Himself to Israel, and Israel to God. Covenant was no longer theoretical; it carried consequence.

This teaches us that covenant always involves responsibility. Privilege and obligation walk together. God's commitment invites human faithfulness—not perfection, but alignment.

Formation reaches a new depth when relationship is sealed by covenant. What God establishes by blood, He intends to sustain by faithfulness.

Key Lessons & Life Applications

- **Teaching:** Covenant establishes binding relationship.
- **Reproof:** Covenant should never be treated lightly.
- **Correction:** God anchors commitment through sacrifice.
- **Instruction:** Live with awareness of covenant responsibility.
- **Righteous Living:** Faithfulness honors covenant.

Prayer Points

1. Father, help me honor covenant responsibility.
2. Teach me the weight of sacred commitment.
3. Align my life with Your covenant expectations.
4. Guard me from casual obedience.
5. Establish faithfulness in my walk with You.

Meditation / Reflection

Do I live with awareness of the covenant I am part of?

Words of Wisdom: *Covenant carries weight, not convenience.*

June 26

Theme: Glory Requires Separation

Anchor Scripture - "So Moses went into the midst of the cloud and went up into the mountain. And Moses was on the mountain forty days and forty nights." **Exodus 24:18**

Devotional Thought

Before instruction descended, separation occurred. Moses ascended alone into the cloud, demonstrating a vital principle: **glory requires withdrawal before impartation.**

God separated Moses not to elevate him above others, but to prepare him to serve them rightly. Intimacy preceded instruction. Isolation preceded revelation.

This reveals that formation includes seasons of separation—times when distractions are removed so clarity can emerge. Not everyone ascends at the same time or in the same way.

Separation is not rejection; it is preparation. God withdraws leaders to deposit what will later benefit the community.

Key Lessons & Life Applications

- **Teaching:** God prepares leaders through separation.
- **Reproof:** Avoiding solitude can limit growth.
- **Correction:** God withdraws to impart clarity.
- **Instruction:** Embrace seasons of focused intimacy with God.
- **Righteous Living:** Preparation precedes influence.

Prayer Points

1. Father, help me embrace seasons of separation.
2. Remove distractions that block clarity.
3. Prepare me for deeper responsibility.
4. Teach me to value intimacy over visibility.
5. Deposit what is needed for service.

Meditation / Reflection

What might God be preparing me for through separation?

Words of Wisdom: *Separation precedes revelation.*

June 27

Theme: God Dwells Among His People

Anchor Scripture - "And let them make Me a sanctuary, that I may dwell among them." Exodus 25:8

Devotional Thought

God's ultimate goal was never distance—it was **dwelling**. After deliverance, formation, law, and covenant, God revealed His heart: to live among His people.

The sanctuary was not about confinement, but proximity. God desired nearness within order. His presence required preparation, structure, and alignment.

This teaches that God's dwelling follows formation. Presence rests where order exists. God does not merely visit—He abides where He is honored. Formation culminates in habitation.

Key Lessons & Life Applications

- **Teaching:** God desires to dwell with His people.
- **Reproof:** Disorder disrupts sustained presence.
- **Correction:** God establishes structure for habitation.
- **Instruction:** Prepare space for God's presence.
- **Righteous Living:** God dwells where He is honored.

Prayer Points

1. Father, prepare me as a dwelling place.
2. Align my life with Your presence.
3. Remove disorder that hinders intimacy.
4. Teach me to host Your presence daily.
5. Let my life become a sanctuary.

Meditation / Reflection

Is my life structured to host God's presence?

Words of Wisdom: *God dwells where order honors His presence.*

June 28

Theme: God Designs Order Before Power

Anchor Scripture - "According to all that I show you, that is, the pattern of the tabernacle and the pattern of all its furnishings, just so you shall make it." **Exodus 25:9**

Devotional Thought

Before God released visible power, He revealed **design**. Before manifestation came measurements, patterns, and instructions. This sequence matters.

God does not empower disorder. He establishes structure so power does not destroy what it is meant to advance. The tabernacle was designed in detail because God's presence requires preparation.

This teaches a foundational principle of formation: **power without order leads to chaos**. God was training Israel to understand that spiritual authority rests on alignment, not enthusiasm.

Many desire power, but resist process. Yet God's power flows safely only through systems He designs. Order is not delay—it is protection.

Formation matures when design is honored before desire.

Key Lessons & Life Applications

- **Teaching:** God releases power through divine design.
- **Reproof:** Impatience ignores preparation.
- **Correction:** Order precedes manifestation.
- **Instruction:** Follow God's pattern carefully.
- **Righteous Living:** Alignment protects influence.

Prayer Points

1. Father, align me with Your design before release.
2. Remove impatience that rushes process.
3. Teach me to value preparation.
4. Guard me from premature empowerment.
5. Establish order that can sustain Your presence.

Meditation / Reflection

Am I honoring God's design—or rushing toward power?

Words of Wisdom: *Power is safest where order is established.*

June 29

Theme: Impatience Produces Idolatry

Anchor Scripture - "Now when the people saw that Moses delayed coming down from the mountain, the people gathered together to Aaron…" Exodus 32:1

Devotional Thought

Delay tested loyalty. When Moses did not return as expected, impatience filled the gap that trust should have occupied. The people did not abandon worship—they **redirected it**.

Idolatry was not born from atheism, but from **impatience with God's timing**. They wanted something tangible, immediate, and controllable.

This reveals a dangerous truth: when formation is incomplete, waiting becomes intolerable. Impatience seeks substitutes. The golden calf was not rebellion against God's existence—it was an attempt to manage uncertainty.

God's delay was intentional; the people's response was revealing. Formation had not yet matured trust.

Impatience turns guidance into substitutes.

Key Lessons & Life Applications

- **Teaching:** Delay tests trust.
- **Reproof:** Impatience seeks substitutes.
- **Correction:** Waiting is part of formation.
- **Instruction:** Resist shortcuts during silence.
- **Righteous Living:** Trust honors God's timing.

Prayer Points

1. Father, strengthen my patience in waiting seasons.
2. Guard me from substitutes born of impatience.
3. Teach me to trust Your timing.
4. Help me remain loyal in silence.
5. Complete the work of formation in me.

Meditation / Reflection

How do I respond when God's timing feels delayed?

Words of Wisdom: *Impatience builds idols where trust should stand.*

June 30

Theme: Intercession Restores What Failure Breaks

Anchor Scripture - "So the LORD relented from the harm which He said He would do to His people." Exodus 32:14

Devotional Thought

Failure did not end the covenant—**intercession preserved it**. When Israel broke alignment, Moses stood in the gap. God responded not by abandoning His people, but by engaging mercy through intercession.

This reveals the power of relationship within covenant governance. Judgment was deserved, yet mercy was activated because someone understood God's heart and stood for the people.

Intercession did not erase consequences, but it prevented destruction. God preserved the relationship while continuing formation.

This moment teaches that failure is not final where repentance and intercession exist. God remains committed to His agenda even when human response falters.

Formation includes learning how restoration happens.

Key Lessons & Life Applications

- **Teaching:** Intercession activates mercy.
- **Reproof:** Failure requires accountability.
- **Correction:** God restores through advocacy.
- **Instruction:** Stand in the gap for others.
- **Righteous Living:** Mercy preserves covenant purpose.

Prayer Points

1. Father, thank You for mercy that restores.
2. Teach me to intercede with understanding.
3. Help me respond rightly after failure.
4. Preserve alignment through repentance.
5. Complete formation in me with grace.

Meditation / Reflection

Who has God called me to stand in the gap for?

Words of Wisdom: *Mercy restores what judgment could end.*

JULY
PROVERBS

July 1

Theme: Wisdom Begins with Reverence

Anchor Scripture "The fear of the LORD is the beginning of knowledge, but fools despise wisdom and instruction." Proverbs 1:7

Devotional Thought

Wisdom does not begin with intelligence, experience, or age—it begins with reverence. Proverbs opens by establishing posture before practice. *The fear of the LORD* is not terror; it is recognition. It is the settled awareness that God is God—and we are not. Without this posture, knowledge becomes pride, skill becomes manipulation, and insight turns self-serving.

This truth is reinforced across the wisdom writings. **After exploring life, success, labor, and meaning from every angle, Solomon concludes his lifelong pursuit with this clarity:** *"Fear God and keep His commandments, for this is the whole duty of man"* (Ecclesiastes 12:13). Reverence anchors wisdom with moral weight and spiritual direction. Without it, knowledge may inform, but it will not transform.

James later echoes this distinction by contrasting wisdom that is earthly, self-seeking, and unstable with wisdom from above that is pure, peaceable, and submissive to God (James 3:13–17). Reverence positions the heart to receive instruction rather than resist it.

A redeemed life is not governed by cleverness, but by reverence. When God is rightly positioned, wisdom follows naturally.

Key Lessons & Life Applications

- **Teaching:** Wisdom begins with reverence for God.
- **Reproof:** Knowledge without reverence leads to pride.
- **Correction:** Restore God to His rightful position as the source of understanding.
- **Instruction:** Receive instruction with humility.
- **Righteous Living:** Reverence anchors wise living.

Prayer Points

1. Father, establish reverence in my heart.
2. Guard me from pride disguised as knowledge.
3. Teach me to honor You in all my decisions.
4. Help me welcome instruction.
5. Align my understanding with Your authority.

Meditation / Reflection

Do I approach God—and His instruction—with reverence or familiarity?

Words of Wisdom: *Reverence is the doorway to wisdom.*

July 2

Theme: Wisdom Must Be Sought, Not Assumed

Anchor Scripture "If you seek her as silver, and search for her as for hidden treasures…" Proverbs 2:4

Devotional Thought

Wisdom is not automatic—it is intentional. Proverbs 2 makes it clear that wisdom responds to pursuit. It must be sought, searched for, and valued. God offers wisdom generously, but He does not dispense it casually. Wisdom reveals itself to those who recognize its worth.

Scripture affirms this posture of pursuit. James writes, *"If any of you lacks wisdom, let him ask of God… but let him ask in faith"* (James 1:5–6). Asking requires humility; seeking requires diligence. Together, they form a posture that invites divine insight. Wisdom is rarely received by accident—it is discovered through desire and discipline.

Jesus reinforces this principle when He says, *"Ask, and it will be given to you; seek, and you will find"* (Matthew 7:7). What we pursue intentionally shapes us profoundly. Wisdom pursued becomes wisdom practiced.

A redeemed life understands that spiritual growth does not happen passively. Those who pursue wisdom are preserved not only from error, but from paths that quietly lead away from life.

Key Lessons & Life Applications

- **Teaching:** Wisdom responds to intentional pursuit.
- **Reproof:** Spiritual passivity hinders growth.
- **Correction:** Replace assumption with diligent seeking.
- **Instruction:** Ask, seek, and search consistently.
- **Righteous Living:** Diligence preserves direction.

Prayer Points

1. Father, increase my hunger for wisdom.
2. Teach me to pursue understanding intentionally.
3. Remove complacency from my spiritual life.
4. Sharpen my discernment through diligence.
5. Lead me in paths of wisdom and protection.

Meditation / Reflection

How intentionally am I pursuing wisdom in this season?

Words of Wisdom: *Wisdom reveals itself to those who pursue it.*

July 3

Theme: Trusting God with the Whole Path

Anchor Scripture "Trust in the LORD with all your heart, and lean not on your own understanding." Proverbs 3:5

Devotional Thought

Wisdom is not merely about knowing what to do—it is about trusting who leads. Proverbs 3 shifts the focus from information to dependence. Trusting God with *all* the heart requires releasing partial reliance on self-understanding. Leaning on God means allowing His wisdom to outweigh our own reasoning.

Scripture consistently warns against self-trust disconnected from God. *"There is a way that seems right to a man, but its end is the way of death"* (Proverbs 14:12). Human understanding, though useful, is limited by perspective. Wisdom acknowledges those limits and submits direction to God.

God Himself declares, *"My thoughts are not your thoughts, nor are your ways My ways"* (Isaiah 55:8–9). Trusting God is not the abandonment of thought, but the surrender of authority. When acknowledgment becomes habitual, direction becomes clearer.

A redeemed life does not reject understanding—it submits it. When trust replaces self-reliance, God faithfully directs the path.

Key Lessons & Life Applications

- **Teaching:** Trust invites divine direction.
- **Reproof:** Self-reliance limits clarity.
- **Correction:** Submit understanding to God's authority.
- **Instruction:** Acknowledge God in every decision.
- **Righteous Living:** Dependence sustains alignment.

Prayer Points

1. Father, teach me to trust You fully.
2. Help me release reliance on my own understanding.
3. Direct my decisions with Your wisdom.
4. Align my heart with Your guidance.
5. Establish my path in truth.

Meditation / Reflection

Where might I be leaning on my own understanding instead of trusting God?

Words of Wisdom: *Trust realigns the path wisdom reveals.*

July 4

Theme: Guarding the Heart Protects the Life

Anchor Scripture: "Keep your heart with all diligence, for out of it spring the issues of life." Proverbs 4:23

Devotional Thought

The heart is the command center of life. Proverbs does not instruct us to guard circumstances first, but the inner source from which thoughts, choices, and directions flow. What is allowed to settle in the heart eventually governs behavior and outcomes.

Jesus affirmed this principle when He said, *"Out of the abundance of the heart the mouth speaks"* (Matthew 12:34). The heart silently shapes words, reactions, and decisions long before they are expressed outwardly. This is why Scripture calls for diligence—because influence is constant and subtle.

Jeremiah reminds us that the heart is impressionable and easily shaped (Jeremiah 17:9). Guarding the heart, therefore, is not isolation but discernment. It is choosing carefully what is allowed to form inner posture. Wisdom recognizes that life outcomes are cultivated internally before they are seen externally.

A redeemed life understands that vigilance is not restriction—it is preservation. What governs the heart ultimately governs the life.

Key Lessons & Life Applications

- **Teaching:** The heart determines life's direction.
- **Reproof:** Neglecting the heart leads to drift.
- **Correction:** Practice intentional vigilance over inner life.
- **Instruction:** Filter influences carefully.
- **Righteous Living:** Inner discipline preserves alignment.

Prayer Points

1. Father, help me guard my heart diligently.
2. Reveal influences that weaken my focus.
3. Strengthen my discernment.
4. Align my inner life with Your truth.
5. Preserve my direction through wisdom.

Meditation / Reflection

What influences am I allowing to shape my heart?

Words of Wisdom: *What you protect within determines what you produce without.*

July 5

Theme: Wisdom Establishes Boundaries for Desire

Anchor Scripture: "For the ways of man are before the eyes of the LORD, and He ponders all his paths." Proverbs 5:21

Devotional Thought

Proverbs 5 confronts desire directly—not to shame it, but to govern it. Desire is powerful, persuasive, and persistent. Left unmanaged, it slowly redirects the heart away from wisdom. God does not deny desire; He defines boundaries that preserve life.

James explains this progression clearly: *"Each one is tempted when he is drawn away by his own desires and enticed"* (James 1:14–15). Desire itself is not the enemy—unchecked desire is. Wisdom interrupts this progression by setting limits before appetite becomes authority.

Paul later echoes this principle, reminding believers that freedom is not permission to be governed by appetite (1 Corinthians 6:12). Boundaries are not restraints on joy; they are safeguards for destiny. Wisdom understands that what feels pleasurable in the moment may be costly in the long term.

A redeemed life honors God not only in action, but in appetite. Desire governed by wisdom preserves alignment and peace.

Key Lessons & Life Applications

- **Teaching:** Wisdom establishes boundaries for desire.
- **Reproof:** Unchecked desire leads to loss.
- **Correction:** Submit appetite to godly restraint.
- **Instruction:** Honor boundaries that protect purpose.
- **Righteous Living:** Self-governance preserves freedom.

Prayer Points

1. Father, help me govern my desires with wisdom.
2. Reveal appetites that threaten alignment.
3. Strengthen my capacity for restraint.
4. Align my longings with Your purpose.
5. Preserve my destiny through disciplined choices.

Meditation / Reflection

Which desires require clearer boundaries in my life?

Words of Wisdom: *Ungoverned desire eventually governs direction.*

July 6

Theme: What God Rejects Must Be Avoided

Anchor Scripture: "These six things the LORD hates, yes, seven are an abomination to Him…" Proverbs 6:16

Devotional Thought

Proverbs 6 removes all ambiguity about wisdom by clearly identifying behaviors God rejects. These are not cultural preferences or situational warnings; they are **non-negotiable offenses**. Wisdom demands awareness, because what God calls an abomination cannot be managed, justified, or ignored without consequence.

The seven listed—**a proud look, a lying tongue, hands that shed innocent blood, a heart that devises wicked plans, feet that run swiftly to evil, a false witness who speaks lies, and one who sows discord among brethren**—reveal something striking: **the tongue appears twice**. This repetition signals emphasis. God is not casual about speech. Words shape reality, covenant, trust, and direction. Scripture consistently reinforces this warning. James teaches that the tongue, though small, is powerful enough to defile the whole body and set the course of life on fire. Jesus warned that every careless word would be accounted for. John goes further, stating plainly that all liars align themselves with judgment. These are not isolated cautions—they form a unified witness.

Even Isaiah could not be commissioned until his tongue was purified. Before God entrusted him with divine words, the instrument of speech had to be sanctified.

This reveals a sobering truth: **God restricts access, authority, and assignment where deception is present**.

Wisdom, therefore, is not merely about avoiding great sins—it is about guarding against tolerated behaviors that God clearly rejects. Small compromises become great damage when they normalize what God forbids.

A redeemed life does not negotiate with what God has condemned. Awareness is protection. Alignment is safety.

Key Lessons & Life Applications

- **Teaching:** God clearly defines what He rejects.
- **Reproof:** Tolerating what God forbids invites restriction.
- **Correction:** Examine pride, speech, motives, actions, and relational conduct—especially areas of dishonesty or division that God explicitly rejects.
- **Instruction:** Treat God's warnings as safeguards, not suggestions.
- **Righteous Living:** Alignment with God's standards preserves access and authority.

Prayer Points

1. Father, align my heart with what You honor and reject what You reject.
2. Purify my speech and guard my tongue.
3. Expose any behavior I have tolerated that You forbid.
4. Cleanse my motives and intentions.
5. Preserve my access and assignment through integrity.

Meditation / Reflection

Am I tolerating anything God has clearly identified as unacceptable?

Words of Wisdom: *What God condemns cannot be safely contained.*

July 7

Theme: Discernment Resists Seduction

Anchor Scripture: "Do not let your heart turn aside to her ways; do not stray into her paths." Proverbs 7:25

Devotional Thought

Proverbs 7 reveals that temptation rarely begins with rebellion; it begins with distraction. Seduction works by appealing to desire before reason and emotion before discernment. Wisdom warns the heart first because once the heart is persuaded, direction soon follows. Scripture repeatedly emphasizes vigilance. Peter urges believers to remain sober and alert because the adversary seeks opportunity. Temptation often gains access not through force, but through familiarity and lowered guard. Discernment resists deception not merely through strength, but through awareness.

Jesus taught that deviation begins within, explaining that the heart is the source from which actions flow. Wisdom therefore trains the heart to recognize danger early—before escape becomes costly.

A redeemed life does not rely on willpower alone. It cultivates discernment that recognizes when desire is being misdirected. Seduction loses power where wisdom remains alert.

Key Lessons & Life Applications

- **Teaching:** Discernment guards the heart against deception.
- **Reproof:** Distraction often precedes downfall.
- **Correction:** Strengthen vigilance before temptation intensifies.
- **Instruction:** Pay attention to early warning signs.
- **Righteous Living:** Alertness preserves alignment.

Prayer Point

1. Father, sharpen my discernment.
2. Guard my heart from subtle deception.
3. Help me recognize danger early.
4. Strengthen my inner vigilance.
5. Preserve my path through wisdom.

Meditation / Reflection

Where might I be lowering my guard without realizing it?

Words of Wisdom: *Discernment recognizes danger before desire decides.*

July 8

Theme: Wisdom Is Worth More Than Precious Stones

Anchor Scripture: "For wisdom is more precious than rubies, and nothing you desire can compare with her." — Proverbs 8:11

"For whoever finds me finds life and obtains favor from the LORD." Proverbs 8:35

Devotional Thought

Wisdom Makes Herself Known.

Proverbs 8 opens by showing that wisdom is not hidden or reserved for the elite. She calls openly, inviting all who are willing to listen. Ignorance is not caused by silence from God, but by inattention from people. Wisdom is accessible, but she must be valued to be received.

Wisdom Dwells With Prudence.

Wisdom is not abstract intelligence. She declares, *"I dwell with prudence."* This reveals that wisdom expresses itself through restraint, discernment, and sound judgment. Where prudence is rejected, wisdom cannot function fully. Admiring wisdom without practicing prudence leads to imbalance.

Wisdom Governs Authority.

Proverbs 8 reveals wisdom's reach beyond personal life into leadership and governance: *"By me kings reign, and rulers decree justice."* Authority is sustained not by power alone, but by wisdom. Leadership without wisdom becomes destructive, while wisdom without authority lacks influence. God governs through wisdom.

Wisdom Produces Life and Favor.

The chapter concludes by revealing wisdom's reward: *"Whoever finds me finds life and obtains favor from the LORD."* Wisdom produces alignment, sustainability, and divine advantage. Desire may promise satisfaction, but only wisdom secures life and favor that endure.

A redeemed life learns to value wisdom correctly. What is incomparable should never be competed with.

Key Lessons & Life Applications

- **Teaching:** Wisdom surpasses every earthly treasure in value.
- **Reproof:** Desire distorts priorities when it outranks wisdom.
- **Correction:** Reorder values around wisdom, not appetite.
- **Instruction:** Practice prudence as wisdom in action.
- **Righteous Living:** Wisdom governs life, authority, and favor.

Prayer Points

1. Father, help me value wisdom above all desires.
2. Teach me to walk in prudence and discernment.
3. Govern my decisions and authority through wisdom.
4. Align my priorities with what produces life and favor.
5. Guard me from competing wisdom with lesser pursuits.

Meditation / Reflection

Where might I be valuing desire over wisdom in this season?

Words of Wisdom: *What cannot be compared should never be competed with.*

July 9

Theme: Two Invitations, Two Destinies

Anchor Scripture: "Whoever is simple, let him turn in here." Proverbs 9:4
"But he does not know that the dead are there, that her guests are in the depths of hell." Proverbs 9:18

Devotional Thought

Proverbs 9 presents life as a matter of invitation and response. Two voices call, both sound appealing, and both promise satisfaction—but they lead to very different destinations. Wisdom prepares a table openly, inviting growth, understanding, and life. Folly also invites, but her appeal is rooted in secrecy, immediacy, and the illusion of pleasure without consequence.

This chapter reveals that destiny is not shaped by opportunity alone, but by discernment. Both invitations are accessible, yet only one is anchored in truth. Jesus later echoed this reality when He described two paths—one narrow and one broad—both entered by choice, but only one leading to life. The danger is not that folly calls, but that it disguises its end.

Wisdom does not merely invite; she instructs. She requires humility, correction, and restraint. Folly, by contrast, resists instruction and flatters appetite. What feels easier in the moment often proves costly in the end. Proverbs 9 exposes the deception of immediate gratification by revealing the final outcome: what begins as stolen pleasure ends in loss.

A redeemed life learns to pause before responding. Every invitation accepted shapes direction, and repeated choices determine destiny. Discernment is not about hearing fewer voices, but about recognizing where each voice leads.

Key Lessons & Life Applications

- **Teaching:** Every invitation carries a destination.
- **Reproof:** Appealing choices can conceal destructive ends.
- **Correction:** Evaluate direction before responding to opportunity.
- **Instruction:** Choose wisdom consistently, not impulsively.
- **Righteous Living:** Discernment preserves life and purpose.

Prayer Points

1. Father, sharpen my discernment when choices are presented.
2. Guard me from invitations that appear harmless but lead to loss.
3. Help me value instruction over immediate pleasure.
4. Align my decisions with wisdom and truth.
5. Preserve my destiny through wise choices.

Meditation / Reflection

Which invitations am I currently considering, and where do they truly lead?

Words of Wisdom: *Every invitation carries a destination.*

July 10

Theme: Wisdom Is Revealed in Daily Conduct

Anchor Scripture: "The wise in heart will receive commands, but a prating fool will fall." Proverbs 10:8

Devotional Thought

Proverbs 10 marks a transition from foundational wisdom to practical expression. Wisdom is no longer presented as a call or an invitation; it is revealed through daily behavior. This chapter contrasts the wise and the foolish not by intention, but by conduct. Wisdom shows up in how a person speaks, works, responds to correction, and manages relationships.

The wise are described as receptive—open to instruction, correction, and guidance.

Wisdom does not resist authority; it recognizes that growth requires submission. Foolishness, however, is often exposed through speech. Words become excessive, careless, or self-promoting, revealing a heart resistant to restraint. Scripture repeatedly warns that ungoverned speech leads to collapse because it reflects ungoverned thought.

Proverbs 10 also connects wisdom to diligence and integrity. Righteous living produces stability over time, while shortcuts and laziness undermine provision. Wisdom understands that character is built through consistency, not bursts of effort. Blessing is sustained not by opportunity alone, but by discipline aligned with truth.

This chapter teaches that wisdom is not proven in isolated moments of insight, but in ordinary decisions repeated faithfully. A redeemed life demonstrates wisdom quietly—through reliability, restraint, and alignment with God's order. What is practiced daily eventually defines direction.

Key Lessons & Life Applications

- **Teaching:** Wisdom is demonstrated through daily conduct.
- **Reproof:** Careless speech and resistance to instruction expose folly.
- **Correction:** Cultivate receptiveness to guidance and restraint in speech.
- **Instruction:** Practice diligence and integrity consistently.
- **Righteous Living:** Faithful habits sustain stability and blessing.

Prayer Points

1. Father, let wisdom govern my daily behavior.
2. Guard my speech and align my words with truth.
3. Help me remain receptive to instruction.
4. Strengthen my diligence and integrity.
5. Establish my life through faithful obedience.

Meditation / Reflection

What do my daily habits reveal about the wisdom shaping my life?

Words of Wisdom: *Wisdom is proven in practice, not intention.*

July 11

Theme: Integrity Creates Stability

Anchor Scripture: "The integrity of the upright guides them, but the unfaithful are destroyed by their duplicity." Proverbs 11:3

Devotional Thought

Proverbs 11 reveals integrity as a guiding force, not merely a moral trait. Integrity provides direction when decisions are unclear and restraint when temptation is present. This chapter contrasts the stability of the upright with the instability produced by duplicity, showing that deception is not only wrong—it is destructive. Integrity aligns the inner life with outward conduct, removing the tension that comes from living divided. Wisdom teaches that stability is not achieved through control, manipulation, or advantage, but through consistency of character.

Throughout this chapter, integrity is linked to humility, honesty, and justice. Pride isolates, but humility welcomes counsel. Dishonest gain promises speed but delivers loss. Righteousness, however, quietly preserves life over time. Wisdom recognizes that outcomes are rarely random; they are the result of repeated alignment or repeated compromise. What guides a person internally eventually determines where they arrive externally.

Proverbs 11 also highlights the communal impact of integrity. Righteous living benefits not only the individual but those connected to them, while deception spreads harm beyond its source. A redeemed life understands that integrity is protective. It guards the heart, stabilizes relationships, and sustains favor. When integrity guides, confusion diminishes and direction becomes clear.

Key Lessons & Life Applications

- **Teaching:** Integrity provides guidance and stability.
- **Reproof:** Duplicity leads to destruction.
- **Correction:** Align inner character with outward conduct.
- **Instruction:** Choose honesty and humility consistently.
- **Righteous Living:** Integrity preserves life and influence.

Prayer Points

1. Father, establish integrity as my guide.
2. Expose any areas of compromise or duplicity.
3. Align my inner life with my outward actions.
4. Guard me from dishonest gain.
5. Preserve my stability through righteousness.

Meditation / Reflection

Where might integrity be guiding—or correcting—my choices today?

Words of Wisdom: *Integrity guides life when choices compete*

July 12

Theme: Industry Is an Expression of Wisdom

Anchor Scripture: "He who tills his land will be satisfied with bread, but he who follows frivolity is devoid of understanding." Proverbs 12:11

"The lazy man does not roast what he took in hunting, but diligence is man's precious possession." Proverbs 12:27

Devotional Thought

Proverbs 12 exposes a foundational truth many resist: wisdom expresses itself through industry. Scripture does not romanticize effort, nor does it glorify ease.

It teaches that satisfaction comes from cultivation, not convenience. Tilling the land represents commitment, consistency, and responsibility. Frivolity, by contrast, reflects distraction, impatience, and the pursuit of outcomes without investment. Wisdom identifies understanding not by ambition, but by willingness to labor faithfully.

The contrast deepens with the image of the lazy man who begins but does not finish. He hunts but fails to prepare the harvest. Opportunity is present, yet benefit is lost because diligence is absent. Wisdom reveals that access without follow-through produces no nourishment. Beginning a task is not wisdom; completing it is. **Scripture warns that "a little sleep, a little slumber" is not harmless—it is the posture through which neglect quietly robs a person of what diligence would have preserved.**

This truth speaks directly to a generation drawn to ease, automation, and shortcuts. While tools may evolve and systems may assist, industry remains irreplaceable.

There are forms of work that require judgment, discipline, consistency, and presence—qualities no technology can substitute. Wisdom does not reject advancement, but it refuses entitlement. Ease may promise speed, but only industry preserves capacity and satisfaction.

A redeemed life understands that labor is not beneath dignity; it carries it. Industry forms character, protects provision, and anchors purpose. Wisdom is not merely known—it is practiced through faithful effort.

Key Lessons & Life Applications

- **Teaching:** Industry reveals wisdom in action.
- **Reproof:** Pursuit of ease without effort leads to emptiness.
- **Correction:** Replace frivolity with disciplined responsibility.
- **Instruction:** Commit to finishing what you begin.
- **Righteous Living:** Diligent labor preserves satisfaction and stability.

Prayer Points

1. Father, establish diligence in my work and responsibilities.
2. Deliver me from the pursuit of ease without discipline.
3. Teach me to steward opportunities fully.
4. Strengthen my commitment to consistency.
5. Let my labor produce lasting fruit.

Meditation / Reflection

Am I cultivating what I desire, or avoiding the labor required to sustain it?

Words of Wisdom: *Industry is wisdom made visible.*

July 13

Theme: Discipline Secures the Future

Anchor Scripture: "A wise son heeds his father's instruction, but a scoffer does not listen to rebuke." Proverbs 13:1
"Wealth gained hastily will dwindle, but whoever gathers little by little will increase it." Proverbs 13:11

Devotional Thought

Proverbs 13 shifts wisdom's focus toward time and outcome. This chapter teaches that the future is not accidental; it is shaped by discipline, patience, and responsiveness to instruction. Wisdom listens because it understands that correction protects tomorrow, while scoffing mortgages it. A refusal to receive instruction may feel like independence, but it quietly limits growth and stability.

The chapter repeatedly contrasts haste with patience. Wealth gained quickly diminishes because it bypasses formation, accountability, and stewardship. What is gathered gradually develops capacity alongside increase. Wisdom values sustainability over speed and alignment over appearance. Impatience promises immediacy but often delivers fragility, while discipline builds endurance that lasts.

Proverbs 13 also exposes the danger of desire unrestrained by wisdom. Hope deferred makes the heart sick, not because desire is wrong, but because expectation is disconnected from process. Wisdom aligns desire with diligence and timing. It understands that longing without discipline becomes frustration, but discipline without discouragement produces fruit.

A redeemed life learns to submit appetite, ambition, and expectation to wisdom's pace. Discipline is not delay; it is investment. What wisdom governs today determines what will endure tomorrow.

Key Lessons & Life Applications

- **Teaching:** Discipline shapes long-term outcomes.
- **Reproof:** Impatience weakens sustainability.
- **Correction:** Replace haste with steady obedience.
- **Instruction:** Receive correction as protection for the future.
- **Righteous Living:** Patience preserves growth and stability.

Prayer Points

1. Father, establish discipline in my life.
2. Help me value instruction over impulse.
3. Guard me from impatience and shortcuts.
4. Teach me to trust Your timing and process.
5. Secure my future through wisdom and restraint.

Meditation / Reflection

Where might impatience be tempting me to sacrifice long-term stability?

Words of Wisdom: *Discipline today determines stability tomorrow.*

July 14

Theme: Righteousness Governs Direction

Anchor Scripture: "Fools mock at sin, but among the upright there is favor." Proverbs 14:9

"There is a way that seems right to a man, but its end is the way of death." Proverbs 14:12

"Righteousness exalts a nation, but sin is a reproach to any people." Proverbs 14:34

Devotional Thought

Proverbs 14 exposes the danger of misjudged direction. Fools mock at sin, treating moral boundaries lightly because they measure actions by comfort rather than consequence. Wisdom, however, recognizes that sin is never harmless. What is laughed at today often becomes loss tomorrow. Favor rests with the upright not because they are flawless, but because they take alignment seriously.

The warning that a way can seem right yet end in death reveals how deceptive human reasoning becomes when righteousness is removed from the process. Confidence does not equal correctness, and sincerity does not guarantee safety. Wisdom requires more than personal conviction; it requires submission to God's standards. When righteousness governs perception, discernment sharpens and direction stabilizes.

This truth extends beyond individuals to societies. Scripture declares that righteousness exalts a nation, while sin brings reproach. Moral disorder weakens foundations quietly—eroding trust, judgment, and cohesion over time. Decline is rarely sudden; it is the result of repeated misalignments that were once dismissed or mocked.

A redeemed life learns to treat righteousness not as restriction, but as protection. Wisdom does not follow what feels right; it follows what preserves life. Direction is determined not by intention alone, but by alignment with truth.

Key Lessons & Life Applications

- **Teaching**: Righteousness determines direction and outcome.
- **Reproof**: Treating sin lightly distorts judgment.
- **Correction**: Submit perception to God's standards.
- **Instruction**: Evaluate choices by truth, not feeling.
- **Righteous Living**: Alignment with righteousness preserves life and favor.

Prayer Points

1. Father, align my perception with Your truth.
2. Guard me from paths that seem right but lead to loss.
3. Establish righteousness in my decisions.
4. Expose any areas where I have treated sin lightly.
5. Let my life be governed by alignment, not impulse.

Meditation / Reflection

Am I evaluating my choices by what feels right—or by what is righteous?

Words of Wisdom: *What feels right can mislead; what is righteous preserves life.*

July 15

Theme: Wisdom Diffuses Conflict

Anchor Scripture: "A soft answer turns away wrath, but a harsh word stirs up anger." Proverbs 15:1

Devotional Thought

Proverbs 15 teaches that conflict is not neutral; it moves in the direction it is guided. This verse reveals that the outcome of a tense situation is often determined by the first response, not the original offense. A soft answer does not deny truth or ignore wrongdoing; it chooses restraint over reaction. Wisdom understands that tone governs atmosphere, and atmosphere influences resolution.

Harsh words escalate tension because they signal threat, defensiveness, or dominance. They shift a situation from problem-solving to power struggle. Wisdom, however, recognizes that escalation rarely produces clarity. It hardens positions, intensifies emotion, and reduces the capacity for understanding. A soft answer, by contrast, lowers emotional intensity and reopens space for reason and dialogue.

This proverb also exposes the difference between control and self-control. Responding gently in a tense moment is not weakness; it is strength under governance. Wisdom does not surrender authority—it exercises it. By choosing restraint, wisdom prevents unnecessary damage to relationships and preserves alignment.

A redeemed life learns that conflict is unavoidable, but escalation is optional. Wisdom diffuses tension not by silence or suppression, but by measured response. The way we speak in moments of pressure often determines whether peace is restored or disorder multiplies.

Key Lessons & Life Applications

- **Teaching:** Responses determine whether conflict escalates or resolves.
- **Reproof:** Harsh words intensify tension and damage relationships.
- **Correction:** Choose restraint over reaction in tense situations.
- **Instruction:** Govern tone as carefully as content.
- **Righteous Living:** Peace is preserved through wise responses.

Prayer Points

1. Father, teach me to respond with wisdom under pressure.
2. Guard my words in moments of tension.
3. Help me choose restraint over reaction.
4. Diffuse conflict through my responses.
5. Let my speech preserve peace and alignment.

Meditation / Reflection

How do I typically respond when tension rises?

Words of Wisdom: *Conflict moves in the direction of the response.*

July 16

Theme: Pride Precedes Collapse

Anchor Scripture: "Pride goes before destruction, and a haughty spirit before a fall. Better to be of a humble spirit with the lowly, than to divide the spoil with the proud." Proverbs 16:18–19

Devotional Thought

Proverbs 16 exposes pride not as confidence, but as a dangerous distortion of self-perception. Pride elevates the self beyond truth, correction, and dependence on God. Scripture warns that pride does not merely risk failure—it *precedes* destruction. The fall is not accidental; it is the natural outcome of a posture that resists humility and instruction.

This warning is consistent with God's revealed standards. Pride appears first on the list of what the Lord hates because it competes with God's authority and blinds the heart to accountability. A haughty spirit dismisses caution, minimizes consequence, and assumes immunity from error. Wisdom understands that pride does not announce collapse; it quietly prepares for it.

Verse 19 reframes success. Scripture declares it better to walk humbly with the lowly than to share victory with the proud. This reveals that alignment matters more than advantage. Pride may win temporarily, but humility preserves life. Wisdom chooses posture over position and character over conquest.

A redeemed life learns to measure success differently. Humility is not self-denial; it is accurate self-assessment before God. Wisdom recognizes that what pride builds quickly, humility sustains securely. Collapse is avoided not by strength alone, but by submission to truth.

Key Lessons & Life Applications

- **Teaching:** Pride sets the stage for destruction.
- **Reproof:** Self-exaltation resists correction and invites collapse.
- **Correction:** Choose humility as a protective posture.
- **Instruction:** Evaluate success by alignment, not advantage.
- **Righteous Living:** Humility preserves stability and favor.

Prayer Points

1. Father, expose any pride in my heart.
2. Teach me to walk in humility before You.
3. Guard me from self-reliance and arrogance.
4. Align my success with submission to truth.
5. Preserve me from collapse through wisdom.

Meditation / Reflection

Where might pride be quietly influencing my decisions or posture?

Words of Wisdom: *What pride lifts, pride eventually drops.*

July 17

Theme: Wisdom Preserves Peace and Relationships

Anchor Scripture: "Better is a dry morsel with quietness, than a house full of feasting with strife." Proverbs 17:1

"He who covers a transgression seeks love, but he who repeats a matter separates friends." Proverbs 17:9

Devotional Thought

Proverbs 17 reveals that wisdom values peace over excess and relationships over ego. This chapter contrasts outward abundance with inner stability, teaching that harmony is worth more than comfort, luxury, or appearance. A quiet environment sustained by wisdom is better than abundance surrounded by strife, because disorder erodes what prosperity cannot protect. Wisdom understands that peace is not accidental; it is cultivated through restraint, humility, and discernment.

The chapter also addresses how wisdom handles offense. Covering a transgression does not mean excusing sin or denying truth; it means refusing to weaponize faults. Repeating a matter, by contrast, keeps wounds open and fractures trust. Wisdom recognizes when silence heals more than speech and when discretion preserves relationships better than exposure. Gossip and repetition may feel justified, but they multiply division.

Proverbs 17 further exposes how pride and foolish speech destabilize community. Quick words, mockery, and emotional reactions invite conflict rather than resolution. Wisdom governs the tongue because it understands that unity is fragile. A redeemed life learns that not every truth must be spoken immediately, publicly, or repeatedly. Love seeks restoration, not victory.

Wisdom preserves peace by choosing restraint over reaction and unity over self-importance. Relationships thrive where humility governs responses and discretion guides speech. What wisdom protects quietly, folly destroys loudly.

Key Lessons & Life Applications

- **Teaching:** Peace is more valuable than abundance.
- **Reproof:** Repeating offenses damages trust and unity.
- **Correction:** Choose discretion over exposure.
- **Instruction:** Govern speech to preserve relationships.
- **Righteous Living:** Wisdom sustains peace through humility.

Prayer Points

1. Father, teach me to value peace over appearance or gain.
2. Guard my tongue from unnecessary repetition.
3. Help me respond to offense with wisdom and restraint.
4. Preserve my relationships through humility.
5. Let my words promote healing, not division.

Meditation / Reflection

Do my words restore peace or quietly undermine it?

Words of Wisdom: *Wisdom protects peace; pride provokes conflict.*

July 18

Theme: Words Are Not Neutral

Anchor Scripture: "Death and life are in the power of the tongue, and those who love it will eat its fruit." Proverbs 18:21

Devotional Thought

Proverbs 18:21 is not poetic exaggeration; it is a governing principle. Words are not merely tools for communication—they are instruments of consequence. Scripture presents speech as a carrier of outcomes, declaring that life and death reside in the tongue. This means words do not simply express reality; they participate in shaping it.

The phrase "those who love it will eat its fruit" introduces responsibility. Speech is not judged only by intent, but by impact. What is spoken consistently produces measurable results—relationally, emotionally, spiritually, and even directionally.

Wisdom recognizes that language reinforces patterns. Repeated words train thinking, shape expectations, and normalize outcomes over time.

This verse also dismantles the idea that words are harmless if they are honest, emotional, or reactive. Truth spoken without wisdom can still produce destruction. Emotion expressed without restraint can still carry death. Proverbs does not caution against speaking; it cautions against ungoverned speech. To "love" the tongue is to respect its power, to handle it deliberately rather than casually.

In a culture saturated with constant expression—opinions, reactions, venting, and commentary—this proverb becomes even more critical. The volume of speech has increased, but the discipline of speech has diminished. Wisdom demands awareness. Every word released enters an environment and produces fruit, whether intended or not.

A redeemed life treats speech as stewardship. Words are weighed, not wasted. They are released with accountability, not impulse. Proverbs 18:21 calls for maturity, reminding us that what we permit our mouths to produce will eventually determine what our lives must consume.

Key Lessons & Life Applications

- **Teaching:** Words actively shape outcomes.
- **Reproof:** Careless speech produces unintended damage.
- **Correction:** Govern speech with awareness and restraint.
- **Instruction:** Speak deliberately, knowing words carry consequence.
- **Righteous Living:** Wise speech preserves life and direction.

Reflection Question

What fruit am I currently eating that may have been produced by my own words?

Words of Wisdom: *Words are seeds. They do not return empty; they return with fruit.*

July 19

Theme: Wisdom Requires Responsibility

Anchor Scripture: "Listen to counsel and receive instruction, that you may be wise in your latter days." Proverbs 19:20

Devotional Thought

Proverbs 19 confronts a common misconception: that wisdom is automatic with age or experience. Scripture makes it clear that wisdom is not inherited by time alone; it is formed through instruction received and counsel honored. The promise of being "wise in your latter days" is conditional. It is not guaranteed by intention, sincerity, or effort—it is produced by teachability.

This chapter exposes how responsibility is central to wisdom. Many of life's frustrations are not the result of fate or injustice, but of ignored instruction and resisted correction. Proverbs repeatedly shows that refusing counsel does not eliminate consequences; it only delays understanding until the cost is higher. Wisdom listens early so pain does not have to teach later.

Proverbs 19 also dismantles the habit of blaming circumstances, people, or God for outcomes shaped by personal choices. Scripture notes that a person's own foolishness ruins their way, yet their heart rages against the Lord. Wisdom demands accountability. It recognizes that freedom without responsibility leads to disorder, while instruction provides guardrails for sustainable progress.

In a culture that prizes autonomy and resists correction, this proverb calls for maturity. To receive counsel is not to surrender independence; it is to preserve the future. Wisdom looks ahead. It values the long view over immediate comfort and understands that instruction received today determines stability tomorrow.

A redeemed life treats counsel as an asset, not an insult. Wisdom is proven not by how strongly one feels, but by how faithfully one listens.

Key Lessons & Life Applications

- **Teaching:** Wisdom is formed through instruction and counsel.
- **Reproof:** Ignoring guidance increases future cost.
- **Correction:** Replace resistance with teachability.
- **Instruction:** Listen early to avoid learning through loss.
- **Righteous Living:** Responsibility preserves long-term stability.

Reflection Question

What instruction am I currently resisting that may shape my future?

Words of Wisdom: *The wisdom you acquire today determines your outcome tomorrow.*

July 20

Theme: Wisdom Is Proven by Integrity and Self-Examination

Anchor Scripture: "Who can say, 'I have made my heart clean, I am pure from my sin'?" Proverbs 20:9

Devotional Thought

Proverbs 20 turns wisdom inward. Rather than focusing on external behavior alone, this chapter presses the reader to examine the heart. The question posed is not rhetorical; it is revealing. Scripture exposes how easy it is to assume purity without reflection and to claim integrity without examination. Wisdom does not rush to self-approval. It pauses to assess, correct, and realign.

This proverb teaches that integrity is not the absence of mistakes, but the willingness to confront them honestly. A clean heart is not declared by confidence, but cultivated through humility and repentance. Wisdom understands that unchecked assumptions about one's own righteousness create blind spots that distort judgment and weaken character. Self-examination is therefore not condemnation; it is protection.

Proverbs 20 also highlights consistency as a mark of wisdom. Integrity requires alignment between what is said, what is done, and what is believed. When the inner life is neglected, outer conduct eventually fractures. Wisdom recognizes that sustainable character is formed through regular reflection and responsiveness to correction.

A redeemed life learns to invite God into its inner evaluation. Rather than defending appearances, wisdom seeks truth. Growth begins when self-deception ends.

Integrity is preserved not by perfection, but by continual alignment with God's standard.

Key Lessons & Life Applications

- **Teaching:** Wisdom requires honest self-examination.
- **Reproof:** Assuming purity without reflection invites deception.
- **Correction:** Invite God to examine the heart regularly.
- **Instruction:** Practice humility and repentance consistently.
- **Righteous Living:** Integrity is sustained through alignment, not assumption.

Prayer Points

1. Father, search my heart and reveal what needs correction.
2. Guard me from self-deception.
3. Teach me humility in self-examination.
4. Align my inner life with Your truth.
5. Preserve my integrity through wisdom.

Meditation / Reflection

Where might I be assuming integrity instead of examining it?

Words of Wisdom: *Integrity is preserved through honest self-examination.*

July 21

Theme: God Weighs Motives, Not Just Actions

Anchor Scripture: "Every way of a man is right in his own eyes, but the LORD weighs the hearts." Proverbs 21:2

Devotional Thought

Proverbs 21 reveals a sobering truth: sincerity is not the same as alignment. A person can feel justified, convinced, and confident, yet still be misaligned with God's standard. Scripture makes clear that human judgment often evaluates actions, but God examines motives. What appears right externally may still be flawed internally. Wisdom therefore requires more than correct behavior; it demands an honest heart.

This verse exposes the limitation of self-assessment. People naturally interpret their actions through personal reasoning, emotion, or intention, often excusing what God is still correcting. Wisdom understands that justification is not validation. God's evaluation penetrates beneath behavior to the heart's posture, uncovering pride, fear, self-interest, or obedience that may not be visible to others.

Proverbs 21 also teaches that outcomes are governed by God's evaluation, not human approval. Plans, effort, and sacrifice do not override misaligned motives. This is why Scripture later declares that doing righteousness and justice is more acceptable to the Lord than sacrifice. Wisdom aligns motive before it trusts action.

A redeemed life learns to submit intention to God's scrutiny. Rather than asking, "Does this make sense to me?" wisdom asks, "Is my heart aligned with God?" Growth accelerates when self-justification gives way to honest surrender. What God weighs determines what endures.

Key Lessons & Life Applications

- **Teaching:** God evaluates motives, not just actions.
- **Reproof:** Self-justification can conceal misalignment.
- **Correction:** Submit intentions to God's examination.
- **Instruction:** Align the heart before trusting behavior.
- **Righteous Living:** Right motives sustain lasting outcomes.

Prayer Points

1. Father, examine my heart and my motives.
2. Guard me from self-justification.
3. Align my intentions with Your truth.
4. Purify my desires and decisions.
5. Let my actions flow from a right heart.

Meditation / Reflection

What motives might God be weighing beneath my current decisions?

Words of Wisdom: *What God weighs determines what lasts.*

July 22

Theme: Formation Shapes the Future

Anchor Scripture: "Train up a child in the way he should go, and when he is old he will not depart from it." Proverbs 22:6

Devotional Thought

Proverbs 22 highlights a principle that governs more than childhood—it governs life itself. Formation precedes outcome. What is repeatedly taught, modeled, and reinforced shapes direction long before results are visible. This verse is often limited to parenting, but its wisdom extends to habits, values, thinking patterns, and spiritual posture. Training is not a moment; it is a process. It establishes pathways that later feel natural, familiar, and difficult to abandon.

Wisdom teaches that direction is set early, whether intentionally or by default. What is not trained will still be learned—often through exposure, imitation, or necessity. Proverbs 22 warns that neglect does not leave a person neutral; it leaves them unguarded. Formation fills that space, either with wisdom or with distortion. This is why humility and instruction appear repeatedly in this chapter. A teachable posture allows correction to shape character before consequences are required to do so.

This proverb also emphasizes alignment. "The way he should go" speaks to purpose, design, and fit—not uniformity. Wisdom does not impose one path on every life; it discerns the right path for each one. Formation anchored in truth equips a person to navigate seasons, pressures, and transitions without losing direction.

A redeemed life recognizes that tomorrow's stability is built through today's formation. What is practiced consistently becomes character, and character determines outcome. Wisdom invests early because it understands that the future is not guessed—it is prepared.

Key Lessons & Life Applications

- **Teaching:** Formation determines long-term direction.
- **Reproof:** Neglect allows distortion to shape outcomes.
- **Correction:** Be intentional about what is taught and practiced.
- **Instruction:** Embrace training as preparation, not restriction.
- **Righteous Living:** Early alignment preserves future stability.

Prayer Points

1. Father, align my formation with Your truth.
2. Expose habits or patterns that need correction.
3. Help me value training and discipline.
4. Establish right pathways in my life and those I influence.
5. Prepare my future through wisdom today.

Meditation / Reflection

What patterns am I forming now that will shape my future?

Words of Wisdom: *The future is formed long before it is seen.*

July 23

Theme: Wisdom Governs Desire

Anchor Scripture: "For as he thinks in his heart, so is he." Proverbs 23:7

Devotional Thought

Proverbs 23 exposes the inner life as the true battleground of wisdom. This chapter repeatedly addresses appetite—what is desired, consumed, and pursued—because wisdom understands that unchecked desire shapes identity long before it produces behavior. The heart is not merely the seat of emotion; it is the center of thought, intention, and inclination. What occupies the heart gradually defines who a person becomes.

This proverb reveals that identity is formed internally before it is expressed externally. Actions follow thoughts, and habits follow desires that have been entertained without restraint. Wisdom therefore does not begin with behavior modification; it begins with inner governance. When desire is left unmanaged, it quietly assumes authority, directing choices in ways that feel natural but may lead to loss.

Proverbs 23 also warns against external influences that appeal to appetite—excess, comparison, and indulgence—while concealing long-term cost. Wisdom teaches discernment, restraint, and delayed gratification. It recognizes that not everything available is beneficial and not every invitation deserves acceptance. Appetite must be disciplined if purpose is to be preserved.

A redeemed life learns that freedom is not the absence of restraint, but the presence of wise self-governance. Wisdom does not suppress desire; it orders it. When the heart is governed by truth, identity stabilizes and direction becomes clear. What the heart consumes ultimately determines what the life produces.

Key Lessons & Life Applications

- **Teaching:** Desire shapes identity before behavior.
- **Reproof:** Ungoverned appetite leads to misdirection.
- **Correction:** Discipline inner thoughts and desires.
- **Instruction:** Practice restraint to preserve purpose.
- **Righteous Living:** Self-governance sustains alignment.

Prayer Points

1. Father, govern my heart with wisdom.
2. Expose desires that compete with truth.
3. Teach me restraint and discernment.
4. Align my thoughts with Your purpose.
5. Preserve my direction through self-control.

Meditation / Reflection

What desires am I allowing to shape my thinking and direction?

Words of Wisdom: *What the heart entertains, the life eventually reflects.*

July 24

Theme: Wisdom Sustains Strength in Adversity

Anchor Scripture: "If you faint in the day of adversity, your strength is small." Proverbs 24:10

Devotional Thought

Proverbs 24 reframes adversity as a test of inner strength rather than an interruption of purpose. Scripture does not deny the reality of pressure; it evaluates the capacity revealed under it. The day of adversity exposes what has been built within. When strength collapses under pressure, it is not the adversity that is at fault, but the lack of preparation before it arrived. Wisdom understands that endurance is cultivated long before resistance is required.

This proverb teaches that resilience is not accidental. Strength is developed through discipline, instruction, and alignment over time. Those who rely on emotion, momentum, or circumstance often falter when opposition arises. Wisdom, however, anchors strength in truth and character, allowing stability even when conditions shift. Adversity does not create weakness; it reveals it.

Proverbs 24 also reminds us that wisdom is communal and purposeful. Strength is not hoarded for self-preservation alone; it is meant to sustain responsibility, justice, and perseverance on behalf of others. Wisdom resists retreat when courage is required and refuses passivity when action is necessary. Endurance becomes an ethical responsibility, not merely a personal virtue.

A redeemed life learns to prepare for adversity before it appears. Wisdom builds strength quietly through consistency, restraint, and faithfulness. When pressure comes, what has been formed internally determines whether one stands or collapses. Strength sustained by wisdom does not faint—it endures.

Key Lessons & Life Applications

- **Teaching:** Adversity reveals the measure of inner strength.
- **Reproof:** Neglecting preparation weakens endurance.
- **Correction:** Build strength through consistent wisdom.
- **Instruction:** Develop resilience before pressure arrives.
- **Righteous Living:** Endurance preserves purpose and responsibility.

Prayer Points

1. Father, strengthen my inner life through wisdom.
2. Prepare me for adversity before it appears.
3. Teach me endurance grounded in truth.
4. Guard me from fainting under pressure.
5. Let my strength sustain purpose and responsibility.

Meditation / Reflection

What have I been building internally that will be revealed under pressure?

Words of Wisdom: *Strength is revealed in adversity but built beforehand.*

July 25

Theme: Wisdom Knows When and How

Anchor Scripture: "A word fitly spoken is like apples of gold in settings of silver." Proverbs 25:11

Devotional Thought

Proverbs 25 teaches that wisdom is not only about *what* is said or done, but *when* and *how*. A word spoken at the right time, in the right manner, carries weight, clarity, and beauty. Wisdom understands timing. Truth delivered without discernment can lose its power, while restraint allows meaning to land with impact. This chapter repeatedly emphasizes discretion, patience, and self-control as marks of maturity.

The imagery of a word fitly spoken highlights precision. Wisdom is careful, measured, and intentional. It does not rush to display knowledge or assert opinion. Instead, it waits for the appropriate moment, recognizing that timing can either enhance understanding or provoke resistance. What is correct but poorly timed may harm rather than heal.

Proverbs 25 also warns against excess—too much speech, too much self-promotion, too much indulgence. Wisdom values moderation because it preserves dignity and influence. Overexposure dulls respect, while restraint strengthens credibility. The wise understand that influence is not maintained by constant expression, but by disciplined presence.

A redeemed life learns that discernment governs both silence and speech. Wisdom knows when to step forward and when to hold back. What is released thoughtfully carries lasting value, while what is rushed often requires repair. Timing transforms truth into treasure.

Key Lessons & Life Applications

- **Teaching:** Wisdom is expressed through discernment and timing.
- **Reproof:** Truth without restraint can lose its effectiveness.
- **Correction:** Practice patience in speech and action.
- **Instruction:** Weigh timing as carefully as content.
- **Righteous Living:** Disciplined expression preserves influence.

Prayer Points

1. Father, teach me discernment in speech and action.
2. Help me recognize the right time to speak and act.
3. Guard me from impulsive expression.
4. Align my words with wisdom and grace.
5. Let my restraint preserve clarity and influence.

Meditation / Reflection

Am I more focused on being right—or on being wise in timing?

Words of Wisdom: *Timing turns truth into treasure.*

July 26

Theme: Wisdom Refuses to Enter Foolish Cycles

Anchor Scripture: "As a dog returns to his own vomit, so a fool repeats his folly." Proverbs 26:11

Devotional Thought

Proverbs 26 exposes the exhausting nature of folly: it repeats itself. This chapter reveals that foolishness is not merely a lack of knowledge, but a resistance to correction. The image of returning to what was already rejected underscores a deeper issue—failure to learn. Wisdom understands that progress requires change, while folly circles back to familiar errors, habits, and arguments, mistaking familiarity for safety.

This proverb highlights the danger of engaging foolish patterns without discernment. Repetition is not perseverance when it lacks learning; it is stagnation. Wisdom discerns when dialogue becomes debate, when correction becomes contention, and when engagement only fuels disorder. Proverbs 26 repeatedly warns against responding to folly in ways that entangle the wise in the same confusion.

Not every issue deserves a response, and not every person is ready for instruction.

The chapter also teaches that folly often seeks validation. It draws others into its cycle through provocation, exaggeration, and mischief. Wisdom resists the pull to react. Silence, distance, and restraint are sometimes the most effective responses. To disengage is not avoidance; it is discernment that protects clarity and peace.

A redeemed life learns to identify cycles that do not produce growth. Wisdom refuses to rehearse what has already proven destructive. Freedom is sustained not by repeated confrontation, but by intentional disengagement from patterns that do not change. Growth begins when repetition ends.

Key Lessons & Life Applications

- **Teaching:** Folly reveals itself through repeated patterns.
- **Reproof:** Engaging foolish cycles drains clarity and peace.
- **Correction:** Learn from error rather than returning to it.
- **Instruction:** Practice discernment in when to respond or withdraw.
- **Righteous Living:** Wisdom preserves progress by ending destructive cycles.

Prayer Points

1. Father, expose cycles in my life that do not produce growth.
2. Give me discernment to disengage from folly.
3. Teach me to learn quickly from correction.
4. Guard me from unnecessary conflict.
5. Preserve my peace through wisdom.

Meditation / Reflection

What patterns might I be repeating that wisdom is calling me to end?

Words of Wisdom: *Wisdom ends cycles that folly repeats.*

July 27

Theme: Wisdom Is Refined Through Accountability

Anchor Scripture: "As iron sharpens iron, so a man sharpens the countenance of his friend." Proverbs 27:17

Devotional Thought

Proverbs 27 reveals that wisdom is not formed in isolation. Growth requires friction—not conflict for its own sake, but honest interaction that exposes blind spots and refines character. Just as iron sharpens iron through contact, wisdom is clarified through relationships that are truthful, courageous, and committed to growth. Flattery dulls discernment, but faithful engagement sharpens it.

This chapter emphasizes the value of honest feedback over surface harmony. Open rebuke is presented as more beneficial than hidden love because wisdom prioritizes alignment over comfort. Correction offered in love preserves direction, while silence motivated by fear allows error to harden. Wisdom understands that accountability is not control; it is care expressed through truth.

Proverbs 27 also warns against self-reliance and misplaced confidence. Boasting about tomorrow reveals a lack of awareness, while humility keeps a person grounded in reality. Wisdom recognizes that perspective is sharpened when others are allowed to speak into one's life. Strength grows when accountability is welcomed rather than resisted.

A redeemed life chooses relationships that refine rather than merely affirm. Wisdom values sharpening because it leads to clarity, maturity, and stability. What is refined through honest connection becomes stronger, more accurate, and more useful.

Growth accelerates where accountability is embraced.

Key Lessons & Life Applications

- **Teaching:** Wisdom is refined through honest relationships.
- **Reproof:** Isolation weakens discernment.
- **Correction:** Welcome accountability and truthful feedback.
- **Instruction:** Choose relationships that sharpen character.
- **Righteous Living:** Growth is sustained through humility and openness.

Prayer Points

1. Father, place wise and truthful voices in my life.
2. Help me receive correction with humility.
3. Guard me from flattery that dulls discernment.
4. Strengthen me through accountable relationships.
5. Refine my character through wisdom.

Meditation / Reflection

Who has permission to sharpen me through honest truth?

Words of Wisdom: *Growth accelerates where accountability is welcomed.*

July 28

Theme: Mercy Responds to Repentance

Anchor Scripture: "He who covers his sins will not prosper, but whoever confesses and forsakes them will have mercy." Proverbs 28:13

Devotional Thought

Proverbs 28 confronts a misconception about mercy: mercy is not automatic, and it is not detached from truth. This verse establishes a clear boundary—concealment blocks prosperity, while confession and forsaking open the door to mercy. Wisdom teaches that covering sin is not protection; it is self-deception. What is hidden does not disappear; it accumulates weight and eventually restricts progress.

Scripture makes an important distinction between regret and repentance. Confession without forsaking preserves patterns that continue to produce loss. Wisdom requires both honesty and change. Mercy responds not to excuses, rationalization, or secrecy, but to repentance that turns away from what God rejects. This is not punishment; it is restoration through alignment.

Proverbs 28 also reinforces a recurring biblical theme: integrity sustains freedom. Concealed sin fractures inner confidence, distorts judgment, and erodes peace. Repentance, by contrast, restores clarity and reopens access to grace. Wisdom understands that God's standards are not barriers to mercy; they are the pathway into it.

A redeemed life learns that mercy has order. God is gracious, but He is not casual about truth. Prosperity—spiritual, relational, and practical—flows where honesty and repentance are practiced consistently. Wisdom does not fear exposure; it fears stagnation. What is confessed and forsaken loses its power to control.

Key Lessons & Life Applications

- **Teaching:** Mercy follows repentance, not concealment.
- **Reproof:** Hiding sin restricts progress and clarity.
- **Correction:** Practice confession paired with change.
- **Instruction:** Align repentance with forsaking harmful patterns.
- **Righteous Living:** Integrity preserves access to mercy.

Prayer Points

1. Father, give me grace to walk in honesty before You.
2. Expose any areas I am tempted to conceal.
3. Help me forsake what You reject.
4. Restore clarity and freedom through repentance.
5. Let mercy flow where truth is embraced.

Meditation / Reflection

Is there anything I am covering that wisdom is calling me to confront?

Words of Wisdom: *Mercy flows where repentance is practiced.*

July 29

Theme: Correction Preserves Freedom

Anchor Scripture: "He who is often rebuked, and hardens his neck, will suddenly be destroyed, and that without remedy." Proverbs 29:1

Devotional Thought

Proverbs 29 issues a sober warning about repeated resistance to correction. Wisdom teaches that rebuke is not an attack, but an intervention designed to preserve life, direction, and freedom. This verse reveals that destruction is rarely sudden in origin; it is sudden in manifestation. It follows a pattern of ignored warnings, resisted instruction, and hardened posture over time.

The hardened neck represents stubborn refusal to adjust. Wisdom understands that flexibility is essential for growth. Correction creates opportunity for realignment, but when consistently rejected, it loses its protective effect. What begins as resistance eventually becomes incapacity. Destruction arrives not because correction was absent, but because it was repeatedly dismissed.

Proverbs 29 also highlights the role of authority and governance. Where wisdom is honored, people flourish; where restraint and correction are despised, disorder increases. Freedom is sustained by alignment, not autonomy. Wisdom recognizes that boundaries and instruction are safeguards, not limitations.

A redeemed life learns to respond quickly to correction. Humility keeps the heart pliable and the path adjustable. The goal of rebuke is restoration, not punishment. But wisdom also acknowledges a boundary: there comes a point where refusal to listen produces irreversible consequence. Freedom is preserved by teachability, and life is sustained by responsiveness to truth.

Key Lessons & Life Applications

- **Teaching:** Correction is a safeguard, not a threat.
- **Reproof:** Resisting rebuke hardens the heart.
- **Correction:** Respond to instruction before patterns solidify.
- **Instruction:** Remain teachable and flexible.
- **Righteous Living:** Freedom is preserved through humility.

Prayer Points

1. Father, keep my heart responsive to correction.
2. Guard me from stubborn resistance to truth.
3. Teach me to adjust quickly when instructed.
4. Preserve my freedom through humility.
5. Align my life continually with wisdom.

Meditation / Reflection

How do I usually respond when correction challenges my posture or plans?

Words of Wisdom: *Correction resisted becomes consequence.*

July 30

Theme: Wisdom Begins with Humble Dependence

Anchor Scripture: "Surely I am more stupid than any man, and do not have the understanding of a man." Proverbs 30:2

Devotional Thought

Proverbs 30 opens with an unexpected posture: humility. Rather than asserting knowledge or authority, the writer begins by acknowledging limitation. This is not self-contempt; it is wisdom. Scripture reveals that true understanding starts where self-sufficiency ends. Wisdom recognizes the boundary between human reasoning and divine truth and refuses to pretend that intellect alone is sufficient.

This chapter exposes the danger of intellectual pride. When knowledge is detached from reverence, it becomes distorted. Wisdom is not diminished by admitting what it does not know; it is protected. Proverbs 30 reminds us that God is not discovered through cleverness, but through humility that seeks Him rightly. The questions posed throughout the chapter highlight how limited human perception is when measured against divine order.

Proverbs 30 also teaches contentment and restraint. The request for neither poverty nor riches reflects wisdom's desire for balance rather than excess. Dependence on God replaces anxiety about provision and temptation toward pride. Wisdom understands that extremes often destabilize faith, while humility keeps the heart anchored.

A redeemed life learns that humility is not weakness—it is alignment. Wisdom does not claim mastery over life; it submits to the One who governs it. Clarity increases when arrogance decreases. True wisdom begins by acknowledging need and ends in trust.

Key Lessons & Life Applications

- **Teaching:** Wisdom starts with recognizing human limitation.
- **Reproof:** Intellectual pride distorts understanding.
- **Correction:** Embrace humility as a pathway to truth.
- **Instruction:** Depend on God rather than self-sufficiency.
- **Righteous Living:** Humility preserves clarity and balance.

Prayer Points

1. Father, keep my heart humble before You.
2. Guard me from pride in my understanding.
3. Teach me to depend on You fully.
4. Align my desires with wisdom and balance.
5. Increase clarity through humility.

Meditation / Reflection

Where might I be relying on my own understanding instead of God?

Words of Wisdom: *Humility opens the door that pride keeps closed.*

July 31

Theme: Wisdom Is Strength Lived with Honor

Anchor Scripture: "Strength and honor are her clothing; she shall rejoice in time to come." Proverbs 31:25

Devotional Thought

Proverbs 31 concludes the book of wisdom by revealing what wisdom looks like when fully formed and faithfully lived. This chapter is not merely a description of a woman; it is a portrait of mature wisdom expressed through character, discipline, and responsibility. Strength and honor are not inherited or assumed—they are cultivated through consistent alignment with wisdom over time.

This proverb emphasizes that true strength is not loud or forceful; it is steady, reliable, and grounded. Honor flows from integrity practiced daily, not from public recognition. Wisdom here is shown through diligence, foresight, restraint, and care for others. Each action reflects inner order. The confidence to rejoice in time to come comes from preparation, not presumption. Wisdom anticipates the future by stewarding the present well.

Proverbs 31 also reframes value. Worth is not measured by appearance or applause, but by reverence for God and faithfulness in responsibility. Wisdom integrates the private and public life seamlessly—what is practiced in obscurity sustains what is visible. Strength is expressed through service, discipline, and consistency rather than domination or self-promotion.

A redeemed life understands that wisdom's goal is not admiration, but trustworthiness. Proverbs closes by showing that wisdom, when embraced fully, produces a life marked by strength, honor, and enduring impact. What wisdom forms quietly becomes a legacy that speaks long after words end.

Key Lessons & Life Applications

- **Teaching:** Wisdom matures into strength and honor.
- **Reproof:** Superficial measures of success distort true value.
- **Correction:** Cultivate character through consistent alignment.
- **Instruction:** Practice wisdom daily in visible and hidden ways.
- **Righteous Living:** Reverence for God sustains lasting impact.

Prayer Points

1. Father, form wisdom deeply in my character.
2. Clothe my life with strength and honor.
3. Help me steward today in preparation for tomorrow.
4. Align my private and public life with truth.
5. Let my life reflect enduring wisdom.

Meditation / Reflection

What kind of strength am I building for the future?

Words of Wisdom: *Wisdom lived daily becomes strength that endures*

AUGUST PSALMS

August 1

Theme: God Welcomes Honest Emotion

Anchor Scripture - "Trust in Him at all times, you people; pour out your heart before Him; God is a refuge for us." Psalms 62:8

Devotional Thought

God does not require filtered emotions—He invites honest ones. The Psalms reveal a God who welcomes the full range of human experience: joy, fear, grief, confusion, and hope.

Pouring out the heart is not weakness; it is trust expressed honestly. Suppressed emotions often harden the heart, but expressed emotions—brought before God—open the way for healing.

A redeemed life learns that prayer is not performance. God is not threatened by what we feel; He is present within it. Refuge is found not by hiding emotions, but by bringing them to Him.

Honesty is the doorway to healing.

Key Lessons & Life Applications

- **Teaching:** God welcomes honest prayer.
- **Reproof:** Suppressed emotions distort healing.
- **Correction:** Bring the heart fully before God.
- **Instruction:** Practice emotional honesty in prayer.
- **Righteous Living:** Trust deepens through transparency.

Prayer Points

1. Father, help me bring my heart honestly before You.
2. Remove fear of expressing my true emotions.
3. Heal what I have hidden or suppressed.
4. Teach me to trust You with my inner life.
5. Be my refuge in every season.

Meditation / Reflection

Am I honest with God about what I truly feel?

Words of Wisdom: *Healing begins where honesty is welcomed.*

August 2

Theme: The Language of Lament

Anchor Scripture - "How long, O LORD? Will You forget me forever? How long will You hide Your face from me?" Psalms 13:1

Devotional Thought

Lament is the language of faith under pressure. It gives voice to pain without surrendering belief. The Psalms teach us that questioning God is not unbelief—it is relationship expressed honestly.

Lament allows sorrow to speak without letting despair dominate. It acknowledges pain while still turning toward God. This posture keeps the heart engaged, even in confusion.

A redeemed life understands that silence is not the absence of faith, and lament is not rebellion. It is prayer that refuses to disconnect.

God listens even when the heart is weary.

Key Lessons & Life Applications

- **Teaching:** Lament is a valid form of prayer.
- **Reproof:** Suppressing grief delays healing.
- **Correction:** Express pain without abandoning trust.
- **Instruction:** Bring unanswered questions to God.
- **Righteous Living:** Faith remains engaged through lament.

Prayer Points

1. Father, help me express sorrow honestly.
2. Give me words when pain feels overwhelming.
3. Guard my heart from despair.
4. Teach me to lament without losing faith.
5. Remind me that You hear even my questions.

Meditation / Reflection

What pain have I avoided bringing before God?

Words of Wisdom: *Lament keeps faith engaged in suffering.*

August 3

Theme: Fear Brought into God's Presence

Anchor Scripture - "I sought the LORD, and He heard me, and delivered me from all my fears." Psalms 34:4

Devotional Thought

Fear loses power when it is brought into God's presence. The Psalms teach that deliverance begins not with denial, but with seeking.

Fear thrives in isolation. When fears remain unspoken, they grow unchecked. But when brought before God, fear is confronted by truth, presence, and reassurance.

A redeemed life does not pretend fear is absent—it refuses to let fear govern. Seeking God redirects the heart from threat to trust.

Freedom begins when fear is named before God.

Key Lessons & Life Applications

- **Teaching:** God responds to those who seek Him.
- **Reproof:** Unaddressed fear grows stronger.
- **Correction:** Bring fear into God's presence.
- **Instruction:** Seek God intentionally during anxiety.
- **Righteous Living:** Trust replaces fear through pursuit.

Prayer Points

1. Father, I bring my fears before You.
2. Deliver me from anxiety that overwhelms my heart.
3. Help me seek You instead of hiding fear.
4. Replace fear with trust in Your presence.
5. Anchor my heart in Your peace.

Meditation / Reflection

What fears do I need to bring honestly before God?

Words of Wisdom: *Fear loses strength in God's presence.*

August 4

Theme: When God Feels Distant

Anchor Scripture - "Why do You stand afar off, O LORD? Why do You hide in times of trouble?" Psalms 10:1

Devotional Thought

There are moments when God feels distant—not because He has withdrawn, but because circumstances have overwhelmed perception. The Psalms give language to this experience without condemnation.

Feeling distance does not equal abandonment. It reveals the tension between faith and feeling. The psalmist speaks honestly, not to accuse God, but to remain connected through questioning.

A redeemed life learns that seasons of perceived distance are invitations to deeper trust. God does not fear our questions; He remains present even when unseen.

Faith continues, even when feeling lags behind.

Key Lessons & Life Applications

- **Teaching:** Feeling distant does not mean God is absent.
- **Reproof:** Interpreting silence as abandonment weakens trust.
- **Correction:** Bring confusion honestly before God.
- **Instruction:** Stay engaged with God during uncertainty.
- **Righteous Living:** Faith persists beyond emotion.

Prayer Points

1. Father, help me trust You when You feel distant.
2. Strengthen my faith beyond my feelings.
3. Teach me to remain connected through questioning.
4. Reveal Your presence in hidden ways.
5. Anchor my heart in truth.

Meditation / Reflection

How do I respond when God feels distant?

Words of Wisdom: *God's presence is not measured by feeling.*

August 5

Theme: Trusting God in Uncertainty

Anchor Scripture - "When I am afraid, I will trust in You." Psalms 56:3

Devotional Thought

Uncertainty exposes where trust truly rests. The Psalms teach that trust is not the absence of fear—it is the decision to rely on God in its presence.

Fear often arises when outcomes are unclear. Trust responds by choosing dependence over control. This choice does not eliminate uncertainty, but it stabilizes the heart within it.

A redeemed life learns to trust God not because circumstances are resolved, but because His character is consistent.

Trust anchors the soul when clarity is delayed.

Key Lessons & Life Applications

- **Teaching:** Trust is exercised in uncertainty.
- **Reproof:** Control weakens reliance on God.
- **Correction:** Choose trust when fear arises.
- **Instruction:** Anchor confidence in God's character.
- **Righteous Living:** Dependence produces peace.

Prayer Points

1. Father, teach me to trust You in uncertainty.
2. Help me release control.
3. Strengthen my reliance on Your character.
4. Calm my heart amid fear.
5. Anchor my trust in You.

Meditation / Reflection

Where am I struggling to trust God because outcomes are unclear?

Words of Wisdom: *Trust steadies the heart when clarity is absent.*

August 6

Theme: The Cry for Help

Anchor Scripture - "I cried out to the LORD with my voice, and He heard me from His holy hill." Psalms 3:4

Devotional Thought

Crying out to God is not desperation—it is recognition of need. The Psalms affirm that God responds to sincere cries, not polished prayers.

The cry for help arises when strength is insufficient. Rather than viewing this as failure, Scripture presents it as humility. God hears the cry that acknowledges dependence.

A redeemed life learns that reaching out to God is an act of faith. Help begins when the heart turns outward instead of inward.

God hears the honest cry.

Key Lessons & Life Applications

- **Teaching:** God hears sincere cries for help.
- **Reproof:** Pride delays seeking help.
- **Correction:** Turn to God instead of isolating.
- **Instruction:** Cry out in faith, not despair.
- **Righteous Living:** Dependence strengthens trust.

Prayer Points

1. Father, I cry out to You for help.
2. Teach me to depend on You fully.
3. Remove pride that resists asking.
4. Hear my cry and respond in mercy.
5. Strengthen my faith through reliance.

Meditation / Reflection

Do I allow myself to cry out to God when overwhelmed?

Words of Wisdom: *Help begins when the heart reaches out.*

August 7

Theme: God as Refuge

Anchor Scripture - "God is our refuge and strength, a very present help in trouble." Psalms 46:1

Devotional Thought

A refuge is not an escape from trouble; it is a place of safety within it. The Psalms repeatedly present God as refuge—near, available, and responsive in times of distress.
God does not remove us from every storm immediately, but He provides shelter while we endure. Refuge speaks of protection, not avoidance. It is where strength is renewed and fear loses its grip.
A redeemed life learns to run toward God, not away from Him, when trouble arises.
Refuge is relational, not geographical.
Safety is found in God's presence.

Key Lessons & Life Applications

- **Teaching:** God is a present refuge in trouble.
- **Reproof:** Running elsewhere delays comfort.
- **Correction:** Seek God as shelter, not distraction.
- **Instruction:** Remain near God during hardship.
- **Righteous Living:** Trust strengthens resilience.

Prayer Points

1. Father, be my refuge in trouble.
2. Strengthen me through Your presence.
3. Help me run toward You in difficulty.
4. Guard my heart from fear.
5. Renew my strength through trust.

Meditation / Reflection

Where do I instinctively seek refuge when trouble comes?

Words of Wisdom: *Refuge is found in God's nearness.*

August 8

Theme: Waiting Without Losing Hope

Anchor Scripture - "Wait on the LORD; be of good courage, and He shall strengthen your heart; wait, I say, on the LORD!" Psalms 27:14

Devotional Thought

Waiting is often misunderstood as inactivity. The Psalms redefine waiting as **active trust**—a posture of expectancy anchored in God's faithfulness.

Waiting tests patience, but it also strengthens the heart. It reveals where hope is rooted. When hope is anchored in outcomes, waiting feels unbearable. When hope is anchored in God, waiting becomes formative.

A redeemed life learns that delay is not denial. God uses waiting to refine trust and deepen endurance.

Strength grows in the waiting.

Key Lessons & Life Applications

- **Teaching:** Waiting strengthens trust.
- **Reproof:** Impatience weakens endurance.
- **Correction:** Anchor hope in God, not timing.
- **Instruction:** Practice courage while waiting.
- **Righteous Living:** Endurance matures faith.

Prayer Points

1. Father, help me wait with hope.
2. Strengthen my heart during delay.
3. Guard me from discouragement.
4. Teach me patience rooted in trust.
5. Renew my courage as I wait.

Meditation / Reflection

How do I respond during seasons of waiting?

Words of Wisdom: *Waiting strengthens what rushing weakens.*

August 9

Theme: Remembering God's Faithfulness

Anchor Scripture - "I will remember the works of the LORD; surely I will remember Your wonders of old." Psalms 77:11

Devotional Thought

Memory is a powerful spiritual tool. The Psalms teach that remembrance stabilizes faith when present circumstances feel uncertain.

Remembering God's faithfulness reframes perspective. It reminds the heart that past deliverance informs present trust. Forgetfulness often fuels fear, while remembrance restores confidence.

A redeemed life intentionally recalls God's works, anchoring hope in proven faithfulness rather than current emotion.

What God has done before informs trust today.

Key Lessons & Life Applications

- **Teaching:** Remembrance strengthens faith.
- **Reproof:** Forgetting fuels fear and doubt.
- **Correction:** Recall God's past works intentionally.
- **Instruction:** Build faith through reflection.
- **Righteous Living:** Gratitude stabilizes trust.

Prayer Points

1. Father, remind me of Your faithfulness.
2. Help me recall past deliverance.
3. Strengthen my trust through remembrance.
4. Guard my heart from forgetfulness.
5. Renew my confidence in You.

Meditation / Reflection

What past faithfulness of God can I recall today?

Words of Wisdom: *Remembrance restores trust.*

August 10

Theme: Deliverance Recounted

Anchor Scripture - "Many are the afflictions of the righteous, but the LORD delivers him out of them all." Psalms 34:19

Devotional Thought

The Psalms do not deny affliction—they place it within the larger story of deliverance. Remembering how God has delivered us before strengthens faith for present challenges.

Deliverance is not always immediate, but it is consistent with God's character. Recounting past deliverance reframes current struggle, reminding the heart that affliction is not the final word.

A redeemed life learns to testify not only in victory, but in remembrance. What God has done before becomes a witness to what He is able to do again.

Hope is sustained by remembering deliverance.

Key Lessons & Life Applications

- **Teaching:** God delivers the righteous.
- **Reproof:** Forgetting past deliverance weakens hope.
- **Correction:** Recount God's faithfulness intentionally.
- **Instruction:** Let testimony strengthen endurance.
- **Righteous Living:** Hope is anchored in remembrance.

Prayer Points

1. Father, thank You for past deliverance.
2. Remind me of how You have rescued me before.
3. Strengthen my hope through remembrance.
4. Help me trust You in present affliction.
5. Let testimony renew my faith.

Meditation / Reflection

What past deliverance can I recall that strengthens my faith today?

Words of Wisdom: *Remembered deliverance restores hope.*

August 11

Theme: Grief Without Shame

Anchor Scripture - "The LORD is near to those who have a broken heart, and saves such as have a contrite spirit." Psalms 34:18

Devotional Thought

Grief is not weakness—it is human response to loss, pain, and unmet expectations.
The Psalms affirm that God draws near to the brokenhearted, not away from them.
Grief does not disqualify faith. When brought before God, it becomes a place of encounter rather than isolation. Shame often accompanies grief, but Scripture removes that burden.
A redeemed life learns that God meets us in brokenness, not after it is resolved.
Healing begins when grief is acknowledged, not denied.
God is near to the brokenhearted.

Key Lessons & Life Applications

- **Teaching:** God draws near in grief.
- **Reproof:** Suppressing sorrow delays healing.
- **Correction:** Bring brokenness honestly before God.
- **Instruction:** Allow God's nearness to comfort you.
- **Righteous Living:** Vulnerability opens the door to healing.

Prayer Points

1. Father, meet me in my grief.
2. Remove shame associated with sorrow.
3. Heal my broken heart.
4. Draw near to me in this season.
5. Restore hope gently and faithfully.

Meditation / Reflection

Am I allowing myself to grieve honestly before God?

Words of Wisdom: *God is closest where hearts are broken.*

August 12

Theme: God Knows the Heart

Anchor Scripture - "O LORD, You have searched me and known me." Psalms 139:1

Devotional Thought

God's knowledge of us is intimate and complete. The Psalms reveal a God who knows not only actions, but motives, fears, and unspoken thoughts.

This knowledge is not invasive—it is compassionate. God's awareness does not expose us for condemnation, but invites us into deeper trust. We do not need to explain ourselves to a God who already understands.

A redeemed life finds comfort in being fully known. There is freedom in realizing that nothing must be hidden from God.

To be known by God is to be safe.

Key Lessons & Life Applications

- **Teaching:** God knows the heart completely.
- **Reproof:** Hiding from God breeds fear.
- **Correction:** Trust God with your inner life.
- **Instruction:** Live transparently before Him.
- **Righteous Living:** Security grows through openness.

Prayer Points

1. Father, thank You for knowing me fully.
2. Help me trust You with my inner life.
3. Remove fear of being seen.
4. Align my heart with Your truth.
5. Let Your knowledge bring comfort and peace.

Meditation / Reflection

How does knowing that God fully understands me affect my trust in Him?

Words of Wisdom: *To be fully known by God is to be fully safe.*

August 13

Theme: Repentance as Return

Anchor Scripture - "The sacrifices of God are a broken spirit, a broken and a contrite heart—These, O God, You will not despise." Psalms 51:17

Devotional Thought

Repentance in the Psalms is not punishment—it is **return**. It is the movement of the heart back toward God after distance, failure, or misalignment.

God is not impressed by performance; He responds to posture. A contrite heart signals awareness, humility, and willingness to realign. Repentance is not about rehearsing guilt—it is about restoring relationship.

A redeemed life understands that repentance is not a one-time event, but a rhythm. Whenever alignment is lost, return is possible.

God does not despise the heart that comes back.

Key Lessons & Life Applications

- **Teaching:** Repentance restores fellowship.
- **Reproof:** Pride resists return.
- **Correction:** Respond to conviction with humility.
- **Instruction:** Let repentance realign the heart.
- **Righteous Living:** Restoration begins with return.

Prayer Points

1. Father, I return my heart to You.
2. Create in me a posture of humility.
3. Heal areas of misalignment.
4. Restore fellowship where distance has formed.
5. Renew my joy in walking with You.

Meditation / Reflection

Where might God be inviting me to return rather than hide?

Words of Wisdom: *Repentance is the courage to return.*

August 14

Theme: Healing After Failure

Anchor Scripture - "He heals the brokenhearted and binds up their wounds." Psalms 147:3

Devotional Thought

Failure wounds more than reputation—it wounds identity. The Psalms reveal a God who does not abandon us after failure, but draws near to heal.

Healing is not denial of failure; it is God's response to it. Shame often keeps wounds open, but grace binds them gently. God restores not only what was broken, but also how we see ourselves afterward.

A redeemed life learns that failure is not the end of the story. God heals, restores, and strengthens those who bring their brokenness to Him.

Healing follows honesty.

Key Lessons & Life Applications

- **Teaching:** God heals after failure.
- **Reproof:** Shame delays restoration.
- **Correction:** Bring wounds to God, not away from Him.
- **Instruction:** Allow grace to restore identity.
- **Righteous Living:** Healing strengthens resilience.

Prayer Points

1. Father, heal wounds left by failure.
2. Remove shame from my heart.
3. Restore my sense of worth and identity.
4. Help me receive Your healing fully.
5. Strengthen me for the journey ahead.

Meditation / Reflection

What failure might God be inviting me to bring to Him for healing?

Words of Wisdom: *Grace heals what shame keeps open.*

August 15

Theme: The Comfort of God's Presence

Anchor Scripture - "Yea, though I walk through the valley of the shadow of death, I will fear no evil; for You are with me." Psalms 23:4

Devotional Thought

Comfort is not the absence of hardship—it is the assurance of presence. The Psalms remind us that God does not always remove the valley, but He never withdraws from it. God's presence reframes fear. Knowing He is with us steadies the heart and restores courage. Comfort flows not from explanation, but from companionship.

A redeemed life learns to rely on presence rather than certainty. God walks with us through valleys, not around them.

Presence is the deepest comfort.

Key Lessons & Life Applications

- **Teaching:** God's presence dispels fear.
- **Reproof:** Fear grows where presence is ignored.
- **Correction:** Focus on companionship, not circumstance.
- **Instruction:** Trust God's nearness through difficulty.
- **Righteous Living:** Courage grows through awareness of God.

Prayer Points

1. Father, thank You for Your presence with me.
2. Help me recognize You in difficult seasons.
3. Replace fear with confidence in You.
4. Walk with me through every valley.
5. Let Your presence comfort my soul.

Meditation / Reflection

How does knowing God is with me change how I face difficulty?

Words of Wisdom: *God's presence turns valleys into places of courage.*

August 16

Theme: Peace in Chaos

Anchor Scripture - "Be still, and know that I am God." Psalms 46:10

Devotional Thought

Peace is often sought by changing circumstances, yet Scripture teaches that peace begins with **stillness of the heart**. In the midst of chaos, God calls His people to pause—not because the storm has ended, but because He remains sovereign.

Stillness is not passivity; it is recognition. It acknowledges God's authority over what feels overwhelming. When the soul becomes still, perspective is restored and fear loosens its grip.

A redeemed life learns that peace is accessed through trust, not control. Knowing God as God stabilizes the heart when everything else feels uncertain.

Peace begins where surrender replaces striving.

Key Lessons & Life Applications

- **Teaching:** God's sovereignty anchors peace.
- **Reproof:** Striving often fuels anxiety.
- **Correction:** Choose stillness over agitation.
- **Instruction:** Rest in God's authority.
- **Righteous Living:** Surrender produces calm.

Prayer Points

1. Father, quiet my heart amid chaos.
2. Help me rest in Your sovereignty.
3. Deliver me from anxious striving.
4. Restore peace through trust in You.
5. Teach me to be still before You.

Meditation / Reflection

What chaos am I being invited to surrender to God today?

Words of Wisdom: *Stillness restores perspective.*

August 17

Theme: Confidence in God's Character

Anchor Scripture - "The LORD is good, a stronghold in the day of trouble; and He knows those who trust in Him." Psalms 9:10

Devotional Thought

Confidence grows not from circumstances, but from **knowing who God is**. The Psalms consistently anchor trust in God's character—His goodness, faithfulness, and reliability. When outcomes are unclear, character becomes the foundation of confidence. God's goodness does not fluctuate with circumstance. His strength does not diminish in trouble. A redeemed life learns to trust God not because life is predictable, but because God is consistent. Confidence rests in who He is, not in what is happening.
Trust deepens when character is known.

Key Lessons & Life Applications

- **Teaching:** Confidence is rooted in God's character.
- **Reproof:** Circumstance-based trust is fragile.
- **Correction:** Anchor faith in who God is.
- **Instruction:** Recall God's goodness intentionally.
- **Righteous Living:** Trust grows through knowing God.

Prayer Points

1. Father, deepen my confidence in who You are.
2. Help me trust Your character over my circumstances.
3. Strengthen my faith in times of uncertainty.
4. Remind me of Your goodness.
5. Establish my trust firmly in You.

Meditation / Reflection

Is my confidence rooted in God's character or in favorable outcomes?

Words of Wisdom: *Confidence grows from knowing who God is.*

August 18

Theme: Trust That Stabilizes the Soul

Anchor Scripture - "Truly my soul silently waits for God; from Him comes my salvation." Psalms 62:1

Devotional Thought

A stable soul is one that has learned to wait quietly before God. The Psalms describe a trust that calms internal unrest and anchors the heart.

Waiting silently does not mean inactivity—it reflects settled confidence. The soul rests because it knows where help comes from. Noise diminishes when trust is secure.

A redeemed life develops stability through dependence. Trust aligns the inner life, quiets anxiety, and restores balance.

Stability is the fruit of surrendered trust.

Key Lessons & Life Applications

- **Teaching:** Trust stabilizes the soul.
- **Reproof:** Restlessness reveals misplaced reliance.
- **Correction:** Return to quiet trust in God.
- **Instruction:** Wait on God with confidence.
- **Righteous Living:** Inner stability reflects trust.

Prayer Points

1. Father, quiet my soul before You.
2. Teach me to wait with confidence.
3. Remove restlessness from my heart.
4. Anchor my trust in You alone.
5. Restore stability through dependence.

Meditation / Reflection

What does my soul need to surrender to experience rest?

Words of Wisdom: *Trust quiets the soul.*

August 19

Theme: God's Nearness to the Broken

Anchor Scripture - "The LORD is near to those who have a broken heart, and saves such as have a contrite spirit." Psalms 34:18

Devotional Thought

Brokenness does not repel God—it draws Him near. The Psalms consistently reveal a God who moves toward wounded hearts, not away from them.

God's nearness is not dependent on strength or composure. He comes close to those who are honest about their fragility. Brokenness becomes a meeting place rather than a disqualifier.

A redeemed life learns that vulnerability invites presence. God saves, restores, and strengthens those who no longer pretend to be whole.

Nearness is God's response to humility.

Key Lessons & Life Applications

- **Teaching:** God draws near to the broken.
- **Reproof:** Hiding pain delays encounter.
- **Correction:** Allow brokenness to lead you to God.
- **Instruction:** Approach God honestly in weakness.
- **Righteous Living:** Humility invites divine nearness.

Prayer Points

1. Father, draw near to my broken places.
2. Help me stop hiding my pain.
3. Heal my wounded heart.
4. Restore my strength through Your presence.
5. Teach me to trust You in vulnerability.

Meditation / Reflection

What broken area of my heart needs God's nearness today?

Words of Wisdom: *God comes close where hearts are honest.*

August 20

Theme: Strength Renewed Through Praise

Anchor Scripture - "But those who wait on the LORD shall renew their strength; they shall mount up with wings like eagles." Psalms 34:1

Devotional Thought

Praise is not denial of difficulty—it is acknowledgment of God's sovereignty within it.
The Psalms teach that praise shifts focus from limitation to faithfulness.
Waiting and praising are intertwined. Praise sustains hope while strength is renewed.
It reorients the soul, lifting the heart above present strain.
A redeemed life learns to praise not only after victory, but during endurance.
Strength is renewed as the heart aligns with God's greatness.
Praise recalibrates the soul.

Key Lessons & Life Applications

- **Teaching:** Praise renews strength.
- **Reproof:** Fixating on difficulty drains energy.
- **Correction:** Redirect focus through worship.
- **Instruction:** Practice praise during waiting.
- **Righteous Living:** Alignment restores strength.

Prayer Points

1. Father, renew my strength through praise.
2. Help me worship amid difficulty.
3. Lift my focus beyond my struggles.
4. Restore endurance to my soul.
5. Let praise realign my heart.

Meditation / Reflection

How does praise shift my perspective during difficulty?

Words of Wisdom: *Praise lifts the soul above strain.*

August 21

Theme: Reframing Pain Through Worship

Anchor Scripture - "You have turned for me my mourning into dancing; You have put off my sackcloth and clothed me with gladness." Psalms 30:11

Devotional Thought

Worship does not erase pain—it **reframes it**. The Psalms show how worship shifts interpretation, allowing pain to be seen within the context of God's redemptive work.

Mourning and joy are not opposites; they are often connected through process.

Worship opens space for God to transform sorrow into strength over time.

A redeemed life learns that worship is not escape, but engagement. It allows God to reinterpret suffering and restore hope.

Pain reframed becomes testimony.

Key Lessons & Life Applications

- **Teaching:** Worship reframes suffering.
- **Reproof:** Unprocessed pain hardens the heart.
- **Correction:** Bring sorrow into worship.
- **Instruction:** Allow God to reinterpret pain.
- **Righteous Living:** Worship restores perspective.

Prayer Points

1. Father, help me bring my pain into worship.
2. Reframe my sorrow through Your presence.
3. Restore joy where mourning has lingered.
4. Heal my heart through praise.
5. Turn pain into testimony.

Meditation / Reflection

How might worship help me see my pain differently?

Words of Wisdom: *Worship transforms how pain is understood.*

August 22

Theme: Hope Anchored in God

Anchor Scripture - "Why are you cast down, O my soul? And why are you disquieted within me? Hope in God, for I shall yet praise Him." Psalms 42:11

Devotional Thought

Hope in the Psalms is not optimism—it is **anchorage**. The psalmist speaks directly to the soul, recognizing inner unrest while deliberately choosing hope in God.

Being cast down does not cancel faith. It reveals the need to re-anchor the heart. Hope steadies the soul when emotions fluctuate and circumstances remain unresolved.

A redeemed life learns to address inner turmoil with truth. Hope becomes an intentional posture, not a passive feeling. When anchored in God, the soul regains stability.

Hope restores balance to a weary heart.

Key Lessons & Life Applications

- **Teaching:** Hope stabilizes the soul.
- **Reproof:** Unchecked discouragement deepens unrest.
- **Correction:** Re-anchor hope in God.
- **Instruction:** Speak truth to the soul intentionally.
- **Righteous Living:** Hope sustains endurance.

Prayer Points

1. Father, anchor my hope in You.
2. Help me speak truth to my soul.
3. Restore balance where discouragement lingers.
4. Strengthen my heart through hope.
5. Renew my confidence in You.

Meditation / Reflection

Where does my soul need to be re-anchored in hope?

Words of Wisdom: *Hope steadies what discouragement unsettles.*

August 23

Theme: Gratitude as Healing

Anchor Scripture - "Oh, give thanks to the LORD, for He is good! For His mercy endures forever." Psalms 107:1

Devotional Thought

Gratitude is more than expression—it is **restorative**. The Psalms reveal thanksgiving as a pathway that redirects focus from loss to mercy.

Gratitude does not deny pain; it reframes perspective. It acknowledges God's goodness even when circumstances remain imperfect. This shift softens the heart and opens space for healing.

A redeemed life learns to practice gratitude intentionally. As thanksgiving grows, bitterness loosens and hope strengthens.

Gratitude heals by restoring perspective.

Key Lessons & Life Applications

- **Teaching:** Gratitude restores perspective.
- **Reproof:** Ingratitude sustains bitterness.
- **Correction:** Choose thanksgiving intentionally.
- **Instruction:** Practice gratitude daily.
- **Righteous Living:** Thankfulness nurtures healing.

Prayer Points

1. Father, cultivate gratitude in my heart.
2. Help me recognize Your goodness daily.
3. Heal bitterness through thanksgiving.
4. Restore joy through appreciation.
5. Let gratitude renew my perspective.

Meditation / Reflection

How does gratitude change how I see my circumstances?

Words of Wisdom: *Gratitude heals by restoring perspective.*

August 24

Theme: Resting in God's Care

Anchor Scripture - "Cast your burden on the LORD, and He shall sustain you." Psalms 55:22

Devotional Thought

Rest is not avoidance—it is **trust expressed through release**. The Psalms invite us to cast burdens onto God, recognizing His capacity to sustain what overwhelms us.

Holding burdens too long exhausts the soul. Resting in God's care requires surrender, not strength. It acknowledges that God is able to carry what we cannot.

A redeemed life learns that rest is an act of faith. Trust deepens when burdens are released intentionally.

Rest begins where trust is exercised.

Key Lessons & Life Applications

- **Teaching:** God sustains those who trust Him.
- **Reproof:** Carrying burdens alone leads to exhaustion.
- **Correction:** Release what overwhelms you to God.
- **Instruction:** Practice intentional surrender.
- **Righteous Living:** Trust restores rest.

Prayer Points

1. Father, I release my burdens to You.
2. Teach me to rest in Your care.
3. Sustain me where I feel weak.
4. Help me trust You fully.
5. Restore peace through surrender.

Meditation / Reflection

What burden do I need to release to God today?

Words of Wisdom: *Rest follows surrender.*

August 25

Theme: Praise Beyond Circumstances

Anchor Scripture - "I will bless the LORD at all times; His praise shall continually be in my mouth." Psalms 34:1

Devotional Thought

Praise that depends on circumstances is fragile. The Psalms reveal a deeper posture—praise that flows from trust in God's unchanging nature rather than temporary conditions. To bless the Lord "at all times" does not deny hardship; it refuses to let hardship define God. Praise becomes a declaration of alignment, affirming that God remains worthy regardless of season.

A redeemed life learns that praise is not reactionary—it is intentional. When praise is rooted in truth, it stabilizes the heart and restores perspective.

Praise anchors the soul above circumstance.

Key Lessons & Life Applications

- **Teaching:** Praise transcends circumstance.
- **Reproof:** Conditional praise weakens trust.
- **Correction:** Choose praise as posture, not reaction.
- **Instruction:** Cultivate continual thanksgiving.
- **Righteous Living:** Praise sustains alignment.

Prayer Points

1. Father, help me praise You in every season.
2. Guard my heart from conditional worship.
3. Align my focus with Your unchanging nature.
4. Strengthen my faith through praise.
5. Let thanksgiving shape my posture.

Meditation / Reflection

Is my praise tied to circumstances or to who God is?

Words of Wisdom: *Praise anchored in truth transcends circumstance.*

August 26

Theme: Joy as Strength

Anchor Scripture - "You have put gladness in my heart, more than in the season that their grain and wine increased." Psalms 4:7

Devotional Thought

Joy in the Psalms is not dependent on abundance—it is imparted by God. This joy strengthens the heart beyond what external success can provide.

Circumstantial happiness fluctuates, but God-given joy remains steady. It fortifies the soul, enabling endurance even when conditions are unfavorable.

A redeemed life learns that joy is not something to manufacture—it is something to receive. God places gladness within the heart as a sustaining gift.

Joy strengthens from the inside out.

Key Lessons & Life Applications

- **Teaching:** Joy is imparted by God.
- **Reproof:** External success cannot sustain inner strength.
- **Correction:** Receive joy as God's gift.
- **Instruction:** Guard joy as a source of strength.
- **Righteous Living:** Inner gladness sustains endurance.

Prayer Points

1. Father, restore joy in my heart.
2. Help me receive joy beyond circumstance.
3. Strengthen my soul through gladness.
4. Guard my heart from despair.
5. Let joy renew my strength.

Meditation / Reflection

Where might God be inviting me to receive joy rather than pursue happiness?

Words of Wisdom: *Joy given by God sustains strength*

August 27

Theme: God's Faithfulness Across Generations

Anchor Scripture - "Your faithfulness endures to all generations; You established the earth, and it abides." Psalms 119:90

Devotional Thought

The Psalms consistently place personal experience within a larger story—God's faithfulness across generations. This perspective stabilizes faith beyond individual circumstance.

God's work did not begin with us, and it will not end with us. His faithfulness spans time, holding generations together through covenant and promise.

A redeemed life gains strength by recognizing continuity. What God has sustained across generations can be trusted in the present.

Faith is steadied by remembering that God endures.

Key Lessons & Life Applications

- **Teaching:** God's faithfulness transcends generations.
- **Reproof:** Short-term thinking limits trust.
- **Correction:** View life within God's larger story.
- **Instruction:** Anchor confidence in God's enduring work.
- **Righteous Living:** Stability grows through generational perspective.

Prayer Points

1. Father, thank You for Your enduring faithfulness.
2. Help me trust You beyond my present season.
3. Anchor my life in Your eternal purposes.
4. Strengthen my faith through generational perspective.
5. Let my life reflect trust in Your continuity.

Meditation / Reflection

How does knowing God's faithfulness spans generations affect my trust today?

Words of Wisdom: *Faith is strengthened by remembering God endures.*

August 28

Theme: Worship as Alignment

Anchor Scripture - "Oh come, let us worship and bow down; let us kneel before the LORD our Maker." Psalms 95:6

Devotional Thought

Worship is not merely expression; it is alignment. To bow is to recognize rightful authority and to reorder the heart accordingly. The Psalms teach that worship realigns perspective, priorities, and posture before God.

When life disorients the soul, worship recenters it. Alignment restores clarity and steadiness. Worship is how the heart returns to its proper orientation—under God's lordship.

A redeemed life understands worship as recalibration. When alignment is restored, peace follows.

Key Lessons & Life Applications

- **Teaching:** Worship restores alignment.
- **Reproof:** Pride resists surrender.
- **Correction:** Bow the heart before God's authority.
- **Instruction:** Use worship to recalibrate perspective.
- **Righteous Living:** Alignment sustains peace.

Prayer Points

1. Father, realign my heart through worship.
2. Restore proper order within me.
3. Remove pride that resists surrender.
4. Let worship steady my soul.
5. Establish peace through alignment.

Meditation / Reflection

Where might worship realign my heart today?

Words of Wisdom: *Alignment restores clarity.*

August 29

Theme: Trusting God with the Future

Anchor Scripture - "Commit your way to the LORD, trust also in" Psalms 37:5

Devotional Thought

The future often carries uncertainty, but the Psalms invite trust that releases control.
To commit one's way is to entrust direction, timing, and outcome to God.
Trust does not require full visibility; it requires confidence in God's faithfulness.
Anxiety diminishes when the future is placed in capable hands.
A redeemed life learns to move forward without fear, knowing God governs what lies ahead.
Trust frees the heart from anxious striving.

Key Lessons & Life Applications

- **Teaching:** Trust commits the future to God.
- **Reproof:** Control fuels anxiety.
- **Correction:** Release outcomes to God's care.
- **Instruction:** Practice intentional trust.
- **Righteous Living:** Peace grows through surrender.

Prayer Points

1. Father, I commit my future to You.
2. Help me release control and fear.
3. Strengthen my trust in Your timing.
4. Guide my steps forward.
5. Let peace replace anxiety.

Meditation / Reflection

What part of my future do I need to entrust to God?

Words of Wisdom: *Trust releases the future into capable hands.*

August 30

Theme: God Reigns Despite Turmoil

Anchor Scripture - "The LORD reigns; let the earth rejoice." Psalms 97:1

Devotional Thought

Turmoil does not dethrone God. The Psalms repeatedly affirm divine reign regardless of human disorder or global unrest.

God's rule is not threatened by chaos. His authority remains intact even when circumstances feel unstable. Rejoicing becomes possible when trust rests in God's sovereignty.

A redeemed life anchors joy not in calm conditions, but in the assurance that God reigns. Stability flows from knowing who is in control.

Key Lessons & Life Applications

- **Teaching:** God reigns above turmoil.
- **Reproof:** Fear magnifies disorder.
- **Correction:** Recenter on God's sovereignty.
- **Instruction:** Let confidence replace anxiety.
- **Righteous Living:** Joy flows from trust in God's rule.

Prayer Points

1. Father, help me rest in Your reign.
2. Remove fear fueled by uncertainty.
3. Restore joy through trust in Your authority.
4. Stabilize my heart amid turmoil.
5. Let confidence replace anxiety.

Meditation / Reflection

How does recognizing God's reign change how I face uncertainty?

Words of Wisdom: *Peace follows confidence in God's reign.*

August 31

Theme: A Soul Anchored in God

Anchor Scripture - "You will keep him in perfect peace, whose mind is stayed on You, because he trusts in You." Psalms 26:3

Devotional Thought

An anchored soul is one that remains fixed on God. The Psalms teach that peace is sustained through focus and trust.

Perfect peace does not imply absence of challenge; it reflects steadiness within it. When the mind stays on God, trust stabilizes emotions and guards the heart.

A redeemed life closes the journey of Psalms grounded—not rushed, not restless, but anchored in God.

Anchoring the mind secures peace.

Key Lessons & Life Applications

- **Teaching:** Trust anchors the soul.
- **Reproof:** Distraction destabilizes peace.
- **Correction:** Refocus the mind on God.
- **Instruction:** Cultivate steady trust.
- **Righteous Living:** Peace grows through anchoring.

Prayer Points

1. Father, anchor my mind in You.
2. Guard my peace through trust.
3. Help me remain focused on You.
4. Stabilize my heart daily.
5. Let my soul rest securely in You.

Meditation / Reflection

What helps keep my mind anchored in God?

Words of Wisdom: *A soul anchored in God remains at peace.*

SEPTEMBER
LEADERSHIP &
KINGDOM PATTERNS

September 1

Theme: Authority Comes from God, Not Position

Anchor Scripture - "By Me kings reign, and rulers decree justice." Proverbs 8:15

Devotional Thought

All authority originates from God—but not all authority reflects intimacy with Him. Scripture makes this distinction clear. God grants authority to fulfill His purposes, sometimes long before personal alignment is complete.

Authority is functional before it is relational. God may authorize a person to carry a message, lead a people, or govern a system without that person yet walking in deep fellowship with Him. This does not mean God endorses their inner life—it means He is sovereign over outcomes larger than individuals.

Position amplifies authority, but it does not create it. Authority is entrusted by God for stewardship, not ownership. When leaders confuse position with source, they misuse power. When they remember that authority comes from God, they govern with humility and restraint.

Authority proves God's sovereignty; relationship reveals spiritual maturity.

Key Lessons & Life Applications

- **Teaching:** God alone is the source of legitimate authority.
- **Reproof:** Position does not equal alignment.
- **Correction:** Return authority to God's governance.
- **Instruction:** Steward influence with reverence.
- **Righteous Living:** Humility preserves authority.

Prayer Points

1. Father, align my understanding of authority with Your truth.
2. Guard my heart from pride tied to position or influence.
3. Teach me to steward authority responsibly.
4. Help me remain reverent toward You.
5. Establish authority in my life that reflects You.

Meditation / Reflection

Do I confuse authority with intimacy, or do I recognize their difference?

Words of Wisdom: *Authority reveals God's sovereignty; intimacy reveals maturity.*

September 2

Theme: Power Without Alignment Is Dangerous

Anchor Scripture - "Let him who thinks he stands take heed lest he fall." 1 Corinthians 10:12

Devotional Thought

Power does not transform character—it exposes it. When alignment is absent, power becomes a liability rather than a gift. Scripture repeatedly shows that God may empower individuals whose inner lives are still unrefined.

Power is granted for assignment, not as evidence of approval. God may empower a person to deliver, lead, or build while still intending to confront and correct their inner life. This explains why some operate in undeniable power while living in parallel to righteous alignment.

Alignment governs power. Without it, power becomes self-preserving, fear-driven, and eventually destructive. God does not fear releasing power; He guards against releasing it without restraint.

The greater the power, the greater the need for alignment.

Key Lessons & Life Applications

- **Teaching:** Power requires alignment to remain safe.
- **Reproof:** Confidence without submission invites collapse.
- **Correction:** Submit power to God's rule.
- **Instruction:** Seek alignment before expansion.
- **Righteous Living:** Restraint protects influence.

Prayer Points

1. Father, align my heart before increasing my influence.
2. Protect me from misusing power.
3. Cultivate restraint within me.
4. Teach me to value alignment over ambition.
5. Preserve me from pride.

Meditation / Reflection

What level of power am I asking God for—and am I aligned to steward it?

Words of Wisdom: *Power reveals what discipline conceals.*

September 3

Theme: The Difference Between Anointing and Approval

Anchor Scripture - "Man looks at the outward appearance, but the LORD looks at the heart." 1 Samuel 16:7

Devotional Thought

Anointing and approval are not synonymous. Anointing empowers a person for assignment; approval confirms readiness of the heart. Scripture shows that God may anoint and even approve a person for service without approving them for intimate relationship.

Some are anointed to rule, deliver, fund, or speak—but are not yet aligned relationally with God. Others carry real power while lacking instruction, depth, or obedience. This does not invalidate God's work; it reveals His sovereignty.

God spoke through Isaiah before Isaiah encountered Him. God anointed leaders who later required correction. God empowered deliverers who never sought counsel. Anointing proves God's purpose; approval confirms maturity.

Enduring authority only comes when assignment is governed by relationship.

Key Lessons & Life Applications

- **Teaching:** Anointing empowers function; approval affirms alignment.
- **Reproof:** Giftedness does not equal maturity.
- **Correction:** Allow God to deal with the heart, not just the hands.
- **Instruction:** Do not confuse usefulness with intimacy.
- **Righteous Living:** Relationship governs sustainable authority.

Prayer Points

1. Father, mature my heart beyond gifting.
2. Align my assignment with relationship.
3. Guard me from confusing anointing with approval.
4. Teach me to value intimacy with You.
5. Prepare me fully for what You entrust to me.

Meditation / Reflection

Am I more focused on being used by God—or walking with Him?

Words of Wisdom: *Anointing enables assignment; relationship sustains authority.*

September 4

Theme: Why God Tests Leaders Privately First

Anchor Scripture - "He who is faithful in what is least is faithful also in much." Luke 16:10

Devotional Thought

Before God entrusts public authority, He examines private faithfulness. Scripture shows a consistent pattern: testing precedes visibility. What is unseen reveals what can be sustained.

Private testing exposes motives, disciplines desire, and trains restraint. It is where God forms character away from applause and pressure. Leaders who fail privately may still function publicly for a season—but they will not endure.

God does not test to disqualify; He tests to prepare. Authority that bypasses private formation becomes unstable under public weight.

A redeemed understanding of leadership honors God's hidden work before visible elevation.

Key Lessons & Life Applications

- **Teaching:** God values private faithfulness.
- **Reproof:** Skipping formation weakens authority.
- **Correction:** Embrace unseen obedience.
- **Instruction:** Allow God to test motives quietly.
- **Righteous Living:** Integrity is formed in private.

Prayer Points

1. Father, refine me in unseen places.
2. Help me honor private obedience.
3. Expose motives that need correction.
4. Prepare me for responsibility with integrity.
5. Form my character beyond visibility.

Meditation / Reflection

How am I stewarding what God has entrusted to me privately?

Words of Wisdom: *What is sustained in public is first proven in private.*

September 5

Theme: Fear as a Leadership Weakness

Anchor Scripture - "The fear of man brings a snare, but whoever trusts in the LORD shall be safe." Proverbs 29:25

Devotional Thought

Fear is one of the most subtle threats to leadership. It disguises itself as caution, wisdom, or diplomacy, yet it quietly governs decisions and compromises integrity.

When leaders fear people, approval replaces obedience. Decisions become reactive rather than principled. Scripture shows that fear entangles authority and limits discernment.

Trust in God releases leaders from this snare. It anchors decisions in conviction rather than popularity. A redeemed leader learns that reverence for God must outweigh concern for opinion.

Authority governed by fear cannot remain free.

Key Lessons & Life Applications

- **Teaching:** Fear undermines authority.
- **Reproof:** People-pleasing weakens leadership.
- **Correction:** Replace fear with trust in God.
- **Instruction:** Make decisions rooted in conviction.
- **Righteous Living:** Reverence for God secures safety.

Prayer Points

1. Father, deliver me from the fear of man.
2. Strengthen my trust in You.
3. Help me lead with conviction.
4. Guard my heart from approval-seeking.
5. Anchor my decisions in reverence for You.

Meditation / Reflection

Where might fear be influencing my decisions more than trust?

Words of Wisdom: *Fear entangles authority; trust secures it.*

September 6

Theme: Obedience as the Safeguard of Power

Anchor Scripture - "To obey is better than sacrifice, and to heed than the fat of rams." 1 Samuel 15:22

Devotional Thought

Obedience is not optional for those entrusted with power—it is protective. Scripture reveals that sacrifice without obedience becomes spiritual noise. God values alignment over performance.

Power without obedience drifts into presumption. Obedience restrains ambition, preserves clarity, and keeps authority aligned with God's will. It is the guardrail that prevents power from becoming destructive.

A redeemed leader understands that obedience is not loss of freedom—it is preservation of purpose. God safeguards authority through submission.

Obedience keeps power clean.

Key Lessons & Life Applications

- **Teaching:** Obedience safeguards authority.
- **Reproof:** Performance cannot replace alignment.
- **Correction:** Submit power to God's instruction.
- **Instruction:** Choose obedience over justification.
- **Righteous Living:** Alignment preserves purpose.

Prayer Points

1. Father, align my heart fully with Your will.
2. Help me choose obedience consistently.
3. Guard me from self-justification.
4. Preserve my influence through submission.
5. Teach me to value obedience over visibility.

Meditation / Reflection

Is there an area where obedience would protect my future?

Words of Wisdom: *Obedience preserves what power exposes.*

September 7

Theme: When Leadership Becomes Self-Preservation

Anchor Scripture - "For you have rejected the word of the LORD, and the LORD has rejected you from being king." 1 Samuel 15:23

Devotional Thought

Leadership quietly shifts when preservation replaces stewardship. What begins as responsibility can slowly become self-protection—defending position, image, or control rather than serving God's purpose.

Self-preserving leaders prioritize survival over obedience. Decisions are filtered through fear of loss rather than reverence for God. Scripture reveals that this shift often happens internally long before authority is removed externally.

God does not withdraw authority suddenly; He responds to gradual misalignment. When leadership centers on self, authority begins to erode—even if the title remains.

True leadership exists to steward God's agenda, not protect personal relevance.

Key Lessons & Life Applications

- **Teaching:** Leadership is stewardship, not self-preservation.
- **Reproof:** Protecting position compromises obedience.
- **Correction:** Return leadership motives to God's purpose.
- **Instruction:** Evaluate decisions through alignment, not survival.
- **Righteous Living:** Faithfulness preserves authority.

Prayer Points

1. Father, guard my heart from self-preservation.
2. Align my leadership with Your purpose.
3. Expose motives rooted in fear.
4. Help me steward, not defend, what You've entrusted to me.
5. Preserve my authority through obedience.

Meditation / Reflection

Where might self-preservation be influencing my leadership decisions?

Words of Wisdom: *Authority erodes when leadership serves self.*

September 8

Theme: Chosen but Not Transformed

Anchor Scripture - "But the Spirit of the LORD departed from Saul." **1 Samuel 16:14**

Devotional Thought

Being chosen does not guarantee transformation. Saul was selected by God, anointed publicly, and affirmed by the people—yet his inner life remained largely untouched.

Transformation requires submission, humility, and responsiveness to God. Saul carried authority without cultivating intimacy. Over time, function replaced formation.

God may choose a person for assignment, but transformation determines longevity. When inner renewal is neglected, leadership becomes hollow and reactive.

A redeemed leader understands that selection begins a process—it does not complete it.

Key Lessons & Life Applications

- **Teaching:** Calling requires inner transformation.
- **Reproof:** Function without formation leads to decay.
- **Correction:** Invite God into inner refinement.
- **Instruction:** Prioritize heart transformation.
- **Righteous Living:** Renewal sustains authority.

Prayer Points

1. Father, transform my heart beyond my calling.
2. Guard me from functioning without renewal.
3. Teach me to welcome Your refining work.
4. Deepen my responsiveness to You.
5. Sustain my leadership through inner alignment.

Meditation / Reflection

Am I relying on my calling while neglecting transformation?

Words of Wisdom: *Calling initiates purpose; transformation sustains it.*

September 9

Theme: Insecurity Breeds Comparison

Anchor Scripture - "Saul eyed David from that day forward." 1 Samuel 18:9

Devotional Thought

Insecurity distorts perception. Instead of stewarding his role, Saul became preoccupied with comparison. David's success felt like a threat rather than confirmation of God's work.

Comparison shifts focus from assignment to competition. Insecure leaders monitor others instead of managing themselves. Authority weakens when attention is divided.

Security in God's calling frees leaders from rivalry. When identity is rooted in God, the success of others does not diminish purpose.

Comparison is not a leadership strategy—it is a symptom of insecurity.

Key Lessons & Life Applications

- **Teaching:** Insecurity fuels comparison.
- **Reproof:** Rivalry weakens leadership focus.
- **Correction:** Anchor identity in God's calling.
- **Instruction:** Celebrate rather than compete.
- **Righteous Living:** Contentment preserves peace.

Prayer Points

1. Father, free me from insecurity.
2. Help me rejoice in others' success.
3. Anchor my identity in You.
4. Guard my heart from comparison.
5. Restore focus to my assignment.

Meditation / Reflection

Where might comparison be draining my effectiveness?

Words of Wisdom: *Insecurity turns leadership into rivalry.*

September 10

Theme: Partial Obedience and Spiritual Rationalization

Anchor Scripture - "But I have obeyed the voice of the LORD." 1 Samuel 15:20

Devotional Thought

Partial obedience often hides behind spiritual language. Saul believed he had obeyed because he fulfilled part of God's instruction. What he spared, he justified.

Rationalization allows leaders to feel righteous while remaining misaligned. God, however, measures obedience by completeness, not intention.

Partial obedience reveals divided allegiance—honoring God where convenient and self where costly. Over time, this fractures authority.

A redeemed leader learns that obedience is not negotiable or selective. Alignment requires full surrender.

Key Lessons & Life Applications

- **Teaching:** Obedience must be complete.
- **Reproof:** Rationalization masks disobedience.
- **Correction:** Submit fully to God's instruction.
- **Instruction:** Examine obedience honestly.
- **Righteous Living:** Alignment requires surrender.

Prayer Points

1. Father, expose areas of partial obedience.
2. Remove rationalization from my heart.
3. Teach me to obey fully.
4. Align my will with Yours.
5. Preserve my authority through surrender.

Meditation / Reflection

Is there an area where I've justified partial obedience?

Words of Wisdom: *Partial obedience is complete misalignment.*

September 11

Theme: When Fear Replaces Reverence

Anchor Scripture - "I feared the people and obeyed their voice." 1 Samuel 15:24

Devotional Thought

Reverence anchors leadership; fear destabilizes it. Saul's confession reveals the internal shift that led to his decline—he feared people more than God.

Fear changes decision-making. Instead of asking what honors God, fearful leaders ask what will preserve approval. Over time, reverence is displaced by anxiety, and obedience becomes selective.

God does not compete with fear. When reverence is replaced, authority weakens quietly. A redeemed leader understands that leadership must flow from awe of God, not pressure from people.

Fear distorts priorities; reverence restores them.

Key Lessons & Life Applications

- **Teaching:** Reverence safeguards leadership.
- **Reproof:** Fear of people compromises obedience.
- **Correction:** Restore reverence for God.
- **Instruction:** Choose God's approval over human approval.
- **Righteous Living:** Awe of God preserves authority.

Prayer Points

1. Father, restore reverence in my heart.
2. Deliver me from fear-driven decisions.
3. Help me honor You above people.
4. Guard my leadership from pressure.
5. Anchor my obedience in awe of You.

Meditation / Reflection

Where might fear be replacing reverence in my decisions?

Words of Wisdom: *Reverence stabilizes what fear destabilizes.*

September 12

Theme: Authority Lost Before the Throne Is Removed

Anchor Scripture - "The LORD has rejected you from being king." 1 Samuel 15:26

Devotional Thought

Authority is lost internally long before position is removed externally. Saul continued to sit on the throne after God withdrew His endorsement.

This gap between position and authority is dangerous. It creates confusion, frustration, and resistance to correction. Leaders may still function publicly while lacking divine backing.

God's withdrawal is not impulsive—it is responsive. When alignment is persistently rejected, authority erodes quietly.

A redeemed leader pays attention to internal alignment, not just external validation.

Key Lessons & Life Applications

- **Teaching:** Authority depends on alignment.
- **Reproof:** Position can outlast approval.
- **Correction:** Monitor internal obedience.
- **Instruction:** Seek God's endorsement continually.
- **Righteous Living:** Alignment sustains authority.

Prayer Points

1. Father, keep my heart aligned with You.
2. Guard me from functioning without Your approval.
3. Help me recognize when correction is needed.
4. Restore sensitivity to Your guidance.
5. Preserve my authority through obedience.

Meditation / Reflection

Am I prioritizing alignment over position?

Words of Wisdom: *Authority erodes before titles disappear.*

September 13

Theme: When the Spirit Departs Quietly

Anchor Scripture - "But the Spirit of the LORD departed from Saul." 1 Samuel 16:14

Devotional Thought

The departure of the Spirit was not dramatic—it was quiet. There was no announcement, no public spectacle, just a subtle loss of sensitivity and clarity.

Spiritual departure often begins with ignored correction. When leaders resist alignment repeatedly, God withdraws His manifest presence while allowing function to continue temporarily.

This silence is merciful—it invites reflection and repentance. But when ignored, it leads to confusion and instability.

A redeemed leader learns to value sensitivity to God more than activity for God. Silence can be an invitation, not a punishment.

Key Lessons & Life Applications

- **Teaching:** God's presence requires responsiveness.
- **Reproof:** Ignoring correction dulls sensitivity.
- **Correction:** Respond promptly to God's conviction.
- **Instruction:** Guard intimacy with God.
- **Righteous Living:** Sensitivity sustains alignment.

Prayer Points

1. Father, restore sensitivity to Your Spirit.
2. Help me recognize Your promptings.
3. Remove hardness from my heart.
4. Draw me into deeper intimacy.
5. Guard my leadership through closeness with You.

Meditation / Reflection

Am I attentive to God's quiet warnings?

Words of Wisdom: *Silence often speaks before judgment does.*

September 14

Theme: Lessons from Saul: What Not to Become

Anchor Scripture - "I have sinned; yet honor me now, please, before the elders of my people." 1 Samuel 15:30

Devotional Thought

Saul's final plea reveals his deepest concern—public honor. Even after acknowledging sin, his focus remained on image rather than repentance.

Saul's story is not meant to shame, but to instruct. It warns against leadership that values appearance over alignment and survival over surrender.

God preserves this account to sharpen discernment, not to condemn. A redeemed leader learns from Saul's failures without repeating them.

Saul teaches us that leadership without humility is unsustainable.

Key Lessons & Life Applications

- **Teaching:** Leadership requires humility.
- **Reproof:** Image-driven leadership resists repentance.
- **Correction:** Value alignment over appearance.
- **Instruction:** Learn from failure without imitation.
- **Righteous Living:** Humility preserves authority.

Prayer Points

1. Father, teach me through Saul's story.
2. Guard me from image-driven leadership.
3. Cultivate humility in my heart.
4. Help me choose repentance over preservation.
5. Preserve my leadership through surrender.

Meditation / Reflection

What lesson from Saul's life should I take seriously?

Words of Wisdom: *Leadership collapses when image replaces humility.*

September 15

Theme: Anointed Before Prepared

Anchor Scripture - "Then Samuel took the horn of oil and anointed him in the midst of his brothers; and the Spirit of the LORD came upon David from that day forward." 1 Samuel 16:13

Devotional Thought

David was anointed long before he was enthroned. God marked him for kingship while he was still a shepherd, unknown and untested in public leadership. This gap between anointing and appointment was intentional.

Anointing reveals calling, but preparation determines stability. God does not rush what He intends to sustain. David's anointing announced destiny; his waiting developed capacity.

Many desire the oil but bypass the process. Yet authority that arrives without preparation collapses under pressure. God knew David would face betrayal, opposition, warfare, and responsibility for a nation. Waiting was not delay — it was divine wisdom.

A redeemed leader understands that anointing is the beginning, not the finish line.

Key Lessons & Life Applications

- **Teaching:** Anointing reveals calling, not readiness.
- **Reproof:** Rushing destiny weakens endurance.
- **Correction:** Embrace preparation before promotion.
- **Instruction:** Allow God to develop capacity privately.
- **Righteous Living:** Wisdom values process.

Prayer Points

1. Father, help me honor Your process.
2. Prepare me before promoting me.
3. Deliver me from rushing destiny.
4. Develop capacity within me.
5. Let Your timing shape my maturity.

Meditation / Reflection

Am I more focused on being anointed or being prepared?

Words of Wisdom: *Anointing announces destiny; preparation sustains it.*

September 16

Theme: Waiting as Active Formation

Anchor Scripture - "I would have lost heart, unless I had believed that I would see the goodness of the LORD in the land of the living. Wait on the LORD; be of good courage, and He shall strengthen your heart; wait, I say, on the LORD!" **Psalms 27:13–14**

Devotional Thought

Waiting is not idleness; it is formation in motion. David understood the internal strain of waiting—the temptation to lose heart when fulfillment delays. Scripture reveals that waiting requires belief, courage, and strengthened resolve.

While David waited for the throne, he was actively growing—learning leadership, navigating conflict, and developing emotional resilience. He served faithfully, fought battles, and built skill. Waiting refined his discernment and sharpened his restraint.

Active waiting trains the soul to govern power responsibly. Leaders who skip this season often lack the emotional and spiritual stability required to withstand pressure. God uses waiting to strengthen the heart so authority can be carried without collapse.

A redeemed leader understands that waiting is God's classroom—where stability is formed before responsibility is expanded.

Key Lessons & Life Applications

- **Teaching:** Waiting develops leadership capacity.
- **Reproof:** Impatience weakens inner stability.
- **Correction:** Choose courage while waiting.
- **Instruction:** Grow faithfully in the present season.
- **Righteous Living:** Faithfulness matures character.

Prayer Points

1. Father, teach me faith-filled waiting.
2. Strengthen my heart during delay.
3. Help me grow where I am planted.
4. Develop wisdom through daily obedience.
5. Prepare me to carry responsibility with stability.

Meditation / Reflection

How am I allowing waiting to strengthen my heart rather than weaken it?

Words of Wisdom: *Waiting is preparation strengthened by belief.*

September 17

Theme: Restraint Under Pressure

> **Anchor Scripture** - "The LORD forbid that I should stretch out my hand against my lord, for he is the LORD's anointed." 1 Samuel 24:6

Devotional Thought

David's restraint was not rooted in fear of Saul—it was rooted in accountability to God. David understood something many miss: **there are battles you are authorized to fight, and there are conflicts you must not touch, even when provoked.**

David could confront Goliath without hesitation because God was not a factor in Goliath's life. Goliath carried no divine assignment, no covenant, and no accountability to God. Saul, however flawed, still bore the mark of God's anointing and divine appointment. David refused to violate what God had established, even when Saul misused it.

This distinction governed David's restraint. He would not take shortcuts that violated divine order. He understood that killing Saul might remove a problem, but it would corrupt his own alignment. David trusted God to resolve what God had permitted.

Restraint is not weakness; it is discernment under pressure. A redeemed leader learns that **not every enemy is meant to be fought**, and not every injustice is meant to be answered by force. Some conflicts must be left in God's jurisdiction.

Key Lessons & Life Applications

- **Teaching:** Accountability to God governs restraint.
- **Reproof:** Reactionary responses often violate divine order.
- **Correction:** Discern who you are authorized to confront.
- **Instruction:** Leave what God established in God's hands.
- **Righteous Living:** Self-control protects alignment and authority.

Prayer Points

1. Father, teach me discernment under pressure.
2. Help me recognize when restraint is required.
3. Guard my heart from impulsive reactions.
4. Help me trust You with justice and timing.
5. Preserve my integrity through accountability to You.

Meditation / Reflection

Are there conflicts I am tempted to fight that God has not authorized me to touch?

Words of Wisdom: *Restraint is obedience when force is available but forbidden.*

September 18

Theme: Submission Without Compromise

> **Anchor Scripture -** "And David behaved wisely in all his ways, and the LORD was with him." 1 Samuel 18:14

Devotional Thought

David's submission during his waiting season was not passive endurance; it was **wisdom under pressure**. Though anointed, David remained in Saul's palace—serving as a musician and warrior—while navigating repeated attempts on his life. His submission was not to Saul's dysfunction, but to **God's order and timing**.

David understood that authority still resided with Saul, despite Saul's instability. To rebel prematurely would have violated divine order and corrupted David's own alignment. Yet David also understood that **submission without wisdom can become fatal**. He did not submit blindly. He exercised discernment—knowing when to serve, when to withdraw, and when to flee.

Submission governed by wisdom preserves alignment and life. David honored God's structure without enabling Saul's behavior. He allowed God—not pressure, ambition, or fear—to orchestrate the transition of authority.

A redeemed leader learns that submission in complex environments requires **discernment, restraint, and spiritual intelligence**, not agreement or silence.

Key Lessons & Life Applications

- **Teaching:** Wisdom governs submission under pressure.
- **Reproof:** Blind submission exposes leaders to unnecessary harm.
- **Correction:** Honor authority without absorbing dysfunction.
- **Instruction:** Let God manage transitions and timing.
- **Righteous Living:** Discernment preserves integrity and life.

Prayer Points

1. Father, grant me wisdom to navigate complex authority.
2. Guard me from rebellion disguised as frustration.
3. Help me submit without compromising alignment.
4. Teach me when to serve, when to withdraw, and when to wait.
5. Preserve my life and integrity as You order my steps.

Meditation / Reflection

Am I exercising wisdom in how I submit, or am I responding from pressure or fear?

Words of Wisdom: *Submission without wisdom can be fatal; wisdom preserves both alignment and life.*

September 19

Theme: A Teachable Heart Under Correction

Anchor Scripture - "So David said to Nathan, 'I have sinned against the LORD.'" 2 Samuel 12:13

Devotional Thought

There are moments in life when even the most aligned can stumble. This is not an excuse for indiscipline or moral failure. Scripture is clear: actions carry consequences. Yet Scripture is equally clear that **posture under correction determines whether failure becomes final or formative.**

David's failure was not minor. Under the Law of Moses, adultery and murder carried the death penalty. The gravity of his sin warranted judgment. What changed the outcome was not denial, explanation, or image management—it was David's posture when confronted. He took full responsibility: *"I have sinned against the LORD."*

David did not argue the judgment; he accepted it. Consequences remained, but restoration was not denied. Fellowship was restored even though loss followed. This distinction is critical: **repentance does not erase consequences, but it preserves relationship and future relevance.**

Leaders who resist correction harden and fracture internally. Leaders who receive correction, though wounded, are refined. A redeemed leader understands that humility under correction keeps the heart accessible to God.

Teachability does not cancel justice; it invites mercy.

Key Lessons & Life Applications

- **Teaching:** Failure does not end destiny; posture determines recovery.
- **Reproof:** Defensiveness delays restoration.
- **Correction:** Accept responsibility without justification.
- **Instruction:** Allow truth to refine, not destroy, the heart.
- **Righteous Living:** Humility preserves alignment and future usefulness.

Prayer Points

1. Father, keep my heart humble and teachable.
2. Help me receive correction without resistance.
3. Remove pride that blocks repentance.
4. Restore alignment where failure has disrupted it.
5. Preserve my future through humility and truth.

Meditation / Reflection

When correction comes, do I defend myself—or do I realign my heart?

Words of Wisdom: *Teachability does not remove consequences, but it preserves relationship and future relevance.*

September 20

Theme: Repentance as Realignment

Anchor Scripture - "Create in me a clean heart, O God, And renew a steadfast spirit within me." Psalms 51:10

Devotional Thought

Restoration is not instantaneous; it is a process—and it is the work of the Spirit.

David understood this. After his failure, he did not attempt to recover through self-effort or public performance. He returned to the secret place, where repentance became a genuine outcry rather than a superficial apology.

David knew the flesh was a liability. He understood that without the Spirit, he could not do right consistently. That is why he prayed, *"renew a right spirit within me."* This request carries weight—it acknowledges that something within him had gone wrong. Repentance, therefore, was not only about behavior; it was about internal realignment.

True repentance does not rush restoration. It allows God to cleanse the heart, recalibrate the inner life, and rebuild what failure disrupted. David did not demand reinstatement; he sought renewal. Authority could wait—alignment could not.

A redeemed leader understands that restoration flows from inner renewal, and inner renewal is the work of the Spirit, not human willpower.

Key Lessons & Life Applications

- **Teaching:** Restoration is a process governed by the Spirit.
- **Reproof:** Ignoring inner misalignment prolongs damage.
- **Correction:** Return to the secret place for genuine renewal.
- **Instruction:** Depend on the Spirit, not the flesh, to walk rightly.
- **Righteous Living:** Inner purity sustains outward authority.

Prayer Points

1. Father, create in me a clean heart.
2. Expose and correct any misalignment within me.
3. Renew a right spirit within me.
4. Help me depend on Your Spirit, not my strength.
5. Restore me according to Your process and timing.

Meditation / Reflection

Have I allowed the Spirit to address my inner life, or am I rushing restoration?

Words of Wisdom: *Restoration begins in the secret place and is sustained by the Spirit.*

September 21

Theme: Why David's Throne Endured

> **Anchor Scripture** - "David did what was right in the eyes of the LORD, and had not turned aside from anything that He commanded him all the days of his life, except in the matter of Uriah the Hittite." 1 Kings 15:5

Devotional Thought

David's throne endured not because he avoided failure, but because of the **posture of his heart before God**. Scripture does not present David as flawless; it presents him as aligned.

Several guiding principles governed David's life and leadership. He was deeply grateful—no other figure in Scripture models praise like David. He adored God openly, consistently giving Him the glory due His name. David was repentant, not defensive; compassionate, not vindictive; prayerful, not presumptuous.

He did not obsess over image or minor offenses. When Shimei cursed him publicly, David refused to retaliate, recognizing that his identity was anchored in God, not public opinion. He discerned when silence was wiser than self-defense.

Above all, David was a man of prayer. His private devotion sustained his public authority. Alignment—not perfection—stabilized his leadership. When David fell, he returned. When corrected, he submitted. When tested, he waited.

A redeemed leader learns that **endurance is sustained by consistent inner alignment**, not occasional external success. David's throne endured because God had continual access to his heart.

Key Lessons & Life Applications

- **Teaching:** Gratitude and worship anchor leadership.
- **Reproof:** Image-conscious leadership fractures under pressure.
- **Correction:** Cultivate repentance, compassion, and prayer.
- **Instruction:** Guard private devotion as fiercely as public responsibility.
- **Righteous Living:** Faithfulness preserves legacy beyond failure.

Prayer Points

1. Father, keep my heart aligned and grateful.
2. Teach me to give You the glory due Your name.
3. Help me respond with humility when corrected.
4. Deliver me from image-driven leadership.
5. Establish my life through prayer and devotion.

Meditation / Reflection

Which inner posture in David's life most needs strengthening in me right now?

Words of Wisdom: *Endurance flows from alignment, not perfection.*

September 22

Theme: Wisdom Requested, Not Power

Anchor Scripture - "Give to Your servant an understanding heart to judge Your people." 1 Kings 3:9

Devotional Thought

Solomon's beginning mirrors the experience of many leaders: when anticipation becomes reality, humility often appears. Solomon did not begin with arrogance; he began with awareness. Having grown up in the palace, he had witnessed instability firsthand—the Absalom rebellion, Adonijah's political maneuvering, and Joab's calculated disloyalty. Raised by a discerning and shrewd mother, Solomon understood that the throne was not merely a position of honor, but a place of danger.

When God invited Solomon to ask for anything, his request for wisdom was not naïve spirituality; it was informed realism. He knew he could not survive leadership without a superior level of understanding. His humility at this stage was commendable, but it was also **situational**—born out of recognition of complexity, not yet fully forged through long-term discipline.

God honors leaders who recognize the weight of responsibility before the privileges of authority. Solomon's request revealed gratitude for the opportunity and reverence for the task. Yet humility that begins as awareness must mature into character.

Wisdom is a gift, but humility is a formation. What is received must later be sustained through alignment.

A redeemed leader learns that good beginnings matter—but they must be guarded, matured, and maintained.

Key Lessons & Life Applications

- **Teaching:** Wisdom is foundational for leadership responsibility.
- **Reproof:** Awareness without sustained discipline can fade.
- **Correction:** Guard humility beyond the beginning stage.
- **Instruction:** Ask for what enables righteous governance.
- **Righteous Living:** Reverence attracts divine trust, but character sustains it.

Prayer Points

1. Father, grant me wisdom equal to my responsibility.
2. Keep my heart humble beyond my beginnings.
3. Help me steward insight with obedience.
4. Teach me to value alignment over intelligence.
5. Guard my leadership from pride as success grows.

Meditation / Reflection

Is my humility rooted in lasting character—or in present awareness of responsibility?

Words of Wisdom: *Good beginnings are gifts; sustained humility is formed.*

September 23

Theme: Wisdom Must Be Sustained

Anchor Scripture - *"And God gave Solomon wisdom and exceedingly great understanding, and largeness of heart like the sand on the seashore."* 1 Kings 4:29

Devotional Thought

God answered Solomon's request abundantly. He granted him wisdom at the **administrative and governance level**—the discernment to judge, organize, and lead a people. Solomon's wisdom became renowned, drawing kings and nations to hear him.

Yet Solomon's request was specific. He asked for wisdom to **govern the people**, not wisdom to govern himself. This is not presented to condemn Solomon, but to reveal an important leadership principle: **wisdom for function does not automatically produce wisdom for formation.**

Wisdom is not static; it must grow. Scripture tells us that Jesus *"increased in wisdom"*—revealing that wisdom is not a one-time impartation but a lifelong process. There is wisdom for doing, and there is wisdom for being. There is the **gift of wisdom** for execution, and there is the **spirit of wisdom** for living.

When wisdom is treated as possession rather than stewardship, dependence quietly fades. Leaders may continue to function brilliantly while inner governance weakens. A redeemed leader understands that **wisdom must be sustained through continued alignment, humility, and dependence on God.**

Initial grace opens doors; sustained wisdom keeps the heart aligned.

Key Lessons & Life Applications

- **Teaching:** Wisdom must be stewarded, not assumed.
- **Reproof:** Functional wisdom without self-governance creates vulnerability.
- **Correction:** Grow wisdom beyond administration into character.
- **Instruction:** Remain dependent on God as wisdom increases.
- **Righteous Living:** Alignment sustains what gifting initiates.

Prayer Points

1. Father, help me steward wisdom with humility.
2. Grow wisdom in me—not only for leadership, but for living.
3. Guard me from self-sufficiency.
4. Teach me to govern myself before governing others.
5. Sustain what You have entrusted to me.

Meditation / Reflection

Am I growing in wisdom for who I am becoming, not just for what I am doing?

Words of Wisdom: *Wisdom received must be sustained; wisdom grown must be guarded.*

September 24

Theme: Expansion Without Inner Governance

> **Anchor Scripture** - "So Solomon ruled over all the kingdoms... and they brought tribute and served Solomon." 1 Kings 4:21

Devotional Thought

Solomon's reign was marked by unprecedented expansion. Wealth increased, influence multiplied, and peace surrounded his kingdom. Yet Scripture quietly reveals a dangerous contrast: **public success coexisted with private vulnerability.**

The missing link was the **law of process**—the disciplined journey of becoming. Like Saul before him, Solomon ascended quickly without enduring the refining pain that builds inner governance. Discipline was not cultivated through waiting, resistance, or prolonged dependence. As a result, compromise became easier because the muscles of restraint were underdeveloped.

David's advantage was not perfection, but process. Waiting forged restraint. Failure produced repentance. Discipline was learned through pain. Solomon, by contrast, inherited glory without the same formation. Even with strategic insight—shaped by palace exposure and a brilliant mother—he lacked the internal structure to carry the weight of expansion sustainably.

Gifts are good, but gifts without process create vulnerability. Expansion magnifies what discipline sustains—or exposes what it never formed. A redeemed leader understands that **growth without inner governance eventually collapses under its own weight**.

Key Lessons & Life Applications

- **Teaching:** Expansion intensifies responsibility.
- **Reproof:** Public success can conceal private weakness.
- **Correction:** Submit to the process of inner formation.
- **Instruction:** Cultivate discipline before influence multiplies.
- **Righteous Living:** Process refines what gifting initiates.

Prayer Points

1. Father, establish inner governance before outward expansion.
2. Deliver me from shortcuts that bypass formation.
3. Strengthen my discipline as You increase my influence.
4. Expose areas where process is lacking.
5. Help me grow in character, not just capacity.

Meditation / Reflection

Have I allowed the process of becoming to shape me as much as success has elevated me?

Words of Wisdom: *Gifting opens doors, but process builds the structure that keeps them open.*

September 25

Theme: Compromise Begins Quietly

Anchor Scripture - "But King Solomon loved many foreign women... and his wives turned away his heart." 1 Kings 11:1–3

Devotional Thought

Solomon's decline did not begin with rebellion; it began with **untamed appetite and tolerated compromise**. What appeared to be political diplomacy—marriages that secured alliances with surrounding nations—slowly became spiritual entanglements that eroded his devotion to God.

Wisdom cannot replace obedience, and diplomacy cannot override divine boundaries. The instruction God gave through Moses did not exempt kings. Solomon's predicament was real: success attracts both good and bad influences. Yet boundaries were not established in advance, and appetite was not restrained early.

Compromise rarely announces itself loudly. It enters quietly through rationalization: *"This is necessary," "This is strategic," "I can handle this."* Applause can create a false sense of immunity, making leaders believe they are beyond vulnerability. Over time, association begins to shape affection, and affection reshapes allegiance.

Solomon's later reflections—captured in Proverbs and Ecclesiastes—reveal deep regret. He documented what wisdom alone could not prevent: **association eventually determines personality**, and untamed appetite will always seek mastery.

A redeemed leader understands that boundaries must be set **before** success tests them. Appetite not governed will eventually govern the leader.

Key Lessons & Life Applications

- **Teaching:** Compromise erodes alignment gradually.
- **Reproof:** Success does not exempt leaders from discipline.
- **Correction:** Establish boundaries before pressure increases.
- **Instruction:** Guard associations and affections carefully.
- **Righteous Living:** Undivided loyalty preserves authority.

Prayer Points

1. Father, help me govern my appetites.
2. Expose subtle compromises before they grow.
3. Teach me to set boundaries ahead of success.
4. Guard my heart from rationalization.
5. Keep my devotion to You undivided.

Meditation / Reflection

Are there associations or appetites quietly shaping my loyalty?

Words of Wisdom: *Untamed appetite will eventually tame the one who feeds it.*

September 26

Theme: Wisdom Without Obedience Is Insufficient

Anchor Scripture - "For Solomon went after other gods." 1 Kings 11:5

Devotional Thought

Solomon's tragedy was not ignorance; it was **progressive disobedience**. He was surrounded by continual negative influence, and compromise gradually shifted into participation. What began as tolerance—allowing foreign wives to retain their gods—eventually became personal involvement in idolatry.

This decline did not happen suddenly. It followed an *"it doesn't matter"* mindset—small concessions justified by wisdom, success, and experience. Over time, repeated exposure weakened conviction. Association reshaped affection, and affection redirected allegiance.

Wisdom alone could not restrain Solomon because **obedience was no longer governing wisdom**. Knowledge did not replace submission. Insight did not override covenant. Solomon knew truth, yet failed to walk in it consistently.

Disobedience hardens incrementally. The danger is not the first compromise, but the gradual dulling of conscience that follows. Eventually, alignment erodes to the point where repentance becomes unlikely—not because mercy is unavailable, but because sensitivity has been lost.

A redeemed leader learns that **obedience preserves what wisdom reveals**, and without it, even great wisdom becomes powerless.

Key Lessons & Life Applications

- **Teaching:** Obedience anchors wisdom.
- **Reproof:** Tolerance of compromise leads to participation.
- **Correction:** Guard conviction before conscience dulls.
- **Instruction:** Align understanding with consistent obedience.
- **Righteous Living:** Faithfulness sustains authority and clarity.

Prayer Points

1. Father, align my actions with the truth I know.
2. Guard my heart from gradual compromise.
3. Strengthen my obedience before sensitivity fades.
4. Deliver me from the "it doesn't matter" mindset.
5. Preserve my leadership through covenant faithfulness.

Meditation / Reflection

Have repeated compromises begun to dull my sensitivity to God?

Words of Wisdom: *Wisdom reveals truth; obedience keeps the heart sensitive to it.*

September 27

Theme: The Cost of Divided Loyalty

Anchor Scripture - *"Therefore the LORD said to Solomon, 'Because you have done this… I will surely tear the kingdom away from you.'"* 1 Kings 11:11

Devotional Thought

The foundation of God stands sure. Covenant does not bend to status, wisdom, or legacy. God shows no partiality, and His standards cannot be defrauded. Solomon's divided heart resulted in divided consequences—not because God was harsh, but because covenant is exact.

Solomon had wisdom, wealth, and renown, yet he lost the **presence**. Wisdom that was once celebrated gradually turned to foolishness because it was no longer anchored in obedience. He possessed many things, but he could not carry the **weight of glory**. When devotion fractured, authority weakened, and eventually, glory departed.

Judgment was delayed for David's sake, but stability was lost. Delay did not equal approval. God does not compete for the heart. When loyalty is divided, leadership becomes unstable, and influence is reduced to form without substance.

This is the sobering truth: **you can retain position and lose presence**. You can hold power and forfeit glory. A redeemed leader understands that covenant leadership demands exclusive loyalty. God entrusts glory only to those who can carry it without compromise.

Key Lessons & Life Applications

- **Teaching:** Divided loyalty weakens authority and forfeits glory.
- **Reproof:** Delay of judgment is not approval.
- **Correction:** Return to wholehearted devotion.
- **Instruction:** Guard the presence of God above success.
- **Righteous Living:** Exclusive loyalty sustains stability and glory.

Prayer Points

1. Father, restore undivided devotion in my heart.
2. Remove every competing loyalty.
3. Help me value Your presence above achievement.
4. Stabilize my leadership through covenant faithfulness.
5. Preserve what You have entrusted to me.

Meditation / Reflection

Have I prioritized success, wisdom, or influence above the presence of God?

Words of Wisdom: *It is possible to have everything and still lose the presence.*

September 28

Theme: Lessons from Solomon: Wisdom Is Not Enough

Anchor Scripture - "Let us hear the conclusion of the whole matter: Fear God and keep His commandments, For this is man's all." Ecclesiastes 12:13

Devotional Thought

Solomon ended his life with clarity that only reflection can bring. After wisdom, wealth, influence, and achievement, he arrived at a sobering conclusion: **wisdom alone is not enough**. What he lacked was the sustaining force that preserves wisdom—the **fear of God**.

The fear of God is not terror; it is conscious accountability. It is living with the awareness that every action, decision, and desire is seen and weighed by God. This was the sustaining principle in the lives of Joseph and Daniel. It governed their private choices long before public success followed.

Solomon possessed wisdom, but reverence did not consistently govern it. Without the fear of God, wisdom became detached from obedience. Choices were no longer anchored in pleasing God, but in managing success, appetite, and alliances.

At the end of his life, Solomon acknowledged what he had missed: inner governance must exceed external achievement. Legacy is not preserved by brilliance alone, but by reverence expressed through obedience.

A redeemed leader learns not only from beginnings and triumphs, but from conclusions. Solomon's final words are a gift—warning future leaders not to repeat his error.

Key Lessons & Life Applications

- **Teaching:** The fear of God anchors wisdom.
- **Reproof:** Wisdom without reverence leads to misalignment.
- **Correction:** Rebuild decisions around pleasing God.
- **Instruction:** Live with conscious accountability before God.
- **Righteous Living:** Fear of God preserves legacy.

Prayer Points

1. Father, cultivate true reverence in my heart.
2. Help me live with awareness of Your presence.
3. Anchor my choices in pleasing You.
4. Preserve my life and legacy through obedience.
5. Teach me wisdom governed by the fear of God.

Meditation / Reflection

Are my decisions guided by brilliance—or by reverence?

Words of Wisdom: *Wisdom without the fear of God cannot preserve legacy.*

September 29

Theme: Why God Removes Some Leaders and Preserves Others

> **Anchor Scripture** - "For the LORD does not see as man sees; for man looks at the outward appearance, but the LORD looks at the heart." **1 Samuel 16:7**

Devotional Thought

Leadership continuity in God's kingdom is not determined by gifting, visibility, or public success. It is determined by **character and inner alignment**. This is why some leaders are removed while others are preserved, even when both appear effective outwardly.

Saul was removed though he was anointed. David was preserved though he failed. Solomon was diminished though he was wise. These outcomes were not arbitrary. God evaluates the heart—its posture, responsiveness, and loyalty—rather than performance alone.

Removal does not always happen immediately. Sometimes God allows leaders to function for a season while internal misalignment is exposed. Preservation, likewise, is not exemption from discipline; it is the result of a heart that remains accessible to correction and repentance.

A redeemed leader understands that continuity is governed by **who you are becoming**, not merely what you are accomplishing. God preserves leaders whose hearts remain teachable, repentant, and aligned—even when imperfect.

Key Lessons & Life Applications

- **Teaching:** God evaluates leadership from the inside out.
- **Reproof:** External success can mask internal decay.
- **Correction:** Prioritize heart alignment over public approval.
- **Instruction:** Guard character as carefully as calling.
- **Righteous Living:** Integrity sustains continuity.

Prayer Points

1. Father, search my heart and align it with You.
2. Preserve me through character, not performance.
3. Remove anything in me that threatens continuity.
4. Keep my heart soft and teachable.
5. Let my leadership please You before people.

Meditation / Reflection

What inner posture might God be evaluating in me right now?

Words of Wisdom: *Continuity is sustained by character, not charisma.*

September 30

Theme: Leadership in God's Kingdom Today

Anchor Scripture - "Not by might nor by power, but by My Spirit," says the LORD of hosts. Zechariah 4:6

Devotional Thought

Leadership in God's kingdom operates by a different standard. It is not governed by ambition, dominance, or image—but by **alignment with the Spirit of God**. Authority flows from submission before it manifests as influence.

Throughout Scripture, leaders who thrived were those who allowed God to govern their inner lives. Those who collapsed often mistook momentum for approval and results for alignment. God's kingdom does not reward self-promotion; it honors obedience, humility, and dependence on the Spirit.

In today's context, this truth remains unchanged. Leadership is not validated by platforms, followings, or accomplishments, but by **spiritual alignment and integrity**. A redeemed leader learns to discern authority by fruit, posture, and faithfulness—not noise. Authority governed by alignment produces stability. Authority driven by ambition eventually fractures. God continues to entrust leadership to those who are willing to be led by Him.

Key Lessons & Life Applications

- **Teaching:** Kingdom leadership flows from spiritual alignment.
- **Reproof:** Ambition distorts authority.
- **Correction:** Submit continually to the Spirit's leading.
- **Instruction:** Evaluate leadership by fruit and faithfulness.
- **Righteous Living:** Dependence on God sustains authority.

Prayer Points

1. Father, align my leadership with Your Spirit.
2. Guard me from ambition that competes with obedience.
3. Teach me to lead from submission, not self.
4. Help me discern true authority in others.
5. Let my influence reflect Your kingdom.

Meditation / Reflection

Is my leadership driven by alignment—or ambition?

Words of Wisdom: *In God's kingdom, authority is governed by alignment, not ambition.*

OCTOBER
FAILURE & PATH RESTORATION

October 1

Theme: Failure Does Not Begin with Rebellion

Anchor Scripture: "The heart is deceitful above all things, and desperately wicked; who can know it?" Jeremiah 17:9

Devotional Thought

Failure rarely begins with defiance. More often, it begins quietly — in the heart. Long before actions drift, internal posture shifts. Assumptions form. Vigilance weakens. Self-awareness dulls.

Scripture does not accuse the heart of being occasionally misleading; it calls it deceitful. This means the heart is capable of convincing us that we are fine when we are already drifting. Many people fail not because they hate God, but because they trusted themselves without examination.

Rebellion is loud. Deception is subtle. One announces itself; the other disguises itself as normalcy. That is why God calls attention to the heart before addressing behavior. Correction begins at the root, not the symptom.

A redeemed life learns to interrogate its own motives. Alignment is not maintained by intention alone, but by continual self-examination in the presence of God.

Key Lessons & Life Applications

- **Teaching:** Failure often starts internally before it becomes visible.
- **Reproof:** Trusting your heart without examination invites deception.
- **Correction:** Allow God to search motives, not just actions.
- **Instruction:** Practice regular internal alignment with truth.
- **Righteous Living:** Honesty before God preserves stability.

Prayer Points

1. Father, search my heart and reveal hidden misalignment.
2. Guard me from self-deception.
3. Help me remain vigilant in my inner life.
4. Teach me to examine my motives honestly.
5. Keep my heart aligned with Your truth.

Meditation / Reflection

Where might I be assuming alignment without examination?

Words of Wisdom: *Failure often begins where self-examination ends.*

October 2

Theme: Indifference Is a Form of Disobedience

Anchor Scripture: "Now Eli was very old; and he heard everything his sons did to all Israel, and how they lay with the women who assembled at the door of the tabernacle of meeting." 1 Samuel 2:22

Devotional Thought

Eli's failure extended beyond parental restraint — it included a **failure of empathy**. Scripture records that he knew his sons abused vulnerable women who served at the tabernacle, yet no decisive action followed.

This was not a private family matter; it was a violation of sacred space and human dignity. Eli's silence toward the victims reveals a deeper dysfunction: when authority protects itself instead of the vulnerable, injustice is normalized.

God took notice.

Position does not immunize anyone from divine judgment. Spiritual office does not excuse moral blindness. When empathy is absent, responsibility collapses. Eli addressed his sons with mild rebuke but left the wounded unseen and unheard.

God's judgment was not sudden — it was measured. Eli was judged not for ignorance, but for **awareness without intervention** and authority without compassion.

Indifference toward suffering is not neutrality; it is participation by omission.

Key Lessons & Life Applications

- **Teaching:** God holds leaders and parents accountable for how they protect the vulnerable.
- **Reproof:** Silence in the face of abuse invites judgment.
- **Correction:** Authority must be exercised to restrain harm, not preserve comfort.
- **Instruction:** Compassion is not optional in stewardship.
- **Righteous Living:** Justice begins with empathy and action.

Prayer Points

1. Father, forgive any silence where You required action.
2. Heal those harmed by negligence and misuse of authority.
3. Remove hardness of heart toward the vulnerable.
4. Teach me to protect what You value.
5. Align my compassion with Your justice.

Meditation / Reflection

Whose pain have I noticed but not addressed?

Words of Wisdom: *Indifference to suffering invites accountability from God.*

October 3

Theme: God Judges What We Tolerate

Anchor Scripture: "Why do you kick at My sacrifice and My offering which I have commanded in My dwelling place, and honor your sons more than Me…?" 1 Samuel 2:29

Devotional Thought

God's response to Eli was direct and piercing: *You honored your sons more than Me.* This was not about favoritism alone — it was about **tolerance**.

Eli did not commit the acts his sons committed, yet God held him responsible for what he allowed to continue. Tolerated wrongdoing becomes endorsed wrongdoing in the eyes of heaven. Silence can elevate human relationships above divine instruction.

God's judgment was not emotional; it was judicial. Eli's tolerance corrupted sacred order, weakened moral boundaries, and communicated permission through inaction. What should have been corrected early was allowed to mature into systemic failure.

This reveals a sobering truth:

God does not only judge actions — He judges **priorities**.

When comfort is preserved over correction, when relationships are protected over righteousness, and when authority refuses to intervene, God intervenes Himself.

Tolerance is not mercy when it shelters injustice.

Key Lessons & Life Applications

- **Teaching:** God evaluates what we permit, not only what we do.
- **Reproof:** Protecting relationships at the expense of righteousness invites judgment.
- **Correction:** Address what is wrong before God is forced to.
- **Instruction:** Honor God above emotional ties and personal convenience.
- **Righteous Living:** Obedience requires decisive action, not passive concern.

Prayer Points

1. Father, show me where tolerance has replaced obedience.
2. Correct my priorities where relationships outweigh righteousness.
3. Give me courage to confront what dishonors You.
4. Remove fear that delays necessary action.
5. Align my responses with Your justice.

Meditation / Reflection

What am I tolerating that God has already addressed?

Words of Wisdom: *What we tolerate, God eventually judges.*

October 4

Theme: Warning Is Mercy, Not Threat

Anchor Scripture: "Behold, the days are coming that I will cut off your arm and the arm of your father's house…" 1 Samuel 2:31

Devotional Thought

Before judgment ever arrives, God sends warning. Warnings are not threats—they are invitations to course-correct. In Eli's case, God spoke plainly, naming the consequence and the cause. The problem was not lack of information; it was lack of response.

Warnings reveal God's restraint. They create space for repentance, change, and alignment. When warnings are ignored, what follows is not sudden—it is permitted. Judgment is rarely abrupt; it is usually the final stage after repeated mercy is dismissed.

This truth applies to every life. God often alerts us through conscience, Scripture, counsel, inner unrest, or repeated patterns. Ignoring these signals hardens the heart and narrows options. He speaks so that outcomes can change.

God's mercy speaks before His justice acts.

Key Lessons & Life Applications

- **Teaching:** God warns because He desires restoration.
- **Reproof:** Ignoring warnings escalates consequences.
- **Correction:** Respond quickly when God brings clarity.
- **Instruction:** Treat repeated conviction as divine mercy.
- **Righteous Living:** Sensitivity preserves outcomes.

Prayer Points

1. Father, sharpen my sensitivity to Your warnings.
2. Help me respond before consequences harden.
3. Remove complacency that delays obedience.
4. Give me courage to change course.
5. Preserve me through timely correction.

Meditation / Reflection

What warnings have I postponed responding to?

Words of Wisdom: *Warnings are mercy in advance.*

October 5

Theme: Position Does Not Cancel Responsibility

Anchor Scripture: "Those who honor Me I will honor, and those who despise Me shall be lightly esteemed." 1 Samuel 2:30

Devotional Thought

Eli's failure exposes a sobering truth: spiritual position does not exempt anyone from responsibility. Being a priest did not shield him from accountability. Being familiar with holy things did not replace obedience. Authority increases responsibility—it does not dilute it.

Eli knew what was happening. He heard the reports. He spoke mild words. But he did not act with the weight the moment required. God judged not only the sins of his sons, but Eli's indifference to them. Silence in the face of wrongdoing became participation by neglect.

This principle applies far beyond priesthood. Parenting, leadership, influence, and access all carry obligation. God does not judge us only by what we do, but by what we allow. Indifference to injustice, abuse, or disorder—especially toward the vulnerable—invites divine response.

God is not impressed by titles. He responds to honor expressed through action.

Key Lessons & Life Applications

- **Teaching:** Responsibility increases with position.
- **Reproof:** Indifference is not neutrality; it is failure to act.
- **Correction:** Address what you have authority to correct.
- **Instruction:** Let reverence shape decisive action.
- **Righteous Living:** Honor God by protecting what He values.

Prayer Points

1. Father, awaken my sense of responsibility.
2. Deliver me from passive indifference.
3. Give me courage to act when action is required.
4. Help me protect the vulnerable entrusted to my care.
5. Teach me to honor You through obedience.

Meditation / Reflection

Where might silence or inaction be costing me alignment?

Words of Wisdom: *What you honor, you prioritize.*

October 6

Theme: Conviction vs Shame

Anchor Scripture: "For godly sorrow produces repentance leading to salvation, not to be regretted; but the sorrow of the world produces death." 2 Corinthians 7:10

Devotional Thought

Conviction and shame are often confused because they feel similar—but they produce opposite results.

Shame pushes people away from God. Conviction draws people back. Shame attacks identity: *"You are wrong."*

Conviction addresses alignment: *"This is wrong."*

God does not use shame to restore people. Shame immobilizes, isolates, and drives hiding. Conviction, however, brings clarity, responsibility, and hope. It exposes error without stripping dignity.

Many people remain stuck not because they sinned, but because they responded to failure with shame instead of repentance. Shame keeps people rehearsing guilt; repentance restores movement toward God.

Godly sorrow is not emotional collapse—it is truthful alignment. It accepts responsibility without self-destruction. It allows correction without resistance. It leads to restoration because it keeps the heart open.

Failure does not end purpose—but refusing conviction does.

Key Lessons & Life Applications

- **Teaching:** Conviction leads to restoration; shame leads to withdrawal.
- **Reproof:** Shame masquerades as humility but produces stagnation.
- **Correction:** Separate behavior from identity.
- **Instruction:** Respond to failure with repentance, not self-condemnation.
- **Righteous Living:** Freedom grows where truth is received without hiding.

Prayer Points

1. Father, help me discern conviction from shame.
2. Remove false guilt that keeps me distant from You.
3. Teach me to respond rightly when corrected.
4. Restore alignment where failure disrupted it.
5. Keep my heart open to truth.

Meditation / Reflection

Do I withdraw from God after failure—or draw nearer in repentance?

Words of Wisdom: *Conviction restores alignment; shame destroys access.*

October 7

Theme: God Works Through Willing Hearts

Anchor Scripture: "But Jonah arose to flee to Tarshish from the presence of the LORD." Jonah 1:3

Devotional Thought

God initiates purpose, but He honors human participation. He works through willing hearts—not forced compliance.

Jonah heard God clearly. His struggle was not confusion; it was resistance. He did not lack direction—he lacked agreement. Rather than wrestle honestly with God, Jonah chose distance.

God does not coerce obedience. He invites alignment. While He may correct and redirect, He does not override the will. Purpose unfolds where willingness meets obedience.

Running does not cancel calling, but it delays alignment. Jonah's story reveals that resistance carries consequences—not as punishment, but as correction designed to bring the heart back into agreement.

God is patient with unwilling hearts, but progress begins when the heart consents.

Key Lessons & Life Applications

- **Teaching:** God partners with willing hearts.
- **Reproof:** Resistance delays alignment.
- **Correction:** Address internal disagreement honestly.
- **Instruction:** Consent of the heart precedes obedience of action.
- **Righteous Living:** Willingness restores forward movement.

Prayer Points

1. Father, reveal where my heart resists Your will.
2. Heal inner conflict that fuels avoidance.
3. Help me respond with willingness.
4. Align my desires with Your purposes.
5. Restore momentum where resistance caused delay.

Meditation / Reflection

Where am I hearing God clearly but struggling to agree?

Words of Wisdom: *Purpose unfolds where willingness meets obedience.*

October 8

Theme: Disobedience Has Collateral Impact

Anchor Scripture: "The LORD sent out a great wind on the sea, and there was a mighty tempest on the sea, so that the ship was about to be broken up." Jonah 1:4

Devotional Thought

Jonah's decision did not end with him. One man's resistance placed an entire ship in danger.

Disobedience is never isolated. Choices—especially unexamined ones—carry consequences that ripple outward. Jonah may not have anticipated the storm, but he became responsible for it. Innocent sailors, unfamiliar with Jonah's God, were forced into a crisis because of a decision they did not make.

One of the marks of maturity is the ability to **weigh impact**, not just intention. Jonah did not consider who would be affected if he ran. Many failures are not rooted in malice, but in thoughtlessness—acting without considering who else will bear the weight of our choices.

God allowed the storm not to destroy Jonah, but to expose the reach of misalignment. Alignment protects more than the individual; it stabilizes everyone connected to them.

Key Lessons & Life Applications

- **Teaching:** Choices affect more than the chooser.
- **Reproof:** Thoughtless disobedience destabilizes others.
- **Correction:** Take responsibility for the impact of decisions.
- **Instruction:** Factor people into obedience, not just outcomes.
- **Righteous Living:** Alignment preserves community stability.

Prayer Points

1. Father, give me wisdom to weigh consequences before I act.
2. Forgive me where my choices have affected others negatively.
3. Restore stability where my misalignment caused disruption.
4. Teach me responsibility without self-condemnation.
5. Align my decisions with Your purposes.

Meditation / Reflection

Who might be affected by my obedience—or my resistance—right now?

Words of Wisdom: *Disobedience is never private; its impact is shared.*

October 9

Theme: Surrender Reopens the Way Forward

Anchor Scripture: "So Jonah said to them, 'Pick me up and throw me into the sea; then the sea will become calm for you. For I know that this great tempest is because of me.'" Jonah 1:12

Devotional Thought

Jonah's turning point did not begin with prayer—it began with ownership.

He did not blame the sailors' skill, the weather, or circumstance. He acknowledged responsibility. Surrender followed recognition. Only then did the storm lose its power.

Surrender is often misunderstood as defeat, but it is actually clarity restored. Jonah did not surrender to despair; he surrendered to truth. He accepted the consequences of resistance without self-pity or accusation.

Many storms persist because responsibility is avoided. Alignment returns when surrender replaces self-defense. God does not calm storms we refuse to confront.

Forward movement often begins the moment we stop explaining and start yielding.

Key Lessons & Life Applications

- **Teaching:** Ownership restores clarity.
- **Reproof:** Deflection prolongs instability.
- **Correction:** Accept responsibility without self-destruction.
- **Instruction:** Yield honestly to God's corrective process.
- **Righteous Living:** Humility restores direction.

Prayer Points

1. Father, help me own my choices truthfully.
2. Remove the need to blame others or circumstances.
3. Teach me surrender without despair.
4. Restore calm where resistance caused turmoil.
5. Realign my heart with Your will.

Meditation / Reflection

What storm may be waiting for surrender rather than explanation?

Words of Wisdom: *Surrender restores clarity and reopens the way forward.*

October 10

Theme: Fear Distorts Judgment

Anchor Scripture: "Should you help the wicked and love those who hate the LORD? Therefore the wrath of the LORD is upon you." 2 Chronicles 19:2

Devotional Thought

Fear has a subtle way of reshaping judgment.

Jehoshaphat was not evil. He loved God, sought counsel, and desired peace. Yet fear—fear of isolation, fear of conflict, fear of political vulnerability—led him into alliance with Ahab. What looked like diplomacy was actually compromise born from insecurity.

Fear often disguises itself as wisdom. It convinces us that proximity will bring protection, that agreement will preserve peace, and that silence will avoid trouble. But fear clouds discernment. It lowers standards while calling it strategy.

Jehoshaphat's mistake was not ignorance of God, but misplaced trust. When fear replaces conviction, judgment becomes negotiable. God's rebuke was not about hatred toward people, but about allegiance toward values that oppose Him.

Fear-driven decisions may feel safe in the moment, but they distort clarity and invite consequences that wisdom would have avoided.

Key Lessons & Life Applications

- **Teaching:** Fear reshapes judgment and weakens discernment.
- **Reproof:** Peace pursued through compromise invites instability.
- **Correction:** Identify fear-based motivations behind decisions.
- **Instruction:** Let conviction—not fear—guide alignment.
- **Righteous Living:** Courage preserves clarity.

Prayer Points

1. Father, expose fear that distorts my judgment.
2. Help me recognize decisions rooted in insecurity.
3. Restore clarity where fear has blurred conviction.
4. Teach me to trust You over human alliances.
5. Align my choices with truth, not pressure.

Meditation / Reflection

What decision might I be justifying out of fear rather than conviction?

Words of Wisdom: *Fear negotiates truth; conviction preserves it.*

October 11

Theme: Wrong Alliances Produce Shared Consequences

> **Anchor Scripture:** "Because you have joined with Ahaziah, the LORD has destroyed your works. And the ships were wrecked, so that they were not able to go to Tarshish." 2 Chronicles 20:37

Devotional Thought

Alliances multiply outcomes—good or bad.

Jehoshaphat aligned himself with Ahaziah for economic and strategic advantage. The plan appeared sound, the venture legitimate, and the intent practical. Yet God disrupted the project entirely. The issue was not the ships, the trade route, or the goal—it was the partnership.

Scripture is clear: *"Because you have joined…"* the work was destroyed. Misalignment can invalidate effort.

This passage reveals that God does not merely evaluate intentions; He examines alignments. When relationships are formed without discernment, consequences become shared. Jehoshaphat did not initiate Ahaziah's corruption, but by joining himself to it, he inherited its outcome.

Some losses are not failures—they are interventions. God wrecked the ships to prevent deeper entanglement. Progress stopped because protection was activated.

Wisdom does not ask only *"Will this work?"* It asks *"Is this aligned?"*

Key Lessons & Life Applications

- **Teaching:** Alignment determines the outcome of shared efforts.
- **Reproof:** Good intentions cannot redeem bad alignments.
- **Correction:** Disengage from partnerships that compromise direction.
- **Instruction:** Evaluate connections by values, not opportunity.
- **Righteous Living:** Discernment preserves future stability.

Prayer Points

1. Father, expose alliances that compromise alignment.
2. Give me courage to disengage where necessary.
3. Protect me from shared consequences of misalignment.
4. Restore losses caused by ungodly partnerships.
5. Align my connections with Your will.

Meditation / Reflection

Are there partnerships in my life producing resistance instead of progress?

Words of Wisdom: *Alignment determines outcome—partnership multiplies it.*

October 12

Theme: Compromise Is Often Disguised as Peace

Anchor Scripture: "Jehoshaphat made peace with the king of Israel." 2 Chronicles 18:1

Devotional Thought

Not every peace agreement produces peace.

Jehoshaphat's decision to align with the king of Israel appeared reasonable on the surface. Peace reduced tension, preserved relationships, and avoided confrontation. Yet beneath the appearance of harmony was compromise.

Compromise often enters quietly. It rarely announces itself as rebellion. Instead, it presents itself as maturity, tolerance, diplomacy, or wisdom. But peace that requires silence about truth is not peace—it is postponement.

Jehoshaphat's peace treaty blurred boundaries that God had already established. What seemed like reconciliation became entanglement. The desire to avoid conflict weakened discernment, and alignment was sacrificed on the altar of comfort.

True peace does not demand the surrender of conviction. God's peace preserves clarity even when it creates tension. When peace costs alignment, it is no longer peace—it is compromise.

Key Lessons & Life Applications

- **Teaching:** Not all peace reflects God's will.
- **Reproof:** Avoiding conflict can weaken conviction.
- **Correction:** Re-establish boundaries where compromise entered.
- **Instruction:** Choose alignment over artificial harmony.
- **Righteous Living:** Truth sustains lasting peace.

Prayer Points

1. Father, reveal peace built on compromise.
2. Restore clarity where boundaries were blurred.
3. Give me courage to uphold truth with humility.
4. Teach me to discern between peace and appeasement.
5. Align my relationships with Your standards.

Meditation / Reflection

Where might I be preserving peace at the expense **my connection with God**??

Words of Wisdom: *Peace that costs fellowship with God is costly—and deadly.*

October 13

Theme: Power Reveals What Was Already Within

Anchor Scripture: "Then he turned back, looked at them, and pronounced a curse on them in the name of the LORD." 2 Kings 2:24

Devotional Thought

Elisha had just received the mantle. The transition was complete. Power had shifted. Almost immediately, he was mocked—*not threatened, not attacked, but ridiculed.* The response was swift and severe. What followed was not a test of prophetic authority, but a revelation of **how power exposes the inner life**.

Power does not create character; it **reveals it**. The authority Elisha carried amplified his response. What might once have been ignored now produced consequences.

This moment forces an uncomfortable truth: **being empowered does not automatically mean being restrained**. God can entrust authority, yet still expect growth in judgment, mercy, and discernment.

This passage is not permission for excess—it is a warning. Power magnifies posture. What we carry inside determines how we wield what God places on us.

Key Lessons & Life Applications

- **Teaching:** Power reveals what already exists in the heart.
- **Reproof:** Unchecked reactions become dangerous when empowered.
- **Correction:** Authority requires maturity to govern response.
- **Instruction:** Learn restraint as influence increases.
- **Righteous Living:** Strength must be guided by wisdom.

Prayer Points

1. Father, refine my heart before increasing my influence.
2. Expose reactions that need restraint.
3. Teach me to govern power with wisdom.
4. Remove pride that seeks immediate retaliation.
5. Align my authority with Your nature.

Meditation / Reflection

How do I respond when I am mocked, challenged, or disrespected?

Words of Wisdom: *Power amplifies character—it does not replace it.*

October 14

Theme: Restraint Is Greater Than Retaliation

Anchor Scripture: "You do not know what manner of spirit you are of." Luke 9:55

Devotional Thought

Jesus' disciples wanted to call down fire. They had precedent. They had Scripture. They had passion.

What they lacked was **discernment**.

Jesus did not deny power—He corrected posture. The issue was not ability, but *spirit*. Authority without restraint becomes destructive. Passion without alignment becomes harmful.

This moment reframes the Elisha narrative through the lens of Christ. What was once permitted under earlier dispensations was now reinterpreted through maturity. Jesus revealed that **the highest expression of power is restraint**.

Not every offense requires response. Not every provocation demands judgment. The ability to restrain action is often the truest sign of spiritual growth.

Key Lessons & Life Applications

- **Teaching:** Restraint reflects spiritual maturity.
- **Reproof:** Passion without discernment misuses authority.
- **Correction:** Evaluate spirit before exercising power.
- **Instruction:** Choose mercy over reaction.
- **Righteous Living:** Self-control preserves fellowship with God.

Prayer Points

1. Father, teach me restraint when provoked.
2. Help me discern the spirit behind my reactions.
3. Remove zeal that lacks wisdom.
4. Align my responses with Your heart.
5. Let maturity govern my strength.

Meditation / Reflection

Do I act from power—or from discernment?

Words of Wisdom: *The greatest strength is the power you choose not to use.*

October 15

Theme: Recognizing Limits Is Wisdom, Not Weakness

Anchor Scripture: "If you will go with me, then I will go; but if you will not go with me, I will not go." Judges 4:8

Devotional Thought

Barak's response has often been misunderstood as fear, but Scripture reveals something deeper—**self-awareness**. He recognized the weight of the assignment and refused to carry it alone. Rather than pretending strength he did not possess, he chose collaboration. God does not measure faith by isolation. Acknowledging limits is not failure; ignoring them is. Barak's willingness to seek support preserved the mission, even though it altered how honor was distributed.

This passage challenges the lie that strength means independence. Wisdom discerns capacity. Humility invites help. God works effectively through those who know where they end and where partnership must begin.

Key Lessons & Life Applications

- **Teaching:** Recognizing limits is an act of wisdom.
- **Reproof:** Pride often disguises itself as self-reliance.
- **Correction:** Admit where help is needed.
- **Instruction:** Choose collaboration over isolation.
- **Righteous Living:** Humility preserves effectiveness.

Prayer Points

1. Father, give me clarity about my limits.
2. Remove pride that resists help.
3. Teach me wisdom in self-assessment.
4. Align me with the right support.
5. Preserve me through humility.

Meditation / Reflection

Where might admitting a limitation actually protect the assignment?

Words of Wisdom: *Wisdom knows when strength requires partnership.*

October 16

Theme: Collaboration Does Not Diminish Calling

Anchor Scripture: "Has not the LORD God of Israel commanded…?" Judges 4:6

Devotional Thought

Deborah affirmed Barak's calling without replacing it. She did not compete for position; she supplied clarity. Collaboration did not diminish Barak's assignment—it stabilized it. God often confirms calling through community. Independence is not proof of maturity. In fact, many failures occur not because God was absent, but because help was refused. Collaboration multiplies strength. It balances perspective. It introduces accountability. When God assigns a task, He often provides people—not just instruction—to carry it out. Calling is not threatened by partnership. It is protected by it.

Key Lessons & Life Applications

- **Teaching:** God affirms calling through others.
- **Reproof:** Isolation weakens execution.
- **Correction:** Welcome reinforcement, not replacement.
- **Instruction:** Value shared discernment.
- **Righteous Living:** Cooperation strengthens obedience.

Prayer Points

1. Father, help me recognize support as provision.
2. Remove fear of collaboration.
3. Teach me to honor shared insight.
4. Strengthen my ability to work with others.
5. Align my calling with community.

Meditation / Reflection

Do I see collaboration as threat—or as provision?

Words of Wisdom: *Calling is not diminished by support—it is strengthened by it.*

October 17

Theme: Refusing Help Can Delay Victory

Anchor Scripture: "Woe to him who is alone when he falls." Ecclesiastes 4:10

Devotional Thought

Scripture is direct: isolation increases vulnerability. Strength is not proven by standing alone; it is sustained by support.

Many collapses are not caused by lack of ability, but by refusal of help. When assistance is rejected, recovery becomes harder and falls become deeper.

God designed humanity to function communally. Ignoring this design introduces unnecessary risk. Help does not weaken faith—it reinforces stability.

Victory delayed is often the result of pride disguised as independence.

Key Lessons & Life Applications

- **Teaching:** Support preserves momentum.
- **Reproof:** Isolation invites unnecessary failure.
- **Correction:** Reconnect where independence has isolated you.
- **Instruction:** Build systems of support.
- **Righteous Living:** Community strengthens endurance.

Prayer Points

1. Father, expose areas where I have isolated myself.
2. Heal pride that resists help.
3. Restore supportive relationships.
4. Teach me interdependence.
5. Preserve my stability through connection.

Meditation / Reflection

Where might refusing help be slowing progress?

Words of Wisdom: *Isolation delays victory; community sustains it.*

October 18

Theme: Confidence Without Wisdom Becomes Presumption

Anchor Scriptures: "Let another man praise you, and not your own mouth; a stranger, and not your own lips." Proverbs 27:2

"If I bear witness of Myself, My witness is not true." John 5:31

Devotional Thought

Confidence is valuable—but when it is no longer governed by wisdom, it quietly becomes presumption.

We live in a world saturated with self-help language and do-it-yourself confidence. Self-belief is celebrated, self-affirmation is normalized, and independence is often treated as maturity. Yet Scripture draws a necessary distinction: **confidence is not the same as wisdom, and self-validation is not the same as truth**.

Presumption assumes capacity without assessment. It moves ahead without counsel, correction, or confirmation. What begins as healthy confidence can harden into self-trust that no longer checks alignment.

Jesus made a striking statement: *"If I bear witness of Myself, My witness is not true."* This was not insecurity—it was integrity. Even the Son of God refused self-validation.

He submitted His authority to truth beyond Himself.

Scripture consistently warns against self-affirmation not because confidence is wrong, but because **unchecked confidence blinds discernment**. When a person begins to validate themselves, wisdom is often sidelined. Momentum is mistaken for approval. Activity is mistaken for alignment.

Biblical wisdom does not dismantle confidence—it **reorders it**. Confidence is meant to flow from alignment, accountability, and truth, not from self-assertion.

Key Lessons & Life Applications

- **Teaching:** Confidence must be governed by wisdom and truth.
- **Reproof:** Self-validation replaces accountability.
- **Correction:** Submit strength to external truth and godly counsel.
- **Instruction:** Let alignment, not affirmation, define progress.
- **Righteous Living:** Humility preserves discernment.

Prayer Points

1. Father, guard my heart from self-validation.
2. Teach me to welcome correction and truth.
3. Expose presumption disguised as confidence.
4. Restore humility where strength has grown unchecked.
5. Align my confidence with wisdom.

Meditation / Reflection

Where might I be affirming myself instead of submitting to truth?

Words of Wisdom: *In a culture obsessed with self-confidence, wisdom still requires submission to truth.*

October 19

Theme: Misjudging Capacity Produces Collapse

Anchor Scripture: "Both you and these people who are with you will surely wear yourselves out. For this thing is too much for you; you are not able to perform it by yourself." Exodus 18:18

Devotional Thought

One of the quiet dangers of confidence is **overestimating capacity**.

Scripture does not condemn strength, ability, or responsibility—but it consistently warns against carrying more than one is designed to bear. Misjudging capacity is not always pride; sometimes it is pressure, urgency, or the fear of letting go.

Moses was not rebuked for loving the people or wanting to help. His failure was structural, not moral. He assumed responsibility without limits, and exhaustion became inevitable. What God called him to lead, he was never meant to carry alone.

Capacity is not only spiritual—it is emotional, physical, relational, and mental. When limits are ignored, even good intentions become destructive. Many breakdowns do not happen because people are unwilling, but because they are **overextended without discernment**.

God often sends wisdom before collapse, not after. Jethro's counsel was not a demotion—it was preservation. Delegation did not weaken Moses' authority; it protected his longevity.

Ignoring limits does not make one faithful—it makes one vulnerable.

Key Lessons & Life Applications

- Teaching: Capacity must be acknowledged and stewarded.
- Reproof: Doing everything yourself invites exhaustion.
- Correction: Build structures that support sustainability.
- Instruction: Learn to release responsibility without guilt.
- Righteous Living: Wisdom preserves strength over time.

Prayer Points

1. Father, help me recognize my limits honestly.
2. Deliver me from carrying what You did not assign.
3. Teach me to release control without fear.
4. Restore balance where I am stretched too thin.
5. Preserve my strength for long obedience.

Meditation / Reflection

Where might I be confusing responsibility with overreach?

Words of Wisdom: *Strength without structure eventually becomes strain.*

October 20

Theme: Restoration Sometimes Requires Transition

Anchor Scripture: "So Moses heeded the voice of his father-in-law and did all that he had said." Exodus 18:24

Devotional Thought

Restoration does not always mean returning to the same structure. Sometimes, it requires **change**.

Moses did not lose his calling—he adjusted his approach. Listening to Jethro required humility, not repentance. It demanded the willingness to acknowledge that what once worked could no longer sustain what was growing.

Transition is often resisted because it feels like loss. Yet in God's economy, transition is frequently the means of preservation. Refusing to adapt can quietly sabotage what obedience built.

Many people remain exhausted not because God has abandoned them, but because they are trying to sustain a season that has outgrown its original framework. Growth demands reorganization. Expansion requires redistribution.

Moses' authority was not diminished by delegation—it was strengthened. By releasing control, he preserved clarity, endurance, and focus. Restoration came not through effort, but through **alignment with wisdom**.

God restores by rearranging, not by reinforcing strain.

Key Lessons & Life Applications

- **Teaching:** Restoration may involve structural change.
- **Reproof:** Resisting transition prolongs exhaustion.
- **Correction:** Listen when God sends wise counsel.
- **Instruction:** Adjust systems as seasons shift.
- **Righteous Living:** Humility preserves longevity.

Prayer Points

1. Father, give me grace to embrace necessary change.
2. Remove fear that resists transition.
3. Help me discern what must shift in this season.
4. Teach me to listen without defensiveness.
5. Restore sustainability to my life and assignments.

Meditation / Reflection

What structure in my life may need to change for restoration to occur?

Words of Wisdom: *Restoration is not always about returning—it is often about rearranging.*

October 21

Theme: Sustainability Is a Spiritual Responsibility

Anchor Scripture: "You will surely wear out, both you and these people who are with you; for this thing is too much for you; you are not able to perform it by yourself." Exodus 18:18

Devotional Thought

God is not glorified by burnout. Exhaustion is not proof of faithfulness; it is often evidence of imbalance.

Jethro identified what Moses could not see clearly from within the pressure—what he was carrying was unsustainable. Not sinful. Not rebellious. Just too heavy for one person to bear long-term.

Sustainability is not optional in God's design. When responsibility exceeds capacity, something eventually breaks—health, clarity, relationships, or judgment. God intervenated early, not as rebuke, but as preservation.

Many failures occur not because people stopped loving God, but because they refused to adjust how they served Him. Carrying everything alone may feel noble, but it quietly violates God's design for shared responsibility.

God does not ask one person to be everything. Longevity requires structure. Wisdom requires delegation. Faithfulness requires limits.

Ignoring sustainability is not spiritual strength—it is spiritual negligence.

Key Lessons & Life Applications

- **Teaching:** God values endurance, not exhaustion.
- **Reproof:** Overextension weakens judgment.
- **Correction:** Redesign what drains life excessively.
- **Instruction:** Share responsibility wisely.
- **Righteous Living:** Steward strength with humility.

Prayer Points

1. Father, show me where I am overextended.
2. Help me release what I was never meant to carry alone.
3. Teach me sustainable obedience.
4. Remove guilt associated with setting limits.
5. Restore balance where strain has accumulated.

Meditation / Reflection

Where might sustainability be God's invitation to obedience—not compromise?

Words of Wisdom: *What God assigns, He also designs to be sustainable.*

October 22

Theme: Success Can Mask Weakness

Anchor Scripture: "As long as he sought the LORD, God made him prosper." 2 Chronicles 26:5

Devotional Thought

Prosperity can conceal weakness long before it reveals it.

Uzziah's success was real. His achievements were visible, measurable, and undeniable. Scripture is clear that his prosperity flowed from one source—**he sought the LORD**. Yet the very success God enabled became the environment where hidden vulnerabilities went unnoticed.

Success has a numbing effect. It quiets self-examination and creates the illusion that everything is well simply because outcomes are favorable. When progress is steady and results are positive, weaknesses often remain unaddressed—not because they are absent, but because they are unnecessary for the moment.

God's help does not eliminate the need for vigilance. Prosperity tests the inner life differently than adversity. Where hardship exposes dependence, success tests restraint, humility, and continued reverence.

Weakness masked by success is dangerous because it feels like strength. A season of visible growth can quietly become a season of internal neglect if seeking God is replaced by relying on momentum.

The lesson is not that success is wrong—it is that success must never become the measure of health.

Key Lessons & Life Applications

- **Teaching:** Prosperity flows from seeking God, not self-sufficiency.
- **Reproof:** Success can dull spiritual awareness.
- **Correction:** Examine foundations even when outcomes are favorable.
- **Instruction:** Continue seeking God beyond breakthrough.
- **Righteous Living:** Sustained reverence preserves integrity.

Prayer Points

1. Father, keep my heart anchored to You in seasons of success.
2. Expose any weakness hidden by progress.
3. Guard me from relying on momentum instead of obedience.
4. Help me seek You continually, not selectively.
5. Preserve my humility as You prosper my efforts.

Meditation / Reflection

What areas of my life feel "fine" simply because things are working?

Words of Wisdom: *Success reveals outcomes; it does not guarantee alignment.*

October 23

Theme: Strength Can Breed Presumption

Anchor Scripture: "But when he was strong, his heart was lifted up, to his destruction." 2 Chronicles 26:16

Devotional Thought

Strength becomes dangerous when it lifts the heart beyond its boundaries.

Uzziah did not fall in weakness; he fell in strength. The very capacity that enabled him to achieve also became the platform for presumption. His heart was "lifted up"—not with gratitude, but with entitlement. What began as God-enabled success slowly morphed into self-assumed authority.

Presumption is subtle. It does not announce rebellion; it assumes permission. It convinces the heart that past victories justify present overreach. Strength begins to speak louder than instruction, and confidence replaces reverence.

God never opposed Uzziah's strength—He opposed the posture that strength produced. When strength is no longer governed by submission, it drifts into territory God did not assign. The issue was not ability; it was **unauthorized access**.

This is the quiet danger of growth: when competence outpaces obedience. A strong life must still be a submitted life, or strength will become the very thing that undoes it.

Key Lessons & Life Applications

- **Teaching:** Strength must remain submitted to God's order.
- **Reproof:** Confidence can drift into presumption if unchecked.
- **Correction:** Re-anchor authority in obedience, not achievement.
- **Instruction:** Let reverence govern strength.
- **Righteous Living:** Humility preserves what strength builds.

Prayer Points

1. Father, guard my heart as You strengthen me.
2. Deliver me from presumption disguised as confidence.
3. Keep my authority aligned with Your boundaries.
4. Teach me to honor instruction even when I am capable.
5. Preserve my life from being undone by my own strength.

Meditation / Reflection

Where might my strength be tempting me to overstep God's boundaries?

Words of Wisdom: *Strength that is not governed by submission eventually becomes presumption.*

October 24

Theme: Crossing Boundaries Invites Consequences

Anchor Scripture: "It is not for you, Uzziah, to burn incense to the LORD, but for the priests, the sons of Aaron, who are consecrated to burn incense." 2 Chronicles 26:18

Devotional Thought

Boundaries are not barriers to greatness; they are protections for sustainability. Uzziah's mistake was not worship—it was **overreach**. He did not deny God; he ignored order. Strength and success had convinced him that access was transferable, that effectiveness in one area justified intrusion into another.

But God's design includes boundaries for every role. Calling does not cancel order. Authority in one sphere does not grant permission in all spheres. When boundaries are crossed, the issue is not intention but **alignment**.

The priests did not challenge Uzziah's kingship—they defended God's structure. Their resistance was mercy, not hostility. Yet Uzziah interpreted correction as opposition and pressed forward anyway.

Many failures begin when correction is viewed as interference instead of protection. God establishes boundaries not because He withholds favor, but because He preserves life, order, and reverence.

Crossing boundaries may feel bold, but it always carries consequences—because order is the framework through which God sustains what He builds.

Key Lessons & Life Applications

- **Teaching:** God's order assigns roles and limits for preservation.
- **Reproof:** Ignoring boundaries invites unnecessary consequences.
- **Correction:** Receive correction as protection, not threat.
- **Instruction:** Stay within God-assigned jurisdiction.
- **Righteous Living:** Obedience sustains favor.

Prayer Points

1. Father, help me honor the boundaries You have set.
2. Deliver me from confusing access with assignment.
3. Give me a teachable heart when corrected.
4. Preserve me from overstepping through pride.
5. Align my authority with Your order.

Meditation / Reflection

Where might I be assuming permission without assignment?

Words of Wisdom: *Boundaries do not limit favor—they preserve it.*

October 25

Theme: God Resists Unauthorized Access

Anchor Scripture: "Leprosy broke out on his forehead, before the priests in the house of the LORD, beside the incense altar." 2 Chronicles 26:19

Devotional Thought

Unauthorized access always triggers resistance—not from people, but from God Himself. Uzziah's leprosy did not appear in private; it appeared **in the place of overreach**. The consequence was immediate, visible, and instructional. God was not reacting in anger—He was enforcing order.

Access in God's kingdom is regulated by calling, consecration, and obedience. When those are bypassed, resistance follows. Scripture is clear: *God resists the proud, but gives grace to the humble.*

This moment reveals a sobering truth—**nearness to holy things does not equal permission**. Passion without submission becomes presumption. Desire without discipline becomes danger.

Uzziah did not lose favor because he worshiped; he lost protection because he ignored alignment. God resists unauthorized access not to humiliate, but to prevent contamination—of the person and of the order He established.

Correction at the altar is severe because misalignment at the altar affects everything else.

Key Lessons & Life Applications

- **Teaching:** God governs access through order and obedience.
- **Reproof:** Presumption invites divine resistance.
- **Correction:** Honor process before proximity.
- **Instruction:** Seek permission through obedience, not desire.
- **Righteous Living:** Humility preserves access.

Prayer Points

1. Father, keep me from presumption.
2. Teach me to honor Your order.
3. Guard my heart from pride disguised as passion.
4. Align my access with Your will.
5. Preserve me through humility and obedience.

Meditation / Reflection

Where might I be assuming access without alignment?

Words of Wisdom: *Access without authorization invites resistance, not favor.*

October 26

Theme: Pride Is Often the Root of the Fall

> **Anchor Scripture:** "Pride goes before destruction, and a haughty spirit before a fall." Proverbs 16:18

Devotional Thought

Pride rarely announces itself loudly. It often enters quietly—through confidence that is no longer accountable, strength that forgets its source, and success that begins to feel self-generated.

Uzziah's fall did not begin at the altar; it began in the heart. Pride is not merely arrogance—it is **self-reliance that no longer checks in with God**. It is the subtle shift from gratitude to entitlement, from stewardship to ownership.

Scripture reveals a consistent pattern: destruction is not sudden, but **preceded by elevation of self**. Pride distorts judgment. It dulls discernment. It convinces the heart that boundaries are optional and that past success guarantees future safety.

God opposes pride not because He resents strength, but because pride disconnects a person from truth. When humility departs, wisdom follows. When wisdom leaves, collapse becomes inevitable.

The fall is not punishment—it is exposure. Pride removes the safeguards that once preserved alignment.

Key Lessons & Life Applications

- **Teaching:** Pride precedes collapse, not because God is harsh, but because pride blinds.
- **Reproof:** Confidence without accountability is dangerous.
- **Correction:** Return to humility before consequences force it.
- **Instruction:** Continually acknowledge God as source and sustainer.
- **Righteous Living:** Humility preserves stability.

Prayer Points

1. Father, search my heart for hidden pride.
2. Guard me from self-reliance that excludes You.
3. Restore humility where success has elevated me.
4. Keep my heart teachable and submitted.
5. Preserve me through reverence and dependence.

Meditation / Reflection

Where has confidence subtly replaced dependence on God?

Words of Wisdom: *Pride removes the safeguards that humility provides.*

October 27

Theme: Living With Consequences Is Still Mercy

> **Anchor Scripture:** "King Uzziah was a leper until the day of his death. He dwelt in an isolated house, because he was a leper; for he was cut off from the house of the LORD." 2 Chronicles 26:21

Devotional Thought

Mercy does not always look like reversal. Sometimes, mercy looks like **preservation within consequence**.

Uzziah's story is sobering because repentance is not recorded, and restoration of position never came. Yet even in judgment, God was merciful. Uzziah was not destroyed; he was restrained. He lived. His lineage continued. The kingdom did not collapse overnight.

Consequences are not always proof of God's absence. In many cases, they are evidence of His restraint. Immediate removal would have meant total loss, but containment preserved what could still be preserved.

There are moments when God allows consequences to remain—not to shame, but to **prevent further damage**. The isolation protected the priesthood. The restriction protected the nation. Mercy limited the spread of what pride could have corrupted further.

God's mercy is not always corrective; sometimes it is **containment**.

This is a hard truth: some doors do not reopen, yet God still sustains life, purpose, and impact in altered form. Grace does not always restore function—but it preserves existence.

Key Lessons & Life Applications

- **Teaching:** Consequences and mercy can coexist.
- **Reproof:** Not all mercy looks like restoration.
- **Correction:** Accept restraint as protection, not rejection.
- **Instruction:** Learn humility through limitation.
- **Righteous Living:** Gratitude survives even when position does not.

Prayer Points

1. Father, help me recognize mercy even when consequences remain.
2. Guard my heart from bitterness when outcomes are altered.
3. Teach me humility through limitation.
4. Preserve what still can be preserved in my life.
5. Help me learn obedience through restraint.

Meditation / Reflection

Can I recognize God's mercy even when restoration does not look like I expected?

Words of Wisdom: *Mercy sometimes limits what judgment could have destroyed.*

October 28

Theme: God Helps, But He Will Not Be Replaced

Anchor Scripture: "The LORD is our judge, the LORD is our lawgiver, the LORD is our king; He will save us." Isaiah 33:22

Devotional Thought

God helps people—but He does not surrender His position.

Uzziah's failure was not ambition alone; it was **replacement**. Help from God slowly became confidence in self. What began as partnership drifted into presumption. He moved from dependence to entitlement, from stewardship to substitution.

God gladly empowers human effort, but He will not be displaced by it. The moment strength, success, or gifting attempts to occupy the space of divine authority, alignment fractures. God remains faithful, but access narrows.

This is the quiet danger of progress: success can blur roles. When achievements grow, the temptation is to assume autonomy. Yet Scripture is clear—God alone remains Judge, Lawgiver, and King. Help does not equal handover.

The lesson is sobering and protective: God's assistance is an invitation to humility, not independence. He empowers hands while guarding the throne.

Key Lessons & Life Applications

- **Teaching:** God empowers, but He remains sovereign.
- **Reproof:** Self-reliance can quietly replace dependence.
- **Correction:** Restore proper order between help and authority.
- **Instruction:** Keep God central as success increases.
- **Righteous Living:** Humility preserves access.

Prayer Points

1. Father, keep me aware of Your sovereignty.
2. Guard me from replacing dependence with confidence in self.
3. Help me steward success without drifting from You.
4. Restore proper order in my heart and decisions.
5. Let my strength never compete with Your authority.

Meditation / Reflection

In what areas of my life might success be slowly replacing dependence on God?

Words of Wisdom: *God empowers our hands, but He never relinquishes the throne.*

October 29

Theme: Repentance Reopens Relationship

Anchor Scripture: "If My people who are called by My name will humble themselves, and pray and seek My face, and turn from their wicked ways, then I will hear from heaven, and will forgive their sin and heal their land." 2 Chronicles 7:14

Devotional Thought

Repentance restores access.

When God speaks through this promise, He does not say He will erase history, undo consequences, or rewrite human nature. He promises **restored relationship**—*"I will hear... I will forgive."*

Repentance does not negotiate with God; it realigns with Him. It humbles the heart back into its rightful posture. Access is reopened, communication is restored, and fellowship resumes.

Yet notice what repentance does *not* promise. It does not eliminate weakness. It does not cancel the need for growth. It does not prevent future testing. It restores **connection**, not perfection.

God responds to humility because humility acknowledges truth. And truth restores access.

Key Lessons & Life Applications

- **Teaching:** Repentance restores access to God.
- **Reproof:** Pride blocks communication with heaven.
- **Correction:** Humility realigns relationship.
- **Instruction:** Seek God's face, not just relief from outcomes.
- **Righteous Living:** Restored fellowship precedes restored influence.

Prayer Points

1. Father, restore access where pride created distance.
2. Teach me to value Your presence over outcomes.
3. Cleanse my heart through humility.
4. Reopen lines of fellowship that were disrupted.
5. Heal what repentance allows You to reach.

Meditation / Reflection

Am I seeking restored relationship—or merely relief from consequences?

Words of Wisdom: *Repentance restores access, not immunity.*

October 30

Theme: Repentance Does Not Remove Human Limitation

Anchor Scripture: "I have heard of You by the hearing of the ear, but now my eye sees You." Job 42:5

Devotional Thought

Job repented—but his humanity remained.

Repentance brought clarity, not transformation of nature. His eyesight changed; his structure did not. Job moved from assumption to revelation, from explanation to surrender.

Repentance exposes limits—it does not remove them. It brings understanding without granting omniscience, humility without eliminating vulnerability.

Job's repentance did not turn him into something other than human. It turned him into someone more aware of God. And awareness, not power, is what repentance restores.

This is an essential distinction: repentance realigns perception, not capacity. It restores sight, not strength.

Key Lessons & Life Applications

- **Teaching:** Repentance restores vision, not nature.
- **Reproof:** Expecting repentance to eliminate limitation breeds frustration.
- **Correction:** Accept humanity while honoring God's sovereignty.
- **Instruction:** Let revelation reshape posture.
- **Righteous Living:** Humility grows through awareness.

Prayer Points

1. Father, refine my vision of You.
2. Teach me to live wisely within my limits.
3. Deliver me from false expectations of self.
4. Anchor my faith in revelation, not control.
5. Keep my posture humble before You.

Meditation / Reflection

Am I expecting repentance to change my nature—or my posture?

Words of Wisdom: *Repentance restores sight, not structure.*

October 31

Theme: Humanity Needs More Than Correction

Anchor Scripture: "Who can bring a clean thing out of an unclean? No one!" Job 14:4

Devotional Thought

Correction cannot cure nature.

This is the unresolved tension of Scripture before Christ. Repentance restores relationship. Instruction improves behavior. Correction restrains damage. But none of these regenerate the human condition.

Job's question exposes the limit of moral repair. An unclean source cannot produce a clean outcome. Humanity does not merely need better discipline—it needs **renewal**.

This is why **October** ends without resolution. The Law corrects. Repentance reopens access. Wisdom restrains excess. But none of them recreate the heart.

Correction can manage behavior; only redemption transforms nature.

And that answer does not arrive until Christ.

Key Lessons & Life Applications

- **Teaching:** Humanity's problem is deeper than behavior.
- **Reproof:** Moral effort cannot regenerate nature.
- **Correction:** Discipline restrains but does not renew.
- **Instruction:** Recognize the limits of self-repair.
- **Righteous Living:** Long for transformation, not adjustment.

Prayer Points

1. Father, help me recognize the limits of correction.
2. Guard me from relying on effort alone.
3. Prepare my heart for true transformation.
4. Increase my hunger for renewal, not reform.
5. Lead me toward what only You can do.

Meditation / Reflection

Am I trying to correct what needs to be redeemed?

Words of Wisdom: *Correction can restrain behavior; only Christ renews nature.*

NOVEMBER
THE KINGDOM REVEALED

November 1

Theme: The Kingdom Is God's Central Message

Anchor Scripture - "From that time Jesus began to preach and to say, Repent, for the kingdom of heaven is at hand.'" Matthew 4:17

Devotional Thought

Jesus did not begin His ministry with morality, miracles, or church structure. He began with a message: **the Kingdom**. This was not a new religion—it was a revelation of divine government returning to humanity.

The Kingdom was God's original intent from creation. Sin disrupted humanity's alignment with God's rule, but redemption restores access. When Jesus announced the Kingdom, He was declaring that God's authority was once again available to govern human life.

Prayer becomes powerful when it aligns with Kingdom reality. Asking without understanding governance produces frustration. The Kingdom explains *why* prayer works, *how* authority functions, and *what* alignment requires.

A redeemed believer does not pray from desperation, but from awareness of divine rule.

Key Lessons & Life Applications

- **Teaching:** The Kingdom is the core message of Jesus.
- **Reproof:** Focusing on religion without Kingdom understanding limits authority.
- **Correction:** Recenter prayer around God's rule, not personal urgency.
- **Instruction:** Study the Kingdom to pray with clarity.
- **Righteous Living:** Submission to God's reign produces stability.

Prayer Points

1. Father, open my understanding to Your Kingdom.
2. Align my prayers with Your rule and authority.
3. Deliver me from religious thinking without governance.
4. Teach me to live under Your reign.
5. Let my life reflect Kingdom order.

Meditation / Reflection

How does my understanding of God change when I see Him as King, not only Savior?

Words of Wisdom: *Prayer gains authority when it aligns with God's Kingdom.*

November 2

Theme: The Kingdom Is Not a Place but a Rule

> **Anchor Scripture** - "The kingdom of God does not come with observation; nor will they say, 'See here!' or 'See there!' For indeed, the kingdom of God is within you." Luke 17:20–21

Devotional Thought

The Kingdom is not a destination—it is a **dominion**. Jesus corrected the assumption that God's reign would arrive visibly through political or religious systems. Instead, He revealed that the Kingdom begins internally.

When God's rule governs the heart, it transforms behavior, decisions, values, and priorities. External change without internal submission produces hypocrisy. True Kingdom living flows from internal alignment with God's authority.

Prayer that seeks results without submission struggles. But prayer rooted in internal governance releases peace, clarity, and authority. When the King reigns within, life comes into order.

A redeemed believer allows God's rule to shape the inner life before expecting external outcomes.

Key Lessons & Life Applications

- **Teaching:** The Kingdom operates through internal alignment.
- **Reproof:** External compliance without inner submission is insufficient.
- **Correction:** Allow God's rule to govern motives and decisions.
- **Instruction:** Cultivate Kingdom awareness within.
- **Righteous Living:** Internal governance produces outward integrity.

Prayer Points

1. Father, reign fully in my heart.
2. Align my desires with Your authority.
3. Remove resistance to Your rule.
4. Establish Kingdom order within me.
5. Let my inner life reflect Your government.

Meditation / Reflection

What areas of my heart resist God's rule?

Words of Wisdom: *The Kingdom advances where God's rule is welcomed within.*

November 3

Theme: Repentance Is a Change of Government

Anchor Scripture - "Repent, for the kingdom of heaven is at hand." Matthew 3:2

Devotional Thought

Repentance is not emotional regret—it is a **governmental shift**. The Greek word *metanoia* means a change of mind, direction, and authority. Repentance transfers control from self-rule to God-rule.

John the Baptist did not preach behavior modification; he announced regime change. Repentance prepares the heart to receive Kingdom governance. Without repentance, the Kingdom remains inaccessible—not because God withholds it, but because resistance remains.

Prayer becomes effective when repentance has settled authority. A life still governed by self cannot fully experience divine order.

A redeemed believer understands repentance as alignment, not humiliation.

Key Lessons & Life Applications

- **Teaching:** Repentance reassigns authority.
- **Reproof:** Regret without alignment changes nothing.
- **Correction:** Yield governance to God.
- **Instruction:** Continually realign thinking with Kingdom truth.
- **Righteous Living:** Submission produces peace and clarity.

Prayer Points

1. Father, realign my thinking with Your Kingdom.
2. Help me surrender self-rule.
3. Teach me daily repentance as alignment.
4. Establish Your authority in every area of my life.
5. Let my prayers reflect Kingdom order.

Meditation / Reflection

Who truly governs my decisions—God or self?

Words of Wisdom: *Repentance is not sorrow—it is surrender of rule.*

November 4

Theme: Kingdom Before Church

> **Anchor Scripture** - "And I also say to you that you are Peter, and on this rock I will build My church, and the gates of Hades shall not prevail against it. And I will give you the keys of the kingdom of heaven…" Matthew 16:18–19

Devotional Thought

Jesus introduced the **Kingdom** before He introduced the **church**. The church was never meant to replace the Kingdom—it was designed to advance it. When the church loses Kingdom understanding, it becomes institutional rather than governmental.

Keys belong to the Kingdom, not the building. Authority flows from alignment with heaven's government, not proximity to religious activity. The church exists to steward Kingdom authority on earth.

Prayer weakens when the church becomes the destination instead of the training ground. A redeemed believer understands that gathering is important—but governing is essential.

Key Lessons & Life Applications

- **Teaching:** The church serves the Kingdom, not the reverse.
- **Reproof:** Institutional focus can replace Kingdom purpose.
- **Correction:** Reclaim Kingdom identity beyond religious structure.
- **Instruction:** Use church as equipping for Kingdom living.
- **Righteous Living:** Authority flows from alignment with heaven.

Prayer Points

1. Father, restore my understanding of Kingdom purpose.
2. Deliver me from institutional dependency without authority.
3. Teach me to steward Kingdom keys responsibly.
4. Align my service with Kingdom advancement.
5. Let my life reflect heaven's government.

Meditation / Reflection

Do I see church as a destination—or as preparation for Kingdom living?

Words of Wisdom: *The church gathers believers; the Kingdom governs life.*

November 5

Theme: The Kingdom Requires New Thinking

Anchor Scripture - "And do not be conformed to this world, but be transformed by the renewing of your mind…" Romans 12:2

Devotional Thought

Kingdom life cannot be lived with unrenewed thinking. The values, priorities, and systems of God's reign often contradict the patterns of the world.

Transformation begins in the mind because governance begins with perception. Without renewed thinking, believers attempt to operate Kingdom authority using worldly frameworks—resulting in confusion and frustration.

Prayer deepens when the mind aligns with Kingdom truth. A renewed mind interprets challenges through authority, not fear; through purpose, not panic.

A redeemed believer allows the Word to retrain thought patterns until Kingdom thinking becomes instinctive.

Key Lessons & Life Applications

- **Teaching:** Kingdom living requires transformed thinking.
- **Reproof:** Worldly patterns hinder Kingdom authority.
- **Correction:** Submit thoughts to God's truth.
- **Instruction:** Renew the mind daily through the Word.
- **Righteous Living:** Alignment of thought produces discernment.

Prayer Points

1. Father, renew my mind with Kingdom truth.
2. Expose thinking patterns that resist Your rule.
3. Transform my perspective on life and authority.
4. Help me discern Your will clearly.
5. Establish Kingdom thinking in me.

Meditation / Reflection

Which of my thought patterns reflect the world rather than the Kingdom?

Words of Wisdom: *Kingdom authority flows through a renewed mind.*

November 6

Theme: Seeing vs Entering the Kingdom

Anchor Scripture - "Most assuredly, I say to you, unless one is born again, he cannot see the kingdom of God… unless one is born of water and the Spirit, he cannot enter the kingdom of God." John 3:3, 5

Devotional Thought

Jesus distinguished between **seeing** the Kingdom and **entering** it. Awareness is not participation. Many recognize Kingdom truth yet remain governed by old systems.

Seeing reveals possibility; entering requires surrender. New birth is not religious affiliation—it is transformation of identity and allegiance. Entry demands submission to God's authority, not admiration of His power.

Prayer matures when believers move from observation to participation. Kingdom authority is accessed through alignment, not curiosity.

A redeemed believer does not settle for understanding the Kingdom—they live under it.

Key Lessons & Life Applications

- **Teaching:** Awareness of the Kingdom is not the same as participation.
- **Reproof:** Knowledge without surrender limits authority.
- **Correction:** Yield fully to spiritual rebirth.
- **Instruction:** Live from Kingdom identity.
- **Righteous Living:** Submission grants access.

Prayer Points

1. Father, move me from seeing to entering.
2. Align my identity with Kingdom citizenship.
3. Remove partial surrender from my life.
4. Teach me to live under Your authority.
5. Let my prayers flow from alignment.

Meditation / Reflection

Am I observing the Kingdom—or living under its rule?

Words of Wisdom: *Seeing reveals the Kingdom; surrender enters it.*

November 7

Theme: Why Many Miss the Kingdom

Anchor Scripture - "Because seeing they do not see, and hearing they do not hear, nor do they understand." Matthew 13:13

Devotional Thought

Jesus made it clear that access to the Kingdom is not limited by availability, but by **perception**. Many miss the Kingdom not because it is hidden, but because their hearts are misaligned.

Familiarity, pride, religious assumptions, and hardened expectations dull spiritual sensitivity. When hearts resist correction, revelation cannot land. The Kingdom requires humility of posture before clarity of understanding.

Prayer becomes shallow when hearts are closed. But when the heart remains soft, understanding deepens and alignment follows.

A redeemed believer guards perception carefully, knowing that receptivity determines access.

Key Lessons & Life Applications

- **Teaching:** Kingdom access requires spiritual perception.
- **Reproof:** Familiarity can block revelation.
- **Correction:** Guard the heart from hardness.
- **Instruction:** Remain teachable before God.
- **Righteous Living:** Sensitivity preserves alignment.

Prayer Points

1. Father, soften my heart toward Your truth.
2. Remove familiarity that dulls perception.
3. Open my eyes to Kingdom realities.
4. Guard me from pride and resistance.
5. Keep me receptive to Your instruction.

Meditation / Reflection

What attitudes might be limiting my spiritual perception?

Words of Wisdom: *The Kingdom is revealed to the receptive, not the resistant.*

November 8

Theme: Blessed Are the Poor in Spirit

Anchor Scripture - "Blessed are the poor in spirit, for theirs is the kingdom of heaven." Matthew 5:3

Devotional Thought

Poverty of spirit is not weakness—it is awareness. It recognizes total dependence on God's rule rather than self-sufficiency.

The Kingdom does not rest on confidence in ability, but surrender of control. Those poor in spirit acknowledge that without God's governance, life becomes disordered.

Prayer deepens when dependence replaces entitlement. Kingdom authority flows most freely through humility.

A redeemed believer embraces poverty of spirit as strength under divine rule.

Key Lessons & Life Applications

- **Teaching:** Humility qualifies Kingdom access.
- **Reproof:** Self-reliance resists divine rule.
- **Correction:** Yield control to God fully.
- **Instruction:** Cultivate dependence daily.
- **Righteous Living:** Humility sustains authority.

Prayer Points

1. Father, deliver me from self-sufficiency.
2. Teach me true dependence on You.
3. Align my confidence with Your authority.
4. Keep my spirit humble.
5. Establish Kingdom order in my life.

Meditation / Reflection

Where have I relied on myself instead of God's rule?

Words of Wisdom: *The Kingdom belongs to those who know they need a King.*

November 9

Theme: Meekness as Kingdom Strength

Anchor Scripture - "Blessed are the meek, for they shall inherit the earth." Matthew 5:5

Devotional Thought

Meekness is strength under control, not passivity. It is power submitted to God's authority rather than driven by ego.

In the Kingdom, dominance does not inherit territory—discipline does. Meekness trusts God with outcomes and refuses manipulation or force.

Prayer becomes authoritative when power is restrained by submission. The meek inherit not because they are weak, but because they are aligned.

A redeemed believer understands that restraint preserves influence.

Key Lessons & Life Applications

- **Teaching:** Meekness governs power rightly.
- **Reproof:** Aggression often signals insecurity.
- **Correction:** Submit strength to God's control.
- **Instruction:** Trust God with outcomes.
- **Righteous Living:** Alignment sustains influence.

Prayer Points

1. Father, teach me true meekness.
2. Help me govern strength wisely.
3. Remove ego-driven reactions.
4. Align my power with Your will.
5. Let restraint preserve my influence.

Meditation / Reflection

How do I respond when my strength is tested?

Words of Wisdom: *Meekness is power that trusts God with control.*

November 10

Theme: Hunger and Thirst for Righteousness

Anchor Scripture - "Blessed are those who hunger and thirst for righteousness, For they shall be filled." Matthew 5:6

Devotional Thought

The Kingdom responds to appetite. Jesus did not bless talent, position, or effort— He blessed hunger. Hunger and thirst describe intense desire, not casual interest.

Righteousness here is not moral superiority; it is alignment with God's ways. Those who hunger for righteousness crave God's order more than personal comfort or convenience.

Prayer becomes effective when it flows from desire for alignment rather than outcomes. God fills those who want His ways more than His benefits.

A redeemed believer cultivates appetite intentionally, knowing that what we hunger for determines what fills us.

Key Lessons & Life Applications

- **Teaching:** Hunger attracts divine filling.
- **Reproof:** Casual desire produces shallow alignment.
- **Correction:** Refocus appetite toward God's ways.
- **Instruction:** Cultivate spiritual hunger daily.
- **Righteous Living:** Desire for righteousness sustains growth.

Prayer Points

1. Father, increase my hunger for righteousness.
2. Deliver me from appetite for lesser things.
3. Align my desires with Your will.
4. Fill me with Your order and truth.
5. Let my life reflect Your ways.

Meditation / Reflection

What am I truly hungry for in this season?

Words of Wisdom: *The Kingdom fills those who hunger for alignment, not advantage.*

November 11

Theme: Mercy as Kingdom Currency

Anchor Scripture - "Blessed are the merciful, for they shall obtain mercy." Matthew 5:7

Devotional Thought

Mercy is not weakness—it is Kingdom strength. In God's economy, mercy sustains authority. Those who rule harshly eventually lose influence; those who extend mercy mirror the King.

Mercy does not excuse wrongdoing; it opens space for restoration. Jesus reveals that mercy governs relationships in the Kingdom the same way grace governs access to God.

Prayer becomes restricted when hearts grow hard. A merciful posture keeps spiritual channels open.

A redeemed believer understands that mercy is not optional—it is Kingdom culture.

Key Lessons & Life Applications

- **Teaching:** Mercy sustains Kingdom authority.
- **Reproof:** Harshness erodes influence.
- **Correction:** Extend mercy without lowering truth.
- **Instruction:** Reflect God's compassion daily.
- **Righteous Living:** Mercy preserves relational authority.

Prayer Points

1. Father, cultivate mercy in my heart.
2. Heal hardness caused by offense.
3. Teach me compassion without compromise.
4. Align my responses with Your grace.
5. Let mercy govern my relationships.

Meditation / Reflection

Where might God be calling me to extend mercy?

Words of Wisdom: *Mercy keeps the Kingdom flowing through relationships.*

November 12

Theme: Purity of Heart and Kingdom Sight

Anchor Scripture - "Blessed are the pure in heart, for they shall see God." Matthew 5:8

Devotional Thought

Purity of heart determines clarity of vision. Jesus taught that seeing God is not about physical sight, but spiritual perception.

A divided heart blurs vision. Mixed motives distort discernment. Purity aligns intention, desire, and obedience under God's rule.

Prayer becomes clear when the heart is undivided. Kingdom sight flows from internal alignment, not external activity.

A redeemed believer guards motives carefully, knowing that clarity follows purity.

Key Lessons & Life Applications

- **Teaching:** Purity produces spiritual clarity.
- **Reproof:** Mixed motives distort discernment.
- **Correction:** Align intentions with God's will.
- **Instruction:** Guard the heart diligently.
- **Righteous Living:** Undivided devotion sharpens vision.

Prayer Points

1. Father, purify my heart.
2. Expose mixed motives.
3. Align my desires with Yours.
4. Restore clarity of spiritual vision.
5. Let my devotion remain undivided.

Meditation / Reflection

Are my motives aligned—or divided?

Words of Wisdom: *Clarity of vision flows from purity of heart.*

November 13

Theme: Peacemakers and Kingdom Authority

Anchor Scripture - "Blessed are the peacemakers, For they shall be called sons of God." Matthew 5:9

Devotional Thought

Peacemaking is not conflict avoidance—it is **authority-driven reconciliation**.

Kingdom peace does not ignore truth; it restores order where disorder exists.

Peacemakers are called sons of God because they reflect the King's nature. God governs through reconciliation, not chaos. Those who carry Kingdom authority do not inflame division; they steward resolution.

Prayer matures when believers move beyond emotional reaction and choose alignment. Peace rooted in truth stabilizes relationships, families, and systems.

A redeemed believer understands that peace is an assignment, not a personality trait.

Key Lessons & Life Applications

- **Teaching:** Peace is an expression of authority.
- **Reproof:** Avoidance is not peacemaking.
- **Correction:** Address conflict with truth and humility.
- **Instruction:** Reflect God's reconciling nature.
- **Righteous Living:** Peace sustains Kingdom order.

Prayer Points

1. Father, make me an instrument of Your peace.
2. Teach me to steward conflict wisely.
3. Remove fear of confrontation.
4. Align my responses with truth.
5. Let reconciliation reflect Your Kingdom.

Meditation / Reflection

How do I respond when conflict challenges my alignment?

Words of Wisdom: *Kingdom peace restores order—it does not ignore truth.*

November 14

Theme: Kingdom Citizenship vs World Approval

Anchor Scripture - "If you were of the world, the world would love its own. Yet because you are not of the world... therefore the world hates you." John 15:19

Devotional Thought

Kingdom citizens operate under a different allegiance. Approval from the world often conflicts with obedience to God.

Jesus made it clear that alignment with the Kingdom may result in rejection. This is not punishment—it is evidence of distinction. Kingdom values challenge systems built on self-interest and pride.

Prayer becomes compromised when approval becomes priority. Authority weakens when allegiance is divided.

A redeemed believer chooses Kingdom loyalty over popularity.

Key Lessons & Life Applications

- **Teaching:** Kingdom allegiance creates distinction.
- **Reproof:** Seeking approval dilutes authority.
- **Correction:** Clarify loyalties.
- **Instruction:** Live from Kingdom identity.
- **Righteous Living:** Faithfulness sustains influence.

Prayer Points

1. Father, anchor my identity in Your Kingdom.
2. Remove fear of rejection.
3. Help me choose obedience over approval.
4. Strengthen my resolve.
5. Preserve my allegiance.

Meditation / Reflection

Whose approval shapes my decisions most?

Words of Wisdom: *Kingdom loyalty may cost approval—but it secures authority.*

November 15

Theme: All Authority Belongs to Jesus

Anchor Scripture - "All authority has been given to Me in heaven and on earth." Matthew 28:18

Devotional Thought

Authority in the Kingdom is not seized—it is delegated. Jesus does not share authority; He **dispenses it**.

Every expression of Kingdom authority flows from Christ's lordship. When authority is exercised apart from submission to Him, it becomes dangerous. True authority reflects obedience, not independence.

Prayer gains confidence when it is rooted in Christ's authority rather than personal effort. The believer operates boldly because Christ governs completely.

A redeemed believer functions under authority before functioning with authority.

Key Lessons & Life Applications

- **Teaching:** All authority originates with Christ.
- **Reproof:** Independent authority invites error.
- **Correction:** Reaffirm submission to Christ.
- **Instruction:** Exercise authority through obedience.
- **Righteous Living:** Submission sustains power.

Prayer Points

1. Father, establish Christ's lordship in my life.
2. Teach me to operate under authority.
3. Align my actions with Your governance.
4. Guard me from independent ambition.
5. Let Your authority flow through me.

Meditation / Reflection

Do I exercise authority from submission—or self-effort?

Words of Wisdom: *Kingdom authority flows from submission to Christ.*

November 16

Theme: Authority Flows from Submission

> **Anchor Scripture** - "For I also am a man under authority, having soldiers under me… And Jesus marveled at him." Matthew 8:9–10

Devotional Thought

The centurion understood a Kingdom principle many miss: authority is accessed through submission. He recognized that power does not originate from position, but from alignment under rightful authority.

Jesus marveled—not at faith alone—but at understanding. The centurion knew that one who is truly under authority can exercise authority legitimately. This insight unlocked miraculous intervention without Jesus needing to be physically present.

Prayer carries weight when the one praying understands authority structure. A redeemed believer does not attempt to command outcomes while resisting submission.

Key Lessons & Life Applications

- **Teaching:** Authority operates through alignment.
- **Reproof:** Resistance to submission weakens authority.
- **Correction:** Submit willingly to God's order.
- **Instruction:** Recognize authority structure in Kingdom life.
- **Righteous Living:** Obedience sustains authority.

Prayer Points

1. Father, teach me true submission.
2. Align me under Your authority.
3. Remove resistance to Your order.
4. Help me steward authority rightly.
5. Let my prayers reflect alignment.

Meditation / Reflection

Where might resistance to submission be weakening my authority?

Words of Wisdom: *Authority is strongest when submission is complete.*

November 17

Theme: Power Without Relationship Is Dangerous

Anchor Scripture - "And then I will declare to them, 'I never knew you; depart from Me.'" Matthew 7:22–23

Devotional Thought

Spiritual power can operate without intimacy—but only temporarily. Jesus warned that miracles, prophecy, and authority exercised without relationship are ultimately rejected. These individuals were active, gifted, and effective—yet unknown relationally. God values alignment over activity. Relationship validates authority.

Prayer that prioritizes results over relationship eventually collapses. A redeemed believer pursues intimacy first, knowing that authority flows naturally from being known by God.

Key Lessons & Life Applications

- **Teaching:** Relationship validates authority.
- **Reproof:** Activity cannot replace intimacy.
- **Correction:** Recenter devotion on knowing God.
- **Instruction:** Measure success by alignment, not output.
- **Righteous Living:** Intimacy sustains power.

Prayer Points

1. Father, draw me deeper into relationship with You.
2. Remove reliance on gifting without intimacy.
3. Teach me to value being known by You.
4. Align my service with devotion.
5. Preserve my walk through intimacy.

Meditation / Reflection

Am I prioritizing relationship—or results?

Words of Wisdom: *Power may impress people; relationship pleases God.*

November 18

Theme: Kingdom Power Is for Service, Not Status

Anchor Scripture - "Whoever desires to become great among you, let him be your servant." Matthew 20:26–28

Devotional Thought

Jesus redefined greatness by reversing hierarchy. In the Kingdom, power exists to serve—not to elevate self.

Authority divorced from service becomes oppressive. Kingdom authority reflects the heart of the King, who gave Himself for others. Leadership that seeks status contradicts Kingdom order.

Prayer gains integrity when motives align with service. A redeemed believer measures greatness by impact, not recognition.

Key Lessons & Life Applications

- **Teaching:** Service defines Kingdom greatness.
- **Reproof:** Status-seeking corrupts authority.
- **Correction:** Reframe leadership as stewardship.
- **Instruction:** Serve intentionally and humbly.
- **Righteous Living:** Humility preserves influence.

Prayer Points

1. Father, purify my motives in leadership.
2. Teach me servant-hearted authority.
3. Remove desire for status.
4. Align my influence with impact.
5. Let my leadership reflect Christ.

Meditation / Reflection

What motivates my desire for influence?

Words of Wisdom: *In the Kingdom, authority is measured by service, not status.*

November 19

Theme: Authority Is Recognized, Not Announced

Anchor Scripture - "And they were astonished at His teaching, for His word was with authority." Luke 4:32

Devotional Thought

True authority does not need self-promotion. When Jesus taught, people recognized authority without Him declaring it. Authority revealed itself through substance, alignment, and clarity.

In the Kingdom, authority is discerned by impact, not asserted by title. It is recognized because it carries weight—spiritual, moral, and relational. Authority that must be announced often lacks grounding.

Prayer gains credibility when life and alignment confirm it. A redeemed believer allows authority to speak for itself through consistency and truth.

Key Lessons & Life Applications

- **Teaching:** Kingdom authority is evident through alignment.
- **Reproof:** Self-promotion weakens credibility.
- **Correction:** Let substance speak louder than position.
- **Instruction:** Grow in depth rather than display.
- **Righteous Living:** Consistency validates authority.

Prayer Points

1. Father, establish true authority in my life.
2. Remove the need to announce myself.
3. Align my life with truth and integrity.
4. Let substance define my influence.
5. Teach me to walk quietly in authority.

Meditation / Reflection

Is my authority recognized by fruit—or asserted by position?

Words of Wisdom: *Kingdom authority is recognized by weight, not words.*

November 20

Theme: The Kingdom Advances by Authority, Not Force

Anchor Scripture - "From the days of John the Baptist until now the kingdom of heaven suffers violence, and the violent take it by force." Matthew 11:12

Devotional Thought

Kingdom advancement is often misunderstood as aggression. Jesus was not endorsing physical force, but spiritual resolve—alignment that presses through resistance.

The Kingdom advances when believers operate in authority rooted in obedience and faith. It is not forced through manipulation or dominance, but enforced through truth and alignment.

Prayer becomes effective when authority replaces anxiety. A redeemed believer advances the Kingdom by standing firmly in God's order.

Key Lessons & Life Applications

- **Teaching:** Kingdom advancement requires spiritual resolve.
- **Reproof:** Force without authority breeds resistance.
- **Correction:** Replace striving with alignment.
- **Instruction:** Advance through obedience and faith.
- **Righteous Living:** Authority sustains Kingdom progress.

Prayer Points

1. Father, teach me to advance through authority.
2. Remove striving from my walk.
3. Strengthen spiritual resolve in me.
4. Align my actions with Kingdom order.
5. Let truth establish progress.

Meditation / Reflection

Am I advancing through alignment—or striving through force?

Words of Wisdom: *The Kingdom advances through authority anchored in obedience.*

November 21

Theme: When Heaven Backs a Life

Anchor Scripture - "How God anointed Jesus of Nazareth with the Holy Spirit and with power, who went about doing good... for God was with Him." Acts 10:38

Devotional Thought

Heaven's backing is not random—it rests on alignment. Jesus moved with power because God was with Him. Presence authenticated action.

When heaven backs a life, resistance yields, doors open, and purpose advances without manipulation. Authority flows naturally where God's presence rests.

Prayer carries assurance when heaven endorses the life behind the words. A redeemed believer seeks presence before power.

Key Lessons & Life Applications

- **Teaching:** God's presence authenticates authority.
- **Reproof:** Activity without presence lacks endurance.
- **Correction:** Seek alignment over ambition.
- **Instruction:** Walk with God daily.
- **Righteous Living:** Presence sustains effectiveness.

Prayer Points

1. Father, let Your presence rest on my life.
2. Align me so heaven backs my steps.
3. Remove ambition disconnected from intimacy.
4. Strengthen my walk with You.
5. Let my life reflect divine endorsement.

Meditation / Reflection

What evidence shows that God is with me?

Words of Wisdom: *When God is with a life, authority follows naturally.*

November 22

Theme: The Kingdom Grows Quietly

> **Anchor Scripture** - "The kingdom of God is as if a man should scatter seed on the ground, and should sleep by night and rise by day, and the seed should sprout and grow, he himself does not know how." Mark 4:26–27

Devotional Thought

The Kingdom does not always announce its progress. Growth often happens unseen, unnoticed, and uncelebrated. Jesus reveals that Kingdom growth is organic, not mechanical.

Many become discouraged because they cannot see immediate results. Yet God works beneath the surface long before fruit appears. Prayer participates in this unseen work, trusting God's timing rather than demanding visibility.

A redeemed believer learns patience with divine processes. Silence does not mean stagnation.

Key Lessons & Life Applications

- **Teaching:** Kingdom growth is often invisible.
- **Reproof:** Impatience disrupts trust.
- **Correction:** Allow time for God's work.
- **Instruction:** Stay faithful even when results are unseen.
- **Righteous Living:** Perseverance honors God's process.

Prayer Points

1. Father, help me trust unseen growth.
2. Remove impatience from my heart.
3. Strengthen my faith in quiet seasons.
4. Keep me faithful in small beginnings.
5. Teach me to rest in Your timing.

Meditation / Reflection

Am I trusting God's work even when I cannot see it?

Words of Wisdom: *What God grows quietly often lasts longest.*

November 23

Theme: The Kingdom Begins Small but Ends Strong

Anchor Scripture - "The kingdom of heaven is like a mustard seed… the least of all the seeds; but when it is grown it is greater than the herbs." Matthew 13:31–32

Devotional Thought

God is not intimidated by small beginnings. The Kingdom often starts in seed form—ideas, convictions, obedience, prayer. What matters is not size, but life.

Small beginnings demand faith. Many despise what seems insignificant, yet God specializes in disproportionate outcomes. Prayer waters what obedience plants.

A redeemed believer learns to honor beginnings rather than rush outcomes.

Key Lessons & Life Applications

- **Teaching:** God works powerfully through small beginnings.
- **Reproof:** Despising beginnings limits vision.
- **Correction:** Value what God initiates.
- **Instruction:** Nurture seeds patiently.
- **Righteous Living:** Faithfulness multiplies fruit.

Prayer Points

1. Father, help me honor small beginnings.
2. Remove comparison and impatience.
3. Teach me to steward what You start.
4. Strengthen my faith in process.
5. Let growth come in Your time.

Meditation / Reflection

What seed has God placed in my life that needs patience?

Words of Wisdom: *God begins small to grow strong.*

November 24

Theme: Hidden Value Determines True Worth

Anchor Scripture - "The kingdom of heaven is like treasure hidden in a field... for joy over it he goes and sells all that he has and buys that field." Matthew 13:44

Devotional Thought

The Kingdom's greatest value is often hidden. Those who recognize it are willing to reorder priorities, release distractions, and invest fully.

Recognition precedes surrender. The man sold everything not out of loss, but joy—because he understood the worth of what he found. Prayer sharpens spiritual perception. A redeemed believer learns that sacrifice is not loss when value is clear.

Key Lessons & Life Applications

- **Teaching:** The Kingdom carries incomparable value.
- **Reproof:** Misplaced priorities obscure worth.
- **Correction:** Reorder life around eternal value.
- **Instruction:** Seek depth, not display.
- **Righteous Living:** Joy fuels surrender.

Prayer Points

1. Father, open my eyes to Kingdom value.
2. Remove distractions that compete for my heart.
3. Teach me joyful surrender.
4. Align my priorities with eternity.
5. Let me treasure what You treasure.

Meditation / Reflection

What am I willing—or unwilling—to release for the Kingdom?

Words of Wisdom: *True value is revealed by what we are willing to release.*

November 25

Theme: The Kingdom Separates Without Noise

Anchor Scripture - "Let both grow together until the harvest." Matthew 13:30

Devotional Thought

God does not rush separation. Jesus teaches that wheat and tares grow together until the appointed time. Premature judgment damages what God is still forming.

The Kingdom separates through time, truth, and fruit—not through haste. Prayer aligns us with God's patience rather than human urgency.

A redeemed believer trusts God to discern rightly and act perfectly.

Key Lessons & Life Applications

- **Teaching:** God handles separation wisely.
- **Reproof:** Impatience leads to misjudgment.
- **Correction:** Allow God to reveal truth.
- **Instruction:** Focus on growth, not comparison.
- **Righteous Living:** Patience preserves integrity.

Prayer Points

1. Father, teach me patience in discernment.
2. Guard me from premature judgment.
3. Help me trust Your timing.
4. Align my heart with Your wisdom.
5. Let truth mature fully.

Meditation / Reflection

Am I trying to separate what God is still growing?

Words of Wisdom: *God separates perfectly—never prematurely.*

November 26

Theme: Understanding the Mysteries of the Kingdom

Anchor Scripture - "To you it has been given to know the mysteries of the kingdom of heaven." Matthew 13:11

Devotional Thought

The Kingdom is revealed to those who are willing to receive, not merely observe. Mystery is not secrecy—it is depth reserved for the teachable.

Jesus explained that hunger, humility, and openness unlock understanding. Prayer positions the heart to receive insight that transforms perception.

A redeemed believer grows by leaning in, not standing back.

Key Lessons & Life Applications

- **Teaching:** Kingdom understanding is granted, not earned.
- **Reproof:** Familiarity can dull perception.
- **Correction:** Cultivate spiritual hunger.
- **Instruction:** Ask for understanding sincerely.
- **Righteous Living:** Revelation deepens obedience.

Prayer Points

1. Father, grant me Kingdom understanding.
2. Remove dullness from my heart.
3. Increase spiritual hunger within me.
4. Teach me to receive revelation.
5. Let understanding lead to obedience.

Meditation / Reflection

Am I leaning in to understand—or standing back casually?

Words of Wisdom: *The Kingdom reveals itself to the hungry.*

November 27

Theme: The Cost of the Kingdom

Anchor Scripture - "Whoever of you does not forsake all that he has cannot be My disciple." Luke 14:33

Devotional Thought

The Kingdom is free, but it is not cheap. Jesus never hid the cost of discipleship. He invited followers to count the cost before committing their lives.

Kingdom allegiance requires reordered priorities. What we cling to reveals what rules us. Prayer does not negotiate terms with God—it yields to them.

A redeemed believer understands that surrender is not loss; it is alignment.

Key Lessons & Life Applications

- **Teaching:** Discipleship requires total allegiance.
- **Reproof:** Divided priorities weaken commitment.
- **Correction:** Release what competes with obedience.
- **Instruction:** Count the cost honestly.
- **Righteous Living:** Surrender produces freedom.

Prayer Points

1. Father, help me surrender fully to You.
2. Expose attachments that compete with obedience.
3. Strengthen my resolve to follow You wholly.
4. Align my priorities with Your Kingdom.
5. Teach me joyful surrender.

Meditation / Reflection

What am I holding onto that may be hindering full obedience?

Words of Wisdom: *The Kingdom costs everything—but gives far more.*

November 28

Theme: Choosing the Kingdom Over Comfort

Anchor Scripture - "Seek first the kingdom of God and His righteousness." Matthew 6:33

Devotional Thought

The Kingdom demands first place. Jesus did not present it as an addition to life, but as the organizing center of life.

Comfort often competes with conviction. Yet when the Kingdom comes first, provision follows naturally. Prayer reorders desire before it rearranges outcomes.

A redeemed believer chooses Kingdom priority over convenience.

Key Lessons & Life Applications

- **Teaching:** The Kingdom requires first priority.
- **Reproof:** Comfort can dilute conviction.
- **Correction:** Recenter life around God's rule.
- **Instruction:** Trust God for provision.
- **Righteous Living:** Right priorities produce peace.

Prayer Points

1. Father, realign my priorities.
2. Help me seek Your Kingdom first.
3. Remove fear tied to provision.
4. Strengthen my trust in You.
5. Let righteousness guide my choices.

Meditation / Reflection

What currently takes priority over God's Kingdom in my life?

Words of Wisdom: *What you place first will shape everything else.*

November 29

Theme: Responding to the Kingdom Call

Anchor Scripture - "Repent, for the kingdom of heaven is at hand." Matthew 4:17

Devotional Thought

The Kingdom demands a response. Repentance is not merely turning from sin—it is turning toward God's rule.

Jesus' message was clear: alignment precedes participation. Prayer becomes effective when the heart is repositioned.

A redeemed believer understands that the Kingdom is entered through repentance and sustained through obedience.

Key Lessons & Life Applications

- **Teaching:** Repentance opens the door to Kingdom life.
- **Reproof:** Delay hardens the heart.
- **Correction:** Realign thinking and behavior.
- **Instruction:** Respond promptly to God's call.
- **Righteous Living:** Obedience maintains access.

Prayer Points

1. Father, realign my heart and mind.
2. Expose areas needing repentance.
3. Help me respond quickly to truth.
4. Restore obedience where drift occurred.
5. Keep my heart tender before You.

Meditation / Reflection

How am I responding to God's invitation today?

Words of Wisdom: *Repentance is the doorway into Kingdom life.*

November 30

Theme: Living as Citizens of the Kingdom

Anchor Scripture - "Our citizenship is in heaven." Philippians 3:20

Devotional Thought

The Kingdom is not only a future reality—it is a present identity. Citizens live by the laws, values, and culture of their Kingdom.

Earthly systems do not define Kingdom people. Prayer shapes our allegiance, reminding us who we belong to and how we should live.

A redeemed believer lives visibly aligned with heavenly citizenship.

Key Lessons & Life Applications

- **Teaching:** Kingdom identity shapes behavior.
- **Reproof:** Earthly allegiance can distort values.
- **Correction:** Live according to heavenly standards.
- **Instruction:** Reflect Kingdom culture daily.
- **Righteous Living:** Identity directs conduct.

Prayer Points

1. Father, remind me who I belong to.
2. Align my life with Kingdom values.
3. Guard me from worldly compromise.
4. Help me live as Your representative.
5. Let my life reflect heaven's culture.

Meditation / Reflection

Does my daily life reflect my heavenly citizenship?

Words of Wisdom: *Citizens live by the laws of their Kingdom.*

DECEMBER
THE KINGDOM REVEALED

December 1

Theme: The Lamb Foreordained

Anchor Scripture - "...the Lamb slain from the foundation of the world." Revelation 13:8

Devotional Thought

The Cross was not God's response to human failure; it was His eternal intention. Before sin entered history, redemption was already written into God's plan. The Lamb was foreordained before humanity ever fell.

This truth reframes prayer. We do not pray to persuade God to fix a broken world—He already planned restoration before the fracture occurred. Redemption was not improvised; it was premeditated in love.

Understanding this stabilizes the soul. Failure does not surprise God. Seasons of weakness do not derail divine purpose. What feels reactive in time was already settled in eternity.

A redeemed believer learns to pray from assurance, not panic.

Key Lessons & Life Applications

- **Teaching:** Redemption was planned before failure occurred.
- **Reproof:** Fear-driven prayer assumes God is reacting.
- **Correction:** Anchor faith in God's eternal foresight.
- **Instruction:** Pray from confidence, not desperation.
- **Righteous Living:** Assurance strengthens endurance.

Prayer Points

1. Father, thank You that redemption was planned before my failure.
2. Deliver me from fear-based praying.
3. Help me trust Your eternal purposes.
4. Anchor my faith in what You have already settled.
5. Let assurance govern my prayers.

Meditation / Reflection

Do I pray as though God is surprised by my struggles—or as One who already prepared redemption?

Words of Wisdom: *What God planned in eternity cannot be undone by time.*

December 2

Theme: The Cross Was Not an Accident

Anchor Scripture - "Him, being delivered by the determined purpose and foreknowledge of God, you have taken by lawless hands…" Acts 2:23

Devotional Thought

The Cross was not a tragic interruption of Jesus' mission—it was the mission.

Though executed by human hands, it unfolded under divine sovereignty.

This reveals a sobering truth: God can fulfill His will even through broken systems, flawed leaders, and unjust decisions—without endorsing sin. Human agendas may intersect God's plan, but they do not override it.

Prayer gains maturity when we understand this tension. We stop confusing chaos with absence. God was present at the Cross, even when darkness seemed dominant.

A redeemed believer learns to trust God's purposes even when circumstances appear unjust.

Key Lessons & Life Applications

- **Teaching:** God's will stands despite human failure.
- **Reproof:** Confusing disorder with God's absence weakens faith.
- **Correction:** Recognize God's sovereignty in adversity.
- **Instruction:** Trust God's purpose even in painful seasons.
- **Righteous Living:** Confidence grows through understanding God's control.

Prayer Points

1. Father, help me trust You when circumstances seem unjust.
2. Strengthen my faith in Your sovereignty.
3. Guard me from misinterpreting hardship.
4. Teach me to see Your purpose beyond human actions.
5. Let peace replace confusion.

Meditation / Reflection

Do I believe God is still working when life feels unfair?

Words of Wisdom: *God's purpose is never accidental, even when circumstances are.*

December 3

Theme: Love Displayed, Not Explained

Anchor Scripture - "But God demonstrates His own love toward us, in that while we were still sinners, Christ died for us." Romans 5:8

Devotional Thought

God did not explain His love—He demonstrated it. The Cross is not a theological argument; it is a declaration.

Love was shown before repentance, before reform, before worthiness. This dismantles performance-based spirituality. We are not loved because we changed; we are changed because we are loved.

Prayer becomes relational when rooted in this truth. We stop striving to earn affection and begin responding to what has already been given.

A redeemed believer rests in love that preceded obedience.

Key Lessons & Life Applications

- **Teaching:** God's love is proven through action.
- **Reproof:** Performance-based faith distorts grace.
- **Correction:** Receive love before trying to prove worth.
- **Instruction:** Let love motivate obedience.
- **Righteous Living:** Gratitude fuels transformation.

Prayer Points

1. Father, help me receive Your love fully.
2. Remove performance-driven striving from my heart.
3. Teach me to obey from gratitude, not fear.
4. Heal areas where love feels conditional.
5. Anchor my identity in Your demonstrated love.

Meditation / Reflection

Am I trying to earn what God has already given?

Words of Wisdom: *Love that must be earned can never transform.*

December 4

Theme: The Price of Redemption

> **Anchor Scripture** - "But He was wounded for our transgressions, He was bruised for our iniquities; the chastisement for our peace was upon Him, and by His stripes we are healed." Isaiah 53:5

Devotional Thought

Redemption was costly. It required more than compassion—it required substitution.
Jesus absorbed what justice demanded so peace could be restored.

The Cross reveals that forgiveness is never cheap. Sin carries weight, consequence, and cost. God did not ignore it; He addressed it fully through Christ. Healing, peace, and reconciliation were not granted sentimentally—they were purchased.

Prayer matures when we understand the cost behind grace. Gratitude deepens when we realize that mercy was paid for, not overlooked.

A redeemed believer lives responsibly because redemption was expensive.

Key Lessons & Life Applications

- **Teaching:** Redemption required substitution.
- **Reproof:** Casual grace ignores the cost of sin.
- **Correction:** Honor what Christ endured.
- **Instruction:** Let gratitude guide obedience.
- **Righteous Living:** Reverence grows from understanding the price.

Prayer Points

1. Father, thank You for the price paid for my redemption.
2. Help me never trivialize grace.
3. Teach me to live responsibly before You.
4. Let gratitude shape my obedience.
5. Heal every area Christ paid for.

Meditation / Reflection

Do I live with awareness of the cost behind my freedom?

Words of Wisdom: *Grace is free to receive, but costly to provide.*

December 5

Theme: Blood That Speaks Better Things

Anchor Scripture - "To Jesus the Mediator of the new covenant, and to the blood of sprinkling that speaks better things than that of Abel." Hebrews 12:24

Devotional Thought

Blood speaks. Abel's blood cried out for justice; Jesus' blood speaks mercy. Where accusation demands judgment, Christ's blood declares forgiveness.

This changes how we approach God. We do not come pleading our case—we come standing in Christ's finished work. The blood does not minimize sin; it resolves it.

Prayer gains confidence when rooted in what the blood has already accomplished.

Accusation loses authority where mercy speaks louder.

A redeemed believer stands on advocacy, not defensiveness.

Key Lessons & Life Applications

- **Teaching:** Christ's blood speaks mercy.
- **Reproof:** Living under accusation denies redemption.
- **Correction:** Silence condemnation with truth.
- **Instruction:** Approach God boldly through Christ.
- **Righteous Living:** Freedom flows from assurance.

Prayer Points

1. Father, thank You for the blood that speaks mercy.
2. Silence every voice of condemnation.
3. Help me live from assurance, not guilt.
4. Strengthen my confidence in Christ's work.
5. Let mercy define my standing with You.

Meditation / Reflection

Am I listening to accusation—or to what Christ's blood declares?

Words of Wisdom: *Where mercy speaks, accusation must be silent.*

December 6

Theme: It Is Finished

Anchor Scripture - "So when Jesus had received the sour wine, He said, 'It is finished!' And bowing His head, He gave up His spirit." John 19:30

Devotional Thought

When Jesus said, "It is finished," He was not surrendering—He was declaring completion. Redemption was fully accomplished. Nothing remained unpaid. Nothing was left undone. This statement liberates prayer from striving. We do not add to what Christ completed. We respond to it. The work that restores relationship, identity, and access is already done. Many faint in prayer because they believe something is still missing. The Cross answers that lie. Completion precedes endurance.

A redeemed believer rests before working and obeys from rest.

Key Lessons & Life Applications

- **Teaching:** Redemption is complete.
- **Reproof:** Striving denies finished work.
- **Correction:** Rest in Christ's completion.
- **Instruction:** Pray from victory, not anxiety.
- **Righteous Living:** Rest strengthens endurance.

Prayer Points

1. Father, help me rest in Christ's finished work.
2. Deliver me from spiritual striving.
3. Anchor my faith in what is complete.
4. Teach me to obey from rest.
5. Let peace govern my prayer life.

Meditation / Reflection

Am I resting in what Christ finished—or striving to add something?

Words of Wisdom: *Completion produces rest; rest produces endurance.*

December 7

Theme: The Cross Ends Striving

Anchor Scripture - "Having wiped out the handwriting of requirements that was against us... And He has taken it out of the way, having nailed it to the cross." **Colossians 2:14**

Devotional Thought

Striving ends where the Cross is rightly understood. Jesus did not reduce the demands against humanity—He removed them entirely.

The "handwriting of requirements" speaks of legal obligation, debt, and accusation. Christ did not negotiate it; He nailed it to the Cross. This means the believer no longer lives trying to earn acceptance but responding to it.

Prayer becomes distorted when we think we must convince God to act. The Cross already settled the matter. Alignment now flows from assurance, not anxiety.

A redeemed believer does not strive to belong—they live from belonging.

Key Lessons & Life Applications

- **Teaching:** The Cross removed spiritual debt.
- **Reproof:** Striving denies finished redemption.
- **Correction:** Stop trying to earn what was given.
- **Instruction:** Pray from assurance, not pressure.
- **Righteous Living:** Rest strengthens obedience.

Prayer Points

1. Father, free me from spiritual striving.
2. Help me live from assurance, not fear.
3. Anchor my faith in the finished work of Christ.
4. Teach me to obey from rest.
5. Let peace govern my walk with You.

Meditation / Reflection

Where might I still be striving to earn what Christ already secured?

Words of Wisdom: *What the Cross finished, striving cannot improve.*

December 8

Theme: From Sinner to Son

> **Anchor Scripture** - "But as many as received Him, to them He gave the right to become children of God." John 1:12

Devotional Thought

Salvation is not merely forgiveness—it is adoption. The Cross did not just remove guilt; it restored identity.

Sonship replaces fear with belonging. Access replaces distance. Authority replaces insecurity. This shift is foundational—how we see ourselves determines how we pray, obey, and endure.

Prayer matures when identity is settled. Sons do not beg; they approach confidently. Daughters do not hide; they draw near.

A redeemed believer prays from relationship, not status anxiety.

Key Lessons & Life Applications

- **Teaching:** Salvation restores identity.
- **Reproof:** Living like a stranger denies adoption.
- **Correction:** Embrace sonship fully.
- **Instruction:** Relate to God as Father.
- **Righteous Living:** Identity shapes behavior.

Prayer Points

1. Father, help me live as Your child.
2. Heal identity wounds rooted in fear.
3. Strengthen my confidence in You.
4. Remove orphan-hearted thinking.
5. Let sonship govern my prayers.

Meditation / Reflection

Do I approach God as a son—or as a stranger?

Words of Wisdom: *Identity settled brings confidence restored.*

December 9

Theme: Justified, Not Tolerated

> **Anchor Scripture** - "Therefore, having been justified by faith, we have peace with God through our Lord Jesus Christ." Romans 5:1

Devotional Thought

Justification is more than forgiveness—it is legal clearance. God does not merely tolerate the redeemed; He declares them righteous.

Peace with God replaces fear of rejection. This peace is not emotional calm—it is relational security. There is no hostility left to manage.

Prayer becomes stable when justification is understood. We stop fearing rejection and start walking in peace. Endurance becomes possible because relationship is secure.

A redeemed believer stands accepted, not on probation.

Key Lessons & Life Applications

- **Teaching:** Justification restores peace with God.
- **Reproof:** Living under guilt denies righteousness.
- **Correction:** Receive God's declaration fully.
- **Instruction:** Pray from peace, not fear.
- **Righteous Living:** Assurance fuels consistency.

Prayer Points

1. Father, thank You for justifying me.
2. Remove fear of rejection from my heart.
3. Help me live from peace with You.
4. Anchor my confidence in Christ alone.
5. Let assurance strengthen my faith.

Meditation / Reflection

Am I living as justified—or as if still on trial?

Words of Wisdom: *God does not tolerate the redeemed—He declares them righteous.*

December 10

Theme: No Condemnation Remains

Anchor Scripture - "There is therefore now no condemnation to those who are in Christ Jesus." Romans 8:1

Devotional Thought

Condemnation is not a tool God uses to mature His children. Conviction restores; condemnation paralyzes. The Cross removed condemnation entirely for those in Christ. Many believers continue to punish themselves for what God has already forgiven. This weakens prayer and erodes confidence. Freedom begins when we accept God's verdict over our feelings.

Prayer becomes effective when condemnation loses its voice. Endurance is sustained when guilt no longer dictates posture.

A redeemed believer learns to live unburdened by accusations already silenced.

Key Lessons & Life Applications

- **Teaching:** Condemnation has been removed in Christ.
- **Reproof:** Self-punishment denies redemption.
- **Correction:** Accept God's verdict fully.
- **Instruction:** Silence accusation with truth.
- **Righteous Living:** Freedom produces consistency.

Prayer Points

1. Father, thank You that condemnation is removed.
2. Silence every accusing voice in my heart.
3. Help me live free from guilt.
4. Anchor my confidence in Christ's work.
5. Let truth govern my emotions.

Meditation / Reflection

What accusations am I still carrying that God has already dismissed?

Words of Wisdom: *Where condemnation ends, endurance begins.*

December 11

Theme: A New Creation Reality

> **Anchor Scripture** - "Therefore, if anyone is in Christ, he is a new creation; old things have passed away; behold, all things have become new." **2 Corinthians 5:17**

Devotional Thought

Salvation does not improve the old life—it replaces it. New creation is not a metaphor; it is a spiritual reality.

While memories may remain, identity has changed. The past no longer defines standing or future. Prayer aligns us with who we are becoming, not who we were.

Transformation is progressive, but identity is immediate. A redeemed believer must learn to live from new reality rather than old patterns.

Key Lessons & Life Applications

- **Teaching:** Salvation creates a new identity.
- **Reproof:** Living from the past denies new life.
- **Correction:** Align behavior with new identity.
- **Instruction:** Renew the mind continually.
- **Righteous Living:** Identity directs choices.

Prayer Points

1. Father, help me live from my new identity.
2. Remove old mindsets that conflict with truth.
3. Renew my thinking daily.
4. Strengthen alignment with who I am in Christ.
5. Let transformation flow naturally.

Meditation / Reflection

Am I living from who I was—or who I am now in Christ?

Words of Wisdom: *Identity changes instantly; transformation unfolds intentionally.*

December 12

Theme: Reconciled, Not Distant

Anchor Scripture - "Now all things are of God, who has reconciled us to Himself through Jesus Christ." 2 Corinthians 5:18

Devotional Thought

Reconciliation restores relationship, not merely status. God did not save us to keep us at a distance—He brought us near.

Distance in prayer often stems from misunderstanding God's posture. Reconciliation means hostility is gone, access is restored, and relationship is secure.

Prayer flourishes when we understand we are welcomed, not tolerated. Fellowship replaces fear.

A redeemed believer draws near confidently, knowing separation has ended.

Key Lessons & Life Applications

- **Teaching:** Reconciliation restores closeness.
- **Reproof:** Avoidance reflects misunderstanding.
- **Correction:** Embrace restored relationship.
- **Instruction:** Cultivate daily fellowship.
- **Righteous Living:** Nearness fuels obedience.

Prayer Points

1. Father, thank You for restoring relationship.
2. Remove fear that creates distance.
3. Teach me to draw near confidently.
4. Strengthen daily fellowship with You.
5. Let intimacy govern my prayer life.

Meditation / Reflection

Do I approach God with confidence—or unnecessary distance?

Words of Wisdom: *Reconciliation invites closeness, not caution.*

December 13

Theme: Grace Trains the Redeemed

Anchor Scripture - "For the grace of God that brings salvation has appeared to all men, teaching us that, denying ungodliness and worldly lusts, we should live soberly, righteously, and godly in the present age." Titus 2:11–12

Devotional Thought

Grace does more than save—it trains. Salvation is the doorway; formation is the journey. Grace does not excuse ungodliness; it instructs the redeemed in how to live rightly.

Many misunderstand grace as permission to remain unchanged. Scripture presents grace as a teacher—patient, firm, and purposeful. It retrains desires, reshapes priorities, and disciplines the soul.

Prayer matures when grace is welcomed not only as mercy, but as instruction. A redeemed believer allows grace to govern conduct, not just cleanse conscience.

Key Lessons & Life Applications

- **Teaching:** Grace instructs, not excuses.
- **Reproof:** Using grace to justify compromise distorts truth.
- **Correction:** Submit daily life to grace's guidance.
- **Instruction:** Let grace shape habits and choices.
- **Righteous Living:** Transformation flows from taught obedience.

Prayer Points

1. Father, teach me through Your grace.
2. Retrain my desires and habits.
3. Help me live soberly and righteously.
4. Guard me from abusing grace.
5. Let grace shape my character.

Meditation / Reflection

Am I allowing grace to train me—or only to pardon me?

Words of Wisdom: *Grace that saves also teaches.*

December 14

Theme: Resurrection Power at Work

Anchor Scripture - "And what is the exceeding greatness of His power toward us who believe… which He worked in Christ when He raised Him from the dead." **Ephesians 1:19–20**

Devotional Thought

The power that raised Jesus from the dead is not reserved for history—it is active in the believer's life today. Resurrection power is not hype; it is enabling grace.

This power strengthens endurance, breaks cycles, and sustains obedience. It does not eliminate struggle, but it ensures victory over it.

Prayer becomes resilient when we recognize that God supplies power, not just instruction. A redeemed believer lives strengthened from within, not pressured from without.

Key Lessons & Life Applications

- **Teaching:** Resurrection power is active in believers.
- **Reproof:** Living powerless denies available grace.
- **Correction:** Rely on God's strength, not willpower alone.
- **Instruction:** Draw daily from divine power.
- **Righteous Living:** Strength sustains consistency.

Prayer Points

1. Father, activate resurrection power in me.
2. Strengthen me beyond natural ability.
3. Help me overcome cycles of weakness.
4. Teach me to rely on Your power daily.
5. Let strength flow from intimacy with You.

Meditation / Reflection

Where do I need to rely more on God's power than my own effort?

Words of Wisdom: *God empowers what He expects.*

December 15

Theme: Raised to New Life

> **Anchor Scripture** - "Therefore we were buried with Him through baptism into death, that just as Christ was raised from the dead... even so we also should walk in newness of life." Romans 6:4

Devotional Thought

Resurrection is not only an event—it is a way of life. New life is meant to be lived, not merely believed.

Walking in newness requires conscious participation. Old patterns may still call, but they no longer rule. Prayer aligns daily choices with resurrection reality.

A redeemed believer understands that new life is sustained by daily surrender and intentional obedience.

Key Lessons & Life Applications

- **Teaching:** Resurrection produces a new way of living.
- **Reproof:** Returning to old patterns contradicts new life.
- **Correction:** Choose alignment daily.
- **Instruction:** Walk intentionally in transformation.
- **Righteous Living:** New life expresses itself through obedience.

Prayer Points

1. Father, help me walk in newness of life.
2. Strengthen my resolve to leave old patterns.
3. Align my daily choices with resurrection reality.
4. Teach me consistency in obedience.
5. Let new life be evident through me.

Meditation / Reflection

Does my daily walk reflect resurrection life?

Words of Wisdom: *Resurrection life is meant to be walked out daily.*

December 16

Theme: Death No Longer Rules

Anchor Scripture - "Knowing that Christ, having been raised from the dead, dies no more. Death no longer has dominion over Him." Romans 6:9

Devotional Thought

The resurrection did not merely defeat death—it stripped it of authority. Death no longer governs Christ, and therefore it no longer governs those united with Him.

This truth reshapes how believers face fear, loss, and uncertainty. Death may still exist as a reality of this world, but it no longer has final authority over identity, destiny, or hope.

Prayer gains courage when fear of final loss is removed. Endurance strengthens when death is no longer the ultimate threat.

A redeemed believer lives governed by life, not fear.

Key Lessons & Life Applications

- **Teaching:** Death's authority has been broken.
- **Reproof:** Living in fear contradicts resurrection truth.
- **Correction:** Anchor confidence in Christ's victory.
- **Instruction:** Face life from assurance, not dread.
- **Righteous Living:** Courage flows from eternal security.

Prayer Points

1. Father, thank You that death no longer rules.
2. Remove fear of loss from my heart.
3. Strengthen my confidence in eternal life.
4. Help me live boldly in assurance.
5. Let hope replace anxiety.

Meditation / Reflection

What fears would lose power if I truly believed death no longer rules?

Words of Wisdom: *When death loses dominion, fear loses authority.*

December 17

Theme: Victory Over the Grave

> **Anchor Scripture -** "*But thanks be to God, who gives us the victory through our Lord Jesus Christ.*" 1 Corinthians 15:57

Devotional Thought

The resurrection declares victory, not survival. Jesus did not escape the grave—He conquered it.

This victory reframes suffering. Trials are no longer evidence of defeat but arenas where victory is eventually revealed. Prayer becomes confident when rooted in triumph rather than uncertainty.

A redeemed believer understands that victory is not always immediate, but it is always assured.

Key Lessons & Life Applications

- **Teaching:** Christ's resurrection guarantees victory.
- **Reproof:** Hopelessness denies resurrection power.
- **Correction:** Expect victory even in delay.
- **Instruction:** Persevere with confidence.
- **Righteous Living:** Gratitude fuels endurance.

Prayer Points

1. Father, thank You for victory through Christ.
2. Strengthen my faith during waiting seasons.
3. Help me persevere with hope.
4. Anchor my confidence in Your triumph.
5. Let gratitude replace discouragement.

Meditation / Reflection

Where do I need to trust God's victory despite delay?

Words of Wisdom: *Victory is assured even when timing is unknown.*

December 18

Theme: A Living Hope

> **Anchor Scripture** - "Blessed be the God and Father of our Lord Jesus Christ, who according to His abundant mercy has begotten us again to a living hope through the resurrection of Jesus Christ from the dead." 1 Peter 1:3

Devotional Thought

Hope rooted in circumstances fades; hope rooted in resurrection lives. Scripture calls it a *living* hope—active, sustaining, and resilient.

This hope endures disappointment, absorbs uncertainty, and stabilizes the soul. It is not denial of pain, but confidence beyond it.

Prayer flourishes when hope is alive. A redeemed believer does not pray to escape reality, but to stand firm within it.

Key Lessons & Life Applications

- **Teaching:** Resurrection produces living hope.
- **Reproof:** Despair contradicts eternal assurance.
- **Correction:** Anchor hope beyond circumstances.
- **Instruction:** Let hope sustain endurance.
- **Righteous Living:** Hope stabilizes the soul.

Prayer Points

1. Father, thank You for living hope.
2. Revive hope where weariness has settled.
3. Strengthen my heart in uncertainty.
4. Help me endure with confidence.
5. Let hope govern my outlook.

Meditation / Reflection

Is my hope anchored in circumstances—or in resurrection?

Words of Wisdom: *Hope lives where resurrection is believed.*

December 19

Theme: Power to Live Free

Anchor Scripture - "Stand fast therefore in the liberty by which Christ has made us free, and do not be entangled again with a yoke of bondage." Galatians 5:1

Devotional Thought

Freedom is both a gift and a responsibility. Christ secured liberty fully, yet believers must learn to live within it intentionally. Freedom can be lost experientially when old patterns, fears, or dependencies are revisited.

The resurrection did not only cancel guilt—it broke chains. However, habits formed in bondage do not disappear automatically. Prayer strengthens discernment and reinforces boundaries that protect freedom.

A redeemed believer understands that freedom is sustained through vigilance, not neglect.

Key Lessons & Life Applications

- **Teaching:** Christ established true freedom.
- **Reproof:** Returning to bondage dishonors redemption.
- **Correction:** Guard liberty intentionally.
- **Instruction:** Resist patterns that re-enslave.
- **Righteous Living:** Freedom flourishes within discipline.

Prayer Points

1. Father, thank You for the freedom Christ secured.
2. Strengthen me to guard my liberty.
3. Expose habits that threaten freedom.
4. Help me stand firm in truth.
5. Let freedom shape my daily choices.

Meditation / Reflection

What patterns threaten the freedom Christ has given me?

Words of Wisdom: *Freedom must be guarded to be sustained.*

December 20

Theme: Strength for the Journey

Anchor Scripture - "My grace is sufficient for you, for My strength is made perfect in weakness." 2 Corinthians 12:9

Devotional Thought

God does not promise a journey without weakness, but He guarantees sufficient grace. Strength is not the absence of limitation—it is divine power at work within it.

Many faint because they attempt endurance through self-effort. Prayer realigns us with grace that sustains beyond capacity. Weakness becomes an invitation for divine strength, not a signal to quit.

A redeemed believer learns to lean, not strain.

Key Lessons & Life Applications

- **Teaching:** God's strength operates through grace.
- **Reproof:** Self-reliance leads to exhaustion.
- **Correction:** Depend on grace daily.
- **Instruction:** Acknowledge weakness honestly.
- **Righteous Living:** Endurance flows from grace.

Prayer Points

1. Father, strengthen me through Your grace.
2. Help me rely on You in weakness.
3. Remove pressure to perform beyond capacity.
4. Teach me to receive daily strength.
5. Let grace sustain my journey.

Meditation / Reflection

Where do I need to rely more on grace than effort?

Words of Wisdom: *Grace sustains where strength alone fails.*

December 21

Theme: Hope Anchored Beyond This Life

Anchor Scripture - "This hope we have as an anchor of the soul, both sure and steadfast." Hebrews 6:19

Devotional Thought

Hope anchored in eternity stabilizes the soul in time. Circumstances shift, seasons change, but eternal hope remains unmoved.

This hope does not deny pain—it outlasts it. It anchors faith during storms and steadies prayer during uncertainty. When hope extends beyond this life, fear loses its grip.

A redeemed believer lives grounded, not shaken.

Key Lessons & Life Applications

- **Teaching:** Eternal hope anchors the soul.
- **Reproof:** Short-term focus weakens endurance.
- **Correction:** Lift perspective beyond present trials.
- **Instruction:** Anchor faith in eternity.
- **Righteous Living:** Hope stabilizes spiritual posture.

Prayer Points

1. Father, anchor my hope in eternity.
2. Steady my heart during uncertainty.
3. Help me see beyond temporary struggles.
4. Strengthen my confidence in Your promises.
5. Let hope govern my outlook.

Meditation / Reflection

Is my hope anchored in eternity or in temporary outcomes?

Words of Wisdom: *An anchored soul does not drift.*

December 22

Theme: God With Us

Anchor Scripture - "Behold, the virgin shall be with child, and bear a Son, and they shall call His name Immanuel," which is translated, 'God with us.'" Matthew 1:23

Devotional Thought

Immanuel is not a seasonal idea—it is a permanent reality. God did not merely send help; He came Himself. The incarnation reveals God's commitment to proximity.

"God with us" dismantles the lie of abandonment. He entered human vulnerability, limitation, and suffering—not as an observer, but as a participant. This assures us that no season is faced alone.

Prayer deepens when presence is understood. We do not pray into distance—we pray from companionship.

A redeemed believer rests in nearness, not isolation.

Key Lessons & Life Applications

- **Teaching:** God chose nearness over distance.
- **Reproof:** Feelings of abandonment distort truth.
- **Correction:** Acknowledge God's constant presence.
- **Instruction:** Practice awareness of God with you.
- **Righteous Living:** Presence nurtures trust.

Prayer Points

1. Father, thank You for being with me.
2. Heal areas where I feel alone.
3. Increase my awareness of Your presence.
4. Help me rest in Your nearness.
5. Let companionship replace fear.

Meditation / Reflection

Am I living aware that God is truly with me?

Words of Wisdom: *God's presence is the greatest provision.*

December 23

Theme: Peace on Earth Begins in the Heart

Anchor Scripture - "Glory to God in the highest, and on earth peace, goodwill toward men!" Luke 2:14

Devotional Thought

Peace was announced before circumstances changed. The angels proclaimed peace while oppression still existed. This reveals that Kingdom peace is internal before it becomes external.

Biblical peace is not the absence of conflict—it is the presence of alignment. When the heart is anchored in God, turmoil loses dominance.

Prayer becomes stabilizing when peace is received internally. A redeemed believer carries peace into disorder rather than waiting for calm conditions.

Key Lessons & Life Applications

- **Teaching:** God's peace is internal first.
- **Reproof:** Waiting for perfect conditions delays peace.
- **Correction:** Receive peace as a gift.
- **Instruction:** Let peace govern reactions.
- **Righteous Living:** Peace reflects trust in God.

Prayer Points

1. Father, establish Your peace in my heart.
2. Calm internal unrest and anxiety.
3. Teach me to live from alignment.
4. Let peace guide my responses.
5. Make me a carrier of Your peace.

Meditation / Reflection

Is peace something I am waiting for—or something I am receiving?

Words of Wisdom: *Peace flows from alignment, not circumstance.*

December 24

Theme: The Gift That Changed Everything

Anchor Scripture - "For God so loved the world that He gave His only begotten Son…" John 3:16

Devotional Thought

The greatest gift was not given to impress—it was given to redeem. God gave Himself before asking anything in return.

This gift redefines value. Salvation was not earned, negotiated, or deserved. It was given freely, motivated by love.

Prayer becomes worship when gratitude replaces striving. The redeemed life flows from receiving, not earning.

A redeemed believer lives from gift, not obligation.

Key Lessons & Life Applications

- **Teaching:** Salvation is God's gift.
- **Reproof:** Performance-driven faith denies grace.
- **Correction:** Receive without striving.
- **Instruction:** Let gratitude guide obedience.
- **Righteous Living:** Love produces devotion.

Prayer Points

1. Father, thank You for the gift of salvation.
2. Help me live from gratitude, not pressure.
3. Remove performance-driven fear.
4. Deepen my appreciation for grace.
5. Let love motivate my obedience.

Meditation / Reflection

Am I living as someone who has truly received the gift?

Words of Wisdom: *What is freely given must be humbly received.*

December 25

Theme: Rest for the Weary

> **Anchor Scripture -** "Come to Me, all you who labor and are heavy laden, and I will give you rest." **Matthew 11:28**

Devotional Thought

The invitation of Christ is not to work harder, but to come closer. True rest is not inactivity—it is relief from carrying what was never meant to be borne alone.

Many faint not because they lack faith, but because they carry unnecessary weight: guilt, performance pressure, fear, and self-reliance. Jesus offers rest that reaches the soul, not just the schedule.

Prayer becomes restorative when we release burdens rather than rehearse them. Rest is a spiritual posture before it is a physical state.

A redeemed believer learns that rest is not earned—it is received.

Key Lessons & Life Applications

- **Teaching:** Christ offers soul-level rest.
- **Reproof:** Carrying unnecessary burdens leads to weariness.
- **Correction:** Release what Christ invites you to lay down.
- **Instruction:** Approach God for rest, not relief alone.
- **Righteous Living:** Rest strengthens endurance.

Prayer Points

1. Father, I come to You with my burdens.
2. Teach me to rest in Christ.
3. Remove pressure that You never required.
4. Restore my soul.
5. Let rest renew my strength.

Meditation / Reflection

What burdens am I carrying that Christ is inviting me to release?

Words of Wisdom: *Rest is not weakness—it is trust expressed.*

December 26

Theme: The Promise of Restoration

Anchor Scripture - "Behold, I make all things new." Revelation 21:5

Devotional Thought

God does not merely repair—He restores. Restoration goes beyond recovery; it reestablishes purpose, dignity, and order.

This promise speaks to brokenness that seems irreversible. God's redemptive work includes renewing what was lost, damaged, or distorted.

Prayer matures when hope is anchored in God's restorative power. The past does not intimidate the One who makes all things new.

A redeemed believer looks forward with confidence, not regret.

Key Lessons & Life Applications

- **Teaching:** God restores fully.
- **Reproof:** Hopelessness underestimates God's power.
- **Correction:** Anchor hope in God's promise.
- **Instruction:** Trust God with broken areas.
- **Righteous Living:** Hope fuels perseverance.

Prayer Points

1. Father, thank You for the promise of restoration.
2. Heal areas that feel beyond repair.
3. Renew hope where disappointment has settled.
4. Help me trust You with the future.
5. Make all things new in my life.

Meditation / Reflection

Where do I need to trust God's promise of restoration?

Words of Wisdom: *What God restores carries renewed purpose.*

December 27

Theme: God Dwelling With His People

Anchor Scripture - "Behold, the tabernacle of God is with men, and He will dwell with them." Revelation 21:3

Devotional Thought

The ultimate goal of redemption is not heaven as a place, but God as presence.
Scripture ends with God dwelling permanently among His people.
This reveals the heart of God—relationship over distance, presence over performance.
Prayer is a rehearsal of eternal fellowship.
A redeemed believer values intimacy with God more than outcomes.

Key Lessons & Life Applications

- **Teaching:** God desires permanent fellowship.
- **Reproof:** Prioritizing outcomes over presence distorts purpose.
- **Correction:** Cultivate intimacy daily.
- **Instruction:** Live aware of God's nearness.
- **Righteous Living:** Presence shapes character.

Prayer Points

1. Father, thank You for Your abiding presence.
2. Teach me to value intimacy with You.
3. Remove distractions that hinder fellowship.
4. Help me live aware of Your nearness.
5. Let Your presence shape my life.

Meditation / Reflection

Do I prioritize God's presence or His benefits?

Words of Wisdom: *God's presence is the destination, not the reward.*

December 28

Theme: Hope That Carries Us Forward

Anchor Scripture - "And everyone who has this hope in Him purifies himself, just as He is pure." 1 John 3:3

Devotional Thought

Hope does more than comfort—it purifies. When hope is anchored in God, it shapes conduct, expectation, and endurance.

This hope carries believers forward—not by denying reality, but by anchoring them beyond it. Prayer becomes future-oriented, steady, and confident.

A redeemed believer lives expectantly, knowing the end is secure.

Key Lessons & Life Applications

- **Teaching:** Hope shapes behavior.
- **Reproof:** Hopelessness weakens discipline.
- **Correction:** Anchor hope in Christ.
- **Instruction:** Let hope guide choices.
- **Righteous Living:** Expectation fuels purity.

Prayer Points

1. Father, anchor my hope firmly in You.
2. Let hope shape my choices.
3. Strengthen my expectation of good.
4. Help me live with eternity in view.
5. Carry me forward in confidence.

Meditation / Reflection

Is my hope shaping how I live today?

Words of Wisdom: *Hope anchored in Christ carries us forward.*

December 29

Theme: Faithful to the End

Anchor Scripture - "Being confident of this very thing, that He who has begun a good work in you will complete it until the day of Jesus Christ." Philippians 1:6

Devotional Thought

God finishes what He starts. Our confidence is not in our consistency, but in His faithfulness. The same God who initiated redemption is committed to its completion. Many faint because they measure progress by perfection rather than perseverance. Yet Scripture assures us that completion is God's responsibility. Prayer becomes steady when hope is anchored in God's commitment, not human strength.

A redeemed believer rests in divine faithfulness and keeps moving forward.

Key Lessons & Life Applications

- **Teaching:** God completes what He begins.
- **Reproof:** Self-reliance weakens assurance.
- **Correction:** Trust God's faithfulness over personal performance.
- **Instruction:** Continue faithfully, not fearfully.
- **Righteous Living:** Confidence fuels perseverance.

Prayer Points

1. Father, thank You for Your faithfulness.
2. Strengthen my confidence in Your work in me.
3. Help me trust You with unfinished areas.
4. Guard me from discouragement.
5. Let assurance sustain my journey.

Meditation / Reflection

Am I trusting God to finish what He began?

Words of Wisdom: *God's faithfulness carries what human strength cannot.*

December 30

Theme: Secure in His Hands

Anchor Scripture - "And I give them eternal life, and they shall never perish; neither shall anyone snatch them out of My hand." John 10:28

Devotional Thought

Security in God is not fragile. Jesus affirms that the redeemed are held—not loosely, but securely. Salvation is not sustained by fear of loss, but by the grip of grace.

Prayer stabilizes when security is settled. Anxiety fades when we recognize that our future rests in God's hands, not shifting circumstances.

A redeemed believer lives boldly when security is assured.

Key Lessons & Life Applications

- **Teaching:** God secures His own.
- **Reproof:** Fear-driven faith undermines trust.
- **Correction:** Rest in God's keeping power.
- **Instruction:** Live confidently, not cautiously.
- **Righteous Living:** Assurance produces stability.

Prayer Points

1. Father, thank You for holding me securely.
2. Remove fear of loss from my heart.
3. Help me trust Your keeping power.
4. Let confidence replace anxiety.
5. Anchor my faith in Your promises.

Meditation / Reflection

Am I living from security—or fear?

Words of Wisdom: *What God holds securely does not slip away.*

December 31

Theme: From Glory to Glory

Anchor Scripture - "But we all... are being transformed into the same image from glory to glory, just as by the Spirit of the Lord." 2 Corinthians 3:18

Devotional Thought

Transformation is progressive, not pressured. God moople from glory to glory—not from fear to fear.

This final day does not close the journey; it clarifies it. Growth continues. Alignment deepens. Glory unfolds gradually through obedience and intimacy.

Prayer enters the new year with expectation, not exhaustion. A redeemed believer looks ahead with confidence, knowing transformation is ongoing.

Key Lessons & Life Applications

- **Teaching:** Transformation is continuous.
- **Reproof:** Measuring progress by comparison discourages growth.
- **Correction:** Embrace God's pace of change.
- **Instruction:** Yield daily to the Spirit's work.
- **Righteous Living:** Growth flows from intimacy.

Prayer Points

1. Father, thank You for ongoing transformation.
2. Help me trust Your pace of growth.
3. Align my heart for what lies ahead.
4. Strengthen my desire for intimacy with You.
5. Lead me forward in glory.

Meditation / Reflection

How has God been transforming me—and where is He leading next?

Words of Wisdom: *Transformation continues where surrender remains.*

ABOUT THE AUTHOR

Dr. Joke Solanke is a transformational teacher, author, and thought leader with a deep commitment to spiritual formation, identity, and purposeful living. Her work is rooted in Scripture and shaped by years of teaching, leadership, and engagement across diverse cultural and professional contexts.

As the founder of Blossom Life Outreach and host of Divine Perspectives with Dr. J., she equips individuals to grow *in* clarity, alignment, and endurance spiritually and practically. Her teaching integrates biblical truth with wisdom for everyday life, emphasizing formation over performance and alignment over activity.

Dr. Solanke is the publisher at Purpose and Pathway Publications, where she develops resources designed to cultivate maturity, leadership, and sustained impact. Her writings reflect a conviction that prayer is not merely a response to need, but a curriculum for communion, discernment, and growth in grace.

Through her books, teachings, and global initiatives, Dr. Solanke continues to guide individuals into deeper fellowship with God and a resilient, grounded walk of faith anchored in truth and shaped forlongevity.

Made in the USA
Coppell, TX
28 January 2026

70221161R00213